FLAT EARTH NEWS

Dark Heart: The Shocking Truth about Hidden Britain
White Lies: The True Story of Clarence Brandley, Presumed Guilty in the American South
Murder on Ward Four: The Story of Bev Allitt and the Most Terrifying Crime Since the Moors Murders
The School Report: Why Britain's Schools are Failing

FLAT EARTH NEWS

An Award-winning Reporter Exposes Falsehood, Distortion and Propaganda in the Global Media

NICK DAVIES

Chatto & Windus
LONDON

Published by Chatto & Windus 2008

4 6 8 10 9 7 5

First published in Great Britain in 2008 by
Chatto & Windus
Random House, 20 Vauxhall Bridge Road,
London SW1V 2SA
www.rbooks.co.uk

Addresses for companies within The Random House Group Limited can be found at:
www.randomhouse.co.uk/offices.htm

The Random House Group Limited Reg. No. 954009

A CIP catalogue record for this book
is available from the British Library

ISBN 9780701181451

The Random House Group Limited supports The Forest Stewardship
Council (FSC), the leading international forest certification organisation. All our titles
that are printed on Greenpeace approved FSC certified paper carry the FSC logo. Our
paper procurement policy can be found
at www.rbooks.co.uk/environment

Mixed Sources
Product group from well-managed
forests and other controlled sources
www.fsc.org Cert no. TT-COC-2139
© 1996 Forest Stewardship Council

Typeset by Palimpsest Book Production Limited
Grangemouth, Stirlingshire
Printed and bound in Great Britain by
Mackays of Chatham plc, Chatham, Kent

FOR ROBIN, PEGGY AND JOE

Contents

Prologue

Dog doesn't eat dog. That's always been the rule in Fleet Street. We dig into the world of politics and finance and sport and policing and entertainment. We dig wherever we like – but not in our own back garden. In the last fifteen years, we have at least started running media pages, but the truth is that they are there primarily to attract advertisements; they don't usually put the spade in too deep.

There was a neat illustration of this while I was working on this book. In January 2007, the *Daily Telegraph*'s Washington correspondent, Toby Harnden, was caught out badly when he filed a speculative description of the hanging of Saddam Hussein some six hours before it actually happened, filling out his story with a little imaginary detail which might well have passed unnoticed had it not been for the unfortunate leaking of a video of the execution. Harnden (with some courage) then confessed all on his blog. However, that moment of openness didn't go down well with his bosses at the *Telegraph*. The entry on his blog was rapidly deleted, and a message was sent to all staff warning them to 'think carefully before blogging about journalistic tricks of the trade'. There you have it: imaginary material is nothing worse than a 'trick of the trade'; and we'll have no real reporting about reporting.

This book is a brazen attempt to break that rule.

It started with a single, notorious story – the long and twisting saga of the weapons of mass destruction in Iraq. As the sand settled after the invasion in March 2003 and the weaponless reality slowly began to emerge, journalists across the world finally started looking for the truth and yet almost all of them wrote about it as though this were a screw-up generated only by intelligence agencies and governments, invariably failing to expose their own profession's global contribution.

But this isn't a book about WMD. It's about everything I found when I started trying to explain how we had managed to do so badly in covering what is probably the biggest single story of our era. The more I looked, the more I found falsehood, distortion and propaganda running through the outlets of an industry which is supposed to be dedicated to the very opposite, i.e. to telling the truth. The more I searched for an explanation, the more alarmed I became by the scale of the problem and by the complexity of its causes. By the time I had finished, I looked back in embarrassment at my own naivety.

I've been a journalist for more than thirty years. In the year that I left university, 1974, Carl Bernstein and Bob Woodward from the *Washington Post* forced US President Richard Nixon to resign. What an idea! That two reporters − armed with nothing more than their pens and their notebooks − could bring down the most powerful man in the world, because he was corrupt.

I became wholly addicted to the idea of becoming a reporter − I would travel the globe, I would take a front-row seat on history unfolding and, most of all, I would change the world. I took a job as a messenger boy at the *Guardian*, bought a second-hand Remington typewriter, sat up at night reading the memoirs of old war correspondents and teaching myself shorthand, applied for scores of jobs as a trainee reporter, got rejection letters from every one and then finally got my foot on the ladder that led to Fleet Street.

Over the years which I then spent running around with a notebook in my pocket, of course I came to see that frequently we fail to tell the truth. The unavoidable reality of journalism is that all of our work is tethered by a deadline and we can never be free to roam as far we want in search of the evidence we need. On the best of days, everything we write is compromised by error. And, of course, I knew, too, that from time to time there was some seriously dodgy behaviour going on behind the headlines.

But until I worked my way into this project, I had no idea of just how weakened we had become, just how prone we now are to fail to tell the truth. I'm not talking about journalists making mistakes. Mistakes can be honest. (And it is a very safe bet that there are mistakes in this book.) I'm not talking about the individual dishonest, hack scumbags who bring our whole profession into disrepute. There are still good, brave, honest people working in this industry. I'm talking about the fact that almost all journalists across the whole developed world now work within a kind of professional cage which distorts their work and crushes their spirit. I'm talking about the fact that finally I was forced to admit that I work in a corrupted profession.

Because I'm writing about the world in which I work – the world that has been handing me my pay cheques all these years – I need to say something about conflicts of interest.

I eventually got my first job when I was hired as a trainee with the Mirror Group on a cluster of local newspapers which they used to own in the West Country. I went from there briefly to the *Sunday People* and then for a year to the London *Evening Standard* before I was hired as a news reporter by the *Guardian*, in 1979. And that has been my professional anchor ever since. On the way through, I floated off for about six years, to be home affairs correspondent at the *Observer*, chief feature writer at Robert Maxwell's *London Daily News*, a freelancer in Washington DC and an on-screen reporter for Granada TV's *World In Action*, before going back to the *Guardian*, where I still work on a freelance contract.

Early on in this project, I established several rules. The first was that I would not draw on my personal knowledge of the private lives of the people I have worked with. I know a fair bit about sex and drugs and hypocrisy in Fleet Street: executives whose papers support the war against drugs while shoving cocaine up their nostrils in the office toilets; reporters who attack the sexual adventures of others while routinely dropping their own trousers at the first scent of a willing secretary. I've used none of that: first, because I think we shouldn't be writing about anybody's private life at all unless there is some really powerful public need to know about it; and second, because I don't want to be beaten up by former colleagues who might reasonably complain that I were betraying their confidence.

The second rule was to try to start from a blank sheet. It wouldn't have been fair to target the media outlets for whom I've worked just because I had an inside track on the way they behave. Equally, it certainly wouldn't have been right to ignore them or favour them. So,

I set out to research the media in exactly the same way that I would research any subject. That applies, in particular, to the *Guardian*.

I'm a *Guardian* man. I've read the paper since I was fourteen. I've worked for it for years and, when I came up with this project, the editor, Alan Rusbridger, agreed to support me while I pursued it. It needs to be said that never at any stage has anybody from the *Guardian* tried to impose any kind of restriction or requirement on what I have written, and you will see that both the *Guardian* and its sister paper, the *Observer*, crop up here, rough and smooth. It follows from this that neither the *Guardian* nor anybody who works there is responsible for the content of the book. That's my responsibility.

I've tended to dig out evidence from the UK, but, at points, I've tried to add information which shows that the same picture is true in other countries, particularly the United States. In the same way, I've tended to focus on print, but I've included some material to show how broadcasting is following the same pattern. I've said very little about tabloids. Nobody needs a book to tell them that the tabloids are an unreliable source of information about the world. My focus has been on the most prestigious and trusted of media outlets.

I was given a big boost early on by the Joseph Rowntree Foundation, who provided the funding for a huge piece of empirical research. That research was conducted by Cardiff University's School of Journalism, Media and Cultural Studies, led by Professor Justin Lewis, Dr Andrew Williams, Professor Bob Franklin, Dr James Thomas and Nick Mosdell. I owe deep thanks to all of them.

I would never have been able to set that up without the help of Mike Jempson, director of MediaWise, the national charity which campaigns for ethical behaviour by the media. In spite of apparently endless financial headaches, Jempson works tirelessly in the cause of MediaWise and was a constant source of support for this project.

I was helped along the way by a shifting team of young researchers. Three of them – Jenny Evans, Jaemie Gallie and Jim Mawson – helped me on numerous subjects with real diligence and energy. In addition, Christian Bjornes handled Freedom of Information applications to Whitehall; Zoë Corbyn researched the reporting of science; Robin Davies handled Freedom of Information applications to journalism colleges; Katy Heslop handled database searches; Garnet Roach researched front groups in the PR industry; Natasha Gilbert researched environmental PR; Jennifer Millen researched crime reporting; Vikki Thomas researched the reporting of terrorism; and Ida Tønder analysed statistics and researched the training of journalists. All of them did good work, and none of them is responsible for the way I've used the raw material which they came up with.

I should add that a great many working journalists helped me on this project. They did so willingly, because like me they can see no good reason why journalism should be exempt from the kind of scrutiny which we bring to bear on the rest of the world. For reasons of professional survival, most of them did so on the understanding that I would not name them. But they are there and, to the extent that this book may attract the hostility of some in Fleet Street, I am proud of the fact that numerous colleagues are better than that.

So. Let dog eat dog.

Part One
Flat Earth Stories

'The duty of doctors is to give health to their patients, the duty of the singer to sing, and the duty of the journalist is to write what this journalist sees in reality.'

Anna Politkovskaya

'The Earth is flat.'

Anybody anywhere until somebody checked

1. The Bug that Ate the World

31 December 1999. Millennium Eve. Most of the adults in the Western world are out in search of alcohol and hectic self-indulgence, and almost certainly most of the journalists are out there with them, but a few have stayed back in their newsrooms. Along with the police and the doctors and the fire brigade, the journalists have a job which is too important to drop just because everybody else is out at a party. And this holds some consolation, because Millennium Eve looks like being a good night to be a journalist on a late shift. This is the night when a very big story is going to break, all around the world.

All it needs is for the sun to move across the planet, hauling the darkness behind it, for midnight to strike, and, hour by hour, country by country, computers will die. And with them may die the world's electricity grids, its telecommunications, its water supplies, its defence networks: the entire corpus of veins which carries the lifeblood of an electronic society faces sudden death from the technological equivalent of a cardiac arrest. The journalists know it is going to happen, because they themselves have written the stories which have predicted it. The millennium bug is finally coming.

This is a story with the finest of journalistic pedigrees. It has been running for years at great length, not only in the tabloids but also in the most prestigious newspapers and magazines which are published in the world's most sophisticated communications systems. In Britain, they have explained: 'Life-saving hospital equipment and 999 services in London face total breakdown on January 1 2000' (*Evening Standard*) . . . 'National Health Service patients could die because insufficient time and thought have been devoted to the millennium bug' (*Daily Telegraph*) . . . 'Banks could collapse if they fail to eradicate the millennium bug from their computer systems' (*Guardian*) . . . 'Riots, terrorism and a health crisis could follow a millennium bug melt-down' (*Sunday Mirror*) . . . 'All trace of pension contributions could be wiped out in businesses failing to cope with the millennium bug' (*Independent*). The threat is not merely that systems will fail and cause chaos in the organisations which rely on them, but that some of those systems will carry on working and choose their own terrifying new course. 'The millennium bug could cause prison security doors and cell doors operated by computer to open,' according to the *Independent on Sunday*, while *The Times* has told its readers of a 'Nato alert over Russian missile millennium bug' and reported 'alliance fears of an attack from the East by rogue nuclear weapons systems'.

In the United States, in the same way, the best newspapers in the land have joined the coverage: 'The millennium bug looms' (*New York Times*) . . . 'Year 2000 – a ticket to disaster' (*San Francisco Chronicle*) . . . 'The computer time bomb' (*Seattle Times*) . . . 'A date with disaster' (*Washington Post*) . . . 'Countdown to "Y2K meltdown"' (*Chicago Daily Herald*) . . . 'The day the world crashes' (*Newsweek*). Stories have gone beyond merely describing the threat. Some American journalists have pointed accusatory fingers at the rest of the world, with a sequence of stories such as one in the *Chicago Tribune* in March 1999, headlined 'Many nations are unwilling or unable to fix possible computer woes, leaving the US in peril'. The *LA Times*, in August 1999, revealed that the solution to the threat was itself under threat: 'Some fear sabotage by Y2K consultants; foreign contractors in particular may be infecting programs as they fix 2000 bugs, US security experts warn.'

As it turned out, we know very little of what really happened on that long-awaited night. That is, in part, of course, because very little did happen.

In Britain, a tide gauge in Portsmouth harbour failed. A desktop computer in a weather station in Aberdeen froze. The government minister responsible for dealing with the bug volunteered that these incidents were 'too trivial to mention'. There was also a businessman in Swansea who reported that his computer had more or less blown up on Millennium Eve, but then discovered that he was suffering from a mouse with loose bowels which had made a mess of his circuit board.

Later that night, in the United States, where the finest newspapers had joined the lowliest television networks and supermarket magazines in relaying the scale of the Y2K threat, John Koskinen, the chairman of President Clinton's Council on Year 2000 Conversion, declared: 'At this point we are not aware of anything that is broken as a result of Y2K.' Bruce McConnell, director of the International Year 2000 Co-operation Center, agreed: 'From an infrastructure standpoint, we expect a continuation of the non-event.'

Across the world, it was the same non-story. No planes fell out of the sky. No power stations melted down. And the great non-event struck not only those countries which had spent years defending themselves against the bug, but also those which had done little or nothing to prepare for it. There was no story in China and India where, the world's press had warned, governments had been so lax that the bug would disable their power grids and their communication systems with the possibility of riots as the social infrastructure collapsed. There was nothing, too, from Russia and Belarus and Moldova and Ukraine, countries where the threat had been so recklessly ignored that, as Millennium Eve approached, the US State Department had issued formal travel advisories to alert American citizens to the risk to their health and safety if they were to go there.

There is a second reason why we know so little about what really happened that night: most of those journalists who worked late in search of the promised catastrophe wrote nothing at all about the great non-story. No millennium bug? No global crash? No crash even in those countries which had failed to protect themselves? No truth at all in hundreds of thousands of news reports and background features and confident comment which had run through just about every newspaper and broadcasting outlet in every country on the planet, stories which had been running for years and which were still running only twenty-four hours before the great night finally arrived? No truth in the mass media? Well, there's no story there. So it never got written.

Encouraged by these stories, some governments had spent fortunes in public money (and secured no better result than those who spent next to nothing). Journalists reported that the British government had spent £396 million on Y2K protection. They also reported that it had spent £430 million. And that it had spent £788 million. The

American government had spent far more, they said – $100 billion, or $200 billion, or $320 billion, or $600 billion, or $858 billion, depending on which journalist you were reading. Anyway, it was a lot. Beyond that, the private sector had spawned a mini-industry of companies selling millennium bug kits, while publishers turned out bug books and bug videos, and estate agents sold bug-resistant homes, and a few families sold their houses and fled to remote cabins in order to give themselves a chance to survive the coming bug-related chaos. But this was not a story.

The sun rose on 1 January 2000 like the lights coming on at an orgy. Everybody who had been so busy – the journalists, the governments, the bug-related businesses and the computer experts – all picked themselves up, hoped nobody was looking and quietly tiptoed away.

You could argue that every profession has its defining value. For carpenters, it might be accuracy: a carpenter who isn't accurate shouldn't be a carpenter. For diplomats, it might be loyalty: they can lie and spy and cheat and pull all sorts of dirty tricks, and as long as they are loyal to their government, they are doing their job. For journalists, the defining value is honesty – the attempt to tell the truth. That is our primary purpose. All that we do – and all that is said about us – must flow from the single source of truth-telling.

So, Millennium Eve turned out to be a terrifying night for journalists. It was in itself a stunning example of a failure in truth-telling by the global media. Whatever the truth was about the possible threat to computers that night, the world's journalists clearly had gone a long way beyond it. It was symbolic too: the new millennium arriving in darkness; the truth lost; and the truth about the losing of that truth then lost as well. The millennium bug is only one example of a systemic weakness which quietly has overwhelmed the communications media, leaving governments all over the planet and their billions of citizens embarking on a new era in which they continue to pour time and energy and money into frantic activity which frequently proves to be built out of untruth.

This is Flat Earth news. A story appears to be true. It is widely accepted as true. It becomes a heresy to suggest that it is not true – even if it is riddled with falsehood, distortion and propaganda.

★   ★   ★

Flat Earth news is so widespread that it is itself the subject of Flat Earth stories.

For example, there is a simple perception that media stories are produced by corrupt and cynical journalistic puppets who just couldn't care less whether they tell the truth and simply dance to the tune of whoever is pulling their string.

The fact is that there are some horrible journalists out there – moral cowards, intellectual quislings, boot-lickers, butt-kissers and natural-born liars. Some of them are drunks. Some of them take backhanders from intelligence agencies or government departments. There are plenty of journalists who deserve at least one of those descriptions. There may even be a few who deserve all of them. But the important point is that there are masses of journalists who are none of those things, many of them genuinely dedicated people, and yet frequently they fail to tell the truth.

To imagine, for example, that you can explain the weakness of the *New York Times* by looking at Jayson Blair, who spent several years as a news reporter planting fiction in their pages, is to miss the point entirely. The problem is much more interesting than that. More worrying, too.

There are all kinds of people who try to make sense of media failure – professional politicians, left-wing radicals, right-wing radicals, a small army of media studies academics and their students, multiple millions of consumers who understand that they cannot believe everything they read – and yet repeatedly many of them fall for explanations which are themselves infiltrated by falsehood, distortion and propaganda. There are honourable exceptions, but the mainstream of media criticism is badly polluted with misunderstanding.

These attempted explanations tend to fail for two reasons. First, a lot of media critics are outsiders who recycle evidence from other outsiders and often develop theories which simply don't catch the reality of what goes on inside newsrooms. Second, they are diverted by a noticeable pattern in media failure, that mainstream journalists tend to produce a consensus account of the world which repeatedly reflects the interests of the rich and powerful. If you look back at the cold war, for example, it is relatively easy to see how the totalitarian regime of the old Soviet Union used the tools of propaganda on its captive media to pretend it was a haven of equality and peace. It is far more difficult to understand how the United States, with its startling history of support for repressive dictatorships in the Third World, was able to rely on constitutionally free media to present it as a beacon of democracy and freedom. This produces conspiracy theories which are attractive but heavily overstated.

So, for example, there is a popular theory that mass-media coverage is orchestrated or at least fundamentally restricted in order to win the favour of corporate advertisers. To an outsider's eye, this is very tempting: these advertisers have money, the media outlets need the money, so they must be vulnerable to some kind of pressure from the advertisers to describe the world in a way which suits their interests. It's a fine theory, particularly favoured by left-wing radicals, but its truth is very limited.

There certainly is some evidence that big advertisers can strong-arm small media outlets into misreporting their particular company or industry. So, fashion magazines may go soft on the big fashion houses; local newspapers may steer clear of conflict with major local businesses. The biggest known example of this was the notorious incident at the *Los Angeles Times* in 1999 when the paper's management cut a deal with a local sports arena, which had the paper commissioning positive stories about the arena while the arena's managers leaned on all their subcontractors to pay for adverts in the paper, with both sides splitting the profit.

But when critics try to use this theory to explain the systemic flow of Flat Earth news through the global media with its heavy skew towards the interests of the status quo, the evidence simply expires.

The closest I can get to shoring up the idea is that there certainly are examples of corporations pulling their advertising in order to try to have an impact on the political or general editorial line of a media outlet – but there is a real shortage of examples of their succeeding. A famous and typical case: when the *Observer* attacked the invasion of Suez in 1956, some pro-Israeli advertisers boycotted the paper in protest – and failed entirely to persuade the *Observer* to change its coverage. In thirty years in Fleet Street, I have never come across a case of advertisers influencing an editorial line, directly or indirectly. Nor can I find any other journalist who has ever known it to happen. And nor, as far as I know, can the critics who promote the idea.

In its loosest version, this theory suggests simply that media organisations understand that corporate advertisers have certain political interests and so – without the need for any explicit strong-arming from any particular advertiser – those organisations make sure that their output broadly supports the status quo for fear of seeing their advertising income dribbling away. The truth is that there is ideology in journalism. Our stories overwhelmingly tend to cluster around the same narrow set of political and moral assumptions about how the world should be run. But again, there is no evidence that advertisers, however indirectly, are the source for this; and, as we will see, there is a different and far more powerful source at work.

If advertisers are in any way responsible for Flat Earth news, it is happening on a scale so small as to be not only negligible but a distraction from what is really going wrong. The fact is that the fingerprints of big corporations are all over news coverage – but it's not the advertising department which is letting them into the newsroom.

The other widespread conspiracy theory is that the problem lies with proprietors who lean down from on high and impose their demands on a compliant staff. And this is true. Owners can and do interfere in the editorial process of their outlets. But, again, it is not quite the way that outsiders imagine.

Historically, particularly during the birth and growth of the mass-circulation press in the twentieth century, there was a clear pattern for power-hungry individuals to buy newspapers and then to stick their cigar-stained fingers into the editorial process in order to promote a detailed agenda of government policy, i.e. for the purpose of political propaganda.

Lord Northcliffe, who founded popular journalism in Britain, was a man in love with political power: he not only used his newspapers to topple one government (Asquith's in May 1915) and to create another (led by Lloyd George in December 1916), he also got himself officially appointed as Britain's Director for Propaganda. His brother, Lord Rothermere, openly embraced dictatorship, declaring that Hitler was 'a great gentleman' and ordering his *Daily Mail* to lockstep with British fascism. Well into the Second World War, his compliant staff were still campaigning against Jewish refugees seeking safety in Britain.

A few of this generation of owners used their wealth to protect and promote decent journalism, but most behaved like Lord Beaverbrook, the model of this kind of proprietor, who famously explained his role as owner of the *Daily Express*: 'I run the paper for the purpose of making propaganda and with no other motive.'

But things have changed, because the ownership of the media has changed. Almost all of the old patriarchs who personally owned and abused newspapers have sold out to corporations, whose primary purpose is not propaganda. Their primary purpose simply and uncontroversially is to make money. And this has introduced a whole new set of pressures whose combined effect easily exceeds the impact of the interference of owners. It is these forces of commercialism which now provide the greatest obstacle to truth-telling journalism.

The new corporate owners interfere far less than their propagandist predecessors. Most (though not all) reporters nowadays will tell you that they have never written a story on the instructions, direct or indirect, of an owner or of any editorial placeman employed by an owner. However, it is not that these new owners are more ethical than their predecessors. There is a powerful reason why they limit the scale of their interference: they know very well that it is bad for business.

At best, this has produced a handful of owners who take the view that as long as the bottom line is healthy, they have no interest at all in any editorial line. One of the few corporate owners who earned the respect of his journalists is the Canadian Roy Thomson, who was also one of the first. In his history of Fleet Street, *Press Gang*, Roy Greenslade marks his buying of the *Scotsman* in 1953 as a key moment for UK media: 'A new, but very different kind of press proprietor had arrived in Britain. Instead of an ideologue who saw journalism as a political weapon, here was an apolitical accountant who viewed journalism as a branch of commerce.' In the United States, Thomson was perfectly happy for his papers in the southern states to support segregation while his titles in the north attacked it, just as long as they turned a dollar. As owner of the *Sunday Times*, Thomson famously allowed his journalists complete freedom of editorial and political manoeuvre.

At worst, this has produced corporate owners who continue to interfere, but their interference differs from that of the old patriarchs.

It is less frequent. And it is offered in the style of prostitution, allowing for a flexible range of ideological activities so long as they produce the right reward. You can see this happening most clearly in the behaviour of the world's most powerful media proprietor, Rupert Murdoch.

Murdoch is a highly successful businessman, a moderately competent journalist in his own right and a brutal and unscrupulous bully. His interventions tend to come in three forms.

First, and most important, he uses his media outlets to build alliances with politicians who, in return, will help him with his business. In his highly revealing biography, *The Murdoch Archipelago*, the former *Sunday Times* journalist Bruce Page goes back to January 1968 to provide an early and vivid example of how the man works. Murdoch then was still in the early stages of building his empire from his base in Adelaide and, in search of a political ally, he had started dealing with the Deputy Prime Minister of Australia, 'Black Jack' McEwen. In January 1968, Black Jack found himself at the centre of a crisis.

The Prime Minister, Harold Holt, had drowned while swimming from a beach near Melbourne. Black Jack was suddenly elevated to the post of Acting Prime Minister. However, he knew he couldn't keep the job, because he led the Country Party, which was the minority partner in a coalition government. The bigger party, the Liberals, would choose a new leader, on 9 January. The choice was between two men: John Gorton and Billy McMahon. Black Jack wanted Gorton, a weak boozer of a man. So he had to stop Billy McMahon.

Black Jack publicly declared that his Country Party would refuse to serve under Billy McMahon but mysteriously refused to explain why. Secretly, in his role as Acting Prime Minister, he called in the head of the Australian Security Intelligence Organisation and urged him to investigate a close associate of Billy McMahon, named Max Newton. Black Jack claimed that Newton was a subversive, secretly working to sabotage the Australian economy on behalf of the Japanese. It was a lie, but the head of ASIO agreed to open a file and see what he could find. He found nothing. Nevertheless, the mere existence of the ASIO file was enough for Black Jack.

Four days before the leadership vote, on the evening of 5 January, as Bruce Page recounts, Black Jack called Rupert Murdoch to his suite in the Kurrajong Hotel in Canberra and handed him a dossier on Max Newton's supposed treachery on behalf of the Japanese. This was a double delight for the young media proprietor. It was not only a chance to do a favour for his political ally. It was also a chance to hurt Newton, who had formerly been one of Murdoch's editors and had made the bad mistake of publicly describing him as 'a whippersnapper from Adelaide'.

Later that evening, Murdoch phoned Newton, and said simply: 'This is the whippersnapper from Adelaide. I suggest you read my paper tomorrow.' The paper was the *Australian*. The next day's story did everything that Black Jack McEwen had wanted, destroying the reputation of Max Newton and, with it, the chances of Billy McMahon winning the vote to become Prime Minister. The headline read: 'WHY MCEWEN VETOES MCMAHON: FOREIGN AGENT IS THE MAN BETWEEN THE LEADERS'. And it told the story of Max Newton, the supposed secret agent of Japanese subversion. It was entirely false, though it is always possible that Murdoch himself believed it. There was no reporter's byline on the story. It was the owner's own work, dictated by the politician who was his ally. Four days later, with the rest of the Australian media crawling all over Murdoch's exclusive, Billy McMahon lost the election, and, just as Black Jack wanted, John Gorton became Prime Minister.

A year later, in January 1969, Murdoch tried to make his first big move out of Australia, bidding to buy the *News of the World* in London. But he was trapped by Australian currency regulations, which prevented him exporting his money to the UK. Black Jack McEwen came to his rescue, summoning the servile John Gorton to his hotel suite to sign an authority which would allow Murdoch to get his cash out of the country. Gorton asked if he had any whisky. As McEwen later recalled: 'The papers were signed. Rupert and I were out in the garden. Gorton went off with his Scotch. Rupert went off to buy his newspaper.'

This is how the man works. He uses his media outlets as tools to secure political favours, and he uses those political favours to advance his business. But his politics are never as big as his wallet. He collects politicians and then he dumps them, with profit as his guide. When he wanted the left-wing Gough Whitlam to become Prime Minister of Australia, he abused the *Australian* to help him and then sought favours from Whitlam in return. Three years later, when he decided that the right-wing Malcolm Fraser could do more for his business interests, he abused the *Australian* again with great crudeness to support the bloodless coup which ousted Whitlam. (On that occasion, he inflicted a double betrayal on his journalists, not only distorting their coverage but concealing from them his intimate knowledge of the biggest story of the decade – the plot to topple the elected Prime Minister, in which he was an active participant.)

It was the same in Britain. The late Woodrow Wyatt's diary, published in 1998, traces the long history of Murdoch's deal-making with the Conservative governments of Margaret Thatcher and then John Major, in which Wyatt was often the middleman. Wyatt records Mrs Thatcher, for example, in 1981, blocking the referral to the Monopolies and Mergers Commission which could have stopped Murdoch buying *The Times* and the *Sunday Times*; and the Murdoch papers then giving the beleaguered Prime Minister an easy ride during the crisis over the sale of Westland helicopters, which threatened to end her career. And, as Wyatt goes on to describe, Murdoch then performed a classic body swerve when he saw John Major's Conservatives running out of electoral juice: he dumped them and made a new ally out of Tony Blair. (Wyatt wept into his diary: 'Rupert has behaved like a swine and a pig.')

And it was the same in China, where Murdoch was so keen to win the favour of the autocrats in Beijing that in 1993 he agreed to drop BBC World Television from his Star satellite TV output in the country; then in 1998 blocked his book-publishing arm, HarperCollins, from proceeding with the memoirs of the former Governor of Hong Kong, Chris Patten, because they criticised China's abuse of human rights; while *The Times*'s China specialist, Jonathan Mirsky, in 1997 resigned in protest at the repeated restrictions imposed on his attempts to write about the suppression of dissent in China.

This is how the man works – and how other corporate proprietors also work. Tiny Rowland repeatedly meddled in the inner workings of the *Observer* to win political favours in Africa, where his company, Lonrho, had vast business interests. Robert Maxwell did the same to score political advantage to assist his investments, particularly in the Soviet Union and Eastern Europe.

As a second form of interference, these new corporate owners will impose a political framework on their outlets, but this is much looser than the political control of their propagandist predecessors. Taking Murdoch again as an example: he has a history of complaining when his newspapers are too sympathetic to commies, poofters and blacks, but this knee-jerk ideology falls a long way short of a coherent political programme – and it is always less important than the commerce. After eleven years of working for him, Andrew Neil concluded: 'He is much more right-wing than is generally thought but will curb his ideology for commercial reasons . . . He will always moderate his political fundamentalism if its suits his business.'

When he first bought the *Sun* in November 1969, Murdoch understood that its readers were unionised working-class men, and so he imposed a relatively left-wing framework on it, supporting Labour and running left-wing leader lines, for example attacking the Vietnam War, racism and capital punishment. As the *Sun's* market changed, he started pushing the framework to the right. In his book, *Good Times, Bad Times*, Harry Evans describes how, as Murdoch's first editor at *The Times*, in the early 1980s, he endured a long campaign of bad-mouthing and internal manoeuvring from his new proprietor, which was aimed at bringing him under financial and editorial control but also at imposing a right-wing political agenda on the paper. Evans went; his successor, Charles Douglas-Home, toed the Tory line: and then the line changed, and the paper moved in behind the Blair government.

Lord Rothermere, owner of the *Daily Mail*, reflected this same priority, when he explained in an interview in May 1997 that he often disagreed with his editor, Paul Dacre. Then in a comment which would have floored his interventionist grandfather, he added: 'He is entitled to his views in the paper, but if they start to affect the circulation, that will be different.'

Occasionally, this generation of corporate owners will go beyond imposing a rough framework and will directly interfere in specific political coverage, usually at times of heightened political tension – in the run-up to national elections or when some other defining political issue is on the horizon, such as the invasion of Iraq which was supported by Murdoch outlets across the planet. One striking recent example in Britain has been Rupert Murdoch's role in diverting the

Blair government away from its support for joining the European currency and for signing up to the European constitution. This has involved a mixture of relentless campaigning by Murdoch titles and direct (and secret) meetings between Murdoch and Tony Blair. And in the United States, Murdoch's political framework and his favour-trading with powerful politicians has united in the slavishly pro-Republican performance of his Fox News TV channel. Courtesy of *Outfoxed*, a documentary directed by Robert Greenwald, we know about the daily memos circulated to staff by Fox's vice president for news, John Moody, laying out editorial lines in support of the Bush administration. A sample memo instructed Fox staff to note the President's 'political courage and tactical cunning . . . in our reporting throughout the day'.

And yet Murdoch will turn a blind eye while his newspapers boost their circulation by embarrassing his political allies – unless the threat becomes too great. Andrew Neil says that Murdoch did nothing, for example, when the *Sunday Times* infuriated Margaret Thatcher by exposing her dislike for the Queen and also by conning its way into her son's bank account, but when she was directly threatened by Michael Heseltine's challenge to her leadership in 1990, Murdoch intervened to protect her (and Neil refused to comply).

Finally, the new corporate owners will also interfere aggressively if one of their outlets trespasses on their other business interests, but generally it has to be a direct threat before they do so. For example, Murdoch allowed the *Sunday Times* to contradict his line that the BBC licence fee should be abolished, even though he has a commercial interest in doing so. But when the same paper, in January 1994, attacked the government of Malaysia over corruption in the Pergau Dam project, he saw a direct threat to his Asian satellite TV business, Star, told Andrew Neil to stop 'this Malaysian business', and soon afterwards removed Neil from the paper.

So, it is true that owners interfere. It is also true that, to the extent that they are able to get away with it, they are taking advantage of compliant staff. There are some editors who fight their owners, but there are plenty who simply shrug and say that that is the way of the world. When in 1989, as editor of the *Daily Telegraph*, Max Hastings found some of his leader comments being attacked by Conrad Black, he explained his position in an interview on Channel 4. 'I've never really believed in the notion of editorial independence,' he said. 'I would never imagine saying to Conrad, "You have no right to ask me to do this," because Conrad is . . . richly entitled to take a view when he owns the newspaper.' Andrew Neil, in his autobiography, *Full Disclosure*, described Murdoch as 'an interventionist proprietor who expected to get his way' and then celebrated his own surrender as editor of the *Sunday Times*. 'Why should the owner not be the ultimate arbiter of what was in his paper?' he asked. The answer to that rhetorical question, of course, is that it is a betrayal of the paper's readers.

All this intervention is deeply damaging behaviour – the truth being traded for political favour and commercial advantage. If honesty is the defining value of journalism, then this precisely qualifies as journalism which is entirely bad. This matters. I don't want to diminish the scale or the wrongness of this kind of activity by proprietors. But, as with interference by advertisers, it is essential to recognise that interference by owners falls a long way short of explaining the consistent pattern of media failure across so many stories, big and small. Owners and advertisers are only part of the reason for the ideological problems in the mass media; and ideology is only part of the total problem of the retreat from truth-telling. Journalists with whom I have discussed this agree that if you could quantify it, you could attribute only 5% or 10% of the problem to the total impact of these two forms of interference.

The important point here is that, as the new owners of the mass media have shifted their priority from propaganda to commerce, that shift itself has introduced a whole new set of obstacles for truth-telling journalism. In an imaginary world, we might remove Rupert Murdoch and all his influence on all his outlets; we could replace him with Rupert Bear: the Murdoch newspapers and television stations would continue to pump out falsehood, distortion and propaganda.

Historically, the clearest threats to press freedom (i.e. the freedom to tell the truth) have come from outside of newsrooms; and they have tended to bring pressure to bear at the point of publication. The state did this through formal censorship, reinforced by secrecy, legal restraint and physical intimidation. Media owners, as we have seen, did this through direct and sustained interference. Both threats remain, albeit in more subtle form than in the past.

But now we are deep into a third age of falsehood and distortion, in which the primary obstacles to truth-telling lie inside the newsrooms, with the internal mechanics of an industry which has been deeply damaged. The problem now is not merely at the point of publication but also at the earlier and even more important stage of gathering and testing raw information.

Look back briefly at the story of the millennium bug and watch how it grew.

As far as I can tell, the story first hatched one Saturday morning in May 1993, in Toronto, Canada. Inside the city's *Financial Post*, on page 37, there was a single paragraph. Under the headline, 'TURN OF CENTURY POSES A COMPUTER PROBLEM', the story recorded that a Canadian technology consultant called Peter de Jager was warning that many computer systems would fail at midnight at the start of the new century and that few companies had taken steps to head off the problem.

Rather like the B-movie egg which is laid by the alien in the dark corner of the peaceful suburb, this little story broke out of its shell and slowly started to distribute its offspring around the undefended planet. By 1995, it had spread out of North America into Europe and Australia and Japan. By 1997, bug stories were being sighted all over the globe. By 1998, they had multiplied tenfold, infiltrating media outlets of every kind, and they were still mutating and dividing, still penetrating more and more newspaper columns, more and more broadcast news bulletins until finally, as Millennium Eve approached, they achieved a global conquest of the media, tens of thousands of bug stories infesting almost every news outlet on the planet.

Now, look closer. Look at the sources for the story, and you will see something very striking.

The first sources were computer specialists like Peter de Jager in Toronto. They knew there was a problem, but the important point is that they didn't know how serious it was going to be. They knew that the problem would occur only in computers which had internal clocks (most desktop computers do, but most 'embedded' systems, on which big organisations rely, don't), but only if those clocks calculated time by using a calendar rather than by simply measuring the gap between two dates, and only if those calendars used only two digits to register the years, rather than four, and only if the computer was being used for programs which had to calculate time across the boundary between 1999 and 2000. There were computer specialists who said at the time that, once you recognised all those limiting factors, this was likely to be a small-scale problem.

They also recognised that, even where it did occur, the problem generally would not cause any serious trouble. They knew this because, in truth, the millennium bug was not a new problem. For years, computers had been making calculations across the 99/00 boundary – for life insurance, pensions, mortgages, subscriptions and all kinds of long-term legal agreements. Many of those computers had already taken the boundary in their stride. Some had produced glitches, but they were quite simple – documents with the wrong dates or calculations that were obviously wrong, most of which could be dealt with very easily.

The difficulty for these computer specialists was that they themselves could not be sure how bad the problem would prove to be and, in the early days, when they found it difficult to persuade organisations that they might need to check their systems, some of them started to exaggerate.

When I spoke to Peter de Jager during the research for this book, he admitted that, when his first attempts to draw attention to the problem passed almost unnoticed, he had 'cranked up the anxiety', dealing with the real doubt about the seriousness of the problem by assuming the worst. In May 1996, for example, he gave evidence in the Canadian House of Representatives to the Subcommittee on Government Management, Information and Technology.

He told them: 'When the year 2000 arrives, the programs we used yesterday will be useless.' This was true of some old programs but certainly not of all. He continued: 'Unless the applications are fixed and available on January 1st, all businesses lose the ability to do business.' Some businesses possibly maybe, but certainly not all. He concluded: 'I will leave it to you to contemplate what happens to the worldwide economy if businesses lose the ability to do business.' This was indeed cranking up the anxiety, albeit with the benign intent of drawing attention to a real potential problem.

In 1997, the head of the British government's Taskforce 2000, Robin Guenier, similarly was pushing the anxiety button. He told the *Mail on Sunday*: 'I do not want to seem irrational or a prophet of doom, but there is a possibility of riots'. Years later, after a riot-free Millennium Eve, Guenier acknowledged that: 'If I'd gone around saying, "We'll probably get through this," no one would have printed anything.'

The media duly started to print what they were being told. As the story spread, a second wave of sources joined in, all sorts of people who had the clearest possible interest in hitting the alarm button.

Office managers used the bug to wring new money out of their organisations to update their computer systems, even when there was no risk to them, and journalists started to write stories about them. Property dealers hiked the price of houses which were supposedly remote enough to survive the crisis and fed spine-chilling quotes to the media. So, too, did the authors of survival guides. 'The Millennium Bug threatens our core infrastructure, and if that's not repaired in time, then every business, every home, every church, every synagogue, every entity that depends on that core infrastructure is also at risk.' That was from Michael Hyatt, publisher and author of *The Millennium Bug: How to Survive the Coming Chaos*. And then there were the manufacturers of millennium bug computer kits. 'There certainly will be some companies that go broke, people will be redundant and inevitably some people will die,' predicted Karl Feilder, founder of the company which sold four million copies of Check 2000 at £20 a piece.

Governments joined in. Given the genuine uncertainty about the scale of the problem, it was clearly politically safer to overreact than to under-react. This was particularly true for a British government whose predecessor had been caught out badly a few years earlier when it had tried to placate its beef farmers by under-reacting to the threat of BSE. So they started spending. Governments also started to use the issue to score propaganda points off traditionally hostile nations. So it was that NATO issued its warning about rogue Russian missiles nuking the West on Millennium Eve, while British ministers boasted that they were leading the world, teaching fifty-eight other countries how to handle the bug. 'We have been seen to be a leader,' declared the then Foreign Office minister, John Battle.

Soon, there was a third wave of sources. These were people who genuinely had no idea what they were talking about. 'Tony Blair is being urged to prevent a devastating millennium nuclear meltdown in Eastern Europe. Many of the ageing computers in the former Eastern bloc will crash at the turn of the millennium.' The *Sunday Mirror* got that from a Liberal Democrat MP. 'US military defences, including its nuclear arsenal, could cease to function.' The *Sunday Times*, among others, got that from a White House official. 'Some computer-guided elevators could simply stop in their tracks. You can also have problems with security systems, fire alarms, smoke alarms, thermostats and even heating, ventilation and air-conditioning equipment.' The US press got that from a real-estate lawyer.

By the late 1990s, a final wave of sources joined in as all kinds of maniacs and religious groups cranked up the anxiety to the point of apocalypse. They were led by Gary North of Christian Reconstruction who declared that 'We need times so hard that men will turn to God.' Mr North had got in early, explaining in 1997: 'When I began writing about Y2K, hardly anyone had heard of it. Today, the media cover it sporadically. In a year, there will be a tidal wave of articles. And, month by month, fear will spread. Doom and gloom will sell, as it has never sold before. I have positioned my name, my site, and Christian Reconstruction in the center of this fear. All I have to do now is to report bad news. That's just about all the Y2K news there is. One by one, the media sources will move in my direction.' And so they did.

Along the way, a kind of echo chamber was created, in which the media's cries produced results which themselves encouraged the media to cry still louder. As the scare stories spread, there were economists who were willing to predict the odds of global recession as a result of this bug, so the media reported their fears, so more companies hired consultants to check their systems, which provided more material for more media stories. In the same way, there were military leaders who read these stories and who were willing to predict the risk of a breach in national security as a result of the bug, so the media reported the threat, so, for example, the British government ordered armed troops and SAS special forces to be on standby on Millennium Eve in case the bug knocked out defence systems and let terrorists in to vital installations, and the media reported that, too.

After the great non-event, some of those who had forecast doom tried to claim that the absence of catastrophe must be evidence of their own success in preventing it. This was always hard for them to do, since right up to Millennium Eve, after all of the spending and preparing, they were still predicting disaster. When it didn't happen on 1 January, they continued to predict trouble for 3 January, when the New Year holiday ended. Then they conceded defeat.

On 6 January, Peter de Jager posted a story on his website in which he considered the case of Italy, one of the many countries which had survived unscathed despite refusing to check all of their computing systems: 'My view of the problem is contradicted by a fact I cannot refute, and make no attempt to: Italy has seen no significant effects . . . Countries that did nothing were faced with fewer problems than we expected.' It was the same, for example, with Russia, which spent less on dealing with the bug than a single British company, British Airways, and suffered no appreciable problem. It was the same, too, with the estimated 30% of small- and medium-sized businesses who had done nothing to defend against the bug and who had survived without significant difficulty. De Jager concluded with some courage as well as honesty: 'It turns out that there were fewer 99/00 boundary cross-ings than we feared.'

In the same way, Robert Roskind, founder of the Y2K Solutions Group and co-author of *The Complete Y2K Home Preparation Guide*, which sold tens of thousands of copies alongside its companion video, looked back from the unexpected safey of the year 2000 and admitted: 'The truth is we totally miscalculated the degree of risk. We spent a lot of time, money and angst that was not necessary.'

Many of these sources no doubt were speaking in good faith, but, if you look back at them, they all have in common one very striking characteristic: not one single one of them knew what the truth was. Even the computer specialists who started it were clouded in doubt. They simply could not tell how bad the problem would be. The rest of the media's sources – the vested commercial and political interests, the know-nothings, the religious and the mad – knew even less.

So, why did the journalists run their stories? Telling the truth is their primary purpose. Why would they not do that? The revealing point here is that nobody ordered them to get the story wrong. No corporate advertisers blackmailed newsrooms into running this stuff. No media proprietors leaned down from on high and imposed this story on their compliant staff. Sure, there were plenty of mercenaries and fools who were happy enough to make the most of the story, but they didn't initiate it or even control it. Journalists around the world spontaneously hopped on board a global flight of fiction which took off and left a few sad facts standing flat-footed and forgotten in its wake.

Why? They did it because, just like their sources, the journalists themselves did not know the truth – even though truth is their primary objective. And that is commonplace. Ignorance is the root of media failure. Most of the time, most journalists do not know what they are talking about. Their stories may be right, or they may be wrong: they don't know.

I say this not as an insult to them (well, most of them). Generally, journalists, like any other professionals, prefer to do their job well. I say it because this profession has become damaged to the point where most of the time, most of its members are no longer able to do their job. They work in structures which positively prevent them discovering the truth. Historically, there has always been an element of ignorance in journalism, simply because it attempts to record the truth as it happens. Now, this has become much worse. It is endemic. The ethic of honesty has been overwhelmed by the mass production of ignorance.

The whole story of modern media failure is complicated and subtle. It involves all kinds of manipulation, occasional conspiracy, lying, cheating, stupidity, cupidity, gullibility, a collapse of skill and a new wave of deliberate propaganda. But the story begins with journalists who tell you the Earth is flat, because genuinely they think it might be. The scale of it is terrifying.

In the late 1960s, in London, three doctors were caught selling heroin. There was an outburst of media coverage, driven by the horrifying idea that GPs, who were supposed to protect health, were making money out of selling poison to their own patients. As a result, GPs were told that they could no longer prescribe heroin unless they had a special licence from the Home Office.

The few licences that were issued were given to selected psychiatrists. At first, they ran a liberal regime, prescribing heroin for the several hundred addicts who were then registered in Britain, almost all of them concentrated in Chinatown on the southern side of Shaftesbury Avenue and among the old jazz cats on the northern side.

However, during the 1970s, with the media still mumbling their discontent at the distribution of this poison and with the US government pressing for prohibition, the British government instructed these psychiatrists to cut their prescriptions in an attempt to force the addicts to give up their drug. The addicts started looking for a new supply and so a small black market developed around Piccadilly Circus, at the foot of Shaftesbury Avenue, most of it supplied by breaking in to chemists. In search of funds to buy their heroin, some of those addicts started selling to friends. The black market started to expand.

For the first time, regular supply lines were opened up to import illicit heroin, initially through American GIs in South-East Asia, then through the Pakistani community which had connections in Afghanistan, and, at the end of the decade, through an influx of Iranian exiles who fled the new regime of Ayatollah Khomeini, converting their cash into heroin.

In the early 1980s, with the black market spreading across London and beginning to spill into other cities, there was another outburst of media coverage, alarmed again at the sale of poison to young people. The Thatcher government clamped down hard, joining the American war against drugs. In an attempt to kill the black market, it put new money into police drugs squads and customs teams, and choked off the prescription of heroin by the licensed psychiatrists, replacing it with strictly limited supplies of methadone, a substitute which is unpopular among many heroin users. The price of black-market heroin rose. London criminals who had specialised in armed robbery switched track and set up new and more effective supply lines. The black market boomed.

Twenty years later, the original black market of several hundred registered addicts had been replaced by some 300,000 'chaotic users', many of them suffering from hepatitis, septicaemia, ruptured veins, dramatic weight loss and, occasionally, overdose; some of them had become heavily involved in prostitution and crime. According to an internal Downing Street report, which was leaked in 2005, black-market drug users by then were responsible for 85% of shoplifting, between 70 and 80% of burglaries, and 54% of robberies.

But all of this – the years of media coverage, the public panic, the government policy – was based on falsehood. Heroin is not a poison. Contrary to popular belief, pure heroin, properly handled, is a benign drug. In the words of a 1965 New York study by Dr Richard Brotman: 'Medical knowledge has long since laid to rest the myth that opiates observably harm the body.' Contrary to popular belief, it is rather difficult to kill yourself with heroin: the gap between a therapeutic and a fatal dose is far wider than it is, for example, with paracetamol. It is addictive – and that is a very good reason not to use it – but its most notable side effect on the physical, mental and moral condition of its users is constipation. The truth is that all of the illness and misery and death which are associated with heroin are, in fact, the effect not of the drug itself but of the black market on which it is sold as a result of this war against drugs.

Black-market heroin becomes poisonous and dangerous because unscrupulous dealers cut it with all kinds of pollutants to increase their profit. Black-market addicts contract diseases, because they use dirty injecting equipment. Black-market users overdose accidentally, because they have no idea of the purity of the batch they are using. Black-market addicts are thin, not because the drug makes them thin, but because they have to give all their money to dealers. Black-market addicts commit crime, not because the drug makes them immoral, but because they have no other way to fund their habit.

For decades, pharmaceutical heroin was prescribed by doctors to patients who had become addicted after operations, particularly soldiers who had undergone battlefield surgery. They spent years on a legal supply: it did them no damage, and they led healthy, fruitful lives. Enid Bagnold, for example, who wrote *National Velvet*, was prescribed it after a hip operation and then spent twelve years injecting up to 350mg a day. Enid – as far as history records – never mugged a single person or sold her body in the streets, but died quietly in bed at the age of ninety-one. Until the American prohibitionists closed him down in the 1920s, Dr Willis Butler ran a famous clinic in Shreveport, Louisiana, for some of these 'therapeutic addicts'. Among his patients, he included four doctors, two church ministers, two retired judges, an attorney, an architect, a newspaper editor, a musician from the symphony orchestra, a printer, two glass blowers and the mother of the commissioner of police. None of them showed any ill effect from the years which they spent on Dr Butler's prescriptions. And, as Dr Butler later recalled: 'I never found one we could give an overdose to, even if we had wanted to. I saw one man take twelve grains intravenously at one time. He stood up and said, "There, that's just fine," and went on about his business.'

The truth about the prohibition of heroin is that it creates the very problems which it pretends to solve: causing the sickness and death which it claims to be preventing; provoking the crime and disorder which it wants to stop.

Just as with the millennium bug, a false story which enveloped the world started simply, with expert sources who did not really know the truth. The Americans launched their war against drugs in 1924 after senators took evidence from specialists on heroin who told them that the drug was toxic, unusually deadly and that, as one witness put it, 'there is no greater peril than heroin'. This was untrue but, once injected into the public domain, the falsehood was picked up and spread further, just as with the millennium bug, by others who had some interest in promoting it: racists who used it to attack Chinese migrants, law-enforcement agencies who used it to increase their funding and their powers, and then by genuine know-nothings who thought they were being helpful. The media knew no better and again operated as an echo chamber, spreading the untruth, stimulating activity which took the untruth for granted, and then reporting that activity as though it were well founded. Delusion and reality became locked together.

And just as with the millennium bug, governments spend colossal amounts on the delusion. By 2003, the US federal government was spending $19 billion a year on its war against drugs. That is $600 a second. State and local governments were spending a further $30 billion. And since then, they have raised the budget. The Transform Drugs Institute in Bristol estimates that for every pound which the British government now spends on prohibition, it stimulates four pounds' worth of crime. If, on occasion, it succeeds temporarily in cutting the supply of heroin, it pushes up the price of the drug, thereby stimulating yet more crime by users who need more money to fund their habit. The impact of all this on the health of addicts is beyond measurement.

This is Flat Earth news. The heroin story appears to be true. It is widely accepted as true. It becomes a heresy to suggest that it is not true. The most powerful institutions on the planet insist that it is true, but it is riddled with falsehood, distortion and propaganda.

It is inherently difficult to establish the real scale of Flat Earth news. The first difficulty is that, precisely because these stories are so widely believed, any reader can be forgiven for holding on to the familiar false-hood. So, I have set up a Flat Earth News website (www.flatearthnews.net) where I have posted a much fuller account of the heroin story and others like it which we will touch on later.

Beyond that, there is a deeper difficulty that, since we are talking about the failure of media on a global scale, the problem is simply too big to be measured with any accuracy. It is like an ant trying to measure an elephant.

At a local level, Philip Meyer, professor of journalism at the University of North Carolina, in his 2004 book, *The Vanishing Newspaper*, records the results of a study which he organised in Oregon and North Carolina, checking with more than 5,000 people who had been the sources of news stories in twenty-two local papers over a two-year period, to discover their view of whether the stories were accurate. Meyer found that the sources reported that 21% of the stories had simple, objective errors, such as names being misspelled; 18% of the stories had mathematical errors; and 53% of them contained 'soft' errors, which were a matter of judge-ment rather than proof, such as distortion, exaggeration and quotes used out of context. Combining all three kinds of reported error, Meyer found that the sources of these stories were claiming inaccuracy of some kind in 59% of them, i.e. three stories out of every five.

It may or may not be that we would find the same alarming level of falsehood if we could conduct that kind of experiment on a global scale. But even if we can't be entirely accurate in our measurement, we can nevertheless clearly see the elephant. Look back over the last ten years at some of the great, global news stories.

Throughout the late 1990s, the biggest political story in the world was the flood of scandal rising up around President Bill Clinton. The global media ran stories which accused him of fraud in the Whitewater property deal, importing drugs through an airstrip in Arkansas and conspiring to murder his friend Vince Foster. All of these stories were false. Much of the detail of his alleged sexual misbehaviour was also false. These stories were picked up and repeated by the familiar range of self-serving and unreliable sources through journalists who simply did not know what was true. After the scandal had done its damage, it emerged that the allegations had originally been promoted by a group of right-wingers who were determined to destroy Clinton and who used the American *Spectator* magazine to insert their stories, true or false, into the mass media. One of them, David Brock, later broke cover and admitted his part in the plot.

In an interview, broadcast in October 2004, the BBC journalist Adam Curtis asked Brock: 'Did those promoting these stories know that they were not true?'

'They did not care,' replied Brock.

'Why not?'

'Because they were having a devastating effect.'

And the global media went along with the tale.

These were the same media outlets who at the same time, with rare exceptions, were misreporting the millennium bug right up to the great non-event; and the dot.com boom of the late 1990s right up to the moment when it collapsed in debt and disarray; and the huge success of the giant energy company Enron right up to the moment when its accounts were exposed as a giant work of fiction; and the almost equal success of the telecoms company WorldCom right up to the point when it collapsed into the biggest bankruptcy in the history of the United States.

Undaunted, these outlets then spent the first twenty months of the new millennium consistently failing to report the threat from Osama bin Laden before the attacks of 11 September 2001. Tom Fenton, then a senior foreign correspondent with CBS News, describes in his book, *Bad News*, how during this time he tried repeatedly to get stories about bin Laden on air but was blocked at every attempt. This was in spite of the fact that bin Laden was already believed to be responsible for a sequence of vicious attacks, including the massacres at US embassies in Kenya and Tanzania in 1998. In the three months leading up to 11 September, Fenton records, al-Qaeda was not mentioned on any of the three main US network evening broadcasts – not once. During that same period, the *New York Times* was given a video of bin Laden explicitly threatening violence. One of their senior reporters wrote up a story about it, headlined 'ON VIDEOTAPE: BIN LADEN CHARTS A VIOLENT FUTURE'. It was posted on their website, which then had only a tiny readership, but it never made it into the paper. Why? They didn't know it was important.

Terrorism, in turn, after the attacks on the US in September 2001, became the biggest story on the planet, and the media joined in with a steady flow of 'terror error' stories.

Some of these were non-events, like the false alerts about expected terrorist attacks in the United States in the autumn of 2001: on 20 September ('aeroplane hijackings this weekend'); 22 September ('Boston later today'); 27 September ('truck bombs in New York City imminent'); 6 October ('major attack highly likely in near future, 100% certain after invasion of Afghanistan'); 12 October ('more attacks highly probable in next several days'); 30 October ('specific, credible threat of very serious attacks in following week'); 2 November ('credible threat of attacks on suspension bridges in California in following five days'); 4 December ('general alert to risk of imminent attack'). All these reports, like many others since, in the US, the UK and the rest of the world, were false, pumped into the media by official sources who either genuinely did not know the truth or did not care but hoped for some political advantage.

Some of the terror error stories were fabricated plots which were built around the genuine arrests of suspects, including the three men from Leicester, who were said to have been planning to fly a helicopter bomb into the US Embassy in London (released without charge and handed over to immigration authorities); the Swede who was said to have been trying to fly a plane into a US Embassy in Europe (the Swedish prosecutor said there was never any evidence of any such plan); the eight men from Manchester who were said to have been plotting to blow up Manchester United's football ground (all released without any charge); the six men in London who were arrested for planning ricin attacks (five cleared of all criminal activity, one convicted of 'conspiracy to cause public nuisance', no ricin ever found); the three men who were said to have been planning a cyanide attack on the London Underground (no evidence of any such plan).

This sort of terror error hit a peak in July 2005, after the bombing of a London bus and three trains. British newspapers spent several days blaming the attack variously on 'white mercenary terrorists' (*Independent on Sunday*) and 'a foreign-based Islamic terrorist cell' (*Sunday Telegraph*) before discovering that, in fact, all four bombers were British-born. *The Times* reported that 'the London rush-hour bombers are alive and planning another attack' before admitting that, in fact, they were all dead. Between them, Fleet Street newspapers identified four different 'masterminds' behind the plot; warned that a fifth terrorist was on the loose (*Daily Mail*); and, after the failed attempt at further bombings two weeks later, that there was a third cell on the loose (*Sunday Times*) – all of which was directly contradicted by the subsequent investigation by police and intelligence agencies.

In the background, some genuine attacks did take place around the world in the months following the September 2001 massacre. By early 2002, the prospect of invading Iraq to deal with this threat had become the world's single biggest story. In the now familiar pattern, that long-running tale began with the cautious estimates of intelligence experts, who happened to be wrong. They were picked up and exaggerated by politicians and Iraqi exiles who had a vested interest in promoting them. They were spread still further by politicians and pundits who genuinely knew nothing at all about Iraqi weapons. And the global media recycled the lot. Professor Justin Lewis of Cardiff University, for example, studied British broadcast news reports in the build-up to the invasion of Iraq and found that 86% of them assumed that Iraq had these weapons and only 14% of them registered any doubt at all about their existence.

Despite that debacle, journalists slid effortlessly into repeating precisely the same process in reporting that Iran was planning to develop nuclear weapons. All through this coverage, the Iranian government insisted that its sole aim was to generate electricity, not to manufacture nuclear weapons. Reporters across the developed world attacked that position, recycling into print and broadcast outlets untested claims from precisely the same intelligence sources and neoconservative politicians who had been so deeply wrong about the Iraqi weapons. Perhaps this time the reporters were right. I don't know. It's a very safe bet that they don't know either.

Alongside this catalogue of global error, there is another kind of Flat Earth news – the non-stories which the global media simply fail to report. In May 2006, the United Nations produced a list of what it regarded as the ten most under-reported stories on the planet: the aftermath of the tsunami which struck countries around the Indian Ocean in December 2004; the lives of millions of economic refugees on the move in search of work; the global shortage of water with all its political implications; violence in Ivory Coast; children all over the world in conflict with the law; Liberia after the end of the war there; the legal obstacle course now facing genuine asylum seekers; the elections then due in the Congo in the midst of a war which had already killed some 3.8 million people; children caught in the crossfire of the long conflict in Nepal; the impact of drought on the fighting in Sudan.

You could add to that list of non-stories almost all scientific activity, almost all trade union activity, almost all European Union politics, almost all the activities of the World Bank, the IMF and the world's NGOs, as well as:

- the global surge in poverty since the early 1980s, which, according to a January 2002 report by a World Bank economist, Branko Milanovic, had reached the point where 80% of the world's population were living below the poverty line; and 1% of the planet's population were enjoying the same annual income as the poorest 57% put together. Over several decades when global consumption of goods doubled and the richest fifteen individuals in the world accumulated more wealth than the whole of sub-Saharan Africa, the average income in more than seventy of the hundred poorest countries fell, leaving the UN to estimate that one billion people now 'cannot satisfy even their elementary needs'.
- the vast expansion of secretive offshore tax havens which, by 2003, was allowing British corporations to avoid handing over some

£20,000 million a year which, in theory, they owed their government. At that time, bankers estimated that a third of the gross domestic product of the entire planet was being channelled through offshore accounts, and the Organisation for Economic Cooperation and Development (OECD) estimated that 60% of world trade consisted of transfers made within multinationals, passing their profits to anonymous subsidiaries in tax-free jurisdictions, while some three million corporations were avoiding tax simply because they had no identifiable owner.

- most, if not all, of the internal political, social and cultural life of most nations on the planet – not only the very poor ones, but also the 'Second World' nations with their growing economic and political importance and even some of the developed nations such as Australia, Canada and New Zealand.

- the surge in inequality within the developed nations, which, according to Professor Loic Wacquant of the University of California, saw 95% of the extra $1,100 billion generated by the booming US economy between 1979 and 1999 go into the pockets of just 5% of the population; while, in the UK, in just about every year since 1979, the official measure of inequality has risen relentlessly, increasing the number of children living below the poverty line from 7% in 1979 to 30% in 1997, a figure which has since begun to fall.

Omission is the most powerful source of distortion. The fact that these non-stories achieve only the most marginal coverage in global media is just as important as the falsehoods embedded in those stories which are covered. And this falsehood and distortion passes into government policy.

The millennium bug and the heroin story are microcosms of the way in which a Flat Earth story can end up being passed backwards and forwards between government and media, like a mud pie in some children's game, until between them they create something which delights their imagination but which, in reality, is just a mess. The truth about this kind of big policy story tends to be very deeply buried.

For example, I spent two years examining the work of the criminal justice system and found it impossible to make sense of what was happening inside it until the Home Office sent me some internal statistics, which revealed that, with a typical one hundred offences, only three are brought to justice (which means a conviction, a caution or being taken into consideration at sentencing). To put it the other way round: 97% of offences are never dealt with. Then I found statistics on the people in Britain's prisons and found that 90% of them were addicted to drugs and/or addicted to alcohol and/or suffering from at least two diagnosable mental disorders. How could a system which was based on detection and punishment be controlling crime if a) it failed to detect and bring to justice 97% of offences, and b) it used punishment to try to change the behaviour of those it caught, even though they were being driven into crime by addiction and mental disorder? (Much more of this on www.flatearthnews.net.)

By the time I had finished my research, I had spoken privately to chief constables who said it was a waste of time arresting criminals; judges who said it was a waste of time sentencing them; and prison governors who said it was a waste of time locking them up. I was confronted with the realisation that the criminal justice system is rather an effective way of regulating the behaviour of law-abiding citizens, who pick up the deterrent signal and react; but a strikingly ineffective way of controlling offenders. So we spend some £17 billion a year on a criminal justice system which, as so many people told me, 'doesn't catch criminals, doesn't dispense justice, and certainly isn't a system'. And we do that even though a mass of people within the system and a mass of criminologists outside the system have a wealth of evidence about tactics which are far more likely to succeed. Why? The answer at root, of course, is ignorance – in the media and, therefore, among voters and very often among politicians. And you can see this flowing down into policy.

For years, a weighty alliance of Fleet Street titles earnestly demanded that the government crack down on crime by putting 'more bobbies on the beat'. They liked to conjure up the image of the old BBC copper, George Dixon, quietly patrolling his patch and preserving the Queen's peace. Dixon, of course, is a fictional character, and there is absolutely no evidence to support the idea that police patrols cut crime. Indeed, there is a great deal of powerful evidence to demonstrate that it is a peculiarly wasteful use of manpower (see www.flatearthnews.net).

I met chief constables who were red-faced with rage at the prospect of their officers being diverted from the kind of sophisticated work which might genuinely help to reduce offending, so that they could wander the streets in haphazard fashion relying on mere chance to encounter some kind of crime. But, locked into media ignorance, David Blunkett, as Home Secretary, went ahead and pleased media consumers by pouring multiple millions of pounds into pushing officers onto the pavement. He even top-sliced the money off police budgets, so that chief constables could not get their funding unless they went along with it. And to the sound of chief constables hurling their hats to the floor, Blunkett called this money 'the crime-fighting fund'.

There was a similar incident in the mid 1990s when the Murdoch press took up the work of an American sociologist, Charles Murray, who, in the teeth of evidence to the contrary, argued that imprisonment cut offending, persuading the then Home Secretary, Michael Howard, to introduce the 1996 Crime (Sentences) Bill, which was greeted in the House of Lords by the Lord Chief Justice, Peter Taylor, declaring: 'Never in the history of our criminal law have such far-reaching proposals been put forward on the strength of such flimsy evidence.' Nevertheless, the bill passed into law and is credited with sucking petty offenders into jails at the rate of up to 30,000 a year.

A few years later, there was another media frenzy in the UK over 'zero tolerance' policing, an idea which was said to have been used successfully in New York City – even though the police there had never engaged in any such thing. The NYPD had had a dramatic impact on crime by collecting rapid data on crime hot spots, pushing responsibility for tactics down to local commanders, looking to solve the problems which provoke crime, working intensely with community agencies, forging strong links with other criminal justice agencies, developing new and imaginative strategies for serious crime and, where appropriate, in some places, using foot patrols to deal with low-level disorder, including mending broken windows, to turn an area around. It was this last 'broken windows' element which was seized and distorted into the zero-tolerance idea. George Kelling, the academic who developed the idea, told my researcher he was aghast that his subtle, clever strategy had been reduced to a campaign to arrest beggars and squeegee merchants, but the media liked it. Delusion and reality.

If you look deep enough into almost any area of government activity, you will find the same pattern. From whole policy areas like education, transport, health and energy to specific issues like the MMR vaccine and genetically modified food, there are governments spending huge amounts of money on pseudo-solutions which are proven failures but which match the misconceptions of the media. (Again, see www.flatearthnews.net for detail on some of this.) Often, this is not even a case of cynical populist politics, merely the hideous offspring of the obsessive copulation of government ignorance with media ignorance.

As one final example, there is a fascinating dispute emerging about the safety of nuclear energy, an issue with huge implications for the economy, the environment and public spending. There is some powerful evidence to suggest that the left's hostility to nuclear energy may be based on Flat Earth news.

Anti-nuclear campaigners often cite the accident at the Chernobyl nuclear power plant in April 1986 as evidence of the danger of nuclear energy. Certainly, there was a cloud of media coverage which drifted across the planet in the weeks after the accident, reporting the hundreds who had been killed by radiation sickness in what soon became known as 'the death zone' around the plant. Within the first few days, some said 2,000 were already dead. One report spoke of 15,000 bodies bull-dozed into a mass grave.

The World Health Organisation organised a three-year study of the health impact of Chernobyl and reported in September 2005: a clear increase in thyroid cancer among children who had drunk milk from cows which had grazed on contaminated grass in the week after the explosion, most of whom had been treated successfully; no hard evidence of any increase in any other kind of cancer, whether solid tumours or leukaemia; nor of stillbirths nor of deformed babies; nor of mutated animals or plants. They found that the total number of people who had died as a result of the accident was not thousands or even hundreds. It was fifty-six.

Environmental groups complained bitterly that the WHO report made a series of optimistic assumptions and that it focused only on the 600,000 people who had been most affected by the accident. Greenpeace, in particular, hit back with its own report, based on the research of more than fifty different scientists. This was published in April 2006, producing numerous headlines like this one, from the *Scotsman*: 'CHERNOBYL'S REAL DEATH TOLL 90,000, SAYS GREENPEACE'.

However, a close reading of the material behind these headlines reveals that they were an inaccurate account of a Greenpeace press release which was itself an inaccurate account of the organisation's own report which was itself somewhat problematic. The figure of 90,000 deaths came from one single study which was mentioned in the Greenpeace report, among a mass of other studies which put the estimated total deaths from Chernobyl at anywhere between dozens and up to six million. The report itself was honest enough to admit that all this research included 'high levels of speculation and general uncertainty'. In other words, they really could not be sure.

The Greenpeace press release failed to spell out this enormous range of estimates, although it did refer to 'wide variations in available data', and it presented the findings of the one single study as the 'results of recent studies', as though there were more than one source for it. The headlines then removed all remaining uncertainty and furthermore failed to reflect the fact that these were deaths which were estimated for the seventy years up to 2056, not deaths which had already occurred.

The Greenpeace report as a whole was presented as the work of fifty scientists. That was true in the technical sense that it selected research papers which had been written by fifty scientists, but those scientists had no control over the report itself nor over its conclusions. All that happened was that their work was wrapped into a report which was edited by a total of seven people, all of whom were working for Greenpeace at the time, though the report did not mention that. Its introduction was written by a Russian scientist, Dr Alexey Yablokov, who is a bona fide marine biologist, but who was described as a member of the European Committee on Radiation Risk without acknowledging that this committee is the creation of the Green Group in the European Parliament and, furthermore, the source of the claim that Chernobyl would kill six million people; nor that Dr Yablokov was the founder of Greenpeace in Russia. None of which inhibited the media story. (WHO and Greenpeace reports and other material on www.flatearthnews.net.)

The facts about Chernobyl are obscured by at least three problems: the old Soviet government's intense secrecy about the accident; the difficulty of disentangling the impact of the explosion from the impact on health of the subsequent collapse of the Soviet Union with its huge increase in poverty and inequality; the risk that, by focusing on Chernobyl survivors, researchers are picking up illness which would otherwise have been missed. To the extent that the truth is shrouded in real doubt, it is possible that both the WHO and Greenpeace have been doing exactly what Peter de Jager did with the millennium bug – 'cranking up' the facts – and taking the media along for the tale. However, there is one other strand of evidence, which appears important, from scientists who specialise in studying the health impact of radiation.

In 2006, BBC's *Horizon* broadcast a programme, made by the independent production company Dox, in which radiation scientists queued up to argue that radiation is simply not as dangerous as we have been led to believe. They argued that for years our understanding of the health impact of radioactivity was based on the bombings of Hiroshima and Nagasaki, but that those victims had been exposed to extremely high doses – far higher than anything released by any nuclear power plant, far higher even than the dose experienced by the vast majority of those who have been affected by the catastrophic explosion at Chernobyl.

They endorsed the World Health Organisation's conclusion on the very small number of people who had been killed by the accident and cited extensive research into the condition of mice, voles and other small mammals at the Chernobyl site. Unlike the humans who had lived there, these animals have not been evacuated; over the years, they have been thoroughly irradiated. And yet they show no sign at all of any of the cancers or of the ill health or genetic damage which have been attributed to the Chernobyl accident. Some scientists insisted that low-level radiation was not harmful and indeed that it could even be positively good for health by stimulating the body to resist genetic damage.

Dr Antone Brooks, professor of radiation toxicology at Washington State University, who has spent years studying radiation sickness, told the BBC programme: 'In my opinion, low doses of radiation are a piss–poor carcinogen and just not a big hitter when it comes to health effects. We have through our fear of radiation parlayed it into a major player when it is not.'

I found this very difficult to accept. And so, with the help of a researcher, I tried to check, with the Health Protection Agency, the Environment Agency, the Health and Safety Executive, NIREX which manages radioactive waste in the UK, the UN Scientific Committee on the Effects of Atomic Radiation, and the Centre for Ecology and Hydrology. In short, they agreed with the thrust of the BBC programme.

Tracking the sources of radiation in Britain, they say variously that 85% of it occurs naturally as a by–product of our planet; 14% of it comes from X-rays and other medical activity; only 1% comes from the nuclear industry. We found that nuclear power workers are exposed to less radiation than coal miners or even air crews; and, in spite of the continuing restriction on eating sheep from areas where rain brought down particles from the Chernobyl plume, they told us that you could eat a chop from those sheep every day for a year and still absorb less radiation than you would from a single hospital X-ray.

Flat Earth news about radiation has become twisted with Flat Earth terror error to produce one particularly powerful media tale – the idea of terrorists using a 'dirty bomb'. Multiple stories around the world have described the alarming likelihood and the even more alarming consequences of terrorists detonating such a weapon in a busy city. Numerous specialists have tried to warn the media that the story is false, and that the repetition of this falsehood is creating the risk of causing needless public panic.

In a June 2005 paper for the Oxford Research Group, for example, Dr Frank Barnaby, a nuclear physicist and specialist on military tech-nology, explained that if terrorists were able to detonate a nuclear weapon with plutonium, the effect would be highly destructive, but that this is very different from a dirty bomb, using conventional explo-sives to scatter radioactive material of the kind which is rather easily available from, for example, hospital waste: 'Generally, the explosion of the conventional explosive would be the most likely cause of any immediate deaths or serious injuries. The radioactive material in the bomb would be dispersed into the air but would be soon diluted to relatively low concentrations . . . Deaths and injuries caused by the blast effects of the conventional explosives and long-term cancers from radiation would likely be minimal. The true impact of a dirty bomb would be the enormous social, psychological and economic disruption caused by radioactive contamination. It would cause considerable fear, panic and social disruption, exactly the effects terrorists wish to achieve. The public fear of radiation is very great indeed, some say irrationally so.'

The effect is that, in the dirty bomb, terrorists have a particularly dangerous weapon only if the media continue to mislead people into believing that it is particularly dangerous.

It is fair to say that, for as long as there have been newspapers, there has been some serious Flat Earth news: the easy collusion of British journalists with the hunt for non-existent German spies before the First World War; the equally easy collusion of American journalists with the hunt for commie spies led by Senator Joseph McCarthy; the prolonged misinformation over the military threat presented by the Soviet Union (which began with the *New York Times*, as Walter Lippmann once noted, reporting the imminent or actual collapse of the Soviet regime ninety-one times between 1917 and 1921 as well as numerous other false stories about the flight, imprisonment and death of both Lenin and Trotsky).

Reporting without the benefit of facts, the global media carried some classic stories at the end of the Second World War when journalists refused to accept that Hitler was dead and solemnly reported that he was working as a waiter in Grenoble. They also reported that he was working as a fisherman in Ireland and as a shepherd in Switzerland and that he was a hermit in Italy and that he had made it to South America and to Eastern Europe and to Spain having escaped simultaneously by plane and by submarine.

The great American political reporter, David Broder, captured this basic level of error in a speech which he made honouring Pulitzer Prize-winners in 1979: 'I would like to see us say − over and over until the point has been made − that the newspaper that drops on your doorstep is a partial, hasty, incomplete, inevitably somewhat flawed and inaccurate rendering of some of the things we have heard about in the past twenty-four hours – distorted, despite our best efforts to eliminate gross bias – by the very process of compression that makes it possible for you to lift it from the doorstep and read it in about an hour. If we labelled the product accurately, then we could immediately add: "But it's the best we could do under the circumstances, and we will be back tomorrow, with a corrected and updated version."'

But the media's ignorance quotient has risen sharply since then. As two other prominent American journalists, Bill Kovach and Tom Rosentiel, put it, in their book *The Elements of Journalism*: 'The need for truth is greater, not less, in the new century, for the likelihood of untruth has become so much more prevalent.'

When you stand back and see the scale of this – the penetration of falsehood deep into the foundations of our collective thinking; the construction of so much activity on top of those false foundations; the money, the time, the energy which are thrown into them; the sheer waste of opportunity – you see a kind of madness, a kind of psychotic society which has started to lose contact with reality and believes its own delusions. If we could prove that this were being organised by some malign conspiracy, it would be a great relief since we could oust the conspirators and cure the sickness. What really makes this frightening is that this group psychosis is now the natural creation of our information industry.

In the 1960s, as a network of communication links finally enabled the mass media to embrace the entire planet, it was reasonable to copy a cool cat like the media theorist Marshall McLuhan and feel excited about the creation of a global village in which anybody anywhere could find out what anybody anywhere else was doing or saying. It was reasonable to see the mass media as a global village schoolteacher educating an entire world in politics and culture and sport and ideas. This is no longer reasonable. The mass media now operate more like a global village idiot, deeply ignorant and easily led.

Why would a profession lose touch with its primary function? Why would truth-telling disintegrate into the mass production of ignorance? Now, there's a real story.

Part Two
The News Factory

'The best journalism is often done in defiance of management.'

Bob Woodward

2. The Workers

A few weeks before the start of the 2006 football World Cup, the Press Association in London put out a story about an England fan named Paul Hucker, from Ipswich, who was so worried about the risk of England failing in the tournament that he had paid £100, plus £5 tax, to insure himself against emotional trauma.

The PA story explained that, if England went down badly and he could provide medical evidence that he had suffered severe medical trauma, Mr Hucker would receive a payout of £1 million from a web-based insurance company, called britishinsurance.com. 'I find when it goes to penalty shoot-outs it gets very difficult and I wanted to insure myself against psychological trauma,' Mr Hucker was said to have said.

Any experienced journalist – and, indeed, any human being with their wits switched on – would look at that story and consider the very clear possibility that it was not exactly reliable. Was any football fan really that neurotic? And that greedy? And that stupid, to imagine that he could prove 'severe medical trauma'? And what kind of insurance company would sell that kind of policy? One that wanted publicity perhaps.

It was easy enough to check. It took less than a minute to Google 'Paul Hucker'; and only a minute or two more to find out that this was not Mr Hucker's first appearance in stories about insurance. A year earlier, he had popped up in a story in the *Daily Mail*, as a member of the public buying a house and looking for the right policy to cover his mortgage. Luckily he had found just the right one 'which has saved me £600 a year'. And he had helped out, too, with a story on an insurance website, as a member of the public celebrating the comfort of being covered against losing his job. The policy was 'excellent value for peace of mind', he said.

Another couple of minutes revealed that, in both of these cases, the policies which had so pleased Mr Hucker were being sold by a Mr Simon Burgess of Braintree in Essex – who also turned out to be the managing director of britishinsurance.com, which had created the policy for Mr Hucker in his state of anxiety about English football. At the same time, Google revealed that Mr Hucker is a marketing director who specialises in promoting web-based companies, including those of Mr Burgess, with whom he has shared several business ventures.

So, within a maximum of five minutes, it became clear that the Press Association should not be running this story. It was a publicity stunt, a neat little tale designed to promote an insurance company. Five more minutes revealed that the story was not only unreliable, it was also old.

Mr Paul Hucker had appeared in exactly the same story before – as the football fan insuring himself with the same Mr Simon Burgess for fear of the same emotional trauma – in the run-up to the previous World Cup, in Japan, four years earlier in June 2002. Mr Hucker was living in Newmarket then, not Ipswich, but the story in the *Sun* was the same and even the quote was similar. 'I am scared that one day I will finally be pushed over the edge – especially if there is a penalty shoot-out,' he was said to have said.

Like any wire agency, PA sells its stories to all kinds of media outlets, which are under no obligation at all to run them. PA's clients can check them and chuck them whenever they want. But within twenty-four hours of its appearance in May 2006, the story about Mr Hucker's World Cup anxiety had appeared in print in the *Western Mail*, the *Newcastle Evening Chronicle*, the *Hull Daily Mail*, the *Liverpool Daily Echo* and the *Daily Telegraph* as well as on the websites of the *Daily Mail*, the *Scotsman*, the *Guardian* and *The Times*. It had broken into television, on the websites of the BBC, ITV and Sky as well as being picked up for radio bulletins by the BBC and commercial stations.

Then it went international. It was posted on Yahoo!'s UK news website; and two American wire agencies, AP and UPI, started pushing it out to their clients around the world. Within forty-eight hours, it was running, either electronically or in print, in the *Sydney Morning Herald*, the *Washington Post*, the *Malaysia Star*, the *Sunday Times* of Zambia, the *Financial Mail* in South Africa and the *Haveera Daily* in the Maldives. It also found its way to India, Finland, New Zealand, Canada and Ireland.

It was translated into Italian and German, into Polish, Romanian, Dutch and Chinese. Here's what the story looked like in Indonesia: 'Paul Hucker membayar 100 pounds ditambah lima pounds untuk pajak asuransi untuk polis yang tidak biasa dari broker British Insurance Limited'. And in Turkey: 'Ingiltere'nin Ipswich kentinde yaayan Paul Hucker, 100 sterlin ödeyerek kendisini "milli takım kökenli" depresyona karı sigortalattı.'

You might think that Mr Hucker and Mr Burgess would have hesitated to put out a story which was so obviously flaky, knowing that the media were bound to check it and chuck it. But they knew better than that. They had played this game before, and not just on that earlier occasion, in 2002, when they put out the story about the neurotic football fan. Over the years, they had also dreamed up the story about the policy to insure yourself against becoming ugly; and the one to protect yourself against being kidnapped by aliens; and against being spooked by ghosts on Halloween; and against being turned into a werewolf or a vampire. All good stories. Not to mention their 'party safe' policy to protect people against not having a good time on Millennium Eve, or their Christmas present policy in case you didn't like your gifts, or their 'immaculate conception' policy which was apparently taken out by three unnamed women from Inverness who were worried about giving birth to the new messiah. All these stories ran through the unguarded gates of the media with the ease of a Brazilian striker penetrating the England defence.

The story of the neurotic football fan contains within it the essential ingredients for the concoction of all Flat Earth news – an unreliable statement created by outsiders, usually for their own commercial or political benefit, injected via a wire agency into the arteries of the media through which it then circulates around the whole body of global communication. And, most important, at every stage, as it passes through the hands of all those journalists into all those outlets, nobody checks it.

Journalism without checking is like a human body without an immune system. If the primary purpose of journalism is to tell the truth, then it follows that the primary function of journalists must be to check and to reject whatever is not true. But something has changed, and that essential immune system has started to collapse. In a strange, alarming and generally unnoticed development, journalists are pumping out stories without checking them – stories which then circle the planet. And so now, in a way that was not true in the past, the global mass media are not merely prone to occasional error but are constitutionally and constantly vulnerable to being infected with falsehood, distortion and propaganda.

There are loads of little Huckers out there.

I commissioned specialist researchers from the journalism department of Cardiff University to investigate a sample of the stories running through the British media. I asked them to focus only on the most prestigious and serious media outlets in the country: four quality daily newspapers (*The Times*, the *Guardian*, the *Independent* and the *Daily Telegraph*) and the *Daily Mail* as the biggest and most influential mid-market title.

They chose two random weeks and analysed every single domestic news story put out by those outlets, a total of 2,207 pieces. With the help of the *Guardian* newsdesk, they then attempted to capture all of the incoming material which had been passed on to reporters during those two weeks. Where there was any doubt about the origin of stories, they interviewed reporters from the different newspapers and then tracked backwards to find their source material.

At the end of this unique investigation, they came up with a striking finding – that the most respected media outlets in the country are routinely recycling unchecked second-hand material. And, just as with Paul Hucker and his World Cup insurance, this tends to come from two primary sources: wire agencies like the Press Association, and public-relations activity which is promoting some commercial or political interest.

They found that a massive 60% of these quality-print stories consisted wholly or mainly of wire copy and/or PR material, and a further 20% contained clear elements of wire copy and/or PR to which more or less other material had been added. With 8% of the stories, they were unable to be sure about their source. That left only 12% of stories where the researchers could say that all the material was generated by the reporters themselves. The highest quota proved to be in *The Times*, where 69% of news stories were wholly or mainly wire copy and/or PR. Even the paper with the lowest quota, the *Guardian*, compiled just over half of its stories in this way.

Newspapers do not admit to this. The Cardiff researchers found that only 1% of wire stories which were carried by Fleet Street papers admitted the source. Most carried misleading bylines, 'by a staff reporter' or even by a named reporter who had rewritten the agency copy. The denial of PR input is at least as thorough: PR professionals generally aim specifically to make their own role in a story invisible, and journalists are happy to go along with that. As the Cardiff report put it: 'We found many stories apparently written by one of the newspaper's own reporters that seem to have been cut and pasted from elsewhere.'

The researchers went on to look at those stories which relied on a specific statement of fact and found that with a staggering 70% of them, the claimed fact passed into print without any corroboration at all. Only 12% of these stories showed evidence that the central statement had been thoroughly checked.

And these are conservative figures. They left out the tabloids, which carry far more celebrity stories dominated by PR material. They ignored the *Financial Times* and the quality finance pages, where City reporting is flooded with PR. They left out the quality feature pages, whose agenda is heavily influenced by film companies, television channels and book publishers promoting their work. They excluded sport, where access to stars is run by PR. These were simply the stories that were being presented by the best daily newspapers in the UK as an account of the most important or interesting events in the country over the preceding twenty-four hours.

The Cardiff researchers concluded: 'Taken together, these data portray a picture of journalism in which any meaningful independent journalistic activity by the press is the exception rather than the rule. We are not talking about investigative journalism here, but the everyday practices of news judgement, fact-checking, balance, criticising and interrogating sources, etc, that are, in theory, central to routine, day-to-day journalism.'

This is not the whole picture. There are still safe havens. There are still journalists who check their stories and publish the truth. But what the Cardiff research suggests is that the 'everyday practices' of journalism are now the exception rather than the rule. Something fundamental has changed. And if you look back at what has been going on inside Fleet Street offices, you can see exactly what has happened.

★　★　★

Take two reporters.

Take, first of all, George Glenton, crime correspondent of the old *News Chronicle*, who recalled his working life in a 1963 memoir:

> Just about noon on Monday, October 10 1960, I was mainly occupied with the grim realities of a skeleton in a cupboard. The macabre discovery had been made in a seaside boarding house in North Wales, and the unhappy landlady was due to stand her trial that week, charged with murder.
>
> I thought about it as I sipped my beer in the oak-panelled bar of an historic City tavern which had prospered in the shadow of crime and its consequences for over 300 years. I pondered the imponderables and laid my plans to leave the vicinity of Newgate and the Old Bailey for a distant Welsh town where the stocks still stand in the council yard and the only excitements are market days and the occasional assize court.

Glenton describes how, in pursuit of the truth about the skeleton in the cupboard, he and his photographer, Freddie Girling, travelled to Ruthin in Denbighshire to cover the landlady's trial. 'In Ruthin that night, we met journalists from every national morning paper. We met men from the London evening papers and men from the agencies – the Press Association and Exchange Telegraph. We met men from Manchester and Liverpool . . . We had with us in Ruthin an army of journalists.'

Glenton recalls many of the journalists he worked with, including with particular affection the legendary Fleet Street industrial correspondent and columnist Ian Mackay, 'who moved indiscriminately among cabinet ministers and cabbies, comedians and clerics and always wore an odd smile . . . He travelled immense distances doing his job. Often his editor only knew where he was, by reading the current day's paper to find Mackay's last dateline . . . His range of contacts stretched from Pierrepoint, the public hangman, to ministers of state. He was a fearless opportunist.'

Now take a young reporter who, a few years ago, wrote an account of his life on a local newspaper in the same city in which Glenton practised his trade. Writing in the *British Journalism Review* in 2004, the young reporter, presumably anxious about reprisals from his employer, adopted as his pseudonym the name of the seventeenth-century scrivener who is generally recognised as the first British reporter, Samuel Pecke. He wrote:

> The owners of my newspaper made a £70 million profit in this country in 2003. Yet . . . reporters are blocked from phoning overseas or even using the directory inquiry services, copies of our own newspapers are rationed in the office, and a current sort of Stalinist stationery embargo means journalists are expected to buy their own notebooks and fax paper . . .
>
> Perhaps one of the most worrying and frustrating aspects of life on local newspapers is being so office-bound. Of all the impressions I had of the profession before getting my first job, relying on telephone interviews and the Internet for so much written work was not one of them. Journalism must allow relationships developing with contacts, whether or not there is a story at stake, and getting to know your patch inside out. Put simply, only lazy reporters spend their days behind desks. Yet such on-the-streets reporting was described to me early on as 'a luxury'.
>
> The newspaper did not have enough journalists to allow staff to go daily to court, let alone out and about. The paper had to be filled and could not wait for as-yet unwritten stories and features to arrive. While the editor preached the virtue of 'interactivity' with the community, the management's own reluctance to employ more staff or give its journalists enough free rein hampered basic reporting. Quality, it seems, is not an issue. Yet across local newspapers, regurgitating press releases and sticking a couple of opposing quotes on the end has become the norm.

George Glenton described the world of journalism as it was less than fifty years ago, but for many journalists in Britain, or indeed anywhere in the developed world, he may as well be describing a dream. It is not just that his cosy world of oak-panelled bars and beery pondering has gone, but that the very practice of old-style reporting generally has gone, too – the army of journalists travelling the country to cover a trial, or any other kind of story; the reporter milking information from contacts among 'cabinet ministers and cabbies'; the intrepid investigator out on the road following the trail of clues. The days of the fearless opportunist are gone. That journalism has been replaced by what Samuel Pecke describes – by what some now call 'churnalism'.

It is a common experience among young journalists that they leave university with a degree in journalism, bursting with enthusiasm, only to end up chained to a keyboard on a production line in a news factory, churning out trivia and cliché to fill space in the paper.

One such graduate, who had just started work on a famous regional paper, sent an email back to her university tutor:

I feel like I am turning out a load of shit, so I expect them to notice. I'm due a review pretty soon, so I'll find out then but settling in here is harder than I thought. We have a new deputy editor. He's pretty good, but the editor is an idiot. He's come from a marketing background not news, and the news editors are all not much older than me and too worried for their own backs to stand up to him and tell him some of the stories he is asking us to follow are just crap. It is really getting me down at the moment, and I'm starting to dislike the job. I just don't know what else to do with myself! It is a sweatshop, but if you'd have told me that, I wouldn't have listened. Arrgghhh – I'm just so frustrated!

Another young graduate agreed to write me a diary of one week in his working life on a regional daily tabloid. This is a paper which produces three editions every weekday, each edition normally containing twenty-four pages of local news and a couple of pages of national news. To produce this, the paper employs seven senior reporters, earning up to £21,500 in 2006; and five trainees, earning £15,500. Here is a glimpse of the modern reporter at work.

Monday. Come in at eight to find the desk asking for a lead story, two 60-line basements [for the foot of a page] and 100 lines of nibs [news in briefs]. And they have no leads. I usually find some stories on my weekend off, but I've had a horrible cold. They tell me to check progress with a building being knocked down in the centre of town. They like stories with pictures, because they fill more space. I phone the developer and the council and turn it into a story. I take my first ever lunch break, wander the streets, copying down details of posters advertising car-boot sales, meditation evenings, whatever. Back in the office, I start turning them into stories. The desk panic because they still have no front-page lead. They steal an old story off the sports desk, about a 12-year-old football star and tell me to call his dad for a quote. The dad hangs up: the last time we wrote about his son, we exaggerated the story. The desk tell me to call him back and threaten to run the story with or without his comment. Reluctantly, he gives me a quote. I file it and spend the rest of the day writing up my poster stories.

Number of stories: eleven
People spoken to: three
People seen face to face: none out of three
Hours out of office: one out of ten

Tuesday. Good news: the sporting boy's dad hasn't complained. Bad news: the desk tell me to call round sports groups to do a follow-up on the same story, just what the dad didn't want. But I can't find anybody to talk to, so the desk tell me to make it up from stuff we've run before and quotes I didn't use from yesterday's call to the dad. It makes a page lead. I feel depressed. Fill some more space inside the paper. Then they tell me to do the Smilies: every day, on page seven, we run three happy, smiling stories, to make the readers feel good, complete with pics. No leads. I call my mum, who lives nearby, and she reads out bits from another local paper. I turn them into Smilies.

Number of stories: ten
People spoken to: eight
People seen face to face: two out of eight
Hours out of office: none out of nine

Wednesday. Out of the office! To another building being demolished – except that the demolition crane is stuck on the motorway, and nobody at the site wants to talk. Back to the office to turn it into a story, which makes a page lead. Try working up some new leads by phoning round likely sources. Feel ill with my cold and head off early. That upsets the other trainee in the office, who is told to find a lead out of nowhere because one which the desk were relying on has suddenly fallen through.

Number of stories: seven
People spoken to: five
People seen face to face: one
Hours out of office: two out of nine and a half

Thursday. A real story walks in the front door: a young woman who has had her children taken into care because they say she has learning disabilities so can't make a decent mum. She is desperate, been standing in the rain waiting for the doors to open. I tell her I'll call her. I know I won't: the desk aren't interested. They want a quick page lead. I end up phoning a guy who has just run a marathon. Well, three weeks ago, but I can bury that. And he only came 50th, but I can bury that too. Then a basement and masses of nibs. No leads at all. I recycle some old stuff from my notebook and download a few upcoming events off the council website.

Number of stories: thirteen
People spoken to: six
People seen face to face: one out of six
Hours out of office: none out of nine

Friday. The desk want me to write a feature about a new supermarket which is going to steal business from local shops. I'm happy but they only give me two hours to do it. Plus they want more stories. I phone round the shops and get some quotes. Can't get hold of the supermarket. Bang out the feature, then start turning out other stuff. For once, the desk have some leads. A good day.

Number of stories: seven
People spoken to: four
People seen face to face: none out of four
Hours out of office: none out of eight

Totals for the week

Number of stories: 48 (9.6 per day)
People spoken to: 26
People seen face to face: 4 out of 26
Total hours out of office: 3 out of 45.5

This is life in a news factory. No reporter who is turning out nearly ten stories every shift can possibly do his or her job properly. No reporter who spends only three hours out of the office in an entire working week can possibly develop enough good leads or build enough good contacts. No reporter who speaks to only twenty-six people in researching forty-eight stories can possibly be checking their truth.

This is churnalism. This is journalists failing to perform the simple basic functions of their profession; quite unable to tell their readers the truth about what is happening on their patch. This is journalists who are no longer out gathering news but who are reduced instead to passive processors of whatever material comes their way, churning out stories, whether real event or PR artifice, important or trivial, true or false.

All local and regional media outlets in Britain – print and broad-cast – have been swamped by a tide of churnalism. As we shall see, the scale and quality of coverage has been swept away. But the tide has not stopped in the provinces. The big national outlets can still support some real journalism – that is where most of the safe havens survive – but here, too, churnalism has swept through newsrooms, forcing the mass of reporters to spend hours recycling second-hand wire copy and PR material without performing the 'everyday practices' of their trade.

The reality of national newspaper life came shining through when the Cardiff researchers interviewed national journalists about their work. The health editor of *The Times*, Nigel Hawkes, captured the view of many: 'We are churning stories today, not writing them. Almost everything is recycled from another source . . . Specialist writing is much easier, because the work is done by agencies and/or writers of press releases. Actually knowing enough to identify the stories is no longer important. The work has been deskilled.'

Another national writer spoke of working in conditions which 'prevent me from going on the road to find stories, from conducting interviews and from going out to develop contacts'. Yet another national journalist, a high-profile specialist who has been doing his job for twenty-five years, described how he had simply given up fighting the tide of churnalism: 'One day, I just thought, "OK, I'm not going to bother now. I'm just going to churn out everything that comes in." . . . The agenda has totally changed. All bets are off, really.'

This is the heart of modern journalism, the rapid repackaging of largely unchecked second-hand material, much of it designed to service the political or commercial interests of those who provide it. This is why Paul Hucker can simply slide his unreliable publicity stunt direct into the mass media and see it relayed around the world. This is why the Cardiff researchers found that, even in the best national papers in the country, only 12% of their stories were their own work and that only 12% of key facts were being checked. This is why we have so much Flat Earth news.

This all began when grocers climbed on top of warhorses. It was James Cameron who first spotted them in the saddle.

By chance, it happened just as the old crime reporter George Glenton and his colleagues lost their jobs, when the old *News Chronicle* was killed off by its owners in October 1960. By that time, Cameron was probably the best-known foreign correspondent in Britain and a favourite son of the *News Chron* for whom he had spent seven years gently exposing humbug and horror, racism and empire. So it was that several of the other newspapers turned to him to write a stylish obituary to their dead competitor. He turned them down.

Cameron chose instead to write his valedictory in his local newspaper, the *West London Press*, where he described the end of the *News Chronicle* as 'the most meaningful collapse the newspaper business has seen this generation'.

Looking back at the death of a newspaper which had done so much to encourage fearless opportunism among its reporters, Cameron asked the question which lies at the heart of Fleet Street's decline: 'Here is the most insoluble problem of what we rather fulsomely call the "free press": how is it possible to equate the commercial success that is indispensable to a liberated paper with the business interests that will always encroach upon that liberation?'

And when he spoke about the encroachment of business interests, he was referring not to censorship by owners, but to the role of the new corporate owners who for some years had been taking over newspapers and imposing their commercial logic on the journalists they had acquired.

He explained: 'The *News Chronicle* was founded by considerable and dedicated men; its function was defined and its patronage identifiable. Latterly, it drifted by default into the hands of lesser people, who thought greatly about commerce and casually about journalism; who permitted its affairs to be run by mediocrities on one floor and sharpshooters on another; who felt that the way to compensate for thoughtfulness in one column was by banality in the next; and who, when both things failed together, were brave enough to tell their staff on Monday that there would be no paper on the Tuesday. The trouble was, the people they so summarily wrote off, were the only ones who cared.'

With one final, wounding stab at his old Remington typewriter, Cameron concluded that the once great *News Chronicle* had died 'a potential warhorse ridden by grocers'.

It is rare in history to be able to identify the precise date of a turning point. In the case of the fall of Fleet Street, however, we can. Those 'business interests' which had so offended James Cameron in their casual killing of the *News Chron*, went on to spend years laying siege to the national newspaper industry, infiltrating occasionally to grab some new booty, gathering strength, gathering power until at last, more than a quarter of a century later, on the bitter cold night of Saturday 25 January 1986, they finally broke down the gates and conquered Fleet Street.

That was the night when Rupert Murdoch moved his UK newspapers behind the barbed wire and security guards of his new fortress at Wapping. In doing so, he broke the print unions and removed the final obstacle to the rule of corporations 'who thought greatly about commerce and casually about journalism'. Those unions were notorious for their greed and bad practice, but they were also the only force strong enough to resist the new corporate owners. And without them, the journalists' union, which had always relied on the printers to stop the paper coming out when they were in dispute, lost its power too. Now, the grocers could rein in all the warhorses.

Newspaper historians tend to see this change as inevitable. They may well be right. There is some powerful evidence that, despite the rewards of political power, the old family proprietors simply could not afford to continue running newspapers with their huge costs of production and distribution aggravated by old technology and by the overmanning imposed by the print unions. The new owners had the cash to carry losses and then, through Rupert Murdoch, the guile and ruthlessness to enforce their power. Once the unions were broken, the new corporate owners simply applied the logic of commerce – cut costs and increase revenue. All of that may well have been inevitable. The point is that, with equal inevitability but less notice from the outside world, that process released a chain reaction of internal changes which have had a devastating effect on truth-telling journalism.

Commercial logic is not necessarily destructive. Applied, for example, to the production of cars or computers, it may well generate significant benefits: the introduction of a production line cuts out human error and saves time, producing cars or computers in greater numbers at greater speed and of better quality. But, applied to news, that logic is highly damaging, cutting out human contact and with it the possibility of finding stories; cutting down time and with it the possibility of checking; thus producing stories in greater numbers at greater speed and of much worse quality.

Free to impose their will, the new owners started to cut costs. At first, in the late 1980s, they did it simply because the demise of the unions allowed them to: they replaced the old hot-metal production with computerised technology, disposing for ever of multiple thousands of highly paid printers. Then, in the early nineties, they cut more costs to improve their profit margins. From 1993, they cut again to finance the price war which was launched in London by the Murdoch papers. In the late nineties, they cut again as the Internet began to suck readers and advertisers out of the traditional mass media, replacing widespread profit with heavy loss. (By 2005, a survey found that UK households under the age of thirty were spending more on chocolate than on newspapers. By 2006, the advertising giant WPP was forecasting that advertising on the Internet was about to surpass that in national newspapers.)

Along the way, these corporations made massive amounts of money. For example, in 1985, the year before Wapping, Murdoch's UK titles declared a total pre-tax profit of £35.6 million. By 1988, with Wapping settled into the low-cost new technology, that figure had more than quadrupled, to £144.6 million. (During the same period, they had cut their total staffing from 8,731 to only 949.) The profits went back to the parent companies; to shareholders; and to 'directors' emoluments', some of which were huge. A fraction of the profits found their way back into the Fleet Street newsrooms, first in the production of new supplements and later in the creation of new free newspapers, both earning extra revenue by carrying more advertising, and finally in the launch of websites.

I suspected but could not prove that something fundamental had changed for Fleet Street journalists in the midst of all this. So I asked the researchers from Cardiff University to find all the information they could on two key points: the amount of space which Fleet Street papers were filling with editorial copy; and the number of staff who were being hired to do so. They gathered this data covering twenty years, starting in 1985 – the year before Wapping.

To check the space, they simply counted the pages in each paper for each year since 1985 and subtracted the space that was used for advertisements. To check the staffing levels, they ploughed through annual reports for every Fleet Street company and, where necessary, spoke off the record to senior executives. It should be said that there are some gaps in this information where companies failed to disclose figures for particular years; and some complications when Fleet Street companies bought non-national titles and included those figures in their total of employees and also failed to include freelance hiring. But the crude underlying trend which they found is overwhelming.

Twenty years after Wapping, after many cuts and occasional bouts of new hiring, average staffing levels across Fleet Street companies were slightly lower than they had been in 1985. But the amount of editorial space which those journalists were filling in their papers had trebled. To put it another way, during those twenty years, the average time allowed for national newspaper journalists to find and check their stories had been cut to a third of its former level. Even allowing for the role of journalists on freelance contracts who won't show up in these figures, if you include their extra work on free sheets, websites, blogs, podcasts and vodcasts, you see that their time has been cut still further. That is a disaster.

It shoves a blade right into the heart of the practice of journalism. If truth is the object and checking is the function, then the primary working asset of all journalists, always and everywhere, is time. Take away time, and you take away truth. 'Somebody says something? Well, that's good enough for me . . . You say there are WMD out there? OK, honey, get me rewrite . . . Clinton did what? Hey, it's a story.'

To check their findings, the Cardiff researchers surveyed national news reporters. Two-thirds of them said that they were now producing more stories; and two-thirds of them said they were doing less checking. Their comments made it very clear why. One told them: 'Newspapers have turned into copy factories. This leaves less time for real investigations, or meeting and developing contacts. The arrival of online editions has also increased demand for quick copy, reducing the time available for checking facts.'

Another, from a different paper, said: 'I think the time available to be thorough has decreased . . . The main consequence of that is that, if things require lots of work, they are less likely to be embarked on.' And another: 'I'm exceptionally busy . . . Journalism has always required investment in time for contacts, but invariably these are now made on my own time – at breakfasts and dinners.' And another: 'I insist on making at least two check calls on every story, but this is becoming increasingly difficult to do, because of time constraints.'

And the reality of the disaster is even bigger than that. Sitting in the national news factory, journalists have always relied on a network of local journalists to gather the raw material from which their stories are built. Reporters on local newspapers, freelancers in local agencies and, more recently, journalists on local radio and television have been their workforce on the ground, digging out information from their communities for their own outlets and then relaying the best of it to the nationals. The grocers have cut those supply lines.

By the mid-1990s, the tide of corporate ownership that had broken through at Wapping was sweeping through the provinces as corporations saw the chance to make similar easy money. Professor Bob Franklin of Cardiff University has specialised in studying this process. In one year, 1996, he found that a third of all local papers were sold to new owners. The *Yorkshire Post*, which until 1995 had belonged effectively to the same owners for 240 years, changed hands four times in ten years. The result was that, whereas in 1992 some two hundred companies owned local papers, by 2005, according to the media analysts Mintel, ten corporations alone owned 74% of them.

All of these papers were then subjected to the logic of pure commerce. Professor Franklin found that hundreds of them were simply killed off, their town-centre offices often sold for profit. In the ten years after Wapping, according to the Newspaper Society, 403 local titles were closed – 24% of the 1,687 which had been supplying news to their areas and to the nationals. Those which survived saw their staffing cut to the bone with just over half of the 8,000 journalists working in the provinces losing their jobs between 1986 and 2000; some local newsrooms were replaced by regional hubs, cut off from their communities; and senior reporters were replaced with low-paid trainees. With rare exceptions, these papers were reduced to mere churnalism of the kind described in the young reporter's diary earlier in this chapter.

One journalism graduate told me how he had started work on a weekly paper owned by Trinity Mirror, where he was one of only three reporters, all of them trainees. There was no news editor, and so, as soon as he passed an internal exam, he was promoted to take the job. 'They didn't replace me. So there was just me and the two reporters, who were both trainees. Then the editor left, and so I was doing his work, too.' When a big national story broke on their patch, none of them had the time to cover it. 'We ended up lifting stuff out of the nationals.'

Even though this was a disaster for local and national journalism, even though masses of readers reacted by giving up local papers (15% of their readers deserted between 1989 and 2004), the grocers were happy. They didn't need readers to pay for their papers, because the big money was in local advertising, in which they still had a virtual monopoly. And since they had cut their costs, their profits were booming. In 2004, for example, Johnston Press, which had been among the most destructive of the new owners, declared a profit of £177 million, a profit margin of 35%.

With the loss of this crucial supply line from local newspapers, national media might have turned for help to the local freelance agencies which covered the country. But they too were attacked. The Fleet Street grocers cut back the budgets of their national news desks who, in turn, cut back on commissioning stories from the agencies and froze the prices of those they did commission. With no effective union to protect them, the agencies started to shed staff and then to close.

In the Leeds area, there had been five agencies, harvesting stories from the city; only one survived. In Manchester, one closed, one shrank and just one survived at full strength. On Merseyside, three closed and one survived, its staff falling at one point from eighteen to seven. In Sheffied, White's agency cut back from ten staff to only two. In Stoke, two agencies closed and one survived. Raymonds of Derby cut back from thirty staff to fifteen while two other agencies in the city folded. All over rural Britain, the one-man outfits which had covered village life went bust, while the bigger rural agencies shrank. Mid Staffordshire News was cut down to a one-man team. Kent saw two agencies fold and one survive. Anglia Press cut back from ten staff to four. Calyx in Dorset went from six staff to one.

Specialist court-reporting agencies – a major supply line – went the same way. Since 1893, for example, there had been an agency which specialised in covering the magistrates' courts in Horseferry Road and Great Marlborough Street in the West End of London. In 1976, it was bought by Tony Asciak who ran a staff of six who would dig out three or four national stories a day. It was Asciak's, for example, who spotted the wife of the then Chancellor, Nigel Lawson, being hurried into court an hour before the day's normal business began, to deal with a drink-driving offence. By 1994, Asciak had had to let go the entire team and continued as a one-man outfit. In April 2006, he died, and, after 113 years, the agency died with him. Across the country, in civil courts and Crown courts and magistrates' courts, other specialist agencies shrank or died too.

Finally, the supply line from local broadcasters was broken as well. By 2004, the eleven different companies which used to own the ITV network had collapsed into a single monopoly whose regional newsrooms saw their journalists and film crews cut, while young graduate trainees were pulled in on cheap wages to fill the gap. In 2006, ITV announced plans to cut their budget by a further £100 million while giving their shareholders £500 million. Their director of television, Simon Shaps, ominously pointed out that they were spending 29% of their money on factual programmes even though they yielded only 11% of their commercial income.

I spoke to a trainee in one of ITV's regional newsrooms who was being used to cut pictures and write underlays (i.e. the script that is spoken over the pictures) without ever having been taught to do either. She said she had cut pictures too short for their slot with the result that the screen went to black for several seconds, as well as writing underlays that were too long for their pictures so the item ended in mid-sentence. She said normally nobody checked what she had done before it went out; nobody ever held a post-mortem about her errors although sometimes she got shouted at. She said she often worked the late shift, which meant that, after coming in at lunchtime and writing stories off the wire for the next morning's *GMTV* bulletin, she would watch the rest of her colleagues drift off home in the early evening and then be left entirely alone with the presenter to work on the late bulletin.

The BBC, though publicly owned, was caught up in the same logic, introducing an internal market in an attempt to justify its licence fee. In 1994, Professor Franklin calculated that 7,000 BBC jobs had been cut in the previous eight years. At least ninety more went in 1996. In 1997, a further huge 25% cut was announced for the following five years. In March 2005, the new director general, Mark Thompson, proposed another 13% cut, including 12% of the jobs in BBC News and 21% of jobs in Factual and Learning. By October 2007, he was announcing the removal of another 500 journalists from News as well as the loss of half of the remaining 1,200 staff in Factual and Learning. And all this was happening as the corporation was increasing its news output by moving into twenty-four-hour broadcasting. The result, of course, is that the BBC has been invaded by churnalism, particularly in their local newsrooms.

Some of the BBC's provincial TV reporters were forced to become 'video journalists', known as VJs, expected not only to research their story, but also to shoot and edit their own pictures, thus cutting even further the time they had to check. At the same time, former cameramen and editors were put through crash courses in reporting and recycled as VJs even though they lacked both skill and experience. When regional news desks complained that these VJs were producing soft stories with poor picture quality, they were not only brushed aside but given a formal target to use VJs to supply at least four out of every ten reports.

Regional BBC TV reporters who have not become VJs say they frequently have no camera crew to work with. Their stories are delayed or dropped in favour of an item which is quicker to shoot. In some areas, reporters have rebelled and succeeded in persuading their bosses to allow a few of them to work 'off diary', digging out exclusive stories. One such reporter provided a dozen exclusives in a couple of months and went for his annual appraisal expecting a pat on the back. Instead, his line manager, under pressure to fill his bulletins, complained that the reporter was appearing on screen too seldom. The reporter recalled his own reaction: 'Laugh? I was tempted to set about him.'

The BBC's regional radio reporters have suffered in a similar way. In Surrey and Sussex in the mid 1990s, for example, they had ten reporters to cover the two counties, plus two newsreaders who could help them. By 2006, that staffing had been cut to just two reporters to cover both counties, and only one newsreader who was recording and reading headlines and bulletins three times an hour for both counties and was thus effectively unable to help.

Commercial radio news has gone the same way, with local news coverage frequently supplied by a single journalist monitoring a computerised collection of agency stories and then reading them out twice an hour, often as a pre-recorded link from a regional hub. In January 2003, a severe blizzard in East Anglia exposed what was happening there, when commercial stations in the area were unable to put out any news or traffic bulletins because they had not one single reporter on duty. Local radio news coverage now may consist of nothing more than a lone presenter sitting in a darkened room, using computerised news systems, such as AP Newsdesk, which generates a list of agency stories to read out once or twice an hour, often complete with pre-packaged sound bites.

National newspapers themselves might yet have protected some of the supply of information from the provinces, through their own networks of regional staff distributed around the country. George Glenton's *News Chronicle*, for example, had nine district men in the north of England, Wales and Scotland, all working to an office in Manchester, as well as staff reporters in Bristol, Cardiff, Birmingham and Southampton. All the nationals had this kind of set-up. But the grocers cut that back, too, leaving only a thin skeleton behind.

So, in two decades, the entire network of supply lines which once carried a steady flow of raw information from the ground to the national news desks was reduced or removed. Who now is out there picking up news? Who is covering the courts and the council chambers? Who is out in the pubs, talking to drug dealers and car thieves, to detectives and doctors and teachers? Who is watching the businesses and the trade unions and checking on the MPs? There are some – but nothing like enough.

Without that rich supply of raw material, how can any national newspaper or broadcaster possibly know what to say each day about the lives of 60 million people, whose endlessly complex tangle of behaviour is supposed to be their subject? The answer is that they can't. And this has happened at precisely the same time as the reporters on those national outlets themselves have been cut and trapped in the office and made more reliant than ever on those supply lines. So it is that only 12% of their stories turn out to be their own work; and only 12% of their key facts are effectively checked.

Speed. The problems of churnalism have become even worse with the arrival of news websites – some of them staffed by specialist journalists, some of them by mainstream reporters who file copy for the site as well as for their traditional outlets. For all of them, the possibility of filing their stories immediately has become an imperative to spend even less time on their work, even less time checking. Rapid repackaging takes over.

The pressure comes through particularly clearly in some internal memos which I was given from the BBC's online news service, now known as News Interactive. Take one, for example, which was written on 9 December 2005 by the service's chief subeditor, Rob Liddle. You need to know that it was written only six months after the BBC publicly issued new guidelines to its journalists officially advising them that 'for the BBC, accuracy is more important than speed'.

Memo from Rob Liddle to News Interactive editorial. Subject: Speed and breaking news: 'We should be getting breaking news up within five minutes.' This, Liddle explained, meant that, within five minutes, staff should: publish a one-line version of the story on the 'ticker' which runs across the top of the BBC website; possibly send an email to the news desk to warn them about the story; write a four-paragraph version of the story and post it on Ceefax as well as on the website; and, at the same time, do 'checking'. Liddle went on to explain that the next target was then to write a full story of at least ten paragraphs within the following fifteen minutes. He suggested that these same targets should apply to stories which were not 'breaking news' but which 'would benefit the service to have up quickly – a good court case, say'.

This is churnalism at its most manic, not merely recycling but doing so at a speed which must jeopardise the BBC's chances of running accurate stories. Five minutes would never be enough to track down and speak to enough people to check any story, let alone while simultaneously writing tickers, emails and a four-paragraph summary. Liddle anticipated that there might be some worries – but they were not those of the churnalist reporters working for him. 'Grievances: if anyone thinks it has taken too long to get a story up, they can go through me and I'll try to find out what went wrong. This won't be a witch-hunt, but may help to identify any weaknesses in the system.'

Liddle wrote his memo on the instructions of Pete Clifton, the ebullient head of News Interactive. In a memo earlier that day, Clifton had said he was worried that staff might be getting complacent about speed. He suggested that they should produce a weekly report comparing their speed with that of rivals; that they should set up an internal complaints procedure to deal with stories that were held to be too slow; that every new recruit should be given a 'breaking news test'; and that subeditors, who are required to check all stories, should do more of their work by standing behind the reporter and peeping over their shoulder while the story was being written.

One memo from Pete Clifton takes this obsession with speed down to microseconds. Reporting a regular test on the time it takes readers to get access to different news sites, he told staff: 'Our site came on top with a load time of 0.85 secs to beat the likes of ITV and Sky (1.63 secs).' (That's a saving of 0.78 seconds he's cheering there.)

You can see the clash of traditional journalism and the new high-speed churnalism in the official BBC guide which is given to all staff on News Interactive. On the one hand, it urges: 'Your story MUST be accurate, impartial, balanced and uphold the values of BBC News . . . NEVER publish anything that you do not understand, that is speculation or inadequately sourced.' And then, as if there were no contradiction at all: 'Get the story up as fast as you can . . . We encourage a sense of urgency – we want to be first.' It then goes on to recite the five-minute target for breaking news.

This demand for speed is being imposed on reporters who have already been caught in the same pincer movement as their colleagues in the rest of the news industry. First, their resources have been cut, along with the rest of the BBC, so that during the day, they rely on a network of district offices with skeletal staffs – one or two reporters covering three or four counties at a time, some of whom were removed in the wave of cuts announced in March 2005. Overnight, there are no dedicated reporters on the health, entertainment and education sections; only one reporter on business even though their stories are being picked up in the United States whose business day runs into the small hours of the UK morning; only two on UK news; and three on the world desk, which has to cover the whole of the globe.

On the other side of the pincer, their output has been increased since 2000, when they were merged with the old Ceefax service. It is only since then that they have had to write simultaneously for Ceefax as well as the website. Apart from stealing yet more valuable time, this involves their adopting the writing style of a robot: every headline has to have between thirty-one and thirty-three characters to fit the Ceefax box; every story has to be written so that the top four paragraphs can stand alone and be diverted to Ceefax while the full version goes to the website. As one staffer there put it: 'Every story looks like a fat lady in a tight girdle, with all the detail spilling out below.' This robot writing is policed by a robot computer program which automatically lights up the headline in red or changes the typeface of the story to a smaller font, if either won't fit the Ceefax template.

The only escape from this pincer, as with so many other media outlets, is to recycle second-hand stories, from BBC staff and, most of all, from wire agencies. 'We'd fall over if it weren't for PA,' according to one staffer working on UK news.

The job is made even more difficult by the fact that staff say that many of them can't use shorthand. The official News Interactive guide attempts a discreet body swerve around the problem, telling them: 'You must take an accurate shorthand or longhand note of any interview.' The reality is that there is no such thing as an accurate longhand note of an interview with anybody who has not swallowed a fistful of tranquillisers.

Some of the results are worrying. Journalists on News Interactive say the pressure for speed is sometimes so great that they are required to write half of their story before it happens, a job which is made even more difficult by the fact that, in the same five minutes, they are expected to harmonise the story they write with the rest of the BBC's coverage. 'There's a pecking order: TV, radio, then us, and so we have to fit with the other two. Suppose a big football team holds a press conference about a crisis at the club. You sit in the office with Five Live on your headphones and one eye on BBC News 24. Before it even starts, you write paragraphs five to eight, which is all background. Then they start talking. Maybe there are multiple angles – the manager is staying, he's appointing a new captain, the chairman has put up millions to buy new players. So, you have to watch for the angle that the other two pick and then go with that. And you've got five minutes to get it up.

'There is no time at all for calls when you're doing this. If you made calls, people would be cross, they'd start yelling at you to get the story published. The Press Association or somebody might follow up with some reaction quotes and we'd pick them up, but we wouldn't make calls ourselves. If the story is unexpected – a plane crash, for example – you write the ticker and the top four paragraphs and you just have to make up the next four paragraphs of background, off the top of your head.'

News Interactive staff also say they are so short of time that they have taken to covering trials by recycling unchecked summaries of what has happened in court from police press officers, a highly contentious source for a type of story which is required not just by journalistic custom but by law to give an accurate account of the defence as well as the prosecution. According to one staffer in a regional newsroom: 'There's no question of calling the court to get the name of the defence solicitor and calling him or her to check accuracy. We just put it straight out.'

In October 2003, an assistant editor at the News Interactive hub in Birmingham, Hugh Berlyn, had the courage to raise the question of accuracy. In a memo to staff, he wrote: 'Yesterday we carried out a study of how many of your stories were being properly checked by a second pair of eyes before publication. To my surprise and concern, more than 60 stories around the country were apparently published without being second-checked.'

Four months later, in February 2004, he wrote again, warning that the number of 'justified complaints' about the lack of accuracy in spelling, names, grammar or simple detail was growing. He said that every day he was receiving dozens of complaints, many of them the result of their recycling inaccurate stories plucked from regional BBC output. 'We have to accept that the standard of journalism in local radio and regional TV is not the same as that required by News Online . . . I really think the level of complaints is such that our credibility is on the line and that cannot be allowed to continue.'

Pulling all this evidence together, what emerges is that the tendency for the media to recycle ignorance, as in the millennium bug and numerous other Flat Earth stories, flows directly from the behaviour of the new corporate owners of the media who have cut editorial staffing while increasing editorial output; slashed the old supply lines which used to feed up raw information from the ground; and, with the advent of news websites, added the new imperative of speed. Working in a news factory, without the time to check, without the chance to go out and make contacts and find leads, reporters are reduced to churnalism, to the passive processing of material which overwhelmingly tends to be supplied for them by outsiders, particularly wire agencies and PR. In these circumstances, the news factory will produce an effective and reliable product for its readers and viewers and listeners only if those outside suppliers are delivering an effective and reliable account of the world. Are they?

3. The Suppliers

When the Queen wants to talk to the world, she gives a statement to the Press Association. When the Poet Laureate wants to publish a new poem, he files it to the Press Association. Every government department, every major corporation, every police service and health trust and education authority delivers its official announcements to the Press Association. It is the primary conveyor belt along which information reaches national media in Britain.

All of the national daily and Sunday papers, all of the major regional papers, all of the other local papers who want to carry national news or sport, all of the *Metro* freesheets, all of the BBC's outlets around Britain and all of their commercial competitors in television and radio, all of the major websites handling UK news, as well as sixteen wire agencies from other countries, all subscribe to the PA news service. There are a few other, much smaller news agencies in Britain, but as PA's editor, Jonathan Grun, told us: 'The fact is we are the central heart of the media industry.'

The churnalists working on the assembly line in the news factory construct national news stories from raw material which arrives along two primary conveyor belts: the Press Association and public relations. We need to look at those two sources to see, first, whether they provide enough material to allow the news factory to cover the country as a whole, and second, whether the material is truthful.

The Cardiff researchers found that 30% of the home news stories in the five most prestigious Fleet Street titles were direct rewrites of copy from PA or smaller wire agencies. A further 19% of the stories were largely reproduced from the same agencies. A further 21% contained elements from them. That is a total of 70% of their news stories which are wholly or partly rewritten from wire copy, usually PA.

PA has such credibility that media outlets treat it as a reliable source which does not need to be checked. The BBC's internal guidelines, for example, specifically instruct their journalists that they must have at least two sources for every story – unless it is running on PA, in which case they can put it straight out on the airwaves. A special notice issued by the BBC journalism board on 1 December 2004 told staff: 'The Press Association can be treated as a confirmed, single source.' This was in bold type.

In practice, although they like to deny it, the same is more or less true of every national media outlet: they routinely rewrite agency copy with the minimum of check calls. As one national newspaper correspondent told the Cardiff researchers: 'Checking information has decreased, and what is worse, it is not expected by the news desk. I cannot tell you the number of times I am told to "take it off the wires and knock it into shape", which is just terrible.' A national broadcast journalist similarly told them: 'Many more stories are demanded by London desks straight from the wires, with few or no checks.' A section editor on a national daily told them: 'We've always been reliant on wire copy, but we use it a hell of a lot more these days. It's quite common for us to cut and paste a story off PA, renose it a bit to mask where it's come from and then put it out there as our own.'

So great is the influence of PA that I know reporters in local newsrooms who have had a story rejected by their news desks and who have discreetly called PA, given them the story and waited for it to run on the wire, at which point their news desks have asked them to follow it up. As a single example of PA's impact, BBC News 24 on 21 November 2005 ran a story about the Ministry of Defence agreeing to pay £5 million compensation to the family of a banker who had died landing his private plane after an RAF helicopter flew onto the runway. That story had already appeared on the BBC's own website three days earlier, filed to them by Strand News, a surviving news agency which specialises in covering the High Court. But PA had failed to run the story. So BBC News 24 did not run it – until three days later, when PA finally put it out.

The Press Association is honest in intent, efficient in performance, cost-effective as a business – and, I believe, entirely inadequate for the role in which it has now been cast. In spite of its defining impact on

UK news, PA is not reliable as a tool to dig out the most important and interesting events in the country; and it is not reliable as a source of truth about those events which it does choose to cover.

You have to see this in context. As the old network of local staff journalists and freelance agencies was hacked apart by the new corporate owners, PA moved in to take their place – but on nothing like the same scale. To fill the gap left by the thousands of local reporters who had been lost, PA increased its district staff from twenty reporters to seventy and distributed them through offices in the Irish Republic, Northern Ireland, Scotland, Wales and major cities in England. This did not begin to match the numbers in the old network.

PA refused to confirm these numbers for us, but according to staff there, the agency now attempts to cover the whole of Greater Manchester, Lancashire and Cumbria with just five reporters, including trainees, based in Manchester. The Newcastle area has only four. Leeds and Yorkshire has three. Merseyside, Cheshire and North Wales has two. Cardiff has four for the whole of South Wales and the Welsh Assembly. There are fifteen for the whole of Scotland. And these reporters work shift patterns, so there is never a time when they are all at work. With the best will in the world, PA cannot cover the ground as the old network did.

I analysed five days of PA output of UK news – no foreign or City, no sport or weather, just its mainstream supply of home news stories. That analysis suggested that, in place of the old network, PA on any one of those five days was deploying from London and its district offices a total of no more than sixty-nine reporters to cover both Houses of Parliament, 410 local councils, the national network of criminal and civil courts, forty-three police services and police authorities, the environment and transport, 151 primary care trusts, 150 local education authorities, consumer affairs, family finance, science and industry, sudden deaths, human interest, show business, religion and the royal family. On the Sunday which I monitored, they used only twenty reporters. PA staff to whom I spoke say that during the evenings and at weekends, they have just one reporter to cover the whole of the North-West, that is Greater Manchester, Lancashire and Cumbria as well as Merseyside, Cheshire and North Wales.

And that skeletal district staff of PA reporters can't fall back on buying in copy from local freelancers, partly because so many of them have gone out of business; and partly because PA has cut back hard on its budgets for freelance copy. Martin Hamer, a former PA journalist who researched the agency for a thesis at Liverpool John Moores University, cites internal PA audits which suggested that, between 1992 and 1997, their use of local correspondents fell from 40% of their output to only 6%. One former head of a district PA office told me he had been instructed simply to buy no freelance copy at all.

If, as the Cardiff report suggests, national newspapers are relying on this thin network to provide material for 70% of their stories, the inevitable result is that a great acreage of UK life simply remains untouched.

There was a striking example of this in October 2006, when police in Lancashire raided a house in Nelson and found what was believed to be the largest collection of chemical explosives ever found in the UK. One of the two men arrested had strong links to the British National Party. Apparently a big story. The nationals missed it. Replying to complaints, the director of news at the BBC explained what had happened: 'Thank you for your email about the court appearance at Pennine Magistrates of two men accused of possessing chemical explosives. It is indeed interesting. Unfortunately BBC TV news didn't know about the police find . . .' Quite simply, the police chose not to push the story themselves through their press office; no local journalist had the police contacts to pick it up and pass it on to Fleet Street; no court reporter spotted the men being remanded in custody and alerted the nationals; and PA's overstretched district staff missed it altogether. Only one news organisation got the story – the local *Colne Times*, which is a weekly. And by the time they had published it, the story was several days old, the men had been charged, and so the media were not allowed to report the case in any detail until it came to trial.

But it is not just these one-off stories which are now far less likely to make it into national news. The routine sources which fed the old network now also fail to make the news.

Take the courts, for example, which are the most productive single source of stories in the country, not just of human interest but of all the unseen tensions in a community's life which come bubbling up through crime and civil actions. PA has not only failed to replace the local newspaper reporters and specialist agencies who once monitored them, it has actually cut back its own coverage.

At the central criminal court at the Old Bailey, the once comprehensive PA staff, which covered eighteen courtrooms hosting some of the most serious and revealing crimes in Britain, has now been cut back to just two. Many cases there now pass entirely unreported. At the Royal Courts of Justice in the Strand, until the early 1980s, PA had twenty reporters covering criminal appeals, libels, all kinds of industrial, commercial and marital disputes and a string of other major cases which change the content of British law. Now, they have only five, to cover ninety-six courtrooms. In both courthouses, there remains also a clutch of freelancers, much reduced over the past twenty years. Between them, they cannot begin to cover all the hearings. The best they can do generally is to catch the top and tail of the biggest cases.

That reduced coverage of the two most important courthouses in the country is a media frenzy compared to what is happening in the ten other Crown courts in the city, which PA attempts to cover with just one specialist court reporter; let alone in the network of fifty-nine other county courts and magistrates' courts in London, where judges are as likely to see a zebra as a reporter. Across the country, most of the work of the eighty-two regional Crown courts, more than two hundred other county courts and more than 350 other magistrates' courts is invisible to PA and, therefore, to most other media, national and local. Each of these courts houses multiple courtrooms; many of those courtrooms will process multiple cases each day. But while several thousand cases are being heard, only a couple of dozen will make it down the PA wire, from which only a handful will make it into the national media.

When I looked into this in the late 1990s, I found a criminal trial which had been running for three months at Leicester Crown Court, without a word of national coverage, even though it had unearthed Scotland Yard's involvement in unlawfully importing Yardie gangsters from Jamaica who were used as informants and effectively given a licence to commit crime in London. I also found the nationals had said nothing about a gay fifteen-year-old boy who was suing his local authority for the right to be placed with gay foster-parents; a police officer who was confronted with evidence of his own corruption while giving evidence in a Crown court; electricity workers who were suing the privatised energy companies for skimming £1.5 billion off the top of their pension fund; and a long sequence of hearings involving animal rights activists who faced being jailed for conspiracy to commit criminal damage purely on the basis of comments they had made to a newspaper. All unreported.

Local government has fallen even further off the media's radar screen. Where once local papers covered all their local authorities, right down to the smallest parish council, the old network has now almost completely withdrawn. PA used to have a couple of specialist local government correspondents who had a hard time attempting to cover all the 410 local councils as well as some 400 other trusts and authorities which run the hospitals, schools and police. As of 2006, PA has no local government specialist at all. In the twelve months before this book was written, not one national newspaper carried a single story 'by our local government correspondent'. There is the beginning of a justification for this in the loss of powers suffered by local authorities since the Thatcher years. Nevertheless, at the time of writing, local councils collectively were spending just over £100,000 million a year in government grant and local council tax and yet their activities were being covered regularly only by the fortnightly 'Rotten Boroughs' column in *Private Eye* (which turns out a steady flow of otherwise unreported tales of corruption and incompetence). Local authorities nowadays generally choose for themselves what the media will report about them, selecting the news that suits them by posting it on their websites or distributing it in press releases.

Even at the heart of government, media monitoring of Parliament has collapsed. As a Labour shadow minister in 1993, Jack Straw published an analysis of the coverage of parliamentary debates which showed that the major dailies had been running up to eight hundred lines of copy a day, more or less steadily from 1933 until 1988 when there was 'a sudden decline' to less than one hundred lines by 1992. This is, in part, because the grocers shifted their focus to stories which were more likely to sell their papers. But it was also the result of the now familiar destruction of reporting staff.

The number of specialist journalists based in Parliament has been slashed to ribbons. Until the 1980s, all the major dailies had teams of reporters covering the chamber; *The Times* alone had sixteen gallery reporters. Now the gallery is generally only for sketch writers. In the same way, only twenty-three of the 1,200 local newspapers still have their own staff there (although some file to more than one title). A mass of debates in the Commons and the Lords, early day motions and parliamentary questions, hearings by select committees pass unremarked.

In the case of Parliament, PA has increased its staffing to fill the gap, but it has also increased its output. Trying to cover every story for every outlet, PA's political staff are as stretched as their general news reporters. Other political correspondents describe PA reporters in Parliament banging out a story from a press release while simultaneously tape-recording some leading politician on radio news, then banging that out while another press release arrives.

Chris Moncrieff, who has covered Parliament for PA since 1962, told us: 'We have so much monitoring of radio and TV, far more now than ten years ago, that we have less time to get stories ourselves.' He added that PA now covers far fewer political meetings and speeches than it used to and relies far more on government press releases. 'They've won,' he said. 'If they put out in advance a copy of the speech, then we will not go. We now print what they want us to print. We go to far fewer meetings or not at all.'

The problem of the under-reported Parliament has become so serious that both government and media organisations have run inquiries in search of a solution. Their underlying conclusion was expressed well in a report for the Hansard Society in November 2006: 'The public are usually in the dark as to how Parliament works and what legislation actually means to their lives. Westminster, the world of politics and Parliament, remain a closed book to many.' A MORI poll in February 2004, also for the Hansard Society, found that 65% of people wrongly believed there had to be an election every four years; and that only 49% knew that the House of Commons had more power than the House of Lords.

If it can't dig out stories for the nationals in the way that the old local network used to, can PA nonetheless check the truth of what it does put out? The great difficulty here is that PA itself is engaged in churnalism.

In August 1995, the Press Association nearly died when some of its biggest clients attempted to defect to a new challenger, UK News. It fought off the attack, retrieved its clients and rose from its deathbed to be reborn as a highly motivated commercial operation, producing maximum output with minimum staff.

For its reporters, this meant a relentless drive for more and more copy. One of their former reporters who started there as a trainee and rose to senior status, told me: 'Stories that PA would once have spiked, now appear on the wire. There is no such thing as a rubbish story at PA. Each story has its value – if *The Times* doesn't want it, the *Leeds Evening Post* will, and if they don't, the *Halifax Courier* might go for it. PA is writing more copy than ever before – some of it crap.'

The copy from reporters is no longer simply put out on the wire. It is treated as raw material, to be recast repeatedly for different customers. The Paul Hucker story, for example, was sold to the nationals as a story about an English football fan; to East Anglian media as a story about a fan from Ipswich; and to north-eastern media as a story about an England fan who supports Newcastle.

PA developed a new production hub at Howden in Yorkshire essentially as a repackaging plant, where stories are put together and sold as cheap, 'oven-ready' pages for local papers and magazines; four-paragraph summaries for Teletext; one-line texts for mobile phones; as well as being sold to websites, to corporations and hotels, to City brokers and through Mediapoint, PA's specialist service for corporations. They sell sports data, which has been processed at their centre in Mangalore, south-west India; weather forecasts; an archive of pictures; listings for arts and entertainment, both local and national. They even sell TV listings to the BBC's own *Radio Times*.

And they are doing this, as we have seen, with a reporting staff which is spread very thinly in its main newsroom in London, in Parliament and in its district offices. In 2005, the National Union of Journalists conducted a survey among PA staff and found them severely over-stretched, working an average of five hours unpaid overtime every day and frequently stepping in to cover senior posts which were unfilled. The union quoted staff: 'Staff shortages are a big problem and running such a tight ship means that when people are off or ill, the situation gets ridiculous . . . Newcomers are dropped in at the deep end and left to sink or swim. Training is minimal . . . I got the job because I was young and cheap. And the guy who replaces me will no doubt be even younger and even cheaper.' A third of the journalists were juniors earning less than £15,000 a year; some were on less than £12,000.

An NUJ assistant organiser, Jenny Lennox, told the union's annual meeting about her own experience working in PA's new hub at Howden, where the agency subedits and packages material for a mass of clients: 'I've spoken to people there who were firemen, who worked in cake factories and who used to sell cars. The only qualification is that they have a GCSE or equivalent pass in English, and they are subbing national and regional newspapers.'

Just as with all the other media outlets which have been transformed by commercial logic, the practical result is that PA deprives its journalists of their most important working asset – the time to check.

PA reporters told me they routinely start the day by writing stories from press releases and other newspapers and, since they are doing this from 4.30 in the morning, they cannot possibly find anybody to check them with. One of their senior editors agreed that this happens. He had previously worked for a regional newspaper and told me: 'We used to take what we were given from PA and accept it as fact but, once I went to work there, I realised that we couldn't.'

One senior PA specialist told the Cardiff researchers that when he first joined the agency twenty-five years earlier, he had written no more than three stories a day, whereas now he expects to write an average of ten in a single shift: 'I don't usually spend more than an hour on a story. Otherwise, I wouldn't be able to write so many.'

Another agency man told them:'My father was a journalist for Reuters for twenty-five years, and the working conditions were completely different. Stories would take much longer to put together, but when they were, they were more likely to be accurate and close to the truth.'

And, in the same pattern which we have already seen at BBC News Interactive, this underlying problem has been compounded by the need for speed, the constant imperative to file before the competition does. For example, PA executives were furious when their reporter was beaten by ITN with the result of the 2003 trial of the army major who was accused of cheating to win *Who Wants to Be a Millionaire?*

Soon afterwards, one of their reporters went to cover a hearing involving allegations against the TV presenter John Leslie of sex offences. The charges were thrown out. Desperate to beat his rivals, the PA reporter texted the result of the hearing from inside the court. That happens to be illegal. The reporter also happened to be sitting next to two officials from the Lord Chancellor's department. They nabbed him.

At a board meeting on 9 December 2004, PA moved into a whole new area of repackaging by deciding to convert all its reporters into simultaneous broadcast journalists, so that they could file video and/or audio reports alongside their printed stories. And these, too, are repackaged and sold to national newspaper websites (the commentary written in one style for the *Sun* and another for the *Mail*) as well as local newspaper websites, foreign websites, public space TV screens, mobile phones, corporate websites and, if PA's plans succeed, to the new network of more than sixty micro-local BBC news outlets. It is a brilliant operation – but unfortunately it cuts still further the time available for its reporters to do their job.

One PA staffer told me: 'You do the interview in shorthand and then again for radio and you file both separately. It's not just time pressure. There's what it does for your concentration, because you can't focus on the print version.'

Apart from the fact that PA reporters have so little chance to check their material, this churnalism in PA is built on a foundation which crucially – and generally unrecognised in Fleet Street – is inherently weak on the truth. PA is a news agency, not a newspaper. It is not attempting, nor does it claim to be attempting, to tell people the truth about the world. As its editor, Jonathan Grun, put it to us: 'What we do is report what people say and accurately.' The PA reporter goes to the press conference with the intention of capturing an accurate record of what is said. Whether what is said is itself a truthful account of the world is simply not their business. Indeed, PA reporters say they would be breaking their own in-house rules if they started challenging speakers. They would be accused of making the news instead of reporting it. Sleuthing, Grun told us, is not PA's role. 'Our role is attributable journalism – what someone has got to say. What is important is in quote marks.' If the Prime Minister says there are chemical weapons in Iraq, that is what the good news agency will report.

Finally, PA's reliability can crumple under official pressure. Twice in 1998, the agency was exposed by the *Daily Mirror*. On the first occasion, PA's royal correspondent, Peter Archer, had interviewed Prince William, who, the *Mirror* found, had then been allowed to preview the copy: the Prince, or his staff, got away with cutting out some six hundred words from the version which was sent out on the PA wire. On the second occasion, a PA reporter was with a group of other national correspondents when Prince Andrew acknowledged that Palace officials had been misleading the public for years. PA failed to report the remark.

What emerges from all this is a national news factory which is unable to fill its pages with its own high-quality product, because it lacks the staff and the front-line workers on the ground, and which then relies on a wire agency which is itself severely limited. And yet the pressure to carry on producing more and more copy is relentless. Starved of time, desperate for material, a system which should be protecting itself with rigorous checks instead starts to suck in anything which looks like a story. This is where the PR industry comes in.

The local reporter now may not have a single contact in the police station down the street, but the press office at police HQ will tape-record a summary of incidents for the voice bank each morning, and the reporter can turn them into stories. The national reporter may not know a single civil servant in the Whitehall department she is covering today, but the department's press office will supply her with a press release, complete with quotes from a minister and background history. The specialist finance reporter can sit in his office, miles away from the nearest boardroom, and still write four or five stories a day, thanks to the creative work of the PR companies who work for almost every major corporation.

When the Cardiff researchers checked the sources of UK news stories in the five most prestigious daily papers in Fleet Street, they found that more than half of them carried clear signs of PR input: 41% of them were initiated by PR and/or contained material supplied by PR, and a further 13% of stories carried clear signs of PR activity, but the researchers were unable finally to prove the point, because the PR trail was too well hidden, usually through off-the-record briefings.

Later, we will uncover some of the subtle tactics which PR uses to insert its material into every area of news. Chapter 5 shows that this is not simply about holding press conferences and putting out press releases, but also about constructing pseudo-events to generate coverage, creating phoney front groups to make news on specific issues, supplying apparently independent experts who speak to an undisclosed PR agenda, and coordinating campaigns of media coverage with direct lobbying in order to shift government policy. And Chapter 6 tracks the signs of a surge in secretly organised propaganda which has occurred since the terrorist attacks of 11 September 2001, injecting into the mass media whole storylines which are fabricated to manage global perception of events. The common element is the ease with which clever outsiders can manipulate the now vulnerable media.

As Edward Bernays, frequently described as the founding father of PR, put it: 'The conscious and intelligent manipulation of the organised habits and opinions of the masses is an important element in democratic society. Those who manipulate this unseen mechanism of society constitute an invisible government which is the true ruling power of our country. In almost every act of our daily lives, whether in the sphere of politics or business, in our social conduct or our ethical thinking, we are dominated by the relatively small number of persons . . . who pull the wires which control the public mind.'

But, at this stage, I want to look not at the tactics of PR, but at the scale of its activity. When I started as a journalist in the mid 1970s, it was relatively rare to come across PR people. Now, every organisation and every individual with a reasonable expectation of media coverage employs PR specialists who will do their best to choose what will and will not be said about them and to ensure that newsrooms accept that choice. It was during the 1980s, just as journalists were losing their jobs, that PR boomed. Indeed, many of the jobless journalists crossed the bridge into PR with the result that, on the best available estimates, Britain now has more PR people (47,800) than journalists (45,000).

In his 2002 book, *Public Relations Democracy*, Aeron Davis of City University in London tracked the change. He found that in 1979, only 28% of the top fifty companies in *The Times* 1,000 list used PR agencies; just five years later, 90% of them were doing so. And they employed more and more personnel: in the twenty years from 1979, big corporations increased their hiring of PR consultants elevenfold. Throughout the 1980s, the number of PR consultants in the UK increased by between 25 and 30% every single year.

And, of course, the same thing was happening in government. Fleet Street has created one of its Flat Earth stories about this, presenting the growth of political PR as the work of Tony Blair's first press secretary, Alastair Campbell. In fact, the big boom happened during the Conservative years.

When Margaret Thatcher took office in 1979, the British government was spending £27 million on the Central Office of Information, which runs its PR departments. In less than ten years, that figure rose more than 500%, to £150 million in 1988. That meant more Whitehall press officers selecting and promoting stories – their numbers more or less doubled from 628 when Mrs Thatcher became Prime Minister, to 1,163 when John Major left office. And it meant much more spending on outside PR consultants, like Lowe Bell and Shandwick, who did so much to shape news during the Conservative years. The Blair government simply took over where they left off, hiring a further 310 press officers in its first two years, increasing its annual output of press releases by 80% to some 20,000 a year, and continuing to give multiple millions of public money to outside PR agencies.

The political parties themselves followed the same pattern, beginning with the Conservatives' use of Saatchi & Saatchi in 1978. This is reflected in their spending on election campaigns. In 1983, the two main parties spent a total of £10.5 million on the general election. By 1997, they were spending a total of £54.3 million on their campaigns, much of it pouring into PR and marketing.

PR soon spilled over into local government. By 1994, when he wrote *Packaging Politics*, Professor Bob Franklin found that 90% of metropolitan authorities had set up their own PR departments; between them, local councils, police, health and education authorities were employing some 15% of the expanding ranks of PR personnel. Thirty years ago, most of the local limbs of the state allowed their civil servants, health workers, doctors and head teachers to talk to the press. Now, none of them does without the approval of the press office. By the late 1990s, trade unions, churches, charities and pressure groups were all using in-house press officers and/or outside PR agencies to create their news. Even paramilitary organisations in Northern Ireland set up formal press links.

But does this PR conveyor belt, which feeds its material into 54% of Fleet Street's home news stories, provide the right raw material to allow the news factory to cover the country as a whole? And is it truthful?

The answer to the first question is indicated by a simple test which was undertaken by the Cardiff researchers. They took a sample of the stories they had been monitoring from the five daily papers (*Times, Telegraph, Guardian, Independent, Mail*), divided them between those which had no PR input and those which had been generated by PR, and then ranked the news value of each story. They found that among those which had no PR input, only 4% were rated as having 'little or no news value'. But among those which had been generated by PR, 25% of the stories fell into this lowest of rankings. This is a bizarre and worrying development.

For many decades, news editors and reporters used 'news values' and contacts to decide what stories to run. Now, to a decisive extent, that crucial process of news judgement has been taken out of their hands. Indeed, it has been taken right outside of their organisations, so that routinely they find themselves processing stories which have been chosen for them by people whose job is to shape news coverage in the service of powerful interests, whether commercial, political or other.

This is not just about PR inserting the material which it chooses; it also involves suppressing the stories which might cause embarrassment to its clients. In *Public Relations Democracy*, Aeron Davis cites three different surveys to support his conclusion that 'for every story fed to the media, there is one being carefully kept out. For many organisations, half or more of the work of PR practitioners involves restricting reporter access and information and/or attempting to quash negative stories.'

Suppression initially means simply not releasing troublesome information. The police officer who wins a commendation for bravery gets a press release; the officer who is caught drunk on duty gets none. Most central government departments require their middle managers to notify the press office of any incident which may create bad news; the press office then prepares a line to give journalists if they enquire.

Speaking privately, government press officers say the vast majority of these lines are never needed, because journalists simply never hear about the incidents. What they report is what they are given.

Alternatively, if embarrassing information has to come out, suppression means manipulating journalists so that they fail to cover it. A routine example: the Prime Minister commissioned the Social Exclusion Unit to investigate the best way to cut crime; the SEU produced a report in July 2002 and expected a government response six months later; but the government had political problems with the report, which collated a mass of evidence to show that its hard-line approach was counterproductive; it had to respond, but it didn't want the response to be reported. First, the government simply stalled for two long years, while the SEU report slipped off the media radar. Second, it waited until one Monday in July 2004, when the Prime Minister made a major speech, blaming crime on 'the 1960s liberal consensus'. An advanced text of the speech was provided on the Sunday to political correspondents, who ran it prominently on Monday morning. During the day, TV and radio covered the Prime Minister actually making the speech; the government announced a series of new hard-line initiatives; and government press officers supplied briefings. All this generated many thousands of words of coverage, with the impact of the 1960s consensus still being discussed by Sunday columnists six days later. On that Monday afternoon, with Fleet Street successfully diverted, the government quietly placed its response to the SEU report on the Home Office website. It received not one single word of coverage.

The simple everyday power of PR to set the news agenda was captured perfectly by a freelance journalist, Nigel Green, who used the Freedom of Information Act to find out how many incidents Northumbria Police had failed to disclose to the press during a single weekend in June 2006. He discovered that they had dealt with a total of 5,083 incidents, including a man who had gone missing from hospital and been found dead in the sea; a seventy-four-year-old man who had been severely beaten by a group of youths; and a young girl who died when she fell from a tower block. The police PR staff had told the press about precisely none of them. The fact that this was the weekend of the quarter-finals of the football World Cup may have had something to do with it.

When we come to the question of whether or not PR material is truthful, the fact that PR is having such an impact on the selection of Fleet Street's stories is the beginning of the answer. Even if all of the material in all of those stories is true, you can see that this is a process of distortion. The story may be true but, without PR, it would not be making it into the news. The story may be newsworthy but, without PR, it would be being told with a different angle. The story may be true and newsworthy but, because of PR suppression, it never makes it into the news.

Beyond this distortion, now built into the structure of news gathering, PR material is clearly inherently unreliable as a source of truth, simply because it is designed to serve an interest. All the great Flat Earth news stories carry the impact of PR. While dodgy executives fixed the books, it was commercial PR which created the public myth around Enron and WorldCom. It was political PR which pushed the story of the WMD in Iraq, the scandal around Bill Clinton, and so much of the policy distortion in black-market drugs and crime and education. It was PR from pressure groups which pushed the megadeath at Chernobyl. And all of them – commercial, political and NGO – joined in to push the millennium bug. This is routine in the world of the news factory, in stories big and small.

I am not saying that all PR is a lie. It isn't. The real worry is that so much of it flows into the news factory without journalists being able to distinguish between what is true and what is false. This stuff runs in through the entrance of the news factory and frequently pours out the other side unchanged.

As a snapshot at the local level, in his 2004 edition of *Packaging Politics*, Bob Franklin reports a survey of press releases issued over a two-month period by Northumberland County Council: 96% of them were converted into stories by local newspapers. Most made it into more than one paper. While the bigger regional dailies tended to edit them substantially, the smaller weekly papers 'either reproduced the press release verbatim and in full, or simply removed whole paragraphs or changed their order.' Franklin concluded: 'What is significant is that none of the published stories contained any additional information to the original release: the bulk of these releases were swallowed whole and uncritically.'

As an example at the national level, in 1996 Professor David Miller of the University of Strathclyde published a study of the Northern Ireland Office which found that at the height of the troubles the NIO was spending £7.2 million on PR output for a population of only 1.5 million people. Fifty-eight press officers were feeding press releases to Belfast news desks three times a day. Despite the clear journalistic imperative to filter this official account of events in a highly contentious arena, Bob Franklin cites a study of NIO press releases put out over a three-month period which found that one newspaper used 77% of these releases and that 'there is little editing . . . with many being published virtually verbatim'.

The impact is the same across the board. Stories which appear to be the work of journalists turn out to be PR artifice. Three examples among many from the Cardiff research: a story in *The Times* in March 2006, about a British soldier in Iraq who had been awarded the George Cross, which was 'an almost verbatim repetition of a press release issued by the Ministry of Defence'; an article about a new hay fever vaccine in the *Daily Mail* in April 2006, which 'reproduces a press release from the drug company Cytos, without adding any original material'; and a news story in the *Daily Telegraph* in March 2006, about the return of the 1980s TV comedy, *The New Statesman*, which is based entirely on material generated by a stunt 'press conference', held by its star, Rik Mayall, in Parliament Square.

Years ago, the veteran journalist Claude Cockburn said: 'A newspaper is always a weapon in somebody's hands.' In those days, he was talking about owners. Nowadays, you don't have to own a newspaper to manipulate it.

Now come back inside the national news factory and see what it looks like.

Wire copy, according to the Cardiff research, finds its way into 70% of the home news stories put out by the five most prestigious titles in Fleet Street. They also found it in 65% of mainstream broadcast stories (evening bulletins of BBC and ITV plus *Today* and *The World at One* on Radio 4). And, as we have seen, this wire copy, dominated by the Press Association, cannot claim to be covering the country in its selection of stories and cannot be relied on as a source of truth about the stories it does select.

On the second conveyor belt, PR material, according to the Cardiff research, finds its way into 54% of these news stories. And, as we have seen, this material, whether or not it is truthful, is designed specifically to promote and to suppress stories in order to serve the interests of political, commercial and other groups.

It's clear, too, that the PR conveyor belt is not only supplying material direct into the factory but also feeding it indirectly by giving it to wire agencies as well. The Cardiff research found that 41% of wire stories which made it into print contained the clear and usually provable imprint of PR. Some of this material is being inserted at both points, so that national reporters construct stories out of a press release which has been sent to them, together with the PA version of the same press release. Some (like the story of Paul Hucker, the anxious football fan) is being pumped into the Press Association alone and thus arrives at national news desks without an overt PR stamp on it.

I spoke to PR specialists who told me they had seen their press releases running more or less verbatim on the wire with a PA reporter's byline on top of their words. One PR man, who works for a major political party, told us: 'PA is a way for us to disseminate our line; X happens so we say Y. It is infinitely preferable logistically to send it to PA than to try and contact 150 journalists. And we are rarely subjected to the sort of cross-examination that say the *Sun* or *The Times* would give us. PA does not do as much of the probing and difficult questions. They are journalists but to some extent they are an information service.'

One of PA's most senior reporters, the industry correspondent Alan Jones, described his end of this to the Cardiff researchers: 'I've got dozens of contacts who work in PR . . . Some of them are really sound and have a lot of integrity, but there is so much consumer PR where the bottom line is placing the name of a product in a newspaper, and they'll bombard people like me with surveys, reports, research or studies, basically wrapped up as a story. But really, it's just a blatant attempt to get a company name in the paper. And the trouble with being so busy and having to write so many stories a day, is that you don't always get time to research some of these things as thoroughly as you should. Every day stuff comes in to me that I think is ridiculous. I write it up, and it ends up being a page lead or a splash in a national newspaper.'

This is why the Cardiff research found that 80% of news stories included material from one or both of these supply lines.

The immediate impact of this is to create a consensus account of the world, in which most of the outlets draw most of their stories and angles and quotes from a tiny collection of raw material. You can see this best if you look at the twenty-four-hour cycle inside the national news factory.

Every morning, the news editors of national papers have to produce a list of stories to take in to the morning conference. As they arrive at their desks, they will find PA's 'news advisory', which is delivered at six each morning. Martin Hamer's 2000 thesis about PA records an interview with the editor, Jonathan Grun, in which he said: 'If you are a news editor arriving in the office first thing in the morning, you're like a drowning man grasping at any straw that you can while you are trying to get your head round what is actually happening. If a schedule from the PA lists our view of the top twenty stories of the day, you will rely on that.'

Each news desk will have some of its own leads (the 12% of original stories uncovered by the Cardiff research) but it is the same PA advisory which shapes the home news list in every national newspaper and every national broadcaster in the country. That advisory to a significant extent will have been shaped by the input of PR material direct into Press Association offices; and that same PR material often will have arrived at the national news desks as well, to reinforce the selection of the twenty 'top stories' in the news advisory. In parallel, BBC News Interactive, which is now used as a secondary source of material by most news desks, will be putting out its key stories, which are themselves heavily influenced by PA, the one source which, as we have seen, the BBC regards as reliable without the need for checking. ('We'd fall over if it weren't for PA.')

During the day, that select group of stories starts running on national radio and TV and in the London *Evening Standard*, any of whom may add some of their own original work. The national papers monitor them all. So does PA, which runs anything it missed; and the national papers keep monitoring PA. Out in the provinces, the local radio stations and newspapers start the day by cannibalising the national papers, then they cannibalise each other's output and both, in turn, cannibalise PA, which in turn monitors all of their output through their district offices and runs anything it missed.

In the background, press officers and PR consultants in government and the private sector monitor the same PA wire and the same news outlets. Some of them use sophisticated electronic programs, like Media Sense which has been developed by a company called PRNewswire, so that they can track their output and put out new material to try to push their stories and angles along.

Late in the afternoon, PA will put out another news advisory, based on the list they put out in the morning plus whatever other 'top stories' may have gatecrashed the list during the day – unexpected events and any significant material which has been turned up, for example, by Radio 4 or the *Evening Standard*. The national news editors take this advisory, make their final news lists for the day and take them back into afternoon conference – at every national outlet.

As the first editions of the papers emerge shortly before midnight, the night news desks monitor each other and lift any significant story they have missed. In the morning, the news editors read each other's final editions, listen to the *Today* programme, which has already started running PA's selection of stories, which are waiting once more on the news editor's desk, to be taken into conference.

PA runs a total of between 150 and 200 home news stories on any weekday. On average, the Cardiff research shows, the *Independent* carries only eighteen UK news stories a day, the *Guardian* carries twenty, *The Times* twenty-four, the *Telegraph* twenty-eight and the *Mail* thirty-eight. That is a total of 128 stories. The consensus here is twofold. First, as the Cardiff researchers found, 70% of those stories will be wholly, mainly or partly constructed from the PA feed. But, second, because media outlets spend so much time monitoring each other's output, they tend to cluster around the same selection of stories, most of them from PA. The Cardiff research shows that, between them, the five leading national newspapers cover an average of only seventy-five stories a day. And, overwhelmingly, these print stories turn out to be covering the same subjects which are covered by national news bulletins on television and radio: 48% of broadcast stories have been published in papers earlier that day; another 42% show up in the papers the following day; only 10% of broadcast stories are not covered by the five leading Fleet Street papers (usually ones that have made it onto television because they have quirky pictures).

This process of consensus is unreliable – in its selection of stories and in its truth. And if you look closer at the content of this consensus material, you find that the result is often arbitrary and even irrational. You can catch a glimpse of this by looking at non-stories, the ones that don't make it onto the conveyor belts at all.

The Cardiff researchers conducted a revealing experiment, checking community news wires and specialist magazines for stories which had not been reported by the national media during the two random weeks when they were sampling Fleet Street output. They found a mass of them.

These included: an Iraqi refugee in Salford, who had witnessed a shooting in a pub and wanted to go back to Baghdad for his own safety; official evidence of a 'postcode lottery' in sentencing, with different courts handing out different punishments for similar offences; a peace activist jailed under a new law for protesting in Parliament Square; a Department of Health report which white-washed their importing of hepatitis-infected blood from the US for transfusion in the UK; worrying cuts in fire safety on the London Underground. None of those made it into the consensus selection of the national media, not because of any conspiracy but simply because of the inadequate performance of the news factory's supply lines.

Equally clearly, this consensus, with its tendency towards the arbitrary and the irrational, is highly likely to contain falsehood, distortion and propaganda. The wire agency supply line, as we have seen, is structurally vulnerable, staffed by journalists who are denied the time to check and who are encouraged to focus on the accuracy of the quotes they are running, but not their truth. The PR supply line is specifically designed to sell an angle.

And since the national news factory is so beset by churnalism that the Cardiff research found that only 12% of key factual statements were being properly checked, this stuff comes pouring down the conveyor belt, through the media outlets and out into the public domain.

It is not that PA and PR are better than the old system. The attraction for the grocers is simply that they are much cheaper. It is no longer a matter of independent newspapers competing with each other to produce the best stories, but of mutually dependent newspapers working in tandem to produce more or less the same stories – stories which may or may not be 'the best'. Or honest. Or accurate.

There is a danger of exaggerating what is happening here. First, not all of this is new. There never was some kind of golden age when all journalists were free to tell the truth. They have always had to work against the clock and they have always been the targets of attempts to interfere in their stories. They have always been – as they still are – restrained by media law which, in Britain, remains particularly restrictive in its approach to official secrecy and libel. There always were accidental screw-ups and deliberate lies.

Second, even now, it is not all churnalism. The Cardiff statistics suggest that 12% of stories are still being generated entirely by the reporters who write them. The researchers found another 8% of stories whose origin they simply could not be sure about. Arguably, many of those stories might be original work, since original work will tend to have sources which are more difficult to trace, although it is equally likely that these untraced stories include off-the-record PR input. But, in principle, it is possible that as much as 20% of Fleet Street's work is still being produced entirely by independent journalists. That original work needs to be acknowledged. There are still reporters who can negotiate the time to work effectively, and some of them work with extraordinary persistence and sometimes real physical courage to find and tell the truth.

Finally, it should be said, too, that their colleagues who are trapped on the churnalist production line are generally a good deal better than the work they are allowed to produce.

But the bottom line remains. The Cardiff research suggests that at least 80% of the news product of the best and most respected newspapers in Britain contains second-hand material, most of it unchecked, much of it provided by people who are at best unreliable and at worst manipulative. Something fundamental has shifted.

Every day, fiction slides effortlessly around Britain, passing unhindered through media channels which are supposed to be reserved for fact. And then, with equal ease, it slips across the border and flows around the world, while fiction from other parts of the world glides quietly into Britain.

Flat Earth news has gone global because all across the world, media organisations have suffered the same experience as their British counterparts – takeover by new corporate owners, cuts in staff coupled with increases in output, less time to find stories and less time to check them, the collapse of old supply lines, the rise of PR and wire agencies as an inherently inadequate substitute, less and less input being repackaged for more and more outlets, truth-telling collapsing into high-speed processing.

Journalism in the world's most powerful country is deep in the same trap. The American media critic Ben Bagdikian has traced the corporate takeover. In 1997, he wrote about the corporations producing America's newspapers, magazines, radio, television, books and films: 'With each passing year . . . the number of controlling firms in all these media has shrunk: from 50 corporations in 1984 to 26 in 1987, followed by 23 in 1990, and then, as the borders between the different media began to blur, to less than 20 in 1993. In 1996 the number of media corporations with dominant power in society is closer to 10.' By 2004, he found, the US media were dominated by just five companies: Time Warner, Disney, Murdoch's News Corporation, Bertelsmann of Germany and Viacom.

These corporations have imposed their grocers' logic on the profession. According to the Newspaper Association of America, the number of people employed in the industry there fell by 18% between 1990 and 2004. In one twelve-month period in 2004/5, some 450 journalists were pushed out of their jobs at the *New York Times, San Francisco*

Chronicle, Philadelphia Inquirer, Newsday, Philadelphia Daily News, Boston Globe and *San Jose Mercury News*. Soon afterwards, the *Washington Post, USA Today, Time, Newsweek, BusinessWeek* and *Forbes* all followed.

The Times Mirror corporation which owned the *LA Times*, the *Baltimore Sun*, the *Hartford Courant* and *Newsday* in New York, cut deep into their reporting staff during the late 1990s. Their then chief executive, Mark Willes, whose previous experience had been with a food corporation, came to be known as the Cereal Killer. As he cut his staff, the company's share price tripled. In 2000, Times Mirror sold out to the Tribune group, who soon inflicted more cuts, provoking one of their Pulitzer Prize-winning reporters, Laurie Garrett, to resign with a powerful public letter.

'The sad arc of greed has finally hit bottom,' she said. 'The leaders of Times Mirror and Tribune have proven to be mirrors of a general trend in the media world: they serve their stockholders first, Wall Street second, and somewhere far down the list comes service to newspaper readerships.'

Reinforcing her words, the American media analyst, John Morton, reported in October 2005 that the average operating profit margin of these media corporations was 20.5%, which was approximately twice as high as the level among Fortune 500 companies. By then, the coverage of most American cities had been reduced to only one newspaper and to local broadcasting networks supplied by centralised hubs.

And in the United States, just as in Great Britain, there has been a huge expansion of PR to fill the information void – from 19,000 personnel in 1950 to 162,000 by 1990. In 2000, PR agencies were still growing in the US by 32% a year, and the US Council of PR Firms reported that the global earnings of the twenty-five biggest American PR companies had reached nearly $3.5 billion. As a single example of their penetration, when the *Columbia Journalism Review* put one edition of the *Wall Street Journal* under the microscope, they found that more than half of the news stories 'were based solely on press releases'. These were reprinted 'almost verbatim or in paraphrase', with little additional reporting but with the classic and dishonest byline 'By a *Wall Street Journal* staff reporter'.

It is the same in Canada where there has been an explosion of media outlets even though, according to Statistics Canada, the number of journalists has declined since 1991. In June 2000, a Canadian PR man, Eric Sparling, resigned from his job and blew his own cover in an article in the *Toronto Star*. 'I owe you an apology,' he told the *Star's* readers. 'I've lied, cheated and swindled.' He went on to describe how he had watched PR material flowing into Canadian media through journalists who were 'too lazy or overworked' to check it, or even to rewrite it: 'Sometimes the headline we wrote in our news release would be the headline of the article in the newspaper. Sometimes the article was our news release, the only change being the addition of a reporter's name at the top . . . Whole sentences, sometimes entire paragraphs, will be pulled directly from a news release and reprinted in a newspaper, words that were written by guys like me with the specific intent of convincing you to be a customer of my client.'

And it is the same in Australia. I worked at the *Melbourne Age* for four months in the mid-1990s, at a time when it was owned by Conrad Black, who was busy syphoning off the income from its lucrative classified advertising columns, known locally as 'the rivers of gold', to finance his price war with Rupert Murdoch in London. Budgets were so tight that I needed a special dispensation just to fly to Tasmania. The result, in a line, was that reporters looked at the newspaper's stationery which proudly declared that it was one of the world's great newspapers and suggested that they might sub that down so that it said simply: 'The *Melbourne Age*: one of the world's newspapers.'

A 2001 study of major Australian daily newspapers, by Clara Zawawi at Queensland University of Technology, found that 47% of news stories were created by press releases and other PR activity; and that these stories overwhelmingly expressed the angle chosen by the PR firm. As elsewhere, Australian journalists have become willing partners in the exercise. A former journalist and PR man, Jim Macnamara, in a paper on the impact of PR on media, cites an email sent in July 2001 by a researcher on the national Australian TV programme, *Good Morning*: 'Hi all, just a quick reminder. If you have any suitable health/medical stories, please let me know. Cheers.' That was sent to eighty-six PR firms.

The importance of this is not simply that journalists in countries across the developed world are no longer in a position to tell the truth about their own societies, but that all of them collectively have lost each other as a source of news about each other's countries. Simply, the reporter in Melbourne has far less chance of finding out what is happening in Canada if the reporter in Toronto cannot find it out either. There was a time when reporters could turn for foreign news to their own network of foreign bureaux and freelance 'stringers' around the world, but they, too, have been cut to the bone and beyond.

Research prepared at Harvard University by Jill Carroll of the *Christian Science Monitor* suggested that, by 2006, the entire US media – print and broadcast – was supporting only 141 foreign correspondents in the whole world. This reflects a catastrophic fall in foreign bureaux, as media outlets have succumbed to a crude commercial calculation: as a commodity, foreign news is high-cost and low-return. Why invest big money in covering the world, when consumers are happy with local news?

Tom Fenton, who had such trouble persuading his bosses at CBS Television to run stories about al-Qaeda before September 2001, says in his book that when he started work for CBS in 1970 in Rome, he was one of three full-time correspondents in the city and that CBS then also had thirteen other major foreign bureaux, ten mini-bureaux as well as freelance stringers in forty-four countries. Today, that total of twenty-four bureaux has been cut to three. Their entire foreign staff, supposedly covering the world, Fenton says, now amounts to only eight people, four of whom are based in London where their job is to churn out repackaged versions of material supplied by wire agencies. CBS London reporters, he says, are sometimes reduced to doing their pieces to camera outside the mosque at Regent's Park because at least that looks as though they have travelled somewhere.

Newspapers and magazines, which never had such large foreign coverage in the first place, have also cut back. In January 2007, for example, the *Boston Globe* announced that it was closing all its three remaining foreign bureaux – in Israel, Colombia and Germany, having previously closed its bureaux in Africa, Northern Ireland and Tokyo. At the same time, it was revealed that the *Philadelphia Inquirer*, the *Baltimore Sun* and *New York Newsday* were also pulling out of Israel.

Gannett, which sells more US papers than any other title and also owns three hundred local UK titles, now gathers foreign news from only six countries.

US News and World Report, despite its name, has closed all its foreign bureaux. In a speech in Sydney in February 2003, the veteran former *Sunday Times* reporter Phillip Knightley cited another example: '*Newsweek* was once a proud news magazine that prided itself on covering the world. It had a large bureau in Hong Kong which covered India and South-East Asia, and bureaux in both Beirut and Cairo. It now has not a single bureau or staff correspondent in that great arc of the world stretching from Tokyo to Jerusalem. This includes the centre of the world's hottest news source, the Muslim Middle East. This is now covered by reporters working out of those two big Islamic news centres – London and Paris. How it could close its New Delhi bureau, which was vital for covering the period of the Taliban's rise in Afghanistan and the testing by India and Pakistan of their nuclear weapons, beggars belief. So much for covering the world.'

The global network of freelancer stringers, which used to back up these staff foreign bureaux, has also disintegrated, because the big media outlets will not pay. Vaughan Smith, one of the founders of the Frontline TV News agency, complained in the *Guardian* in September 2005 about the 'pasteurised version of the world' which was reaching audiences: 'Prices paid for independent news images have fallen to about a fifth of what was paid at the peak of the market in 1990, and independent pictures have been all but squeezed out,' he said.

The planet is a much less covered place. That in itself has two very important effects. First, it creates a vacuum of information. A survey of US newspapers by the Newspaper Advertising Bureau found that, by 2002, they were devoting only 2% of their news space to foreign stories; thirty years earlier, it was five times that much. Second, it tends to produce a consensus – and conservative – account of the world: reporters are flown out from their home bases at a few hours' notice and arrive in today's trouble spot with nothing but their preconceptions to guide them; then they plug in to a handful of obvious sources, usually including their own embassy, to have those preconceptions reinforced by official sources.

The day-to-day reality of foreign coverage is that, just as the UK now relies for so much of its domestic news on the Press Association, so, too, most of the newspapers and broadcasters and websites in the world rely for most of their international news, pictures and video on just two wire agencies – Associated Press (AP) and Reuters. Many of them take all of their foreign news from these two agencies alone.

In the United States, 1,700 print outlets and 5,000 radio and TV outlets take their foreign coverage from AP. In the rest of the world, a further 8,500 media organisations, including 500 broadcasters in 121 countries, recycle AP stories as their own. Reuters is smaller by comparison but nonetheless files to more than 1,000 newspapers and 500 of the world's largest broadcasters with more than 1,000 channels in 100 countries carrying their reports. Both agencies reckon their news is consumed every day in one form or another by more than one billion people around the planet – the same choice of stories with the same angles and the same quotes and the same pictures. A tiny fragment of the planet's life masquerading as the truth, much of it inevitably shaped by the activities of PR.

The virtual monopoly of these two global agencies has grown as their competition has shrunk: the once powerful UPI went bankrupt in 1985 and again in 1991 and finally ended up being taken over by a company linked to the Unification Church (otherwise known as the Moonies) and is a shadow of its former self; the old Soviet agency, TASS, always tainted by its link to state propaganda, has lost power and scope since the collapse of the Soviet Union; Agence France-Presse survives, with bureaux in 110 countries, but suffers from a small staff and also from a credibility deficit as a result of its links with the French government, which appoints a third of its board. A handful of even smaller agencies, such as Knight Ridder and Dow Jones which specialises in financial news, are also still at work, as well as three other global TV providers – the BBC (bureaux in thirty-three countries), CNN (bureaux in thirty-three countries) and al-Jazeera (bureaux in eighteen countries). All these organisations – print and TV – recycle AP and Reuters as well as whatever they themselves come up with.

AP and Reuters are by no means useless. They have some real strengths. First, they consistently demand accuracy and impartiality from their journalists, some of whom take considerable personal risks to cover their stories. Second, these two agencies are at least still there, attempting to cover the planet, while other supply lines have been cut. Yet both of these strengths have significant limits.

Just like PA, their concern with accuracy is deliberately different from a newspaper's concern with truth. One man who has spent many years as a senior executive from Reuters echoed Jonathan Grun from PA, explaining to me that Reuters was not concerned with the truth. The agency would try to provide an accurate account of what was being said and might sometimes add an accurate account of an opposing point of view: 'But it isn't an agency's job to start choosing between these voices and saying who is telling the truth.'

All the great Flat Earth news stories have travelled via wire agencies into the unprotected global media. It was Reuters and AP who told the world about the millennium bug and the weapons of mass destruction, who carried the myths about drugs and crime and radiation and education and all the other Huckers, big and small. All these stories were accurate, in that they faithfully recorded what somebody had said; none of them was true.

Just like PA in Britain, part of the problem is that reporters in the international agencies are forced into churnalism, because they do not have the time to work effectively. Reuters, in particular, has suffered from job cuts. They froze editorial budgets and cut 3,000 jobs in 2002 and then, in December 2004, announced what they called their 'Fast Forward Plan', which turned out to be a programme of further cuts to save £440 million by 2006, most of it achieved by removing another 2,000 people from their workforce. Based on the numbers of journalists and stories which Reuters now claims for itself, each of its reporters is now filing an average of some five stories each working day, well beyond the scale that would allow them to check. There has been great controversy within Reuters, because some of their journalism is now outsourced to a centre in Bangalore, India, where business news and data are recycled by staff who, with the best will in the world, cannot know the background to the stories they are writing – with the result, for example, that Reuters has placed Cracow in Portugal instead of Poland and described Lynndie England, the US Army reservist who was caught up in the abuse of Iraqi prisoners at Abu Ghraib, as the commander of her unit when she was only a lowly private.

It was unfortunate for David Schlesinger, the global managing editor of Reuters who organised these 'efficiency savings', that, five months later, in April 2005, an internal memo which he wrote for ten senior executives was accidentally sent to thousands of Reuters staff. So, we know that he acknowledges that: 'Our news is perceived as not having enough insight. Our data is perceived as having terrible quality problems.'

Most foreign correspondents, covering an entire country or region on their own, rely for their information on three sources: official PR from government and other major organisations; local media, frequently recycling that PR; each other. Most of the time, they have no option but churnalism. I remember some years ago talking to staff from the *Independent*'s bureau in Washington DC who told me that they had one simple rule: 'no phone calls'. Instead, they used what they called the JCB technique – lifting material out of the big US papers and dropping it into their own columns as if they were using a JCB mechanical digger. It is no different for the correspondents working for AP and Reuters. They are particularly likely to cannibalise each other's material – and always have.

The veteran foreign correspondent Ed Behr, in his book, *Anyone Here Been Raped and Speaks English?*, recalls his early days with Reuters in Paris: ' "Who really makes the news?" I began asking myself. In London, Agence France-Presse correspondents rewrote Reuters copy as fast as they could, and the finished product ended up as part of the AFP news service. In Paris, we shamelessly rewrote Agence France-Presse copy, serving it up as Reuters' fare. All over the world, lesser news agencies were writing up their versions of Reuters' stories and serving them up as authentic.'

Tom Fenton's book quotes the veteran CBS anchorman Walter Cronkite pointing precisely to the danger of news outlets such as the big US TV neworks simply recycling this agency feed: 'If Reuters or AP is the only one to get the story, that's a single source, and we should be double checking it . . . The problem is that you – that is, the organization that is accepting the service or the report – have lost control. You are only circulating something that is already available, not checking those facts against your own expert reporters.'

And the fact that the two agencies are still trying to cover global news does not mean that they are in a position to do so, any more than PA can do so in the UK. Just like PA, Reuters and AP report only a tiny fragment of the world around them.

There are something like two hundred countries in the world (the precise number is a matter of endless political dispute). With their print operations, AP has staff in 121 of them; Reuters in only ninety-two. Some eighty countries, around 40% of the world's nations, have no print bureau from either agency. With their TV operations, the coverage is even less thorough. AP's television news arm, APTN, which claims to supply 88% of the world's broadcasters, has TV crews in only fifty-eight countries; Reuters claims fifty-nine. I have counted 130 countries which have no TV bureau from either agency. This includes, for example, Canada, Ireland, New Zealand, Saudi Arabia, the Congo with its long-running war, Sudan with its war and drought, and masses of other poor nations.

Even where the agencies do have bureaux, their staffing is generally tiny, sometimes just one man or woman. In Kabul, for example, in September 2001, Reuters had only one journalist, who was filing newspaper stories as well as acting as photographer, video crew and picture editor. Similarly, APTN's staff investment in countries such as Australia, Argentina, Brazil, Chile, South Korea and Malaysia consists of just one one-man crew covering millions of people across thousands of miles. In practice, what happens is that the agencies switch print reporters and TV crews around the world as big news stories break with all that that means for lack of background information, lack of analysis and context, and lack of follow-up once the event is over. Or they pick up second-hand material from the surviving network of stringers and from the local media. The bomb goes off, the election result is declared, the plane crashes – and all across the world, media outlets repackage the same small selection of TV shots and interviews and photographs. If they get it wrong, if they miss the story altogether, that's just Flat Earth news.

The agencies' answer to this criticism is that, even if they don't have staff in place, they can cover a country by using stringers and links with local broadcasters. But the limits of their performance in reality were caught neatly in a survey by World Television, who monitored all of the TV stories put out by Reuters and APTN about the nation of New Zealand. They did this twice: first, for the two years from March 2002; and then for the two years from March 2004.

World Television noted first that, throughout this time, neither agency had its own TV bureau anywhere in New Zealand. Their nearest staffers were in Sydney; the next nearest 3,400 miles away, in Jakarta. The two agencies covered New Zealand only if it came across their radar in some other location, or if they heard of something sufficiently attractive to justify paying for something from inside the country, whether by sending in their own crews or by buying from local suppliers.

During the two years from March 2002, World Television established, the two agencies between them put out only 262 stories which even referred to New Zealand. Most of these (140) were produced from other bureaux in other countries. World Television classified all the stories under the conventional headings for different kinds of news and found that more than half of them (147) were soft news – seventy-five sports (mostly rugby, cricket and yachting in the America's Cup), twenty-eight disasters (often angled around international travel and tourism) and forty-four human/bizarre.

In the whole two-year period, only 115 stories covered any kind of hard news and, overwhelmingly, they proved to be stories which were angled around the interests of dominant Western nations. Seventy-one were classified as news/political and tended to focus on international issues such as protests against the war in Iraq and a visit by the Australian Prime Minister. There were forty-one cultural stories (mostly because *Lord of the Rings* and *Whale Rider* were filmed there) and one about tourism. In all the two years, they ran only two business stories: a new design for toilets in New York; and an item on exchange rates between New Zealand and Europe. Under the headings of health, youth, environment and science, they ran nothing at all.

When World Televison repeated the exercise for the two years from

March 2004, they found that coverage by the two agencies had collapsed even further. Mic Dover, one of the few journalists to follow this, recorded in the *New Zealand Listener* in August 2006:

> The data collected shows there has recently been a 50% drop in the amount of domestically produced TV news coverage of New Zealand picked up by the wire agencies for distribution abroad. The decline was caused by less political coverage, fewer sports stories and a collapse in cultural stories. The loss of profile since *Lord of the Rings*, *Whale Rider* and the America's Cup highs has been compared to a similar shift in profile seen in Australia at the end of the *Crocodile Dundee* movies – dubbed the 'Crocodile Dundee effect' due to its economic effect on tourism and the economy.
>
> 'From 2004–06, overseas TV news viewers saw no stories on Kiwi business or trade. They saw various 'bizarre/human interest' stories such as 'Whipper the budgerigar', *Shrek*, and the damage done to a roof by a grapefruit-sized meteor. They saw four election stories: two on the successful election of Helen Clark; one focusing on an incident on election night with a light plane; and one featuring Toby, a Jack Russell terrier in Wanaka that was registered to vote.'

This unreliable and limited flow of information is now spreading further and faster than ever before, because of the role of global news websites, all of whom rely overwhelmingly on AP and Reuters, few of whom submit their copy to anything more than the most cursory checking. Which is why, for example, so many respected media outlets in February 2005 reported that militants in Baghdad were claiming to have kidnapped an American soldier, pictured kneeling, grim and bound, in front of a slogan in Arabic script. The truth was that this 'soldier' was a doll, and the whole story was a practical joke. But it ran on AP, so it ran elsewhere too.

The scale of this global dependence is reflected brilliantly in the work of Dr Chris Paterson, now at the University of Leeds, who has led the way in tracing the flow of planetary news, particularly into the news websites on which some 60% of US adults now rely for their information about the world. Over a period of years, Dr Paterson used a computer program which was designed to spot plagiarism, to sample the extent to which these websites were simply reproducing copy provided to them by Reuters and AP.

When he looked at the most popular websites which are run by major media organisations, he found in 2001 that 34% of what they published was simply reproduced from the two big agencies and their smaller competitor, Agence France-Presse. That figure is highly conservative in that it reflects only those stories which recycled the wire copy verbatim; it excludes stories which were taken off those wires and rewritten in house style. Nevertheless, by 2006, the figure had jumped to 50%. And that was an average. ABC TV's website was recycling agency copy verbatim for 91% of their website stories, MSNBC for 81% of their news, the *Guardian* for 62%, CNN for 59%. The average was pulled down by the websites of the *New York Times* (32%), Sky TV (15%) and the BBC (9%) – either because they were genuinely digging out more of their own original information, or because they were putting more effort into rewriting the agency copy in their own style.

When Dr Paterson then looked at the newly created news portals run by Internet companies, rather than by mass-media organisations, he found the figures were even higher. In 2001, 68% of their work was already simply recycled from agencies. By 2006, the figure had soared to an average of 85%. Excite were rerunning verbatim agency copy for 98% of their news, Yahoo! for 97%, AOL for 94%. The average was brought down only by Altavista, who were using verbatim agency copy for only 50% of their stories.

The biggest news portal, Google News, slipped out of Dr Paterson's analysis, because it did not exist until 2002, a year after his first survey. There is no reason to think that its dependence is any less since, like other major portals, Google does not even pretend to be checking its stories or exercising any kind of journalistic judgement. Google simply presents what everybody else is saying, without scruple to its importance or truth. It does this not with reporters but with computer programs. Krishna Bharat, Google's principal scientist, told *Press Gazette* in 2006 how it selects its editorial content, using mathematical algorithms to analyse global editorial output: 'We look at how many editors have chosen to run brand-new articles on a subject, and we interpret that as the amount of interest in the editorial community and that's the basis of the ranking. It's not like we have an arbitrary process. We just ask the editors of the world what they find interesting.'

The result was detected by the Project for Excellence in Journalism in its 2006 report on the American media. They analysed one day's coverage of Google News and found that it 'offers consumers access to some 14,000 stories from its front page, yet on this day they were actually accounts of the same 24 news events'.

As Dr Paterson concluded: 'A few original producers of content provide the lion's share of the international news for those aggregators, despite the audacious pretence of source diversity which each promotes.'

Ignacio Ramonet, editor-in-chief of *Le Monde Diplomatique*, writing in January 2005, saw the whole picture: 'A journalism of compliance is in the ascendancy and critical journalism on the decline . . . Information may proliferate but we have zero guarantee of its reliability. It may turn out to be false . . . Display and packaging have taken over from verification of facts.'

This is world news. What has been created is a vortex of concentric forces, reducing reality to a small cluster of reports, flowing through a handful of monopoly providers who, in turn, channel each other's stories into their own streams. Frequently unchecked, commonly created by PR, this consensus account of the world is inherently inadequate in its selection of stories, inherently unreliable in its reporting, daily generating the mass production of ignorance.

The point here is not that, in some imaginary non-capitalist world, mass media could have been saved from the grocers' grasp. The point simply is that it has happened.

This is the global village idiot. We're all Huckered.

4. The Rules of Production

On 26 August 2004, the American National Right to Life Committee sent out a press release to journalists. Pursuing its long-standing campaign to restrict the right to abortion, the press release attacked a recent judgement by a federal court, which had upheld US abortion law.

One of the journalists who received the press release was Todd Eastham, then the North American news editor for Reuters. He didn't like what the NRL had to say, and so he sent them an email to tell them so. He asked them: 'What's your plan for parenting and educating all the unwanted children you people want to bring into the world? Who will pay for policing our streets and maintaining the prisons needed to contain them when you, their parents and the system fail them? Oh, sorry. All that money has been earmarked to pay off the Bush deficit. Give me a frigging break, will you?'

This was obviously a risky move. Eastham was using his office email to wave a defiant digit in the face of one of his employer's suppliers. And sure enough, within twenty-four hours, he was taking an incoming volley of verbal fire, but the line of attack had little to do with his rudeness.

Eastham's email rapidly leaked onto a network of websites run by anti-abortionists, including Christianitytoday.com, LifeNews.com, Family News in Focus and the right-wing Weekly Standard. Soon, it reached the national media through the columns of the *Washington Post* and a blog linked to the *Wall Street Journal*. The complaint against Eastham, expressed in tones of outrage, was not his confrontational style, but that he had junked his objectivity and, therefore, could not be trusted in his job.

By 2 September, Reuters' then managing editor, David Schlesinger, had surrendered. He sent the email equivalent of a white flag to NRL, telling them: 'I was personally appalled by Mr Eastham's lapse. It has been handled through our disciplinary process, and he understands the seriousness of what happened. Freedom from bias is integral to all that Reuters represents, and I intend to keep it that way.' It then became clear that Schlesinger had punished Todd Eastham by removing him from his job as North American editor.

Thus, David Schlesinger closed the issue. But, in doing so, he failed to ask or answer the most important question: what should Todd Eastham have done with that press release? What would have been the 'objective' journalist's reaction to the NRL's attack on the federal judge?

Eastham could simply have dismissed the release as an expression of bias in itself and dumped it. At the other end of the scale, he could have sent it to a reporter to be converted straight into a story for the wire. Or, he could have sent it to a reporter with an instruction to flesh it out by contacting pro-abortion groups who opposed the NRL. He could have used it as a news peg for an investigation into the needless deaths of unborn children; or for an investigation into the lobbying power of the NRL; or for a feature about abortion law around the world; or for an inquiry into federal court judgements. He could have stuck with the original thought in his email and dug out the criminological research which does indeed support his contention that one of the outcomes of a clampdown on abortions is a subsequent surge in the number of unwanted children whose childhoods prove to be so difficult that they drift into crime. The reality, which David Schlesinger failed to confront, is that each one of these decisions would have been entirely legitimate journalism.

In his autobiography, *Good Times, Bad Times*, Harry Evans describes an incident which occurred soon after Rupert Murdoch bought Times Newspapers and switched him from editing the *Sunday Times* to running the daily paper. Murdoch appointed as Evans' deputy Charles Douglas-Home, who was a very different kind of journalist to Evans and showed some inclination to stab him in the back.

Evans had been passed a confidential letter from the government's chief medical adviser, warning that hundreds of thousands of children were at risk of brain damage from ingesting the high level of lead in petrol fumes. He commissioned a major front-page story to run on a Monday morning but then fell ill over the weekend and left it to

Douglas-Home to publish it. When Evans looked at the paper on the Monday, he was surprised to see that the story had been played down and then to hear that Douglas-Home was resisting writing a leader on the story, as Evans had requested, saying that he did not want to go beyond 'normal news values'.

Evans wrote: 'What are these normal news values? Is it abnormal to regard the poisoning of children as a subject for persistent inquiry and for vigorous comment? This was the implication and it perfectly reflected the moral torpor of the Douglas-Home horizontal school of journalism: it waits on events. Speeches, reports and ceremonials occur and they are rendered into words in print along a straight assembly-line. Scandal and injustice go unremarked unless someone else discovers them . . . Judgements have to be made about what is important; they are moral judgements. The vertical school is active. It sets its own agenda.'

The heart of Evans' argument is that judgements 'have to be made' – not that they 'may sometimes need to be made' or that they 'will be made by journalists behaving badly'. These judgements are not optional extras. They are not shameful lapses. They are the essential, unavoidable, constant requirements of every journalist on every story – to select this subject and not another, to choose this angle instead of the alternatives, to use this headline, this intro, this language, while rejecting others.

The great blockbuster myth of modern journalism is objectivity, the idea that a good newspaper or broadcaster simply collects and reproduces the objective truth. It is a classic Flat Earth tale, widely believed and devoid of reality. It has never happened and never will happen because it cannot happen. Reality exists objectively, but any attempt to record the truth about it always and everywhere necessarily involves selection, by using the kind of judgements that Harry Evans describes. In this sense, all news is artifice.

All stories have to view reality from some particular point of view – just like somebody walking into a room has to view it from a particular point. The story can't be everywhere at once. Good, healthy news organisations make these judgements case by case, selecting the story and the angle and the language and the presentation which is most likely to reveal what is most important. They do it without restricting those judgements to the demands of any ideology or owner or advertiser or government or any other overarching influence. They do it knowing that other options are always available. They do it 'honestly'.

A lot of senior journalists understand this. As Evans once put it in an article in the *Listener*: 'Facts may be sacred – but which facts? The media are not a neutral looking glass: we select what we mirror.' George Orwell, James Cameron, Martha Gellhorn all poured scorn on the idea of objectivity. The former *Sunday Times* writer Nicholas Tomalin put it neatly in a feature about reporting: 'The idea of a "fact" is so simplistic, it is a lie. Facts are not sacred; the moment any reporter begins to write his story, he has selected some and not others, and has distorted the situation. The moment he composes the "facts" into a narrative form, he has commented on the situation. The idea of "facts" to be shoved at readers like little lumps, is best forgotten very swiftly. To say a journalist's job is to record facts is like saying an architect's job is to lay bricks – true, but missing the point.'

Reuters missed the point so completely that Todd Eastham lost his job. His real sin, of course, was not to make a judgement about a press release, but to do it openly. Media managers like David Schlesinger enjoy the comfort of life behind the myth of objectivity. It allows them to pretend that they have a special claim on the truth. In reality, what they generally promote is not objectivity at all. It's neutrality, which is a very different beast.

Neutrality requires the journalist to become invisible, to refrain deliberately (under threat of discipline) from expressing the judgements which are essential for journalism. Neutrality requires the packaging of conflicting claims, which is precisely the opposite of truth-telling. If two men go to mow a meadow and one comes back and says 'The job's done' and the other comes back and says 'We never cut a single blade of grass', neutrality requires the journalist to report a controversy surrounding the state of the meadow, to throw together both men's claims and shove it out to the world with an implicit sign over the top declaring, 'We don't know what's happening – you decide.'

Travelling under the alias of objectivity, this approach has become respectable – has made churnalism seem respectable. Even at the BBC, a haven of public-service journalism, the head of editorial policy, Stephen Whittle, in 2006 saw no problem at all in defending the corporation against controversy by proclaiming: 'Our responsibility is to remain objective and report in ways that enable our audience to make their own assessments about who is doing what to whom.'

The damage goes further than merely abandoning the primary purpose of journalism. It actually transfers the truth-telling judgements out of newsrooms and into the hands of outsiders. This is what happens in the news factory. The old model, where news editors and reporters selected stories and angles, is in a state of collapse. We have seen how the structure of corporate news has converted journalists from active news-gatherers to passive processors of material – only 12% of which could be shown to be free of the mark of wire agencies and PR consultants. It is these outsiders who now make the primary judgements on which news organisations rely. Organisations like the NRL send out press releases to agencies like Reuters because they know very well that there is a good chance that they will be allowed to set the news agenda. The invisible 'neutral' journalist in the news factory processes them for publication along the 'straight assembly-line' about which Harry Evans complained.

However, there is something else at work here, apart from the structural weaknesses of corporate news organisation. The fact is that the news factory does not use all of the second-hand material which is placed at the beginning of its assembly lines. Some kind of selection is going on within the factory. Some part of this may still involve journalists making moral judgements, as Harry Evans describes; and owners inflicting their own judgements, as we have seen. But for the most part, selection now consists of rules which are embedded in the process of churnalism, a kind of quality-control system which instantly rejects any raw material which does not meet the factory's requirements.

These rules of production were never formally drawn up in some neatly tabulated summary. They have simply evolved to meet the logistics of the mass production of news. Some of them are old rules which have been adapted. Some of them are new. Some of them overlap. All of them collectively serve as substitutes for the selective judgements without which journalism cannot function.

What is particularly interesting is that these unwritten and unstated rules of production tend to generate an account of the world which, while claiming the virtues of objectivity, generally suffers from three weaknesses which are fatal to truth-telling: an arbitrary selection of subjects, which fundamentally distorts reality by systemic omission; routine use of a host of factual claims which are frequently unreliable and sometimes false; and the steady imprint of a political and moral consensus which tends to reflect the values only of the most powerful groups in the surrounding society.

These are, I should stress, the rules of churnalism. They are still broken by a considerable number of able journalists who despise them. But those reporters repeatedly run into trouble with media managers who prefer to abide by them. In haphazard form, all of them flow from the two guiding principles of commerce: to cut the costs of production, and to increase the flow of revenue.

Cutting the costs

Rule One: Run cheap stories

This rule simply requires the selection of stories which are a) quick to cover, and b) safe to publish. Those are the cheap ones, in the short term and the long term. The impact of the rule is to discourage tricky investigations and to distort the selection of ordinary news stories in favour of those which are simple, uncontentious and easy to obtain.

You can see how the rule works in magnified form in the cautionary tale of Bob Port. He was working as the head of AP's Special Assignments Team in New York when, in April 1998, he was passed a feature which had been filed by a young Korean reporter working for the AP bureau in Seoul. It described how a group of South Korean men and women were suing for damages over an incident nearly fifty years earlier in the Korean War. They were talking about US forces massacring civilians.

The story was that in late July 1950, American troops had ordered the occupants of two villages to leave their homes. As the group of some four hundred women, children and elderly men had made their way down the road near a place called No Gun Ri, they had been strafed by US planes, which had killed about a hundred of them. US ground troops had told the survivors to take shelter in the arches of a concrete bridge. That night, the same troops had set up machine guns in front of the arches, opened fire and killed almost all of them. The motive apparently was that North Korean soldiers might have been hiding among the refugees.

In a book called *Into the Buzzsaw*, a collection of stories about the obstruction of reporting in the US, Bob Port recalls how he decided to check out the story and sent a researcher to see what he could find in military records in the National Archives. Within twenty-four hours, raking through bundles of paperwork which had not been touched for decades, the researcher found a memo, dated 27 July 1950, from a US Army commander, William Kean, who referred to a hundred-square-mile area around the bridge at No Gun Ri and instructed his men: 'All civilians seen in this area are to be treated as enemy and action taken accordingly.' The researcher also found a record of a radio message: 'No refugees to cross the front lines. Fire everyone trying to cross lines. Use discretion in case of women and children.'

Bob Port goes on to describe how he set about pursuing more evidence 'quietly', because he feared his bosses would shut down the story if they realised how much time and money he was going to have to spend on it. This was the nature of AP, he says. 'It was a place filled with excellent journalists but, unfortunately for me, it was also a place whose leaders seemed not the least bit interested in the pursuit of investigative reporting for the good of democracy. At the AP, the emphasis is on simple stories and neutrality.'

Three months later, in July 1998, he had produced a story which now included eyewitness accounts from US Army veterans who said they had taken part in the massacre. But his managers didn't like it, saw it as 'big trouble', accused Port of practising 'gotcha journalism', ordered one rewrite after another, stalled for months and finally, in December 1998, formally killed it. Port succeeded in reviving it but only on condition that a senior executive rewrote it yet again and this time without Port or any other reporter who had worked on it being allowed to see it.

Finally, in September 1999, fourteen months after Port first submitted a draft of the story, AP published it. It conspicuously avoided the word 'massacre'; told most of the story from the point of view of the US troops whom it described sympathetically as 'young, green and scared';

pushed the text of the crucial memo ordering the shooting of civilians down into the forty-fifth paragraph; aired doubts about what had really happened – and nevertheless won a Pulitzer Prize for AP.

But the cautionary tale does not end there. The final version of the story was based, among other evidence, on the word of six US veterans who said they had shot at the refugees and six others who said they had witnessed the shooting. Eight months later, US News and World Report attacked the story, revealing that one of these veterans, Ed Daily, who had provided a graphic account of the killings, had not been there and had not even been a member of the army unit which was involved. Daily admitted he had lied and indeed that he had fabricated an entire military career in such vivid detail that other veterans thought they remembered him. This had allowed him to collect medals and financial compensation to which he was not entitled.

AP found itself under a barrage of criticism. The agency defended the story, arguing that the loss of one witness did not undermine the truth of a story which was supported by eleven other veterans, twenty-four Korean survivors and the internal military paperwork. The Pulitzer committee agreed and confirmed their award. The US Army, who had originally denied that any of their forces had been anywhere near No Gun Ri, eventually reported that civilians had indeed been killed there. Nevertheless, the furore was deeply embarrassing for AP. And, in a sense, it proved the point of the managers who had been so anxious and even obstructive: stories like that are big trouble. They are expensive and time-consuming and they provoke a backlash. One of the things which helped them to defend the story was precisely that they had published it in such a tentative form. And who among AP's clients would have complained if they had never run the story at all? There was plenty of other news on the assembly line.

Along the way, AP closed down the Special Assignments Team which Bob Port had run for three years and moved him to a sideline job dealing with the office computer system. He resigned. In his account of events, Port ends by saying: 'What troubles me is this: What other stories like No Gun Ri are waiting out there to be told? And who at AP will be working hard to tell them?'

The logic of AP's managers – which is entirely reasonable from their point of view – has spilled over into a general neutering of investigative work at most media organisations. In their book, *The Elements of Journalism*, Bill Kovach and Tom Rosentiel trace the collapse of investigative reporting since its peak with the Watergate scandal in the mid-1970s. They focus, as an example, on American television 'I-teams', which claim to be investigative but which steer well clear of tough subjects involving government or the abuse of power.

'Local television news often employs its I-teams in such stories as "dangerous doors", reporting on the hazards of opening and closing doors; or "inside your washing machine", a look at how dirt and bacteria on the clothes consumers put in their washers, get on other clothes.' They cite, too, an investigation which used hidden cameras to prove that you can't really get all your carpets cleaned for only $7.95; and an investigation into a bra whose metal wiring could poke its owner. They also point to the role of the PR industry in selecting these subjects by providing TV stations with pre-packaged 'just add water' investigative reports: 'These come from TV news consultants who literally offer stations the scripts, the shots, the experts to interview or the interviews themselves already on tape.'

The same logic has infiltrated current affairs television in Britain, where journalists who work on those programmes parody their own low-cost, low-risk human-interest output. As one experienced editor put it to me: 'We've done "Fuck me, I'm fat". We've done "Fuck me, I'm thin". We're just working on "Fuck me, I'm fucked up".'

Beyond that, this logic has left a deep imprint on the everyday judgement of which news stories should be covered. It is a key factor in the collapse in foreign coverage, which is simply and always much more expensive than domestic news. Hurricane Katrina killed more than 3,000 people in New Orleans, ruined a major city and became a global news story. In the same summer, Hurricane Stanley killed 654 people, left 828 others missing suspected dead and 120,000 people without homes. But that was in Guatemala, where Western media have just about no news resources. So it was that, according to a study by Carmen International media analysts, Katrina quite rightly got 3,105 references in the UK press, but Stanley got only thirty-four. According to the Third World and Environment Broadcasting Project, the amount of factual international programming on the four largest terrestrial channels in the UK in 2003 was 40% lower than in 1989.

The rule also skews domestic coverage. The closer to Fleet Street a story is, the more likely it is to be covered. In the late 1990s, I covered an official hearing into sexual abuse in children's homes. Former staff and residents, giving evidence on oath, provided moving, graphic accounts of the fondling and rape of young boys, variously naming police officers and social workers among the offenders, and described how official lethargy had allowed this to continue for years. At the back of the hearing, there were two rows of seats which had been reserved for the press. All of them were empty, not because this was a bad story, but because it was happening in North Wales, simply too far away for Fleet Street to be bothered with.

Supply comes to dictate demand, as the easy story automatically goes to the head of the queue. It would be hard to imagine, for example, the world's press picking up on a murder allegedly committed by an Irish hurling player – a man they had never heard of, who played a sport they did not follow – even if it was a big story in Ireland, even if the player, for example, was a Catholic who was accused of killing a Protestant woman, so the story had a political edge. It would be a mad fantasy to imagine that the story would be picked up and given many months of global coverage of such saturation that, for example, the British Prime Minister would complain that his keynote address to his party conference was bumped down into second place on the evening television news to make way for the result of the hurling player's trial. But it did happen – only it was an American football player who was a black man accused of killing a white woman. It could have made sense for non-US media to cover the trial of O. J. Simpson once or twice, because of its meaning for race relations in the United States, but the one and only reason that that story became global news was that masses of text and pictures were being pumped out of the United States every day, so it was cheap and easy.

Rule Two: Select safe facts

This rule encourages journalists to favour factual statements which are safe, especially those which can be attributed to official sources.

On Sunday 19 March 2006, the Knight Ridder agency filed a story from Baghdad, based on a leaked Iraqi police document which recorded that eleven people – two men, four women, four children and a six-month-old baby – had been herded into a room in a village called Abu Sifa and shot dead by American troops who had then killed their animals and blown up their house. The report quoted a US military spokesman, who said: 'We're concerned to hear accusations like that, but it's also highly unlikely that they're true.'

In the UK, the story was picked up and published in full by only one paper, the *Guardian*, who ran it as a lead on one of their foreign pages. Apart from that, the *Independent* ran it in one paragraph, and the BBC mentioned it at the bottom of a story about another incident. Nobody else in the UK touched it. In the whole of the United States, it was run in full only by two regional papers. Fourteen other regionals mentioned it in a single paragraph or less. Not one of the major dailies touched Knight Ridder's story.

Earlier that week, on Tuesday 14 March 2006, Iraqi police released information about fifteen men who had been found dead in an abandoned vehicle in west Baghdad. Their hands and feet were bound, their bodies showed signs of torture and they appeared to have been strangled. Reuters filed a report, which suggested that they were the Sunni victims of Shia death squads.

The story was picked up and run in the United Kingdom by the *Guardian*, the *Independent*, *The Times*, the *Telegraph*, several provincial papers and the BBC, as well as being mentioned in a round-up of the day's violence by the *Mirror* and the *Sun*; and in the US by the *New York Times*, the *Washington Post*, the *LA Times* and fourteen other regional papers, as well as being mentioned in a round-up of the day's violence by the *Chicago Tribune*, *USA Today* and numerous other regionals.

Why the difference? Judged purely on traditional news values, both these stories were equally powerful: multiple dead in both; the death of women and children in one arguably matched by the extreme violence in the other; the political implications of Iraqi police formally recording the shooting of civilians by US troops matched by the political impact of the drift to civil war.

In terms of evidence, however, Knight Ridder's story about the eleven

dead civilians was certainly the stronger. It was based on an internal
police report, which the agency supplied in English translation as well
as in its original language; the report was authenticated by a named
senior Iraqi police officer; and it was supported by eyewitnesses in the
village and by a second named Iraqi police officer who said autopsies
revealed that 'all the victims had bullet shots in the head and all bodies
were handcuffed'. By contrast, the story of the fifteen dead men was
based solely on a statement by Iraqi police.

There are probably several different factors at work here: the fact
that Knight Ridder files to far fewer papers than Reuters; a kind of
story fatigue about Iraq; the hint of 'big trouble' in accusing US troops
of murder, as there was with AP's Korean story. But the decisive difference, I believe, is that while the story of the fifteen dead men was
uncontested and supported by an official source, the facts in the Abu
Sifa story were rendered unsafe because they were being denied by
an official source. As soon as news of the incident in Abu Sifa reached
Baghdad, a US military spokesman challenged the story, claiming that
only four people had died in the incident and that one of them was
a member of al-Qaeda who had provoked attack by firing on US
troops from inside the house. This official account was directly contradicted by pictures which ran on Arabic TV on the night of the incident and which clearly showed eleven bodies, including children. Yet
the official statement served to blunt the coverage.

There was a four-day gap between the incident, which happened
on the Wednesday, and Knight Ridder filing their report on the Sunday.
During that time, the *LA Times* and the *New York Times* did run short
versions, both of which took the classic neutral route, balancing the
allegation of a massacre with the official US denial. They did this in
spite of the evidence of the television pictures. I don't intend any of
this as a criticism of the reporters on the ground: it is overwhelmingly difficult to verify stories in conditions of such chaos and violence;
and it is standard, approved practice to produce this kind of truth-
avoiding coverage. When I contacted the foreign desks of the papers
concerned, most stressed this need to verify. Nonetheless, the fact
remains that leading newspapers in the UK and the US consistently
chose not to run the Knight Ridder story which was supported by

documents, eyewitnesses and TV pictures but which was being challenged by an official source; and yet they did run a story – about the fifteen dead men – which was based on nothing more than an official statement without any supporting evidence at all.

Reporters rely on official sources. This is partly because they are well organised, with press officers and websites and press releases and background material, so they provide quick copy. But, more than that, it is because reporters know that they are far less likely to be attacked if they go with the official line. The official line is safe.

There is a graphic example of this in the experience of Andrew Gilligan, the former BBC radio reporter whose story attacking the government's handling of intelligence on Iraqi weapons saw him put through the professional equivalent of being burned at the stake. The formal inquiry, conducted by Lord Hutton, concluded in January 2004 that his story was 'unfounded'. And yet we know that most of the stories put out by most of the reporters who wrote about Iraqi weapons also were 'unfounded': they assumed that the weapons existed. With the one exception of Judith Miller from the *New York Times*, who eventually lost her job amid other scandal, the mass of those other reporters suffered not even a hint of heat for their failure. Because they had the official sources on their side.

Gilligan's experience is a high-profile example. There are plenty of lower-profile examples of officialdom attempting to enforce its line with punishment. Ministers in the Blair government, for example, privately approached senior news executives with explicit invitations to sack Andy McSmith, the political editor of the *Independent*; Paul Eastham, the political editor of the *Daily Mail*; Christian Wolmar, the transport correspondent of the *Independent*; Mark Mardell, political correspondent for *Newsnight*; and Andrew Marr when he was editor of the *Independent*. Ivo Dawnay, as chief political correspondent of the *Financial Times*, wrote a story which irritated Peter Mandelson, who reacted by calling Dawnay's girlfriend late on the night of its publication with a simple message: 'Just tell Ivo he's dead. He doesn't exist.'

In the UK, the safety of following the official line is reinforced in law. The 1952 Defamation Act protects journalists against being sued for libel if their story is based on an official statement 'by or on behalf of any government department, officer of state, local authority or chief officer of police'. In 1996, that protection was expanded to include official statements from the European Union as well as British officialdom. In short, if an official statement accuses a man of being a criminal, the press can't be sued for using it; but if a man accuses a government official of being a criminal, the press can be sued for repeating it.

Rule Three: Avoid the electric fence

This extends the rule of safe facts from favouring official sources to an encouragement of deference to any organisation or individual with the power to hurt news organisations. It works like the kind of electric fence which is used by farmers to control their cattle. The farmer puts the fence across the field; some of the cows wander into it and get hurt; the farmer then takes the fence away; none of the cows crosses the line.

In the UK, the oldest electric fence is media law. The Official Secrets Act tends to deter journalists and to inhibit potential sources by threatening imprisonment for those who are caught trying to publish whatever the government deems secret. Libel law is even more powerful, because its reach is so much wider, covering any story which could be deemed to damage the reputation of its target. However, its protection tends to apply only to the rich and powerful, simply because it costs a lot of money to sue, and legal aid has never been available for libel actions. So, it is common practice for a newspaper lawyer, confronted with a potentially libellous story, to ask the reporter: 'Does this chap have money?' This was how Robert Maxwell succeeded for years in repelling effective reporting of his corruption. The royal families of the UK and Saudi Arabia have used libel law to stop the publication in the UK of books which are available elsewhere. Doctors, police officers and, to a lesser extent, prison officers have consistently deterred coverage of their malpractice, because their professional bodies have a history of funding libel actions. The impact on cash-starved local media is particularly deadly.

Now, however, there are multiple new electric fences, erected by professional lobbying groups, who are part of the brave new world of PR. In the United States, for example, the Parents Television Council has orchestrated vitriolic campaigns against media outlets who don't accept their conservative Christian values. According to *Mediaweek* magazine, in 2003 the PTC was responsible for 99.8% of indecency complaints to the Federal Communications Commission. In the UK, the Countryside Alliance was highly effective in disciplining coverage of the debate about hunting. But the most potent electric fence in the world is the one erected on behalf of the Israeli government.

Journalists who write stories which offend the politics of the Israeli lobby are subjected to a campaign of formal complaints and pressure on their editors; most of all, they are inundated with letters and emails which can be extravagant in their hostility. Robert Fisk of the *Independent* has been told that his mother was Adolf Eichmann's daughter, that he belongs in hell with Osama bin Laden, that he is 'a hate peddler', 'a leading anti-Semite and proto-fascist Islamophile propagandist' and a paedophile. After broadcasting an ITV programme about the Palestinians, John Pilger was told he was 'a demonic psychopath', a Nazi and that the murder of his family was 'not a bad idea'. In 2006, a German correspondent was simply told by an Israeli government spokesman that he was 'a bag of shit'.

There is now a network of pro-Israeli pressure groups who specialise in orchestrating complaints against the media. HonestReporting has offices in London, New York and Toronto and claims to have 140,000 members on whom it can call to drench media organisations in letters and emails. (One campaign aimed at the *Guardian* landed so many emails on the readers' editor, Ian Mayes, that he developed repetitive strain injury in opening them all and needed three months' physio-therapy.) Camera, the Committee for Accuracy in Middle East Reporting in America, uses street demos, pressure on advertisers, formal complaints and email showers. Giyus, Give Israel Your Support, supplies its members with a browser button which they can hit to send them any article which they deem offensive, and software called Megaphone to assist them in launching mass complaints. Memri (the Middle East Media Research Institute), Palestine Media Watch, Bicom (the Britain Israel Communications and Research Centre) and Israeli Embassy staff all supply more energy for the fence. They share aims and/or funding sources with the immensely powerful network of organisations which lobby governments and political parties on behalf of Israel.

The result is that some facts become dangerous: to report Palestinian casualties; to depict the Palestinians as victims of Israeli occupation; to refer to the historic ousting of hundreds of thousands of Palestinians from their homes; to refer to the killing of Palestinian civilians by Zionist groups in the 1940s. The facts are there, but the electric fence will inflict pain on any reporter who selects them. Words themselves become dangerous: to speak of 'occupied territories'; to describe Palestinian bombers as anything other than 'terrorists'; to reject the Israeli government euphemism of 'targeted killings'. Crucially, there is no lobby of similar force on the Palestinian side. The pro-Israeli groups are able to claim numerous victories.

HonestReporting claims: 'Since 2000, the organisation prompted hundreds of apologies, retractions, and revisions from news outlets.' They cite, in particular, their campaign against CNN, which saw them sending up to 6,000 emails a day to the chief executive and which resulted in their being invited to CNN's headquarters in Atlanta to meet managers who, they say, 'showed a genuine sensitivity to HonestReporting's concerns'. They had complained that CNN was failing to describe Palestinian bombers as 'terrorists'; that too little attention was being given to Israeli victims; and that CNN had been willing to broadcast videotaped final statements by bombers. Following the meeting, they note, CNN.com started referring to 'Palestinian terrorism' and ran a special series on Israeli victims, while the chief executive issued a ban on the use of videotaped statements by bombers. HonestReporting also quotes from transcripts of CNN broadcasts in which the anchor in Atlanta interrupts the correspondent on the ground to put the Israeli case.

HonestReporting also claims credit for Reuters' decision to stop referring to Hamas as a group seeking an independent state and to describe them instead, for example, as 'Hamas, sworn to Israel's destruction'; and for the *Washington Post*'s decision to change a website headline from 'JEWISH TODDLER DIES IN THE WEST BANK' to 'JEWISH BABY SHOT DEAD ON WEST BANK' within ninety minutes of HonestReporting starting to complain. The *New York Times* printed a fulsome apology for publishing a photograph of a pro-Israeli demonstration which showed anti-Israeli protesters in its foreground. A survey by fair.org found that in 90% of references to the Palestinian territories occupied by the Israeli Army,

American cable news described them only as 'contested' or 'disputed' or even as 'Israel'.

The BBC has been targeted particularly heavily, winning HonestReporting's annual award for dishonest reporting. One senior journalist there told me: 'The lobby insinuates a sense of fear. If the editor of the *Today* programme knows that an item will make the phone ring off the hook, he may think twice about running it. Sure, the lobby works. I can think of numerous examples where I have felt the brunt of it.' One member of staff at the BBC recalls the former press officer at the Israeli Embassy in London, David Schneeweiss, persuading a *Today* producer to set up a story about Yasser Arafat's involvement in corruption, even though BBC correspondents in Israel said there was nothing in it. 'You get correspondents there who will file a piece about Palestinians and be told by London "Nice piece, but it needs an Israeli voice." And that would never happen the other way around.' Two extensive academic surveys have found that the BBC routinely gives more airtime to Israeli voices than to Palestinian and that it focuses more frequently on Israeli victims than on Palestinians. The judgements are there to be made.

Rule Four: Select safe ideas

This rule runs parallel to the selection of safe facts by requiring moral and political values also to be safe. There are two important points here. First, moral and political ideas generally are not expressed overtly in the story but are the undeclared assumptions on which it is built and, being undeclared, are safe from scrutiny. Second, they reflect the surrounding consensus.

Some of these ideas apply to particular stories, with a decisive impact. In the mid-1980s, as home affairs correspondent at the *Observer*, I was one of the reporters who led the way in the investigation of the mysterious death of Hilda Murrell, an elderly lady who was found dead after somebody broke into her home in Shrewsbury, ransacked the place and sexually assaulted her. The stories I wrote suggested that this was not merely a violent burglary, but that she might have been attacked either because she was opposing the construction of a new nuclear power station, or because she had sensitive information from her nephew, who had worked in naval intelligence during the Falklands War.

On the tenth anniversary of her death, working for the *Guardian*, I set out to write a retrospective and I was alarmed to discover that my old stories simply did not stand up. What I had written at the time was a collection of fragments, some of which were clearly false, a few of which were open to interpretation, all of which were pushed into the shape I had given them only because of my unstated assumption that the state or the nuclear power industry was likely to have done something like this. It was an assumption which was widely shared at the time, as the Thatcher government used the security services against 'the enemy within' – so widely shared that I did not need to express it explicitly. I simply took it for granted. I wrote an analysis of my error. In 2005, a thirty-six-year-old labourer from Shrewsbury, with no connection to the nuclear industry or the state, was convicted of murdering Hilda Murrell after he was matched to the DNA in semen traces found on her body.

The same impact of unstated moral and political assumptions is at work in the coverage of asylum seekers in the UK. If you look back to the early 1980s, you will find a collection of stories which are highly sympathetic both to the asylum seekers and to their traffickers – written by the same journalists who now devote such energy to attacking them.

Geoffrey Levy, for example, now at the *Daily Mail*, used to work for the *Daily Express* where he profiled a lorry driver who had illegally smuggled a whole family of asylum seekers across Europe and into England. Under a headline 'THE LORRY DRIVER WHO GAVE A FAMILY A LIFT TO FREEDOM', Levy described the dangerous journey across four borders, the 'darkly pretty' girls who were hidden in boxes strapped beneath the truck, and the modest driver who declined to call himself a hero for this 'courageous act of friendship'.

In those days, the *Mail* itself was happy to profile a young couple of asylum seekers who were pictured enjoying their first pints of English beer; to celebrate the arrival of another young couple who 'danced for joy outside a sombre immigration office yesterday'; and to run a series of stories campaigning for the rights of one failed asylum seeker who, they reported, was 'screaming and struggling' as he was 'frogmarched by British officials' onto a plane. 'It could be taking him back to prison or to his death,' said the *Mail*, 'but the Home Office refused to let him stay.' They quoted Amnesty International saying that this was 'a tragedy beyond belief'.

These stories all reflected the unstated assumption that these asylum seekers were 'good' – because they were fleeing countries in the old Soviet bloc. These are the same East European countries, of course, whose migrants more recently have been attacked by these same newspapers as 'bad' – criminals, dole scroungers and carriers of disease. The migration argument is complex, a clatter of economic and social and moral points. It is particularly complex for the *Mail* and the *Express*, because they have been among the most vocal supporters of the creation of free markets; they continue to support the free flow across international borders of capital and services and goods, but not of labour – not if it means Africans, Gypsies and poor people turning up looking for work. As a result, their whole economic model collapses. But just like me with my conspiracy theory about the state and Hilda Murrell, their assumption that East European migrants now are 'bad' is not tested, because it is not expressed. It shapes the story from the safety of its foundations.

Ideas become safe not simply by remaining unstated. More important, they are safe if they reflect what Gramsci called 'the common sense of the era'. They may be entirely outrageous as moral or political statements but, if they are widely accepted, they will rest easy as a safe platform on which stories can be built. You can see this particularly clearly if you look back at journalism from previous eras.

Look, for example, at the coverage of black people by the US press during the late nineteenth century. You will find casual news reports about meetings of the Ku Klux Klan as a good Christian organisation; plenty of comfortable jokes about the stupidity of poor niggers; and a steady flow of news reports, like the one in the *Houston Post* in December 1885, which recorded that a young black man named Bennett Jackson had been accused of attacking a white woman in Montgomery County in east Texas. 'JUDGE LYNCH WILL PRESIDE IN MONTGOMERY TODAY', declared the headline. The story went on to explain that local people had planned to kill Jackson immediately but 'the lynching picnic was postponed until Saturday . . . A thrilling time is expected here.' Only twenty years after the end of the civil war, the 'common sense of the era' simply took it for granted that black people who attacked white people would be murdered as a public spectacle. As the *Post* said: 'Every good citizen approves of the lynching as the negro outrages are too frequent in this section.'

Or consider the more recent case of a book which declared: 'It is clear that America as it now exists must be destroyed . . . Having found you out, we will destroy you or die in the act of destroying you. That much seems inevitable . . . The very act of retribution is liberating . . . It is clearly written that the victim must become the executioner.' It went on to quote a religious leader's reaction to the death of twenty-two Americans in a plane crash: 'Allah has blessed us. He has destroyed 22 of our enemies.'

That book was given a rave review in the *New York Times*. Not now, but in 1969. The reviewer welcomed it as 'a magnificent example of the new black revolutionary writing that could generate the tidal force to sweep aside all the tired and dead matter on our literary shores'. I don't mean to suggest that the *New York Times* was ever committed to black power and revolution. This is to do with the limits of plausibility, the range of ideas which can be taken for granted without controversy. In New York in the late 1960s, somewhere between the birth of the civil rights movement and the end of the Vietnam War, that consensus admitted as reasonable the need for radical change and outspoken protest. (The book is called *Look Out, Whitey! Black Power Gon' Get Your Mama*, written by Julius Lester who went on to become a professor at the University of Massachusetts.)

The years of Reagan and Thatcher demolished that counter-culture and replaced it with a new consensus. So, for example, a database search reveals that, in 2006, Fleet Street papers had almost ceased to refer to the structure of their own society, a subject which generated the most powerful global debate of the twentieth century: in 2006, they referred more often to crap than they did to capitalism. The point is not whether one consensus is inherently better than the other. It is the fact of the consensus which is important, and its decisive influence as a safe platform on which churnalists can build their stories.

This has a formative impact on some of the great Flat Earth stories, particularly when it is coupled with the convention of the invisible reporter, trapped in neutrality. The effect is to rip the rudder off journalism and leave it to be swept along by the current of prevailing prejudice. Moral and political judgements are allowed, but only if they are rendered invisible by reflecting popular belief.

In *A Bright Shining Lie*, the defining journalist's view of the Vietnam War, Neil Sheehan, who covered the war for the *New York Times*, looks back at the failure of the US media and concludes: 'Our ignorance and our American ideology kept us from discerning the larger truths of Vietnam beneath the surface reality we could see. Professionally, we were fortunate in our ignorance. Had any reporter been sufficiently knowledgeable and open-minded to have questioned the justice and good sense of US intervention in those years, he would have been fired as a "subversive."'

There was plenty of negative reporting from Vietnam but it did not – because it could not – expose or attack the underlying assumption that the US was a force for good and that almost any brutality was permissible in order to prevent other countries falling like dominoes to Communist rule. As Sheehan puts it: 'When the press did cause trouble, the argument was over detail, not substance.'

In the same way, more recently, when the North Koreans tested a nuclear weapon for the first time, in October 2006, it was safe for the mainstream media to make routine references to the idea that their President was mad. This extended to the presenter of BBC's *Newsnight* looking into the camera and describing him as 'a crackpot'. No evidence was ever produced to support the allegation (nor was it when the same easy slur was made about Colonel Gaddafi and Saddam Hussein). On the other side of the safety line, in recycling criticism of the nuclear test from the USA, the UK, Russia and China, it was not safe for the invisible reporter to point out that all four nations themselves possessed a considerable store of nuclear weapons and that one of them had used two such weapons to bomb two cities full of civilians.

The unstated consensus assumption becomes particularly dangerous when it becomes part of a running narrative, so that media outlets are trapped by the story they have told so far, unwilling to allow uncomfortable facts to become part of the story. There was a particularly horrific example of this in the case of Gary Webb, an award-winning reporter at the *San Jose Mercury News*, who, in August 1996, ran a series of stories exposing the fact that from the early 1980s the street gangs in Los Angeles had sold tons of cocaine which had been supplied via the Contras, the armed group which was then waging a guerrilla war to overthrow the socialist Sandinista government of Nicaragua.

The problem for Gary Webb was that this story clashed badly with the running narrative of the mainstream US dailies, which had accepted the claim of the Reagan administration that the Contras were freedom fighters who were worthy of support, which they were receiving in large quantities from US security and intelligence agencies, including the CIA. Webb's story put two Nicaraguan CIA 'assets' at the heart of the conspiracy to raise funds for the Contras by selling cocaine into the United States and said that the CIA had known that this was happening. The mainstream dailies, however, had previously considered similar allegations and failed to follow them.

Webb's story was duly attacked mercilessly by the *New York Times*, the *Washington Post* and the *Los Angeles Times*, all of them supported by official sources, including the CIA itself. Webb's bosses started to get nervous, destroying 5,000 reprints of the story because they carried the CIA logo; ordering him to include in follow-up stories a clear statement exonerating the CIA centrally from knowledge of the conspiracy; suppressing his follow-up stories; and finally running a column by an executive editor which formally apologised for 'short-comings' in the series. Webb resigned in December 1997, his highly successful career ruined.

In the year following his resignation, Webb's story was supported by a series of official reports, from the Justice Department and the inspector general of the CIA, which variously confirmed that the Contras had been raising money by trafficking cocaine; that the CIA had known about this, failed to stop it and actively concealed evidence about it; and that at least one of the two Nicaraguan 'assets' named by Webb had been directly involved. Even though the *Washington Post's* in-house ombudsman had published a strongly worded criticism of the *Post's* 'misdirected zeal' in attacking Webb's story, these reports received minimal coverage from the big dailies. On 10 December 2004,

Gary Webb was found dead with two shotgun wounds in his head. The local coroner ruled that he had committed suicide.

Rule Five: Always give both sides of the story

This is the safety net rule. It suggests that, if all else fails and you end up having to publish something which is not 'safe', you bang in some quotes from the other side to 'balance' the story.

Balance means never having to say you're sorry – because you haven't said anything. Applied to statements of opinion, the rule is fine. But applied to statements of fact, the rule is the embodiment of neutrality and with the same result, that journalists are encouraged to abandon their primary purpose, of truth-telling.

A small but perfectly formed example: in December 2005, brokers and dealers in London who picked up a copy of the *City AM* freesheet on their way to work, read a front-page report that the chief executive of Tesco, Sir Terry Leahy, was stepping down. In the City, this was a big story, and Tesco shares immediately dropped. Of course, it was wrong. But rapidly, it reached other news outlets who applied Rule Five by calling the Tesco press office, taking down a statement which dismissed the report as 'complete nonsense', coupling the rumour to this denial, calling it a story and publishing it – on BBC radio, in the *Evening Standard*, the *Guardian*, the *Express*, *The Times* and the *Independent*. This is standard practice in the world of neutral reporting.

Scientists spent two decades warning that the planet was heating up while journalists simply balanced what they were saying with denials from experts and oil companies. It was the same years ago when scientists tried to warn that smoking was linked to lung cancer, and journalists simply balanced their evidence with counterclaims from the tobacco industry. It was the same again in May 2006, when thirteen of the most senior doctors in Britain, including a Nobel Prize-winner and the president of the Academy of Sciences, wrote a public letter calling on the government to stop funding homeopathy and other 'unproven or disproved treatments'. The journalists immediately reached for a homeopath who denounced the doctors' letter snappily as 'medical apartheid', and the facts were soon buried in balance. The truth? Not our job.

The balance rule is fine as a fallback, when the attempt to uncover the truth has failed: then, honesty requires that journalists admit their ignorance and lay out the fragments of truth which they have managed to collect. But to make it the object, to make it a golden rule in the training of journalists, is to embed the fallback as the primary purpose, to ease the flow of churnalism without truth. And it should be added that, in the hands of a malicious reporter, this rule becomes a handy tool in the deliberate publication of lies, since it allows a story which is entirely false in its thrust to be made safe against most complaints by tucking into the final paragraph a 100% denial from the story's victim.

Even when applied without malice, the rule operates in a particularly insidious way. In practice, it is applied only to statements of fact which are maverick, i.e. which contradict the safe, consensus view; the consensus statements of fact, by contrast, run through the media without balance. There was a particularly clear example of this in the build-up to the invasion of Iraq. Throughout the extended global debate, a former UN arms inspector, Scott Ritter, was waving from the side of the pitch, trying to persuade journalists to listen to his evidence, based on first-hand experience, that the Iraqis had no weapons of mass destruction. From time to time, Ritter would succeed in fighting his way into the news factory and getting some coverage, and always his statements were balanced by counter-statements from government sources who insisted he was wrong. But the reverse did not apply. When government officials took media space to put their case, nobody ever said, 'We'd better get hold of someone like Scott Ritter for some balance.'

I had the same experience making a one-hour special for Channel 4 about heroin. I made a programme which was stacked with expert evidence to show that heroin is a benign drug; that it is the black market and not the drug which is responsible for the suffering of its users. That was a statement of fact, amply supported by evidence, but it was a maverick one. And so I was put under extreme pressure by Channel 4 to include material to contradict it. And yet, when those who know no better tell the media that heroin is a poison which, as in the 1980s publicity campaign, 'screws you up', no journalist comes under any pressure at all to call in a source to contradict them. The maverick statement is neutralised; the consensus statement runs unchecked.

The idea of balanced reporting has its roots in the most honourable of journalistic traditions. The convention grew from an era when hack journalists were willing to sell their editorial soul, to write partisan and distorted stories for the greater good of their wallets. In that context, it was a brave and necessary step for honest journalists to declare that they would show no favour, that they would be willing to tell the truth from all sides. Now, however, that context has changed, and the demand for balance has become a gateway through which spokesmen for the consensus are invited to enter our stories with their comments, regardless of whether or not they are false, distorted or propaganda. The honourable convention aimed at unearthing the facts has become a coward's compromise aimed at dispatching quick copy with which nobody will quarrel.

Increasing the Revenue

Rule Six: Give them what they want

This is the rule which is best known by those outside the news factory. Simply, it requires that stories should increase readership or audience. If we can sell it, we'll tell it.

One of the few British journalists to survive a long period as editor with his reputation intact is Arthur Christiansen, who ran the *Daily Express* when it was the most successful newspaper in Britain. He was not a news-factory man. He described his paper's relationship to its readers very simply: 'It is our job to interest them in everything. It requires the highest degree of skill and ingenuity.'

In place of that traditional idea, Rule Six proposes a collapse in editorial judgement under the enormous pressure of consumer demand. This was perfectly captured by the BBC's occasional media critic, Raymond Snoddy, in a review of the week's BBC output in July 2006. Snoddy began by querying the fact that the deaths of two British soldiers in Afghanistan had been knocked into second place in the news by coverage of the tearful resignation of the England football captain, David Beckham. The former BBC war correspondent Martin Bell condemned the decision, saying: 'The BBC has set itself adrift in a whirlpool of trivia.' Snoddy then moved to a second item, reporting on a viewer who had complained that, by comparison with ITV news, the BBC was spending too much time on each story and going into too much detail, and as a result, she said, it had failed, unlike ITV, to run an item about a new film, *Pirates of the Caribbean: Dead Man's Chest*. There you have it: Martin Bell, the veteran journalist, speaking up for editorial judgement; and the consumer speaking up for less information and more entertainment, even if it is nothing more than PR. In a commercial culture, the viewer has more power than the journalist.

Notoriously, this rule defines tabloid coverage, expressed with particular crudeness in a memo from the news editor of the *Sunday Express*, Jim 'Mad Dog' Murray, which was leaked in the summer of 2003: 'We are aiming to have six sex stories a week. In an ideal world, we should have a "cabinet minister affair" story. Sex and scandal at the highest level of society always sells well, but these stories are notoriously difficult to get. We need to be constantly stirring things up. We must make the readers cross: the appalling state of the railways, the neglect of the Health Service, the problem of teenage pregnancies, the inability of bureaucrats to get enough done properly, etc, etc.'

But the same rule now applies in quality media too, because in their commercialised form they need stories which sell. As a single example, in May 2005, three days after Tony Blair won his third general election, the political editor of the *Independent*, Andrew Grice, found that some of the Prime Minister's own Cabinet colleagues were already saying he would have to stand down within eighteen months. As Grice later recalled in a diary in the *Press Gazette*: 'It's the most significant story I've had for ages and I twice plead for it to be the splash. But the paper wants a change of pace after the election so instead, we splash on a story about Britain's vanishing flowers, with a big picture of one on the front page.'

You can see the impact of the rule particularly clearly in ITV's output of current affairs. Until the late 1980s, the channel supported *World In Action*, *This Week* and *First Tuesday*, all digging out original stories of the kind which Arthur Christiansen would have recognised. However, in 1998, in search of bigger audiences, it killed off all three and replaced them with the populist *Tonight with Trevor McDonald*, a programme whose choice of stories attracted an ironic swipe from the head of news and current affairs at Channel 4, Dorothy Byrne, a former *World In Action* producer. In an article for the *Guardian* in January 2007, she wrote: 'I admire *Tonight with Trevor McDonald*. And I especially admire the young journalists who constantly re-invent what is, taken in total, a very narrow consumer agenda. Supermarkets, cars, sick kids, sick kids going to the supermarket in cars, supermarkets which make kids sick, kids' car sickness. They certainly deserve an award for that.'

Aeron Davis's book, *Public Relations Democracy*, quotes two revealing statements from British TV executives. Paul Jackson, as director of programmes at the old ITV company Carlton, said in 1992: 'If *World In Action* were, in 1993, to uncover three more serious miscarriages of justice, while delivering an audience of three, four or five million, I would cut it.' And the former controller of editorial policy at the BBC, John Wilson, said in 1998: 'News is a way of making money, just as selling bread is a way of making money. No one believes that news and journalism are simply a service to democracy.'

The most obvious impact of the rule is that it promotes the trivial. Foreign is boring. War is depressing. CBS in America actually cut short its coverage of the second day of the invasion of Iraq in March 2003, to make way for a basketball tournament. More than that, it distorts the entire output of the news factory.

The wire agencies who provide so much of the factory's raw material, have deliberately shifted their coverage to fit the rule. As the Press Association's communications manager, Elizabeth Castle, told us: 'What customers want drives the editorial judgement.' So while PA provides such fragmented coverage of, for example, local government in Britain, it has opened a whole new agency dedicated to entertainment news, powered by reports on celebrities. In the same way, Reuters, because it earns more than 90% of its revenue from selling news to the world finance industry, is far more likely to cover the price of cotton than the life of the cotton worker, which is why it invested extra money in reporting oil and energy at the same time as it cut its coverage of West Africa. Although AP does not suffer from this skew towards financial news, its coverage is nonetheless clearly distorted in favour of its Western market. In the summer of 2000 the academic specialist Chris Paterson analysed two days' output of APTN and found

63% focused on the developed world and only 28% on the developing countries where the majority of the planet's population live; 37% of the stories focused directly or indirectly on the US.

The rule also encourages wire agencies to cover subjects which will sell in multiple markets. So, they like lifestyle stories, which is why in 2001, Reuters set up TV Life Feed to put out between three and five stories a day on health and holidays and the purchase of happiness, all of which could be sold across the developed world. For the same reason, they like sport and celebrities. Sampling the output of APTN, Dr Paterson found that, in 1995, sport and entertainment accounted for only 1% of its output; by 2000, the figure was 25%. Reuters has been expanding its coverage of football in the United States and the Middle East. Apart from setting up its new entertainment agency, PA now claims to be 'the world's leading supplier of sports news'. A vast mass of human life – domestic poverty, world poverty, labour movements, the whole backstory about Islamist terrorism, real politics, international trade – is consigned to the margins.

And this is one of several factors which tend to produce a conservative account of the world. As Dr Paterson concluded: 'Because news agencies must please all news editors, everywhere, they must work harder than their client journalist to create the appearance of objectivity and neutrality. In so doing, they manufacture a bland and homogeneous, but still ideologically distinctive, view of the world; stories challenging the ideologicial positions of the dominant political players on the world scene (in agency eyes, the US and UK) receive little attention.'

The rule not only distorts the selection of stories, it also distorts their content. A crime story, for example, won't sell unless it is scary. In June 2005, there was a big story in the UK about a gang of feral child bullies who had attempted to murder a five-year-old boy by hanging him from a tree; the boy had managed to free himself. For several days this was a big news story, followed up by solemn comment about the youth of today and the impact of violence on television. The story was not true.

It was obviously not true from the moment it started running. There was the common-sense problem that even a fully grown man with ten years of SAS training who found himself hanging by the neck would have the greatest difficulty in reaching up and lifting his entire body weight with one hand while using the other to remove the noose. How would a five-year-old boy do it? More than that, there was the evidence in the story itself. From the first day, the police refused to say that the boy had been hanged. The parents and neighbours who told the press how shocked they were never claimed to know what had happened. The one and only line on which the whole story was built was a quote from the boy's adult cousin, who said he had told her: 'Some boys and girls have tied a rope around my neck and tried to tie me to a tree.' That's 'tie me to a tree' – not 'hang me from a tree'.

The truth was that this was a nasty case of bullying but not an attempted murder. A 12-year-old girl certainly had put a rope around the boy's neck and led him round like a dog, pulling on it hard enough to leave marks on his neck. That was clearly very dangerous. But the boy never claimed she had hanged him from a tree. Indeed, he never even claimed that she had tied him to a tree, only that she had tried to. To double-check, we spoke to Professor Christopher Milroy, the Home Office pathologist who handled the case. He said: 'He had not been hanged. That was not correct and I couldn't understand why the press were insisting that he was.'

They insisted, of course, because it sold the story, so a bad case of bullying, which would not normally be touched by the national media, became choice output for the news factory. The tabloids ran all over it; and TV and the rest of Fleet Street joined in. The *Evening Standard* calling it a lynching; the *Mail*, the *Guardian* and *The Times* all ran head-lines which stated boldly that the boy had been hanged; the *Independent* ran a moody feature about fear descending on the boy's estate. The rule overwhelmed the facts, even though the facts clearly contradicted the story from the outset.

The rule also favours stories which fit well-known templates. The story of the hanged boy took off because it allowed newspapers to suggest it was a repeat of the genuinely horrifying tale of two young boys who murdered two-year-old James Bulger in February 1993. (The press renamed him Jamie, because it sounded softer.) Often these templates come from fiction. In May 2005, a commonplace court case in Tyneside, involving a twelve-year-old girl on an antisocial behaviour order, was catapulted into national news, simply because a clever reporter linked her to Vicky Pollard, the fictional brat from the BBC series *Little Britain*. The whole story of the joyous marriage of Prince Charles and Princess Diana was based on the model of a fairy tale which sold around the world for years, before it fell apart to be replaced with a different fairy tale, of the evil prince and the beautiful princess, before that, too, fell apart to be replaced with a different fiction, of the scheming tart, before that fell apart with her death, and she became the people's princess.

Reporters now even turn themselves into fictional characters, usually as heroes. The *Daily Telegraph*'s war correspondent, Robert Fox, wrote a telling piece during the first Gulf War, when he saw CNN correspondents wearing gas masks to do their pieces to camera, while their own technicians wandered around without any kind of protection, because, in reality, there was no danger. For the same reason, current affairs programmes send more and more reporters to work under cover, because it gives them the sexy sequence where the reporter looks into his own camera and explains how frightened he feels as he prepares to infiltrate the bad guys. This means that television not only selects stories purely because they can go undercover, it also puts their reporters into situations where they can get hurt even though there are other ways of getting the story.

Rule Seven: The bias against truth

This extends the commercial imperative of Rule Six beyond the selection of stories and into a series of prejudices about the way that stories are told.

In an article in *The Times* on 28 February 1975, John Birt, later to become director general of the BBC, suggested that factual television was so consistently failing to provide context for its stories that it was creating a bias against understanding. More than thirty years later, that article still makes sense. So, I'm going to steal John Birt's idea and apply it more broadly.

As he put it in a subsequent article, co-authored with Peter Jay: 'Reality is a seamless garment of interacting and developing processes while journalism is organised to collect innumerable nuggets of self-contained fact, to report an atomised world of a million tiny tales.' Those tales now are not merely atomised but, more than ever, they are internally constructed in order to sell. The failure to provide context has multiplied and divided into a preference for human interest over issue; for the concrete over the abstract; for event rather than process; for the current over the historic; for simplicity rather than complexity; for certainty rather than doubt. This applies in both print and broadcast, generating patterns of distortion so consistent as to amount to a bias against truth.

Like Rule Six, this bias first makes its mark by rejecting a mass of stories, because they are not 'events'. Slow-burning tales don't fit on the assembly line. The news factory reports the train crash which kills a hundred people; the government sets up a public inquiry. It doesn't report the hundred car crashes which separately kill a hundred people, so there's no inquiry. The most powerful security machine in the world cannot find the man who organised the public massacre of some 3,000 of its citizens. It's one of the biggest stories in the world, but it isn't an event, so the news factory can't process it. The rule particularly favours events which have good pictures. The UK Police National Missing Persons Bureau records 387 children under fourteen who vanished in the most recent calendar year, most of whom never make a headline, and yet the disappearance of Holly Wells and Jessica Chapman in August 2002 was a big story as soon as they went missing, even though there was no evidence of foul play for thirteen days, primarily because there was a brilliant picture, of two pretty little girls in Manchester United shirts, which had been taken on the day they vanished. It is this rule which leaves the US government complaining, possibly with some justice, that the media report the big deaths from Iraq but never the signs of stability.

Then the rule infiltrates the content of stories, with devastating effect. In his book *Bad News*, the veteran CBS correspondent Tom Fenton describes filing a story from Saudi Arabia which included important revelations about the threat from a man called Osama bin Laden. This was before the September 2001 attacks. Fenton describes how he was ordered to remove all references to bin Laden. Conspiracy theorists would smell a cover-up. The banal truth was caught in CBS's explanation to an angry Fenton: 'Too many foreign names in the story.'

It was the same when he tried to file a report on the gassing of thousands of Kurds by Saddam Hussein. He was told to remove all references to the fact that the victims were Kurdish, even though that lay at the heart of the story. It was too confusing, he was told: 'No one knows who the Kurds are.' Fenton comes up with a fine phrase to describe this – 'the natural selectivity of ignorance'.

The news factory drains the detail out of its stories, clears away the complexity, cuts out the context and reduces them to mere events, often devoid of meaning. How would the French Resistance have come across in stories which merely reported that a bomb had been planted in a café by a group which was prepared to kill unarmed targets in order to promote its political ends? The meaning is in the context. When researchers from Glasgow University analysed a sample of British television output on Israel and Palestine, they found 3,500 lines of text – only seventeen of which were devoted to the history of the conflict. As a result, when they sampled public opinion, they found numerous viewers who believed that it was the Palestinians who were occupying the occupied territories, not the Israeli Army; and that 'people simply don't know that the Palestinians lost their homes and land in 1948'. The BBC's former Middle East correspondent, Tim Llewellyn, who has become a vocal critic of the corporation's coverage, says he spoke to a BBC journalist who explained that his managers did not want 'explainers' about Israel. 'It's all bang-bang stuff,' the journalist told him.

A drug addict dies. It's reported as a death caused by heroin. Never mind the complicated stuff about the black market, not the drug, being responsible. A government minister announces more bobbies on the beat. Report the speech; it's concrete; never mind all that abstract research which exposes the futility of the policy. A bomb goes off. It's a story about dead people and flames. Who knows why it happened or what it really means? As Rupert Murdoch put it, in a moment captured in Bruce Page's book: 'I'm not having any of that upmarket shit in my paper.'

The bias against truth is now entrenched by the news factory's move towards shoving its stories into smaller and smaller packages, like a dismembered body being stuffed into a suitcase. Tell it fast, or the punters will lose interest. At the Centre for Media and Public Affairs at Harvard University, Kiky Adatto researched the length of TV news sound bites during American presidential election campaigns: in 1968, they ran to an average of 42.3 seconds; by 1988, they had been slashed to only 9.8 seconds; by 1992, they were even smaller, at 7.3 seconds. It's the same in the UK. July 2005 saw Sir Nicholas Hewitt, president of the Newspaper Society, happily sharing his vision of the future – 'shorter stories, more fun and plenty of variety'.

As an incidental side effect, this, too, tends to confirm the consensus view of the world. Without the time or the incentive to show the meaning of events, they settle easily into the framework of popular assumption, however right or wrong that may be.

Rule Eight: Give them what they want to believe in

This rule runs parallel to Rule Six, requiring that ideas as well as facts should be selected with commerce in mind.

It is neatly caught, in all its cynicism, in a memo written in the spring of 2003 to Sly Bailey, the chief executive of Trinity Mirror, by the then editor of the *Daily Mirror*, Piers Morgan, apologising for the sudden plunge in sales as a result of the paper continuing to oppose the invasion of Iraq even after British troops had started fighting: 'I am afraid I misjudged the way our readers would respond to the start of the war, and our line has clearly been too confrontational and too critical for many of them . . . I am very sorry about this, it means we'll drop below two million for the month and that is desperately unfortunate . . . I will just have to get those readers back as fast as I can. One thing I won't be doing is sitting here defiantly telling myself how I'm right and they are all wrong. The readers are never wrong. Repulsive, maybe, but never wrong.' So regardless of editorial judgement about what was right or wrong, the paper changed its line to feed the values of its consumers.

The rule is potentially highly destructive. In October 2005, the *New Yorker* published a long analysis of the damage caused by the profit-seeking behaviour of the owners of the *Los Angeles Times*. The paper's managing editor, Dean Baquet, acknowledged the danger of the populist idea that editors should give readers whatever they demanded. Baquet, a black American, said: 'It's not always our job to give readers what they want. What if they don't want war coverage or foreign coverage or to see poverty in their communities? Southern newspapers are still hanging their heads because generations ago, they gave readers what they wanted – no coverage of segregation and the civil-rights movement.' (In September 2006, Bacquet resigned under pressure after publicly denouncing the 'irrational era of cost-cutting' in newspapers including the *LA Times*.)

Precisely the same problem in the UK was pinpointed by a senior journalist at White's freelance agency in Sheffield, who told us: 'When it comes to asylum seekers if I'm honest there is an undercurrent of understanding. No red-top or tabloid is going to buy a positive story about an asylum seeker. We know that, we know what they want. And I don't feel bad about it. I'm trying to make a living so I'll get them what they want. We won't look into a story that we know we are going to get no money for.'

Rule Nine: Go with the moral panic

This rule applies only at times of perceived crisis. It combines the recycling of readers' values with the bias against truth, by attempting to sell the nation a heightened version of its own emotional state in the crudest possible form. Unlike the other rules, it is compulsory: waverers who fail to express their part of the moral panic are hunted down and attacked.

Rule Nine is always invoked by big deaths: the nation is in mourning; everybody must mourn; that's the story. The death of Princess Diana in August 1997 saw Rule Nine at its most powerful, recording genuine shock and sorrow, playing it back at increased volume, heightening the shock and sorrow, and then playing that back too, all the time condemning heretic unbelievers with such passion that the Queen herself ended up being denounced for failing to show enough misery.

Rule Nine is capable of generating stunning falsehood as the facts are forced to fit the feeling. There were terrible problems with the death of the Queen Mother in March 2002. She died on a Saturday. Moral panic swept the newsrooms of Sunday newspapers, which started throwing out multiple pages of news to express their feeling. The *Observer*, not historically a monarchist paper, scrapped its front page and the following ten pages of its main news section. In their place it ran a series of headlines which informed readers: 'THE QUEEN MUM — THE CENTURY WAS HERS', 'THE QUEEN MOTHER'S DEATH ROBS A NATION OF ITS FAVOURITE GRANDMOTHER' and 'MILLIONS GRIEVE FOR A GRACIOUS QUEEN'. There was a striking shortage of evidence to support any of this.

The particularly tricky fact was that there was a national shortage of grieving millions, which caused special problems for television. Fiction flowed. That Saturday evening, a crew was dispatched to the West End of London to cover the preordained story about the clubs and cinemas being empty because the mourning millions were too sad to go out and enjoy themselves. In reality, the West End was its normal heaving self, and a highly enterprising reporter dealt with the problem by turning to the camera and telling the nation that the West End was showing the plucky 'spirit of the Blitz': millions were mourning but the show had to go on, he explained. It was the same the next morning outside Buckingham Palace where the absence of a sea of bouquets and a weeping crowd saw one middle-aged, mixed-race woman suddenly elevated into the most famous face in Britain, because, for one reason or another, she was crying within the vicinity of the palace gates. On this occasion, it was the BBC presenter Peter Sissons who was attacked as a heretic, for failing to wear a black tie to read the news.

The rule produced less aggression but even more fiction when Pope John Paul II died in April 2005. Media outlets without question expressed Christian belief as fact. 'SAFE IN HEAVEN', declared the headline on the front page of the *Mail on Sunday*. The Pope had 'a concealed power which draws a person closer to Christ', explained the *Sunday Telegraph*. All of them then reached greedily for the dying man's final words, even though those words showed every sign of being the fictitious product of the Vatican's PR department.

A week before his death, on Easter Sunday, the Pope had appeared at a window overlooking St Peter's Square and attempted to address the crowd. He was too weak to stand or say anything. The following Wednesday, he had tried and failed again to speak. The next day, he suffered a cardio-circulatory collapse, went into a coma and breathed through a pipe inserted into his throat. And yet when he died on the

Saturday afternoon, he was suddenly conscious and articulate. The first Vatican version claimed he had breathed, 'Amen.' The second version upped that, claiming he had declared in his dying moment: 'Let me go to the house of the Father.' The final version went for something more moving, claiming that he had succeeded in dictating a formal statement: 'It is love which converts hearts and gives peace to all humanity, which today seems so lost and dominated by the power of evil selfishness and fear: our resurrected Lord gives us His love, which forgives, reconciles and reopens the soul to hope.'

I spoke to one of the journalists who reported the death and who had included the statement in his story. He said he was 'as sure as I can be' that the Pope had never uttered a word of the statement. He added: 'The Vatican has 2,000 years' experience of putting the best spin on the death of popes. I doubt whether he could have come up with anything as coherent as that, I doubt whether he could have spoken at all. I tried in the nicest possible way to cast a shadow of doubt over this. I think reporters generally knew that he almost certainly had not said this – none of us really thought he had said it.' But they all ran it, just as they all felt compelled to describe the thousands who gathered in St Peter's Square for the subsequent funeral as 'mourners', even though a mass of them were clearly tourists, not crying or throwing flowers, as they had at Diana's funeral, but taking photographs.

In the case of the Pope, the coverage conveyed a powerful political distortion. This was a man with a highly contentious history of conservative belief who had hammered 'liberation theology' priests in Central America when they tried to stand up to murderous pro-Western dictatorships there; and campaigned globally for a ban on contraception with disastrous consequences for those caught in the Aids epidemic in Africa. All this was swept aside by crude mourning for 'the people's Pope'.

Moral panic is also invoked by war. There were some striking examples during the 1982 Falklands campaign where heretic coverage by the BBC's *Panorama* programme, for example, saw it denounced as *Traitorama*, for daring to explore the arguments against the British campaign. The fear of failing to be patriotically correct saw the *Sunday Times* suppress a story which challenged the heart of the British case for war.

That case rested on the claim, articulated by the then Foreign Secretary, Francis Pym, that 'We're not in any doubt about our title to the Falkland Islands and we never have been.' However, an academic called Peter Beck from what was then called Kingston Polytechnic unearthed an archive of Foreign Office paperwork which showed the exact opposite. This included, for example, internal messages from senior officials over the years saying: 'We cannot easily make out a good claim and we have wisely done everything to avoid discussing the subject'; and 'It is not easy to explain our possession of the islands without showing ourselves up as international bandits.' Clearly there was a considerable gap between the public and the private position of the British government and a gap furthermore into which the lives of British and Argentinian soldiers were being hurled. However, the editor of the *Sunday Times*, Frank Giles, refused to run the story while fighting was going on, explaining in an internal memo: 'I don't want it to surface at the moment.'

In an interview with the BBC's *Newsnight* in May 2002, one of the most senior journalists in American television, Dan Rather of CBS, acknowledged the impact of this kind of thinking on his own work in the build-up to the invasion of Iraq: 'What we are talking about here – whether one wants to recognise it or not, or call it by its proper name or not – is a form of self-censorship. It starts with a feeling of patriotism within oneself. It carries through with a certain knowledge that the country as a whole felt and continues to feel this surge of patriotism within themselves. And one finds oneself saying: "I know the right question, but you know what? This is not exactly the right time to ask it . . ." There was a time in South Africa when people would put flaming tyres around people's necks if they dissented, and in some ways, the fear is that you'll be necklaced here. You'll have a flaming tyre of lack of patriotism put around your neck. Now, it's that fear that keeps journalists from asking the toughest of tough questions.'

Rule Ten: Ninja Turtle syndrome

This requires the media to run stories which are being widely published elsewhere, even if those stories clearly lack merit.

The name derives from the problems of parents who attempt to divert their children from television programmes which they deem unsuitable, such as the 1990s American series, *Teenage Mutant Ninja Turtles*, which combined casual violence with the impression that the names of Leonardo and Raphael belonged not to Renaissance artists but to heavily armed reptiles. Those parents who succeeded in keeping their homes turtle-free then found themselves doubting their policy when their children went to schools where every other child was talking turtle, leaving their own offspring isolated. So they succumbed.

In the news factory, highly dubious stories are published and broadcast on the same principle, to prevent their consumers being cut out of popular debate (and possibly tempted to look elsewhere for their news).

This happened in glorious style with the story launched by the *Mail on Sunday* in November 2003, alleging that an unnamed member of the royal family had been having some kind of sexual affair with an unnamed 'senior palace servant'. Within days, it became clear that this referred to Prince Charles and his former aide, Michael Fawcett. The story not only lacked evidence to support it; it relied entirely on evidence which clearly deserved to be rejected.

There were only three possible sources: Prince Charles, who issued an unequivocal denial; Michael Fawcett, who issued an equally unequivocal denial; and George Smith, a former palace footman, now dead, who had suffered a nervous breakdown in 1995, been sectioned several times under the Mental Health Act, suffered from alcoholism and had previously accused Michael Fawcett of raping him during a royal visit to Egypt in 1995, even though no such royal visit occurred. It was clear at the time that there was nothing to justify the story and so it should not be published. Everybody published it, because of Ninja Turtle syndrome.

The rule makes its mark fairly frequently with the mass publication of obviously unreliable small stories. There was a prime example in February 2006, when a Serbian radio station reported that Ratko Mladic, wanted for war crimes, had finally been captured. The sources who could have confirmed it all explicitly denied it, but the story trickled from the radio station into the local media and from there to late-night television bulletins in Britain and then into the daily papers – all of whom calculated that they had to run the story, for fear of isolating their readers, and all of whom thus misled those readers.

The rule is reinforced by the generally unrecognised habit of journalists covering their backs by colluding on stories. It is commonplace for reporters to emerge from a court case or a big speech, to go into a huddle asking 'So, what's the line?', so that they can come up with an agreed version. The same thing happens at very senior level: for years, the editor of the *Observer*, Roger Alton, was in the habit of speaking on Saturday afternoon to Michael Williams, the deputy editor of his supposed competitor, the *Independent on Sunday*, to swap notes on the stories they were planning to run in the following day's papers. In September 2005, it was disclosed that for the last ten years the *New York Times* and the *Washington Post* had been faxing each other an early proof of their front pages, before the presses started to roll.

This is a powerful rule, which has played a decisive role in spreading some of the biggest Flat Earth news. The Clinton scandals are a particularly clear case. Senior journalists all over America worried out loud about stories emerging, for example, from the website run by Matt Drudge, a former sales clerk who became a conduit for right-wing rumours about the President, including some salacious sexual detail and a report that the President's wife was about to be indicted. When *Brill's Content*, a US magazine which scrutinises the quality of journalism, analysed some of his stories, it found that twenty-one out of thirty-one were not true. But if the *Washington Times* were running a Drudge rumour, the *Washington Post* had to run it too. As Drudge himself once put it: 'Screw journalism. The whole thing's a fraud anyway.'

You can see how these rules fit neatly into the new structure of corporate news organisations. Journalists who are denied the time to work effectively can survive by taking the easy, sexy stories which everybody else is running; reducing them to simplified events; framing them with safe ideas and safe facts; neutralising them with balance; and churning them out fast. You can see, too, just how destructive this is, especially when different rules reinforce each other.

The *Columbia Journalism Review* in September 2006 published a lengthy analysis of the history of US coverage of the abuse of prisoners in Afghanistan, Iraq and Guantánamo. It began by tracing the work of a handful of individual reporters who had tried to break the story up to eighteen months before it finally became a scandal. Carlotta Gall, the Afghan correspondent of the *New York Times*, had done a neat piece of research, following up an official announcement that a prisoner had died in custody because he had a weak heart, by tracking down his death certificate which gave his cause of death as 'homicide'. Together with details of a second death, she filed the story in February 2003, but the *New York Times* would not run it.

The *Journalism Review* quoted the then foreign editor, Roger Cohen: 'I pitched it, I don't know, four times at page-one meetings, with increasing urgency and frustration. I laid awake at night over this story. And I don't fully understand to this day what happened. It was a really scarring thing.' The beginning of an explanation is provided by Doug Frantz, then the paper's investigations editor, who explained that the most senior people on the paper 'insisted that it was improbable; it was just hard to get their mind around'. The story didn't fit the running narrative of the US as a force for good; it was not safe; it clashed with official sources; there was a clear electric fence in sight; it ran into the moral panic of war. As Carlotta Gall herself put it: 'There was a sense of patriotism, and you felt it in every question from every editor and copy-editor. I remember a foreign-desk editor telling me, "Remember where we are – we can smell the debris from 9/11."' Her story eventually ran on page 14. A handful of other reporters elsewhere dug into the same area, including one of the few remaining investigators at AP, Charles Hanley, who succeeded in getting a story onto the wire in November 2003. Other news outlets conspicuously failed to follow.

Then, in April 2004, the story suddenly went global. Two things had happened. First, CBS Television had broadcast photographs of Iraqi prisoners being abused in Abu Ghraib. Now, there was a simple, safe event with the bonus of pictures. Even then, as the *Journalism Review* article described, US coverage was slow – until President Bush reacted to foreign stories about the photographs by denouncing the abuse. Now the story was safe: here was an official source acknowledging it. And so the Ninja Turtle rule kicked in: everybody could do it, because everybody else was doing it. The outlets which had ignored the story now pounced on it, producing powerful coverage, some of which used information which had been available for many months.

Yet, even now the rules of the news factory distorted the story. The US government engaged in heavy news management, driving coverage into a cul-de-sac about whether or not there should be coverage. The balance rule made that easy. As the *Journalism Review* put it: 'The argument by the White House and its allies, that there wasn't a need for a debate, was aided by many news organizations' habit of presenting both sides of the story as if they were equal, regardless of the underlying reality.' Coverage remained inhibited by the original fear of challenging the consensus, and the news factory endlessly reran pictures of the US soldier Lynndie England with her naked prisoner like a dog on a lead (concrete and sexy), while ignoring the trickle of leaked memos which exposed the systemic policy behind the abuse (abstract and boring and close to an electric fence).

You can see there how the news factory is not yet a monopoly. There are still reporters who have the time to do their work effectively, and it is still possible to break the rules of production. But the great mass of reporting, even by wealthy and powerful media organisations, remains compliant, selecting stories in an arbitrary, almost irrational way; recycling falsehood and distortion; clinging to the safest of political and moral assumptions.

Sometimes, the result is merely irrational. In January 2005, the BBC published the results of an inquiry into its coverage of the European Union, chaired by Lord Wilson of Dinton. He had unearthed a chaos of conflicting distortions: 'The partiality seems to flow both ways at different times and with different intensities. It is not consistent.' Analysing this, he caught the impact of several factory rules: 'In essence, it seems to be the result of a combination of factors including an institutional mindset, a tendency to polarise and over-simplify issues, a measure of ignorance of the EU on the part of some journalists, and a failure to report issues which ought to be reported, perhaps out of a belief that they are not sufficiently entertaining. Whatever the cause in particular cases, the effect is the same for the outside world and feels like bias.'

He noted how this had virtually killed coverage of key issues, like the working-time directive, the chemical directive, water and air pollution, waste disposal, health and safety, regional policy; and that research with focus groups had revealed large sections of the public with very little understanding of the EU (even though some of them professed to hold very strong opinions on the subject).

In a classic example of the bias against truth, he cited an incident where a senior print journalist was invited to record an item for *The Politics Show*, explaining why Britain should not join the euro. The journalist's argument was entirely about economics. But the script which was provided to the journalist read: 'There's just something about being British that we don't want to lose – our great British traditions, the pub, the great British breakfast . . . That's why I'll never vote for the euro.' Lord Wilson commented: 'A stated aspiration of BBC journalism is to "make the important interesting", but there is a danger that instead they make the interesting important.'

But often, the outcome is more consistent, as the consensus fills the knowledge vacuum. American media consumers may stand back aghast in January 2006 when Bolivia elects a new president, Evo Morales, who immediately declares his antipathy to their nation. They don't know what he's talking about: the news factory has left them in ignorance. It simply has not told them, for example, the story of the Bolivian trade union leader, Casimiro Huanca, who was shot dead in December 2001 by troops which had been trained and supported by the American government to crack down on cocaine production. This incident generated considerable hostility towards the US Embassy there, and no coverage at all in the international mass media. Too far away, too expensive, too boring, too un-American. A left-wing website which did cover the story quoted an American journalist who happened to be in Bolivia at the time: 'You need 20 to 25 deaths on a daily basis in order to get a story into the United States press.' It also quoted a Catholic priest who described the press as 'psychotic' in its pursuit of falsehood in preference to truth.

It was exactly this same blind focus in the news factory which left the American people after the attacks of September 2001 asking in genuine ignorance: 'Why do they hate us?' In the same way, it has left them for decades in overwhelming ignorance of the behaviour of US security and intelligence agencies which has created such hostility to their country.

This is part of an overwhelming pattern, which was well highlighted by AlertNet, a news agency which specialises in international disaster relief (funded, to their great credit, by the Reuters Foundation). In 2005, AlertNet asked more than a hundred organisations working on the ground in trouble spots around the world, to list the ten stories which most deserved to be covered. They produced a list of non-stories, headed by the death of 3.8 million people in the war in the Congo, a tale of economic rape and physical suffering which breaks far too many factory rules to win headlines.

The AlertNet list went on to cover a clutch of other battle zones which were beyond the reach of churnalists, in Sierra Leone, Liberia and Ivory Coast, Chechnya and northern Uganda; as well as the progress of malaria, tuberculosis, diarrhoea and HIV. They also listed 'the progressive slaughter of non-Arabs in Sudan including Darfur'. This was a story which had been standing outside the news factory, begging for coverage, for years. But, with rare exceptions, it couldn't get in until celebrities like the Hollywood actor George Clooney started pushing it. It just broke too many rules – expensive and difficult to cover, too complicated (just who are the good guys out there?), slow-burning, boring, depressing and no Americans.

A report in July 2005, by the Genocide Intervention Fund and the American Progress Action Fund, compared the scale of coverage of three stories on US television during the previous month: the fighting in Sudan which had killed 400,000 people in Darfur and now spread to the east of the country; the activities of Tom Cruise who had announced his engagement and publicly defended his involvement with the Church of Scientology; and the trial on charges of child molestation of Michael Jackson. They found that Tom Cruise got twelve times as much coverage as Darfur, and Michael Jackson got fifty times as much. Highlighting the news factory's urgent requirement for sympathetic Western victims, the same report measured the coverage a year earlier of the deaths of eight white tourists at the hands of guerrillas in Rwanda and found that that single incident received almost exactly the same attention as the deaths of tens of thousands in Sudan over the whole year. The report concluded: 'Put simply, if television does not cover the genocide in Sudan, it does not exist in the minds of many Americans.'

You can see the patterns in here: the arbitrary and the irrational replacing real judgements; the casual recycling of unreliable claims; and the structural bias towards the political and moral beliefs of the most powerful groups in society. This last point is worth dwelling on for a moment, because this is the subject which so often persuades outside critics of the media to guess that there must be widespread conspiracy. There is sometimes conspiracy. But it is building on the power of these rules of production: the selection of safe facts and safe ideas; the fear of the electric fence; the aversion to context and subtlety; the obsessive recycling of the stories which other media are running; the succumbing to moral panic. All of these rules tend to favour the status quo. All of them, furthermore, are reinforced by the impact of PR which (as we shall see in more detail in Chapters 5 and 6) is primarily a tool for the powerful. And all of this is passed on with pride by reporters who believe that their refusal to make judgements amounts to the virtue of objectivity.

This is ideology of a particularly powerful kind. In a totalitarian state, media lies stand up proud and insult their readers direct to their faces. In the free society, the lies rest quietly and in comfort inside clichés – clichés of language and of fact and of value – and slip gently past their readers' defences with the ease of a familiar friend on the doorstep. In a totalitarian state, ideology stands up and announces itself in every sentence – 'the glorious fatherland . . . the heroic soldiers . . . our great leader and immortal helmsman'. In a democracy, the ideology is still there in every sentence, but it lies down and hides beneath the surface. There is no need for a totalitarian regime when the censorship of commerce runs its blue pencil through every story.

I think there is no great conspiracy here (although governments and owners certainly plot when they need to). But I don't see any of this as being planned. If the idea of the news factory captures the image of journalists tied to their keyboards etc., it is in another sense misleading since it suggests conveyor belts smoothly and efficiently conveying each item of information to its correct destination on the production line.

The whole thing is crazier than that. It's more like watching a mouse being thrown into a washing machine. Anything can happen to frail fragments of information as they are hurled from hand to hand, whirled through a clash of conflicting needs – do what the others do, be exclusive, steal other people's exclusives, sell papers, sell a bunch of second-hand ideas, save money, make money, make friends, hurt enemies, hype it, ramp it, tweak it, match it to a picture, match it to a space, splash it on the front, bury it inside. This isn't a conspiracy. It's just a mess.

The picture as a whole is much worse than the one I had expected to find when I set out to write this book. I started with the millennium bug, with the simple idea that the main reason why journalists produce stories which contain falsehood, distortion and propaganda, is that they don't know the truth themselves. Then I began to see the scale of this Flat Earth news.

I found that national newspapers and broadcasters across the developed world have been taken over by a new generation of corporate owners, who have cut their staffing and increased their output, heavily restricting the time available for journalists to check the truth of what they write. I found that the same owners have caused the disintegration of the old network of local, front-line reporters, in domestic and foreign coverage, heavily restricting the flow of raw information to these hard-pressed national newsrooms.

I found that national journalists have been forced to rely overwhelmingly on the output of a tiny number of wire agencies – one for the whole of the UK, just two big ones for the whole of the world – and that none of these agencies has anything like the manpower needed to cover its patch; none of them has anything like the scope of the old network it has replaced; none of them generally gives its own editorial staff enough time to function as effective journalists; none of them generally attempts to check the truth (as opposed to the verbatim accuracy) of its stories.

I found the national news outlets, the remaining local outlets (in the UK and abroad) and the key news agencies are all monitoring each other's output, all focusing on a smaller and smaller selection of stories and angles, a process which has only been reinforced by the arrival of global news portals, which recycle the same output without attempting to check any of it.

Original, truth-telling journalism survives at the margins and commonly tends to be overwhelmed by the consensus account, whether true or false.

What we are looking at here is a global collapse of information-gathering and truth-telling. And that leaves us in a kind of knowledge chaos, where the very subject matter of global debate is shifted from the essential to the arbitrary; where government policy, cultural values, widespread assumptions, declarations of war and attempts at peace all turn out to be poisoned by distortion; where ignorance is accepted as knowledge and falsehood is accepted as truth.

I found that this entire structure – nationally and globally, the news outlets themselves and the agencies which feed them – is now inherently vulnerable to being infiltrated by stories which are generated by PR acting for commercial and political interests.

Within this alarming picture, that may be the most disturbing single element. And it is to the generally unseen world of PR and propaganda that we should turn next.

Part Three
Hidden Persuaders

'Some of these persuaders, in their energetic endeavors to sway our actions, seem to fall unwittingly into the attitude that man exists to be manipulated.'

Vance Packard, *The Hidden Persuaders*

5. The Private Life of Public Relations

When the American energy company Enron collapsed in a cloud of dishonest accounting in December 2001, 21,000 people lost their jobs and thousands of others lost their pensions and life savings. A few months later, the *Sunday Times* came up with a UK end to the story: 'Three British investment bankers were at the centre of the schemes used by Enron, the bankrupt American energy group, to hide hundreds of millions of pounds of losses from the financial markets.'

The story, by one of their City reporters, Paul Durman, revealed that the three British bankers had earned millions of pounds in fees by carrying out dozens of complex deals for the corrupt American company and it described their extravagant self-indulgence as they cemented their 'cosy relationship' with Enron with alcohol, skiing and regular visits to lap-dancing clubs, all on their expense accounts. Such was the excess of the three bankers that a former colleague had written a thinly disguised novel about their adventures in the US, *The Pursuit of Happiness – Overpaid, Oversexed and Over There*. The *Sunday Times* focused, in particular, on the lead British banker, Gary Mulgrew, who was described as 'fiercely competitive' with 'a massive ego' and 'scars on his arms' from his former career as a nightclub bouncer.

Over the following year, there were more embarrassing stories about Enron's three British assistants. A Dutch bank, Rabobank, which had lost money in the Enron collapse, sued them personally for $517 million, accusing them of 'the deliberate looting of Enron assets'. The Dutch writ claimed: 'The participation of these three was grossly morally reprehensible, and involved such wanton dishonesty as to imply a criminal indifference to civil obligations.' There was more coverage of 'the womanising buccaneers' (*Independent*), lots more quotes from the novel based on the activities of 'Gary Mulgrew and his cronies' (*Evening Standard*), and then a burst of prominent news stories in June 2002 when the three of them were formally charged by the FBI with using their Enron contacts for a scam which had conned their own employers, a subsidiary of the National Westminster Bank, yielding a swift $7.3 million which they were said to have split between the three of them.

The *Daily Telegraph* ran the most detailed account of the FBI's allegation. The story claimed that the three bankers had persuaded NatWest to sell its stake in a company at a knock-down price without revealing that the three of them owned an option in the outfit which was buying this stake. Within a week of making this deal, they had sold the stake on to Enron at a hugely inflated price, making a personal profit of $7.3 million while their corrupt Enron contacts pocketed even more for their personal stakes in the same deal. As an exclusive, the *Telegraph* published several emails which were alleged to have been exchanged between the three of them, salivating over the huge profit they were going to make if Enron agreed to pay an inflated price, and discussing the motive for one of their Enron contacts, Andrew Fastow, to help them. One of the three, David Bermingham, was said to have written: 'I will be the first to be delighted if he has found a way to lock it in and steal a large portion himself . . . We should be able to appeal to his greed.'

The story bubbled along gently for two more years until the summer of 2004, when the FBI formally declared its intention to extradite the three men to face trial in Houston, Texas, for their alleged scam. Most newspapers carried a line from an FBI affidavit: 'This was the quintessential inside job because NatWest did not know about the robbery until the collapse of Enron.' In October 2004, Bow Street Magistrates' Court ordered their extradition.

And then a funny thing happened. Fleet Street changed direction. Completely. The 'former bouncer' and his 'cronies' with their alleged corruption and their extravagant lifestyle became the object of an emotional national campaign, which was supported by every major newspaper and which drew in the vociferous encouragement of numerous pressure groups, MPs from all three main parties and a host of senior businessmen, finally generating a rebellion in the House of Lords and an emergency debate in the House of Commons dedicated to defending the three of them. What happened? PR happened.

Just as their case was going to Bow Street Magistrates' Court, the three accused contacted a company called Bell Yard Communications, which specialises in 'public reputation management during times of corporate crisis or dispute' and which claims a particular skill in 'understanding pressure points peculiar to legal actions'. Bell Yard knows how to handle the press.

Most PR activity does not involve outright falsehood. If you trap a press officer in the corner with a hostile question, some of them certainly will lie; and there are some stunning examples (which we will come to) of PR companies engaging in the dirtiest of dirty tricks. Much more often, however, PR will distort – a gentler, albeit almost equally destructive, art which involves the judicious selection of truths and issues, and the often very skilful manipulation of reporters to persuade them to focus only on those chosen angles.

According to some of those closely involved, when Bell Yard took on the case of the three bankers, its founder, Melanie Riley, rapidly saw the story she wanted. Fleet Street must stop talking about the alleged guilt and extravagance of these three men and must focus instead on one single aspect of their case, the new Extradition Act under whose terms the three men now faced trial in Texas. This was indeed a very vulnerable pressure point.

The act had been hurried through Parliament in 2003 primarily as an aid to the extradition of terrorist suspects and yet here it was being used against businessmen. And it was lopsided, in that it now allowed the US to extradite from Britain without having its evidence tested in a British court; but Britain could still extradite from the US only if it produced its evidence and proved there was a case in front of an American judge. Melanie Riley decided to reinforce that angle by arguing that Houston was in such uproar about Enron's many local victims that the three bankers could never receive a fair trial there; and that, since the alleged victim of their fraud was a British bank, a trial should surely take place in Britain.

To convert this chosen story into Fleet Street coverage, Bell Yard went down two routes. On route one, Melanie Riley discreetly contacted politicians and pressure groups who might be sympathetic to this legal cause, with a six-page briefing note headed 'Inherent Injustice of Extradition Arrangements with the US'. Among others, she contacted a Liberal Democrat peer and QC, Lord Goodhart; Liberty, which had already raised doubts about the new law; Justice; and Fair Trials Abroad. They all saw the issue and became sources of quotes and corroboration towards whom Bell Yard could direct journalists.

On route two, Melanie Riley broke up the story into four different angles, to be targeted at different kinds of reporters. First, there was the law, with stories aimed at political and legal specialists. Lord Goodhart himself soon wrote an opinion piece in *The Times*. Second, there was human rights, aimed at liberal papers. The *Guardian* was the first to run . this, quoting the director of Liberty, Shami Chakrabarti. Third, there was the business angle, aimed at City journalists. One of those involved in the campaign told me that the *Evening Standard* City pages were a favourite vehicle: 'You just ring them up and pitch the story. Their City stories tend to run unchanged through the day and they're read by all the nationals, who pick their stories up and then they find it hard to change an angle once they've accepted it.' Finally, there was human interest, aimed at the news pages and broadcast outlets, with lots of stories about British subjects being paraded into an American court in shackles and orange jumpsuits. Again, the *Evening Standard* went first, with a suddenly sympathetic interview with Gary Mulgrew, standing outside the home which he said he stood to lose, as legal costs swallowed his assets.

The PR story started to roll forward. Understanding the rules of production in the news factory, Bell Yard kept the coverage cheap and safe and simple, and looked to generate events as pegs for their material. Melanie Riley, for example, backed a decision to focus the issue by suing the Serious Fraud Office for failing to prosecute them in the UK and decided to seed the story with Andrew Gilligan, the former BBC reporter who by then had moved to the *Evening Standard*. 'He doesn't like the government and he's bright enough to understand the issues,' according to one of those involved. Gilligan ran the story, angled around the wrongness of a US trial; and the following day, the nationals ran it too, with the same angle. David Bermingham had been chosen as the lead man for interviews and rapidly learned to deliver crisp, clear sound bites. 'I cannot imagine anyone has taken the SFO to court for not prosecuting them before,' he told Gilligan. 'I cannot imagine that anyone has ever taken the SFO to court before for not investigating them,' he told the *Daily Telegraph*.

In principle, the media could have refused to go along with Bell Yard's strategy. In practice, they went for it, like a baby fastening on a teat. Melanie Riley pushed the story personally with journalists from PA, Reuters, the Bloomberg financial news agency, the *Financial Times*, the *Guardian*, the *Independent*, the *Telegraph*, *The Times*, the *Evening Standard*, as well as tabloids, Sundays, broadcast outlets and some regional papers. Once the story had been established in a few papers, the others were sucked in by Ninja Turtle syndrome, and she managed to generate hundreds of articles, all of them on her angle. The suspect criminals became victims of the law. The stories about high-living womanisers became features about family men, worried about their children. The former bouncer and his cronies became 'the NatWest Three' with its echo of the wrongly convicted Guildford Four and Birmingham Six. Going with the angle, journalists simply dropped all reference to the Dutch bank suing them for 'the deliberate looting of Enron assets'; and to their alleged emails about stealing and greed; and to their overpaid and oversexed antics in the thinly disguised novel.

Even the *Sunday Times*, which had first broken the story of the three men's involvement with Enron, changed angle: 'Three British bankers are facing extradition to America to answer fraud charges despite the fact that no evidence has been brought before a British court,' the paper told its readers. At one point, the *Sunday Times* ran a background feature of nearly 2,000 words without a single reference to the material which one of its own reporters had originally put into the public domain.

By February 2006, the echo chamber was working well, with high-profile businessmen, MPs and pressure groups all agitating to stop the extradition and providing secondary stories for Fleet Street. The three bankers then opened a second front, employing a further PR company, called M Communications, in search of the parliamentary contacts of one of its consultants, Adrian Flook, a former PR man who had become the Conservative MP for Taunton for four years before losing his seat in April 2005. Flook set about using his knowledge of parliamentary rules to keep the three bankers in the UK by amending the controversial Extradition Act, enlisting the support first of key conservatives including the shadow attorney general, Dominic Grieve, and then of the Liberal leader, Sir Menzies Campbell, and then of numerous backbenchers on both sides of the house – right-wingers who wanted to stand up for British businessmen and left-wingers who wanted to stand up to the perceived aggression of the United States. So it was that the former Tory leader, Michael Howard, found himself in alliance, for example, with the rebellious Respect MP, George Galloway. The more they became involved, the more there were stories for Fleet Street; the more stories there were, the more people became involved.

As the July deadline for the three bankers' extradition approached, Bell Yard cranked up the coverage. They decided to focus stories on the business community and, in June, the agency set up a news event by organising a march through central London by angry businessmen, who presented a petition to the Home Secretary. Far bigger demonstrations go unreported on a regular basis, but Bell Yard used its media contacts to make sure this was a very big story. Bell Yard also stepped hard on the human interest pedal, setting up David Bermingham's wife, Emma, with the *Evening Standard*; Gary Mulgrew's wife, Laura, with the *Mail on Sunday*; David and Emma 'at home' with the *Independent*; David alone with the *Guardian*. There were lots of stories about their having to spend two years in jail awaiting trial and facing thirty-five-year prison sentences and much talk of foot chains and hand chains and leg chains and orange jumpsuits. Aidan Barclay, chairman of the Telegraph Group, took a personal interest, and the *Daily Telegraph*, which had first printed the men's emails about stealing and greed, now launched a campaign called 'Fair Trials for Business' with an open letter to the Home Secretary, a special campaign spot on its website and a torrent of sympathetic stories. David Bermingham became one of the few suspects awaiting trial to be given space to write his own comment piece in the *Daily Mail*.

Bell Yard's story reached a climax in mid July when, following Adrian Flook's work, the House of Lords rebelled against the government, using a police bill to try to amend the Extradition Act; and the House of Commons held a three-hour emergency debate which cornered the tough-on-crime Tony Blair into promising that British officials in the US would do their best 'to see whether there is any support or assurances that we can give'. But the extradition went ahead. On 13 July, David Bermingham stood outside a police station and delivered his final quote to the cameras: 'It is a very sad day for British people. We have been let down by our government.' As the three men set off for the airport to fly to Houston, Sky TV hired a helicopter to follow their journey, and Emma Bermingham was filmed sad and alone at home.

Once the three men got to Houston, it soon became clear that they were not going to have to spend two years in jail awaiting trial: they spent one night in a hotel and were given bail. There were no orange jumpsuits: they wore their own clothes to court, although they did have to wear handcuffs. There was no prospect of a thirty-five-year jail sentence: a prosecutors' memo, lodged with the court, showed that the maximum possible sentence was nine years. And the prosecutors explained that the case had to be heard in Houston, because all the Enron paperwork was there and, more important, their key witness – the three men's old Enron contact, Andrew Fastow – was already serving a prison sentence there.

At this point, the *Guardian* broke ranks and published details of a slide show which the three men had put together in February 2000 as part of their alleged scam to make $7.3 million out of Enron and its limited partners (LPs). In emails, they had worried about the slide show's contents: 'Problem is that it is too obvious [to both Enron and LPs] what is happening [i.e. robbery of LPs], so probably not attractive.' They had worried too about other people at NatWest finding out what they were doing, and so David Bermingham had sent a colleague a message to cover their tracks, which he had then forwarded to his two friends with a note: 'This is an attempt to head the obvious off at the pass and keep the lid on the thing. Large numbers of people are asking what we are up to. I hate lies.'

The *Guardian* story continued by quoting the head of the Serious Fraud Office, Robert Wardle, who said he was astonished that the men had become a cause célèbre: 'In this case, most of the evidence is in America – the main witnesses are there, as are most of the documents. Even if you think the new extradition arrangements are unfair, in this case the evidence that was produced would have been enough to secure extradition even under the old act.'

But he was too late. PR had had its way with Fleet Street.

Years ago, Rupert Murdoch personally intervened in a story which had fallen into the hands of reporters at the old *National Star*, one of his first American titles. They had received an anonymous letter from somebody who claimed to have the inside track on the mysterious disappearance of Jimmy Hoffa, a union leader who had rubbed up too close to the Mafia.

The reporters were told to place an advertisement in the *International Herald Tribune* ('Old French sheet music required') to signal their interest in following up the story. They did so and were soon contacted by a nervous character called Mr Josephs, who explained that he had been hired to kill Hoffa, had turned down the job and now feared he would himself be killed to silence him. With Murdoch's approval, the *Star* paid for Mr Josephs to fly from London to Las Vegas, where one of its reporters arranged to meet him outside the Roxy Theatre on Sunset Boulevard to give him some cash for living expenses: a car pulled up; a rear window wound down; the reporter handed over the cash; Mr Josephs said, Thank you. Over a series of meetings, Mr Josephs met the *Star* reporters and told in some detail how Jimmy Hoffa had been tortured and then murdered in the back of a van before being buried somewhere in New Jersey. The *Star* needed evidence. Mr Josephs said that was no problem: he had it, safely hidden away in a luggage locker at Cologne airport. But he would need money, to get away from the threat to himself from Hoffa's assassins.

Keen for his paper to nail the story, Murdoch sent his secretary with an envelope containing $20,000 in cash for a *Star* reporter, Piers Ackerman, who flew with it to Cologne. Following Mr Josephs' instructions, Ackerman went to a hotel lobby and handed over the cash to an associate of Mr Josephs known only as 'the Dutchman', who then directed him to the Lufthansa desk at the airport. There, the reporter picked up a key and the number of a luggage locker. Inside it, he found an old pair of dirty brown shoes – the very shoes, according to Mr Josephs, which Jimmy Hoffa had been wearing when he met his painful end. The *Star* sent the shoes for spectrographic analysis, which unfortunately yielded no link to Hoffa. They took them to Hoffa's son, who unfortunately said they were nothing like his father's shoes. Still, Rupert Murdoch ran the story.

In truth, the old brown shoes had never been anywhere near Jimmy Hoffa. Nor had Mr Josephs. The shoes came cheap from a second-hand charity shop; and Mr Josephs was a conman, better known as Joe Flynn, also known as Edward Christian, Charles Benson, Harry Banks and Edward Begg, though his real name is Barry Edward Gray, born in south London on 26 January 1934. For his work in selling Rupert Murdoch an old pair of shoes, Gray filched a total of some $30,000 from the press baron's pocket. During a twenty-year career as a specialist in conning the media, Gray went on to earn many thousands more by successfully manipulating some of Fleet Street's finest. Towards the end of this career, he told a French writer, Adam Pianko: 'English journalists – I despise them. One paper called me a low-grade Walter Mitty. But if I'm just a dreamer, what are they? Who published my tall stories?'

Gray's skill as a conman was to understand exactly what journalists wanted and then to fabricate what they needed: the media door opened before him. A good PR works in the same way. Barry Gray fabricated to sell a lie. In PR, the fabrication may well be an attempt to sell the truth (or some distortion of it); it may well be an attempt to promote a story that deserves to be covered (or that richly deserves to be ignored). But fabrication is the heart of PR, the fabrication of news which is designed to open the media door. As Edward Bernays, the formative figure of early PR, put it: 'The counsel on public relations not only knows what news value is; but, knowing it, he is in a position to make news happen.'

Bernays, for example, famously made news happen when the American Tobacco Company in 1929 asked him to help it increase the sales of Lucky Strikes among women. The problem for the tobacco company was that cigarettes were still considered not quite ladylike. Bernays chose his story: this was about freedom. Then he fabricated some news: he hired thirty models to parade through the middle of New York City on Easter Sunday, all smoking Lucky Strikes, which he described to journalists as 'torches of freedom'. His chosen story ran all over the United States. Other women read it and spontaneously held their own 'torches of freedom' events, smoking for freedom, making more news, pushing up the sales of Lucky Strikes.

Journalists in search of quick, easy stories are fundamentally vulnerable to this kind of pseudo-news, contrived by specialists who understand the rules of production in the news factory. In his extraordinarily prescient book *The Image*, published in 1962, the American historian Daniel Boorstin studied the growing torrent of manufactured stories which was already flowing through the US mass media and warned: 'In a democratic society, the people can be flooded by pseudo-events. Freedom of speech and of the press includes freedom to create pseudo-events.'

At its simplest, the pseudo-event simply and overtly couples up journalists with carefully selected information. We have completely lost track of it now, but in the early days of mass-circulation newspapers, the very idea of an interview was regarded as a regrettable artifice. Boorstin suggests that the first occasion on which a journalist was persuaded to stage a formal interview was in August 1859 when the *New York Tribune* ran a verbatim account of a conversation with Brigham Young, leader of the Church of Jesus Christ of Latter-Day Saints (better known as the Mormons). Ten years later, he records, the *Nation* was still warning that this kind of interview 'is generally the joint product of some humbug of a hack politician and another humbug of a reporter'. There is a point here: almost all interviews are generated not by the reporter actively uncovering the truth, but by the interviewee's PR adviser actively making news to sell a policy or a product.

And it is the same with the press conference and the press release and the photo opportunity. The stories which they produce may or may not be legitimate, but all of them are pseudo-events, created to open the media door. Some also convey subtle messages. Dealing with the murder of five prostitutes in Ipswich in December 2006, Suffolk Police consciously set out to reassure the public by having their press conferences led by a detective chief superintendent, Stuart Gull, knowing that reporters would assume they were hearing their news direct from the man who was running the inquiry. In fact, the opposite was true: each murder inquiry was being run by a senior detective; Gull fronted the press conferences precisely because he was not busy with the investigation.

However, just as often, the pseudo-event is disguised. Every PR adviser to whom I have spoken agrees that the best PR conceals its own hand. The overt links to the media and the whole well-worn idea of 'spin' scarcely begin to capture the breadth and ingenuity of the tactics which are now used by the global industry of public relations. And it is this huge industry of manipulation – targeted at a structurally vulnerable media – which feeds falsehood and distortion directly into our news channels, without the old-fashioned need to use proprietors or advertisers as levers.

PR fabricates pseudo-incidents, from Bernay's 'torches of freedom' march to Bell Yard's businessmen traipsing through the centre of London in their suits. When PETA – People for Ethical Treatment of Animals – flour-bombed the London fashion show in February 2006, or when they threw fake blood over the audience at the International Fur Fair, or chucked a tofu pie at Calvin Klein, they were fabricating news. 'We're stunt queens,' according to PETA's director, Ingrid Newkirk, in a *Guardian* interview. What is being fabricated is not just news, but news with a predetermined angle – and pictures are usually the key ingredient.

When President Bush announced 'the end of combat operations' in Iraq in May 2003, he didn't do it from the front door of his ranch or the podium at the White House: his PR advisers arranged for him to put on an airman's combat gear and to fly out to an aircraft carrier full of journalists off the coast of California, where he was thus projected as both victor and combat hero. When he wanted to indicate his solidarity with US troops, still up to their neck in combat operations six months later, he didn't just put out a press release: he flew into Baghdad airport on Thanksgiving Day, kitted out in an army jacket, and was filmed surrounded by beaming soldiers with a large and well-roasted turkey which, as the *Washingon Post* later revealed, turned out to be a stage prop complete with decorative grapes. Two hours later, with the image of his solidarity with the troops already flowing through global media, he flew out again. (Caught out by the continuing fighting in Iraq, the White House eventually changed its website to make it appear that the President had only ever announced the end of 'major' combat operations.)

Some of the reporters and photographers who covered the removal of Israeli settlers from the Gaza Strip in August 2005 strongly suspect that they were watching a sequence of carefully stage-managed pseudo-incidents. The removal was central to the political need for the then Prime Minister, Ariel Sharon, to reposition himself as a man who was willing to compromise for the sake of peace. For six days, global media outlets were flooded with pictures of tearful Israelis being hauled out of their homes by soldiers. The removal was real and doubtless distressing but, according to journalists who spoke to the *Guardian* in January 2006, the incidents which the media covered had been prearranged between the settlers and the Israeli Army: the settlers had agreed to throw only harmless missiles such as flour and tomatoes and 'pickles – as long as the pickles had been removed from the can'; and the army had agreed to use small squads and minimum force to take the settlers away. 'There are numerous reports of hysterics and tears that appeared to be staged for the cameras,' according to the *Guardian* piece, which added that the illegal Israeli settlement of the West Bank was then proceeding 'at a breathtaking pace' without media coverage. In the same way, the removal of thousands of Palestinians from their homes was a media non-story. Reflecting on the coverage of the Gaza settlers, the picture editor of a major news agency said: 'It was a masterpiece. Afterwards, we all felt we played a game and that we had been used, bought with great pictures.'

PR also fabricates pseudo-groups who pump apparently independent stories into the media and sometimes masquerade as spontaneous grass-roots organisations which create a mass of newsworthy activity (known among cynical PR advisers as 'AstroTurf', because their grass roots aren't real).

In their exposé of the PR industry, *Toxic Sludge is Good For You*, John Stauber and Sheldon Rampton cite the promotional material of a US company, Davies Communications, which claims that its founder, John Davies, 'can make a strategically planned program look like a spontaneous explosion of community support'. Davies's website currently boasts: 'At Davies, we don't believe in fate. We make fate happen. We've been crafting the opinions and perceptions that our clients need for 20 years . . . Perception is reality.'

As a result of paperwork disclosed in US court cases, we now know that when the tobacco companies in the 1950s found themselves under pressure from the discovery of the link between smoking and cancer, they hired PR companies to create a network of pseudo-groups to massage public thinking on their behalf. Hill & Knowlton, who were then the biggest PR agency in America, duly created the Council for Tobacco Research and the Tobacco Institute as apparently independent organisations to produce research to defend their sales. Internal memos make it plain that the PR object was certainly not to tell the truth about tobacco but to engage in the judicious selection of facts, specifically to select any kind of scientific reference to any kind of doubt about the link to cancer. As one memo put it: 'Doubt is our product since it is the best means of competing with the "body of facts" that exists in the mind of the general public.'

While Hill & Knowlton's two pseudo-groups hired experts to remould the public consensus, a second PR agency, Burson-Marsteller, created the National Smokers Alliance as an AstroTurf group, to hold public meetings and hassle politicians, changing the tobacco story from a threat to health to a threat to freedom: 'If "Anti America" is pushing a discriminatory smoking ban in your workplace, speak up!' All this opened the media door to coverage which was specifically designed to distort the facts.

Since then, PR companies have created a mass of pseudo-groups to fabricate grass-roots activity on their behalf, including, for example: Cancer United (set up by Weber Shandwick for Roche to push its anti-cancer drugs in Europe); Americans for Constitutional Freedom (Gray and Co. for the porn industry); Americans Against Unfair Gas Taxes (Beckel Cowan for the American Petroleum Institute); the Council for Agricultural Science and Technology (Shandwick for the food industry); CropGen and the Agricultural Biotechnology Association (Lexington for GM food companies); and the Coalition for Health Insurance Choices, created for the Health Insurance Association of America to block President Clinton's plans for new medical insurance and led by a PR specialist called Blair Childs. Childs shared some of his techniques with a 1994 conference in Chicago, titled 'Shaping Public Opinion – If You Don't Do It, Somebody Else Will', where he highlighted the use of 'positive' words for the names of pseudo-groups such as 'fairness', 'choice' and 'alliance' and reflected on the numerous different kinds of people who had been sucked into his AstroTurf: 'It was an amazing array, and they were all doing something.' They were making news.

The food industry in Europe recently has been funding groups to protect its position against public and government alarm over obesity, junk food, misleading food labelling, diabetes and the advertising of fatty foods to children. British newspapers routinely carry reports and quotes on diet from the Social Issues Research Centre, the British Nutrition Foundation and the International Life Sciences Foundation and routinely fail to point out that all three have received significant funding variously from Cadbury Schweppes, Nestlé, Kelloggs, the Dairy Council, Kraft and the Sugar Bureau. In the same way, in 2003, Fleet Street reported the comments of a nutritionist called Dr Susan Jebb who attacked the Atkins Diet as 'a massive health risk', without explaining that her research into the low-carbohydrate diet had been funded by the Flour Advisory Bureau. This kind of research may or may not be accurate; but it is the hidden hand of PR which is paying for it to happen and promoting it into the news.

Reuters was caught out badly in November 2005, when it ran a story about the success of GM crops in Africa, based on quotes from Dr Florence Wambugu who runs a group called Africa Harvest in Nairobi. The agency was forced to correct the story after the British PR-monitoring group Spinwatch pointed out that Africa Harvest had been funded by GM companies and that Dr Wambugu was an adviser to DuPont, one of the giants of the GM industry, none of which had been disclosed in the original Reuters story.

PR also produces pseudo-experts. In December 2003, BBC radio ran a story on *Money Box* which was recycled through its website, claiming that toys were not merely good Christmas gifts but good investments too, and citing specialist auctions run by a company called Vectis. The story quoted one David Barzilay as 'a keen collector of toys' who had made a profit of more than £40,000 with his collection and who agreed that auctions were a good place to start. Two years earlier, the BBC had run a very similar story about the hidden financial value of old toys for sale at auction, quoting one David Barzilay – but, this time, as an official PR spokesman for specialist auctioneers Vectis. (Curiously, the toy industry in the US similarly produced an expert on toys, Christopher Byrne, known as 'the Toy Guy' and widely used in media stories, who turned out to be a PR frontman for toy manufacturers.)

In the same way, think tanks, which are funded by corporations with specific PR interests, award their staff pseudo-titles with the ring of academic respectability, such as 'senior fellow' or 'research director', and see them regularly used in broadcast debates and newspapers as though they were independent experts without any vested interest. Like most PR tactics, this began in the United States where neoconservative think tanks like Heritage have been allowed to slip their ideologues into the news factory as regular guests. But it has spread to Europe.

The Stockholm Network, for example, which was set up in 1997, links more than 115 neocon think tanks across the Continent with funds from giant pharmaceutical and oil companies, and claims to 'influence many millions of Europeans every year'. A Mr Dan Lewis has cropped up all over the quality end of Fleet Street, as a multitalented expert arguing for cuts in public transport and cuts in government spending, for scrapping the Kyoto Protocol on climate change and promoting the role of business in dealing with global warming, and is variously described as the head of research at the Economic Research Council, the director of the Efficiency in Government Unit, the author of *The Official Guide to British Quangos*, the author of a Centre for Policy Studies report – and the environment director of the Stockholm Network.

The media door is so easy to open that some of these experts have simply promoted themselves and skewed news coverage even though they have no compelling qualification in their chosen subject. An outstanding example is Norman Brennan, who set himself up in 1994 as the Victims of Crime Trust and has become a routine source of quotes, promoting the crudest possible line in punitive criminal justice policy (longer sentences, guns for the police, more bobbies on the beat). Brennan has no special qualification to do this: he is a constable in the British Transport Police who is simply recycling his personal opinion as expertise. In the same way, Josephine Quintavalle has given hundreds of interviews as the face of Comment on Reproductive Ethics, promoting a conservative and even religious line on highly complex issues: her only qualification as an expert is that she used to be a counsellor with the anti-abortion group LIFE. Slightly more intriguing is Simon Barrett, who crops up as an expert in hair-raising stories about Arab terrorists. He is described variously as a spokesman for Terror Aware, a British terrorism analyst, director of the

International Coalition Against Terror and director of International Media Intelligence Analysis. The basis on which he claims to be an expert in terrorism is not clear, and his company accounts describe him merely as 'a journalist', but it may be significant that somebody called Simon Barrett used to be a spokesman for the Zionist Federation of Britain.

These self-proclaimed experts at least have a toehold on reality, unlike Mike Kenny who wandered through the media door in 2004 and became an expert on domestic violence against men, telling of his own experience of being beaten up by a girlfriend. With radio, television and *The Times* reporting his views, he set up a pressure group called It Does Happen 2 Men and announced the opening of three refuges, before it was revealed that none of his girlfriends had beaten him up, and he was convicted on two counts of deception. Tom Carew, who became a regular media expert on the SAS and wrote a book about his experiences fighting in Afghanistan, was similarly exposed as a liar by BBC *Newsnight*, punching a cameraman before he disappeared back out of the unlocked media door.

PR fabricates pseudo-evidence – surveys, polls and specially commissioned research. Surveys are a favourite, usually for commercial PR, usually released on a Sunday to fill the news vacuum for Monday morning's papers. A business is looking for free publicity; the PR outfit dreams up a catchy survey; often they simply stick a questionnaire on a website and offer a free mobile phone or a weekend in a hotel as a prize to encourage people to fill it in; they take the result and create news. So newspapers end up publishing stories about the nation's favourite Christmas lunch (promoting a consumer analysis company); the nation's favourite book (book seller); the year's oddest book title (book magazine); the world's sexiest men (women's magazine); women's sexiest bits (another women's magazine); world's sexiest things (sex store); pets getting fatter (animal charity); people's heads getting smaller (US university); soldiers getting more homesick (army); everybody getting more drunk (medical insurance company); everybody doing more sleepwalking (hotel chain); people buying more shredders (supermarket); people buying still more shredders (shredder seller); older people having less money (a bank); children having more money (a building society).

These stories don't just creep into the inside pages of the tabloids:

they swarm across newspapers of every kind. On a single Monday in November 2005, the *Guardian* ran nine different survey stories on its news pages, and the *Sun* ran nine others. Some of them are statistically baseless. One PR outfit, acting for a company who wanted to set up a service for finding lost mobile phones, informed the media that 63,000 mobile phones had been left in London taxis over the previous six months. The real figure, according to the Public Carriage Office, was 779. The survey, it turned out, was based on talking to precisely 131 out of the 24,000 cabbies in London. Still, the story got used.

As an adjunct to this, all kinds of groups now use PR to claim named days or weeks as their own. The first seven days of August 2007, for example, had at least forty-eight different PR causes attached to them in the United States, including National Watermelon Day, National Chocolate Chip Day, National Fresh Breath Day and National Icecream Sandwich Day, while the month as a whole was claimed for at least thirty-six PR causes including eyecare, peaches, parks and international air travel. Having claimed the day, PR can use it as a peg for artificial news.

Political PR also abuses surveys as a source of pseudo-evidence, selecting only the findings which it wants to promote. In early 2004, the Department of Culture organised a major consultation on the future of the BBC, which happened to coincide with the publication of the Hutton Report, which attacked the BBC for its coverage of Iraq in terms that provoked the resignation of its director general and its chairman of governors. The consultation, however, revealed a powerful public backlash against the government. 'The BBC was predominantly viewed as a wronged and wounded beast,' according to the official report of the consultation. 'Indeed, the attacks endured over the past year, perhaps culminating in the findings of the Hutton report, were considered by some respondents to be a badge of honour, symbolising the integrity and independence of the news coverage.' In the referendum of public opinion between BBC and government, it said, 'the BBC wins convincingly'. Even those who agreed that there was 'a culture of arrogance' within the BBC, 'maintained that such arrogance is positively endemic in the present government'. The importance of this backlash was registered in the public response to the central question of whether the BBC should be more accountable to government: 'More than any other single question in the consultation, this one produced remarkably consistent answers: the public want the BBC to remain or even to become more independent of government.'

But when the Department of Culture announced the results of this consultation in July 2004, it put out a press release which said: 'The BBC is still held in high esteem by the British public but there are some concerns about a general decline in quality, a report published today by Culture Secretary Tessa Jowell reveals.' The press release included not one single word about the backlash against the government since the Hutton Report, nor a word about its implications for the future of the corporation's relationship to government. And, as a result, there was not one single word about it in the subsequent media coverage, almost all of which accepted the Department of Culture's choice of angle about the 'general decline' in BBC quality.

There is a kind of pseudo-world being created here. Most of the quotes which come through press offices have never been anywhere near the mouth of those who are supposed to have said them. Reporters know that. As long as the readers don't realise, nobody is worried. The BBC press office was caught out by a rare rebel in March 2005 when the actor Christopher Eccleston loudly objected to their distributing pseudo-quotes in his name without even speaking to him, to explain why he had decided to stop playing Dr Who. Most of the articles which appear in newspapers under the byline of the Prime Minister or other members of the Cabinet have never been anywhere near their keyboards. Alastair Campbell's former deputy, Lance Price, blithely recalls in his *Spin Doctor's Diary* that 'I've written two letters to William Hague this week, one from Ian McCartney and one from Robin Cook.' Even resignation letters turn out to be pseudo: those of Peter Mandelson, Ron Davies and Geoffrey Robinson, for example, were all written by the Downing Street press office.

There are pseudo-leaks, the result not of any kind of digging by reporters but of PR advisers choosing to plant selected angles with selected and compliant reporters. There are pseudo-pictures, too. The US Republican Party, for example, put out a picture of George Bush talking to a crowd of soldiers, with a young boy sitting on his father's shoulders in the foreground waving the US flag. The picture was fake. The original shot showed

Bush speaking to a crowd of civilians, many of whom were holding banners in support of his electoral opponent, John Kerry; the boy in the foreground was wearing a Kerry T-shirt. The Republicans, picking up on a tactic from Stalinist propaganda, simply removed all signs of Kerry and dropped in images of soldiers to conceal their handiwork.

There are pseudo-illnesses, like social anxiety disorder or night-eating syndrome, invented or grossly exaggerated by PR agencies working for pharmaceutical companies. (International PR agents Cohn and Wolfe spread social anxiety disorder – also known as shyness – with such energy that, according to the *Washington Post*, media references to it leaped from fifty in 1997 to more than a billion in 1999 while sales of the drug they were pushing rose by 18%). There are pseudo-wars. At the height of the Monica Lewinsky scandal, President Clinton bombed the stuffing out of a pharmaceutical factory in Sudan on the grounds that it was manufacturing chemical weapons. It wasn't, but it beat Monica out of the headlines for a few days. Clinton may well have been inspired by the precedent of Ronald Reagan, who ordered the invasion of Grenada in October 1983, just as public opinion was turning against him after a suicide bomber killed 240 US marines in Beirut.

The whole business of celebrity reporting is riddled with fabrication. Daniel Boorstin caught the underlying phoniness in his 1962 book, when he observed the way in which the reality of heroism was being usurped by the artifice of celebrity: 'In the democracy of pseudo-events, anyone can become a celebrity, if only he can get into the news and stay there . . . The hero was distinguished by his achievement; the celebrity by his image or trademark. The hero created himself; the celebrity is created by the media. The hero was a big man; the celebrity is a big name.' According to the journalists who specialise in celebrity reporting, the mass of their coverage is contrived by PR agencies: even snatched paparazzi pictures, they say, are often set up by PR agencies, with the connivance of photographers, to look as though they are spontaneous. (One high-profile sportsman is said to use his mother as a go-between: he gets her to set up 'snatched' shots of him for a favoured pap who pays her a handsome commission for her assistance.)

But this pseudo-world is also a dirty world. In *Toxic Sludge is Good For You*, Stauber and Rampton tell of PR companies infiltrating pressure groups who oppose their clients, to gather intelligence and/or to screw up their activities: Hill & Knowlton's attempt to discredit Earth First! by sending out a phoney memo on their headed paper urging violence 'to fuck up the mega machine'; Ogilvy & Mather's PR campaign for Nestlé which included spying on the International Organisation of Consumer Unions, the Pesticide Action Network, trade unions and vicars; Ketchum's campaign for the California raisin industry to sabotage the launch of a book which reported findings of '110 industrial chemical and pesticide residues' in the raisins; Burson-Marsteller's campaign for Monsanto which included using two staff members to infiltrate opponents' meetings under cover of an AstroTurf group which they had created; Kaufman PR's campaign for the US National Dairy Board which contacted local reporters to put them off attending an opposition meeting and, as a fall-back, infiltrated half a dozen supporters into the meeting to speak up and change the angle, just in case any reporters did turn up.

Finally, most recently, PR has found new ways to target its fabrication of news on broadcast outlets. This emerged scandalously in the United States in 2004, when TV news stories which had all the appearance of being mainstream journalism were exposed as pre-packaged 'Video News Releases' produced by numerous branches of the federal government, using actors and PR professionals to pose as on-screen reporters to promote their policies including the invasions of Afghanistan and Iraq. The General Accounting Office in January 2005 ruled that these were illegal 'covert propaganda'. Following that GAO report, the Centre for Media and Democracy in March 2006 traced a further thirty-six VNRs, created for commercial clients including General Motors and Pfizer, which had been broadcast by a total of seventy-seven TV stations, almost always disguised as journalism produced by the TV station by adding its own graphics and/or using its own local anchor to introduce the pseudo-story from a script written by the PR agency.

This practice is now spilling over into European broadcasting. This is partly because American VNRs are distributed globally by Reuters and APTN, but also because European PR agencies have started to produce them. CAN Communicate in London specialises in VNRs for the world of sport, including, for example, promoting Adidas as a leading football brand during the 2006 World Cup. The Television

Consultancy works on 'consumer launches, corporate announcements and government campaigns' and was responsible, for example, for a VNR for the Department of Trade, warning about con men extracting money through the post by offering phoney prizes, which, the company says, 'was used extensively by broadcasters'.

British broadcasters like to claim that they do not use these VNRs. But they do. BBC's *Scotland Today* and *Reporting Scotland*, for example, used an unlabelled VNR funded by an insurance company to interview a would-be Olympic athlete, Joanne Finch, with the insurance company's logo on her shirt and also on a board behind her. More often, they use 'B roll footage', pictures shot by a PR company to push their story up the agenda, but with the script written by the broadcaster's own staff. The same is happening in radio. A company called Radio Lynx ('Create Great Radio') tells its clients: 'For just £500, we target over 500 stations nationwide with your editorial message in the form of pre-recorded interview or pre-packaged sound bite.'

Underlying all this fabrication of news is a consistent and explicit tactical understanding in the history of PR thinking that the best PR appeals to the irrational, that they should focus their work on the subconscious minds of their target audience.

It is no fluke that at the birth of PR, the man who did most to define its tactics was the nephew of Sigmund Freud, Edward L. Bernays. He studied his uncle's work in an attempt to convert its lessons from the assistance of individuals to the influencing of whole societies. As he put it: 'If we understand the mechanism and motives of the group mind, it is now possible to control and regiment the masses according to our will without their knowing it.'

By the 1950s and 60s, this had become a source of concern. Vance Packard published *The Hidden Persuaders* in 1957, with the opening words: 'This book is an attempt to explore a strange and rather exotic new area of modern life. It is about the way many of us are being influenced and manipulated – far more than we realize – in the patterns of our everyday life. Large-scale efforts are being made, often with impressive success, to channel our unthinking habits, our purchasing decisions, and our thought processes by the use of insights gleaned from psychiatry and social sciences.'

Packard went on to quote the president of the Public Relations Society of America, that 'the stuff with which we work is the fabric of men's minds'. He traced the adoption by leading PR companies of the discoveries of 'motivational research' – the use of psychoanalytical techniques to provoke a response which was either just below the conscious mind ('the level of prejudices, assumptions, fears, emotional promptings and so on') or down in the deep subconscious. Packard dug out examples of this at work in the commercial world, like the smokers who had been persuaded that they liked only one particular brand of cigarette but who, when blindfolded, could not tell one brand from another. They did not know it, but the reality was that it was not the cigarette but the 'image' of the cigarette to which they had formed an attachment. Soap was not for cleanliness but for beauty; cars were not for transport but for glamour.

At the same time as these 'depth' techniques were being developed for the commercial world, they were converted for political use too, notably during the First World War when Woodrow Wilson's government created the Committee on Public Information to use the symbolism and language of patriotism and freedom to procure mass support for the war in Europe. As the head of the committee, George Creel, put it: 'People do not live by bread alone; they live mostly by catchphrases.'

Vance Packard was moved to write *The Hidden Persuaders* partly because he could see this kind of appeal to the subconscious at work in the Republican campaign of 1956 when Dwight Eisenhower was returned to the White House with Richard Nixon as his vice president. He saw the PR men making their first appearance as electoral strategists; saw Eisenhower's press officer attending cabinet meetings and directly influencing policy. He saw how Eisenhower's heart attack in 1955, which should have reduced his status as a prospective leader, instead produced an irrational surge of support; saw how the PR men deliberately targeted this irrational level, packaging their candidates like consumer goods, converting them from ordinary humans into 'personalities', projecting Eisenhower as a wise grandfather, providing training in the appearance of 'candour', repeating key phrases on radio and key images on billboards, timing waves of TV adverts to go out after popular comedies, when viewers were, as John Steinbeck noticed, in a 'will-less, helpless state, unable to resist any suggestion offered'.

Packard concluded: 'The goal is mind-molding itself. No longer is the aim just to play on our subconscious to persuade us to buy a refrigerator or new motorboat that we may or may not need. The aim now is nothing less than to influence the state of our mind and to channel our behavior as citizens.'

This attempt to apply the raw material of psychology to the marketing of goods and politics, has developed from the early 'motivational research' which worried Vance Packard, through the programme of the Stanford Research Institute in California in the late 1970s to develop 'psychographic' models of the inner desires of groups of consumers, to the contemporary use of focus groups to link the PR agency's clients with finely tuned campaigns aimed at forming an attachment with the values and self-image of their target audiences.

As a single example of this focus on the subconscious, consider the imagery in an American TV campaign called 'Remember Freedom', broadcast in the period between the terrorist attacks of September 2001 and the invasion of Iraq in March 2003. This was produced by the Ad Council of America, which specialises in 'public service advertising . . . designed to make lasting and positive social change'. One of these ads told the story of a man named only as Tom, who was said to have migrated to the US from Cambodia. Sandor Ligetfalvy, editor of a freedom-of-speech website, analysed its imagery and found, for example, a single sequence which began with Tom asking 'Why did I come here?' and went on to display a quick-fire sequence of pictures of the US bald eagle with its mouth open, the eagle from a different angle, the Congress building, the Golden Gate Bridge, the eagle from yet another angle, the opening shot of the eagle with its mouth open again, the Statue of Liberty against a blue sky, the Statue of Liberty with Manhattan in the background, the Statue of Liberty from the ground with pigeons flying, Mount Rushmore, the word 'FREEDOM' in white on a black background, and, finally, Tom smiling and answering his own question with a single word, 'Freedom'. As the Ad Council itself says on its website: 'The results of our campaigns testify to the power of the Ad Council's messages.'

This deliberate targeting of the subconscious minds of its target audience is coupled with a second consistent and explicit theme in the history of PR thinking, that the masses are a political threat whose thinking must be controlled by the techniques of PR. This sounds like left-wing paranoia, but it is well documented. When he investigated the growth of the PR industry, Professor Stuart Ewen concluded in his book *PR! A Social History of Spin* that: 'A nervous preoccupation with the perils of democracy . . . has chaperoned the growth of corporate public relations for nearly a century.'

He traced this back to the politicisation of the working class in the early twentieth century through their acquisition of the vote and their creation of the trade union movement; through moments of collective panic among the power elite when the great capitalists were exposed as 'robber barons' by muckraking journalists; and then again when the system fell into structural failure during the depression of the 1920s.

In the aftermath of the depression, the head of PR at General Motors was concerned to defend not just his corporation but the capitalism which allowed it to exist: 'The challenge that faces us is to shake off our lethargy and through public relations make the American plan of industry stick. For, unless the contributions of the system are explained to consumers in terms of their own interest, the system itself will not stand against the storm of fallacies that rides the air.'

Ewen follows the long campaign by the corporate umbrella group, the National Association of Manufacturers, from the depression through to the era of communist scares, to use PR to create a consensus for capitalism, or, as they put it, 'to link free enterprise in the public consciousness with free speech, free press and free religion as integral parts of democracy'. So they used radio shows, films, billboards, advertisements and news coverage to hit the emotions of the masses with their catchphrase: 'There's no way like the American way.'

This is the industry which has now become so powerful – so large and so sophisticated in its methods – feeding the news factory with all or most of the material for 54% of the home news stories of the most prestigious media outlets in Britain. This is the industry which is engaged in 'the efficient mass production of pseudo-events', as Daniel Boorstin put it in 1962, adding: 'The media must be fed! The people must be informed! Most pleas for "more information" are misguided. So long as we define information as a knowledge of pseudo-events, "more information" will simply multiply the symptoms without curing the disease . . . We have become eager accessories to the great hoaxes of the age.'

And that was before Rupert Murdoch paid $30,000 for a pair of old boots.

A collection of (slightly elderly) internal paperwork fell into my hands from the back door of Freud Communications, a PR agency which has made an art form of manipulating news media into providing free coverage for its commercial clients. The paperwork captures some of the techniques of the pseudo-world at work, all of them owing more than a little to the con man's art, all of them reflecting the easy presumption that it knows exactly how to get what it wants from supposedly independent media.

For example, there is a proposal document, written in June 1998, to help BT sell a new cut-price deal for Saturday phone calls. Heading 1, Strategy, proposes a classic PR manoeuvre – 'the creation of National Chatterday.' Heading 2, Concept, explains that the aim is 'to name September 5 National Chatterday, so that BT effectively owns the first Saturday in September'. Heading 3, Rationale: 'To use National Chatterday as a springboard for other PR and promotional activity.'

This turns out to involve manufacturing news coverage by hiring celebrities for up to £5,000 each 'to feature in interviews about who they enjoy talking to, why they spend time on the telephone on a Saturday, whether they call friends to organise lunch, shopping or football during the day . . .' It lists eleven target celebrities, most of them TV presenters and chat-show hosts, and proposes to hook them up with Saturday newspaper supplements: 'Incorporated into the interview would be information about the BT Chatterday offer.' Easy enough, and if any of the interviews yields 'any celebrity gossip or previously unknown facts about the celebrity', Freud proposes to pass them on to other media outlets for more stories. The rationale, as spelled out in the paperwork, is 'to receive perceived endorsement from both the Saturday publication and the chosen celebrities'. In parallel to this, they propose straight press releases to national and regional media explaining the cut-price deal, and a double-page spread in a national paper offering a cut-price trip to Disneyland in Paris for some of those who sign up for the deal.

In another proposal for BT, the paperwork shows Freud's staff deliberately selecting story angles to sidestep awkward facts. They want to persuade people to leave competing phone companies, but they have to deal with the unfortunate problem that some of these rival companies are cheaper than BT, so they break up the campaign into different geographical areas in which BT faces different rivals: 'In areas where BT is price-competitive, the campaign will emphasise the value for money offered by BT. In areas where BT is not price-competitive, the emphasis will be on BT's quality of service.' In the same way, the stated aim of the campaign is 'to reduce defections from BT', but the press release will turn that on its head 'to communicate the message that customers are returning to BT'. Easy enough. And the entire campaign will sell the idea of customers coming back to BT as part of a new fashion for everybody to come back to 'retro' style, with pogo sticks and lava lamps as competition prizes, retro musicals as a peg for promotions, and the 'BT Come Back' radio quiz where callers have to answer questions about people or fads which have made a comeback.

The Freud paperwork is littered with plans for the invention of pseudo-events: the high-profile rock show, which is really a vehicle to sell men's deodorant; the glossy fashion shoots which are contrived to promote a new car; the Christmas music CD which is themed to sell a brand of sweets; the party for footballers and their kids, which is really a device to promote a brand of fried chicken; the auction of game-show memorabilia which is contrived to promote a TV channel. You begin to see how PR can create a kind of pseudo-environment in which target populations find themselves sucked into activities and ideas without realising that they have been created with the sole intention of satisfying some vested interest.

Freud Communications is primarily devoted to commercial work, which is where PR started, manipulating the media in order to sell its goods. But now PR has broken out into a mass of other speciality areas as it floods media outlets with self-serving pseudo-events.

'Reputation management' has become a big growth area. There was a stunning example of this after Cardinal Joseph Ratzinger was elected Pope Benedict XVI in April 2005 and was confronted with a trickle of negative stories recalling his past in the Hitler Youth and later as a member of the German armed forces. Although the Pope's supporters insisted that he had never genuinely supported the Nazi cause, this was a particularly potent threat to his reputation, since it revived the long-standing complaint that for many hundreds of years the Catholic Church had actively fostered anti-Semitism and that, during the Second World War in particular, Pope Pius XII had knowingly turned a blind eye to the Nazi persecution of Jews. The new Pope answered this by visiting the Auschwitz concentration camp in Poland in May 2006 and praying for the camp's victims.

The Pope's sorrow may well have been genuine, but the event itself was full of artifice, constructed by a Vatican PR machine which was determined to manage the new pontiff's reputation by injecting its message into the world's media. In principle, the Pope might have gone to pray in the camp privately without anybody knowing about it. In the event, scores of reporters and cameramen were invited to take up position in a press pen by the main gate as, to an agreed timetable, the Pope was dropped off in a car outside the camp so that he could walk slowly through the gate, his hands clasped in prayer, with an escort of clergymen and a bell tolling in the background. In front of the cameras, he kneeled and prayed at a wall where prisoners had been shot dead and then spoke with a group of thirty-two camp survivors who had been assembled for the occasion and who were made available for interviews with reporters.

TV cameras then recorded the Pope entering a dark cell to meditate on the death of a Catholic priest, Maximilian Kolbe, who had been incarcerated there without food after volunteering to take the place of a condemned man. While viewers saw the Pope entering the dark room alone, the fact is that those pictures were shot from inside the cell and he was walking into a staged photo opportunity. The Pope then emerged to make a carefully crafted speech, in which he said nothing about his membership of the Hitler Youth or about the Catholic Church's history of anti-Semitism; and he presented the Holocaust as an attack not on Jews but on all Christians, perpetrated not by ordinary Germans but only by an elite of Nazi criminals who had forced themselves upon the German people. Historians subsequently objected that this was deeply misleading. Still, the global media ran the story.

President Clinton's PR team staged a very similar piece of reputation management in the summer of 1998 after he had been caught out lying about his relationship with Monica Lewinsky: they set him up with a 'prayer breakfast' with a collection of one hundred clergymen, where he made a tearful confession of his sins and begged for forgiveness, all of it televised nationwide.

Whole countries now go in for reputation management. When the Saudis found themselves in the international doghouse after the terrorist attacks of September 2001, they hired Burson-Marsteller to buff up their image (following the precedent of the old Argentinian junta and the Suharto regime in Indonesia, who hired the same agency when they found their devotion to torture and murder was causing them some diplomatic irritation). And it works: when Turkey was accused by the US State Department of violating human rights, it invested more than $3 million in PR firms and was rewarded with $800 million of aid from the same US government.

'Crisis management' is another growth area for PR. Sometimes, it's clever in its distortion of news. On 1 May 2000, P&O's biggest ship, the *Aurora*, set off from Southampton on its maiden cruise after three years of careful commercial PR work by Shandwick. Sixteen hours later, the propeller shaft overheated, and the captain contacted P&O headquarters to tell them he had no choice but to head back to Southampton. Shandwick took over management of the crisis and rapidly saw the threat of Fleet Street taking its angle from 1,800 angry passengers. That day, with the passengers still at sea, the PR agency took control of the story, issuing a press release, briefing 110 reporters, emphasising three angles: that the ship had passed its sea trials, that the passengers would be compensated, and that the *Aurora*'s next scheduled cruise in a fortnight would go ahead as planned. These angles successfully dominated the first day's coverage.

The problem then was how to deal with the second day's coverage, when the passengers would come streaming off the ship in Southampton docks, all potentially available to reporters as a source for damaging stories. Shandwick's strategy was twofold. First, they set up a press conference for the returning captain so that his voice would be prominent in the coverage; and second, they agreed with P&O that, long before they docked, all the passengers should be given a letter promising them a full refund and a free second cruise, and that all the passengers be given unlimited free drinks for the return journey. The plan, as Shandwick's chief executive, Philip Dewhurst, subsequently described it, was that 'the media would be given access to disembarking passengers so that they could reveal details of the generous compensation package'. The result was that the crisis was converted into good news. *The Times* headline compliantly captured the impact of Shandwick's work: 'P&O SAILS BACK ON WAVE OF GOODWILL'.

Sometimes, however, crisis-management PR involves feeding the media with brazen falsehood behind the safety of an off-the-record briefing. When a train crashed into Potters Bar station in May 2002, killing six people, first reports blamed the engineering company responsible for track maintenance in the area, Jarvis. But, within forty-eight hours, 'a senior rail source' was briefing reporters that the crash could have been an act of vandalism and, in spite of the lack of any evidence to support it, this story was picked up and run prominently by most Sunday newspapers and then echoed in subsequent coverage. Three years later, an official inquiry found that vandalism was 'highly unlikely' to have caused the accident and belatedly pointed back to shoddy maintenance by Jarvis as the probable cause.

In the same way, when Scotland Yard officers raided a house in Forest Gate, east London, in June 2006 and shot an unarmed man before being forced to admit that they had made a mistake, a sequence of off-the-record briefings misled the media into reporting, first, that the house had been used to prepare for chemical terrorism (not even a fragment of evidence was ever found to support this); second, that the occupants had a suspicious stash of cash (they did – like many devout Muslims, they regard banks as usurers); and finally, that one of the occupants had been downloading child pornography (a charge that was dismissed for lack of evidence). All of these manufactured news stories served to take the heat off the political crisis that was building around Scotland Yard and the Home Office, although none of them was supported by the facts.

But the really big boom area in PR over the last couple of decades has been 'issue management', which has seen the mass media become the plaything of multinational corporations and opposing pressure groups. The result is a kind of information chaos.

This flows directly from the process of globalisation which was engineered by Western governments from the late 1970s. Corporations rapidly grew in size and soon occupied more than fifty places in the league table of the world's hundred biggest economies. As that was happening, the revolutionary left's attack on capitalism was collapsing. Its activists switched their focus away from the system and towards the corporations themselves.

Now, the corporations who had used PR so effectively to sell their brands found themselves on the receiving end of a highly effective PR counter-attack from pressure groups and, in particular, from the big environmental groups, who learned how to create their own pseudo-events to change the emotional meaning of those brands (burgers are not for hunger but for ill health; pharmaceuticals are not for curing illness but for profiteering). The campaign programme director of Greenpeace, Chris Rose, spelled this out in a speech in December 1995: 'Multinationals and famous brands are the iron-clad battleships of commerce: big, heavily built and, above all, slow-moving targets, vulnerable to torpedo attack unless they alter course or change sides.' Issue management is corporate PR's answer to this. Global warming is the issue they have tried hardest to manage.

The facts of climate change have become the site of a three-cornered battle in which truth, as ever, has been an immediate casualty. In one corner are companies like Exxon fighting a head-to-head war of attrition, denying that global warming is occurring and/or that it is a man-made problem for which they have any responsibility. Against them are groups like Greenpeace, 'cranking up the anxiety' with highly emotive messages about the scale of the threat. The third corner is occupied by companies like BP, who have broken away from Exxon and adopted a strategy of camouflage, radically redrawing their image to cloak their businesses in green credentials. For all three forces, the newly vulnerable mass media have become a weapon of convenience, constantly available to fire off their messages for them. And in the background, rather like the civilian population of a war zone, the billions of people who rely on the mass media for information have suffered the worst injuries of all under a bombardment of falsehood, distortion and propaganda.

It was the Exxon strategy which led the way. Within months of the UN producing its first report endorsing the idea of man-made climate change, in 1989, Exxon and other big corporations started setting up pseudo-groups. The first and biggest was the Global Climate Coalition which was soon lobbying in the corridors of power and exploiting one of the news factory's most powerful rules of production – to give 'the other side of the story' – in order to get through the media door.

As a single example of its activities, the coalition made a classic appeal to the subconscious feelings of its American audience before the Kyoto conference in December 1997, when it spent $13 million on TV advertising, aimed at reining in the Clinton administration. It pitched the whole issue as a matter of freedom and patriotism. 'America has signed many treaties . . . but never a treaty of surrender,' was the key line in one advertisement, over a photograph of the Japanese surrender at the end of the Second World War.

When Kyoto nevertheless produced an agreement to cut emissions, Exxon, in early 1998, helped to set up a new front group, the Global Climate Science Team. A leaked memo, written by a PR executive at the American Petroleum Institute, echoed precisely the work of the old tobacco pseudo-groups in aiming to focus public thinking on doubt. The memo looked forward to a time when 'recognition of uncertainty becomes part of the conventional wisdom'. In order to reshape the global consensus, the memo proposed 'a national media relations program to inform the media about uncertainties in climate science'.

It needs to be said that the uncertainties were real. The mass of scientists who feared that human activity was raising the temperature of the planet necessarily acknowledged that they could not be sure: there were limits to their knowledge of past temperature patterns, limits to their ability to quantify the impact of human activity on the observed changes, limits to their ability to predict future changes. But even though there was a reality to the doubt, the effect of the Exxon-led campaign was to distort public perception of the truth by giving this doubt disproportionate weight.

The leaked memo from the new Global Climate Science Team proposed a budget of $5 million to establish 'cooperative relationships with all major scientists whose research in this field supports our position'. The campaign would produce 'simple fact sheets that present scientific uncertainties in language that the media and public can understand'; set up briefings for science journalists; supply their own scientists for radio talk shows; and produce 'a steady stream of op-ed columns and letters to the editor authored by scientists'. The stated objective was 'to raise such questions about the Kyoto treaty's scientific underpinnings that American policymakers not only will refuse to endorse it, they will seek to prevent progress toward implementation'.

But the GCST was only the beginning of the post-Kyoto blitz of media manipulation. The same leaked memo anticipated the funding of AstroTurf groups to give the impression of popular support for their campaign ('organize, promote, and conduct through grassroots organizations a series of campus/community workshops/debates on climate science'). This took off. Between 1998 and 2005, ExxonMobil alone spent $15.8 million on forty-three different front groups, according to research published in January 2007 by the Union of Concerned Scientists, who described this as 'the most sophisticated and successful disinformation campaign since Big Tobacco misled the public'. Some were well-established right-wing think tanks, like the Cato Institute and the Competitive Enterprise Institute. Others were fringe groups, like the Congress of Racial Equality, which created a pseudo-incident at an Exxon shareholders' meeting by staging a protest against environmental protests. The effect of these groups was to create the illusion of widespread doubt about global warming, when the reality was that they were generally recycling the work of only a dozen or more 'contrarian' scientists.

The research published by the Union of Concerned Scientists named, for example, Sallie Baliunas, whose work was promoted through nine different groups in the Exxon-supported network; Patrick J. Michaels, with eleven groups; and S. Fred Singer, also with eleven. Some of the work of these scientists ran into considerable controversy. Two of them, Sallie Baliunas and Willie Soon, published a paper in the *Climate Research* journal, suggesting that the twentieth century was not unusually warm, and provoked the resignation of three of the journal's editors and the criticism of thirteen other scientists who complained that the paper misrepresented their work. A petition which claimed to carry the signatures of 18,000 scientists who disputed the theory of global warming turned out to have been signed by numerous students with no special qualification as well as the fictional TV detective Perry Mason and somebody claiming to be one of the Spice Girls. A research briefing from the Competitive Enterprise Institute suggested that 'the likeliest global climate change is the creation of a milder, greener, more prosperous world'. It all found its way into the unprotected media.

While this was happening, two of the biggest oil companies – BP and Shell – had seen how the attack by environmental groups was damaging their brands and had resigned from the original Global Climate Coalition. BP, in particular, from 1997 performed the PR equivalent of a sex change, transforming their image from that of a ruthless, profit-seeking predator into a caring green giant.

The move was engineered by the company's new chief executive, John Browne, on the advice of a specialist in issue management, Simon Bryceson, a PR professional who had formerly been national administrator of Friends of the Earth. It was launched when Bryceson wrote a key speech for Browne to deliver at Stamford University in May 1997, accepting that action must be taken to deal with the possibility of climate change and pledging BP to lead the way.

The speech was the beginning of a carefully orchestrated sequence of pseudo-events which saw BP investing in solar energy and marketing itself as an energy company, not an oil company; Bryceson persuading Greenpeace to issue a statement welcoming BP's shift; BP running a huge training scheme for staff to teach them the new line; Browne speaking at a Greenpeace conference (and opening with a joke from Bryceson, that he was happy to be on their platform instead of their protestors occupying his); BP running a campaign of 'TV branding' and hiring the PR network of Burson-Marsteller to target the message into selected quality media which influence 'leg and reg' (legislation and regulation).

As an attempt to reduce global warming, this had only the most marginal of impacts. John Browne announced plans for the company to cut the emissions from its own activities by 10% but, according to one of those closely involved, BP deliberately avoided suggesting specific policies to reduce the immeasurably more significant emissions from the global customers who bought its oil. Browne's line on climate change always put hydrocarbons, particularly oil and natural gas, at the centre of energy policy and argued for cutting emissions by tackling waste and inefficiency without making any kind of cut in global oil consumption.

However, as a commercial manoeuvre to defend the company's market, the new image was highly successful. According to the source who was directly involved, the truth is that the new image was designed: to improve the BP brand with women drivers whose forecourt trade they wanted; to recruit and retain better staff, some of whom had objected to its hard line on global warming; to win round liberal US opponents of its plan to merge with Amoco and Arco; and, above all, to get the company inside the debate on climate change where it could influence the outcome.

And indeed the result, as Bryceson recorded in an item on his website (since removed), was that BP 'moved itself from being a potential victim of the political debate to a participant in that debate'. Soon after the Stamford speech, Browne was in the White House with President Clinton and became the only non-US oilman on Clinton's board on climate change. Clinton's team went into Kyoto with an idea which had been heavily backed by Browne, to allow nations to buy and sell their cuts in emissions, which meant effectively that rich nations could maintain a higher level of emissions by paying poorer nations to cut their levels. There were further commercial benefits for the company. They succeeded in selling their merger with Amoco and Arco, and, as the BP source put it: 'If you want less tax on North Sea oil, it certainly helps if a programme like this is giving you better access to ministers.'

As this battle unfolded, the scientific consensus lined up behind the environmental groups and yet, under hostile fire from the oil lobby, some of these groups began to throw back what looks very much like exaggeration and distortion. For example, for years they had argued against global dependence on fossil fuels such as oil and coal on the grounds that supplies would soon run out ('Due to lack of interest, tomorrow has been cancelled,' in the words of an early green slogan). But, as they moved to push climate change up the agenda, the same groups reversed their position, arguing that governments must stop oil companies opening new fields because the potential reserves were so great.

Greenpeace is particularly skilled at creating pseudo-incidents: its supporters are up Nelson's Column with a banner, they're abseiling onto an oil platform with their own camera crew to film it, they're raiding

Exxon's headquarters dressed as tigers. Like all PR, these stunts are designed to open the media door for the supply of claims which, in the case of some Greenpeace statements, appear to be at best highly contentious. We took four high-profile statements about climate change from the Greenpeace website, asked them to tell us their source for each one and then went to each source to try to establish the accuracy of the Greenpeace version. Here are the results.

Greenpeace claim: 'Climate change kills 160,000 people a year.' Source: Greenpeace referred us to a July 2005 World Health Organisation report. Accuracy: the report does not contain the statement made by Greenpeace. It does warn that global warming presents 'substantial risks to human health' and it suggests that it 'may have caused 150,000 deaths in 2000'. One of the authors of the report, Dr Diarmid Campbell-Lendrum, told us that that figure was qualified by 'a very wide range of uncertainty' – so wide that it was not even possible to say whether the estimate of 150,000 was too high or too low. He added that Greenpeace were not alone in misreporting their findings; the media had done the same.

Greenpeace claim: 'Within the lifetime of a child being born today, [climate change] may challenge our survival as a species.' Source: Greenpeace told us they could not remember the source for this. We asked the Tyndall Centre, which is the world's leading centre for climate change research, if they knew of any evidence to support the claim. They replied: 'Where is the evidence that climate change will extinguish the entire human race? That is clear politics of fear.'

Greenpeace claim: 'By the end of this century, if current trends continue, the temperature will likely climb higher than it has been in the past two million years. The consequences are likely to be catastrophic: mass extinctions, droughts, hundreds of millions of refugees.' Source: Greenpeace pointed us to the reports of the UN's Intergovernmental Panel on Climate Change. Accuracy: Greenpeace are right to say that there are scientific papers, quoted by the UN panel or by other sources, which support the key elements of this claim. However, the Tyndall Centre pointed out that by describing all this as 'likely', the claim failed to reflect the inherent uncertainty of these predictions.

Greenpeace claim: 'Without radical action now, we'll face a dire global emergency in the 2020s.' Source: Greenpeace referred us to the conclusion of a conference on 'Avoiding Dangerous Climate Change', held in Exeter in 2005, which found that 'even delays of five years could be significant in terms of cost'. Accuracy: the report of the conference steering committee does indeed say that 'different models suggest that delaying action would require greater action later for the same temperature target and that even a delay of five years could be significant'. It is not clear how that supports the prediction of a global emergency in the 2020s.

Greenpeace is not alone. A BBC Radio 4 programme, *Overselling Climate Change*, in April 2000 recorded the advocacy director of Tearfund, Andy Atkins, claiming that global warming is allowing mosquitoes for the first time to inhabit the highlands of Ethiopia where they are spreading malaria among farmers. And yet Tearfund's own representative in Ethiopia suggested the highland farmers might be developing malaria because of poor nutrition, or increased resistance to anti-malaria drugs, or a new mobility which meant the highland farmers now visit the valleys where malaria has always been a risk. Scientists who personally believe in man-made climate change complained on the programme of environmentalists making unproved links between global warming and the severity of hurricanes and the extinction of species.

They cited, in particular, the case of the golden toad which, according to environmental groups, was the first casualty of global warming, killed off by a fungus which had flourished as a result of higher temperatures. However, the fungus kills toads at low temperatures. And a toad specialist, Dr Cindy Carey, who herself believes in climate change, complained that no causal link had been established. She pointed out that they might as well argue that global warming had caused an increase in child obesity or an increase in the number of Wal-Mart supermarkets since they too had occurred while global temperatures were rising. One scientist, Dr Hans von Storch, who has spent years arguing that the climate is changing, told the Radio 4 programme: 'The alarmists think that climate change is something extremely dangerous, extremely bad, and that overselling it a little bit, if it serves a good purpose, is not that bad.'

In the midst of this three-cornered battle, the mass media (and their consumers) have been left in a state of some chaos. Newsrooms themselves have been divided under the impact of conflicting PR. At an early stage in the battle, the then news editor of the *Guardian*, Melanie Phillips, instructed the paper's environment correspondent, Paul Brown, to stop using Friends of the Earth and Greenpeace for source material. Brown continued to quote them. Phillips wrote a memo to the then editor, Peter Preston, asking for Brown to be sacked. Preston compromised by sending Brown away on a long trip, ironically with Greenpeace in the Marshall Islands. Brown returned, and the internal clashes continued.

The right-wing press was suffering similar confusion. In her new role as a columnist at the *Daily Mail*, the same Melanie Phillips went on to write a series of outspoken columns denouncing the whole concept of man-made climate change. 'Global warming is a scam,' she wrote in February 2002. 'The latest evidence is provided in a report published today by the European Science And Environment Forum, in which a group of the most eminent scientists from Britain and America shred the theory.' However, the forum whose work she was quoting was, in truth, yet another pseudo-group, created with the help of two PR agencies (APCO Worldwide and Burson-Marsteller) with the specific intent of campaigning against restrictions on corporate activity; and the report to which Phillips referred in such glowing terms was recycled work which had been funded by Exxon. A similar column, in January 2005, stated: 'Far from being proved, the claim of man-made global warming is a global fraud.' This column, too, drew on research from Exxon-funded groups and cited the controversial petition by 18,000 'scientists' to show that the claim of scientific consensus was also 'bogus'. The result was that the *Mail* was attacked by the Royal Society, the UK's academy of science, for 'its faithful reproduction of the propaganda put together by the denial lobby in the US'. The Royal Society's president, Lord May, complained bitterly about misinformation from the oil lobby and, citing in particular the *Mail*'s coverage, concluded: 'There is no danger this lobby will influence the scientists. But they don't need to. It is the influence on the media that is so poisonous.'

The scoreline in the battle thus far reflects real tactical victories for the oil lobby. Even though the environmental groups, backed by the UN and the consensus of scientific opinion, appear to have won the bulk of public opinion, the twin strategies of the oil companies have clearly won favour in government. In 2001, President Bush formally withdrew the United States from the Kyoto process (and the Global Climate Coalition, claiming victory, shut up shop).

From the point of view of media consumers, the chaos continues. In February 2007, the UN's Intergovernmental Panel on Climate Change reported that the evidence of climate change was 'unequivo-cal' and that the chances of its being man-made were as high as 90%. The Fraser Institute of Canada, which has received $120,000 from Exxon, replied within forty-eight hours by publishing a paper claiming that 'there is no compelling evidence that dangerous or unprecedented changes are under way'. And Greenpeace sent forty volunteers up the Eiffel Tower with a banner, dumped four tonnes of coal on the doorstep of the British government's environment department, DEFRA, and claimed on its website that 'within 50 years, one-third of species could face extinction'.

I should stress that the point here is not that PR is to blame for all the falsehood and distortion which run through the global media. Certainly, PR produces plentiful distortion and significant falsehood, but the media themselves, operating as a news factory, as we have seen, first, have become structurally weakened to the point where they routinely betray their own function by passing on unchecked PR to their readers and viewers, and second, work with rules of production which are themselves a significant source of falsehood and distortion.

There was a beautiful little example of all this at work in *Overselling Climate Change*, which punctured some of the more extravagant claims of the environmental lobby.

A group of scientists formed climateprediction.net to run thousands of computerised models, attempting to predict what would happen to global temperatures if carbon dioxide emissions were doubled. The over-whelming majority of the results suggested that temperature would rise by about three degrees Celsius, which was well within the range of earlier findings. Yet when this was published in January 2005, it produced the following coverage: 'Global warming is "twice as bad as previously thought"' (*Independent*); 'Global warming may be twice as bad as feared'

(*Times*); 'Weather trial predicts 10C rise in British temperatures' (*Telegraph*); 'Average temperature could rise 11C' (*Guardian*).

What had happened was a classic example of the internal dynamics of Flat Earth news. First, a press release had been issued to mark the publication of the research in *Nature* magazine. This made no reference at all to the majority finding of a three-degree increase in temperature and focused instead on the finding of a tiny minority of the computerised models, that 'average temperatures could rise by up to eleven degrees'. This, the press release explained, was more than double the maximum rise which previously had been considered by the UN's Intergovernmental Panel on Climate Change.

Trying to explain this, the Radio 4 programme commissioned independent scientists to peer-review the press release. One of them explained: 'It's a difficult line for us scientists to tread, since we need something exciting to get published in places like *Nature* and to justify our funding. I do think that in this case, that clearly overstepped the line.' The principal investigator for climateprediction.net, Dr Myles Allen, shed further light: 'Our press advisers tell us . . . to make sure that the press release could be used by the hard-working journalist on the *Oxford Times* who doesn't have the time to go and read the whole story, so they can essentially copy it out.'

Having fed this essentially misleading line to the media, the scientists then saw it not just recycled but heightened by the news factory's rules of production. What had been framed in the press release as a possibility was converted into a prediction, with stories dropping either the crucial 'could be' and/or the equally crucial 'up to'. And it was not just the local reporter on the *Oxford Times* who didn't have the time to go and read the whole report. On the basis of the stories they published, it seems that none of the national journalists who covered the report actually read it: they relied on the press release and never once mentioned the majority prediction of a three-degree rise. The process as a whole simply shunted the truth into the sidings.

A much bigger example of the combined impact of Flat Earth PR and Flat Earth journalism is the reporting of government. It is notorious among both politicians and journalists that this is badly done. To the extent that this has been the subject of media coverage, it has itself tended to become the subject of yet more distortion, with the whole issue reduced to a single cliché, of 'spin'.

According to this cliché, the Blair government, driven by a pragmatic decision to use the media to consolidate its power, hired a manipulative bully, Alastair Campbell, who proceeded to break the rules of honest government to the point where he had to be driven from office.

This deeply self-serving version of events fails to say anything about the media's own role. There are two points, in particular, which it ignores.

The first is that political reporters – like most of their colleagues – are wholly complicit in assisting PR operatives like Alastair Campbell to have their way with them. Where is it written that reporters must take their stories from press officers? Westminster is full of ministers and MPs and peers, all of whom are potential sources of stories, most of whom are treated like wallflowers in a disco and just never asked to join in. Similarly, Whitehall is full of civil servants, all of whom know far more than their press officers about what is happening in their departments, and yet almost all of whom are similarly ignored as sources of information.

Press officers can be a perfectly legitimate source of information as long as they take their place alongside other sources. But the reality is that, short of time, looking for stories which are quick and safe to cover, and anxious to cover the stories which everybody else is covering, most political correspondents, just like most other reporters, turn to press officers, particularly those who speak for official sources, where they are handed stories on a plate with a sprig of parsley on top.

At its worst, this involves straying over the ethical boundary. In the United States in January 2005, Armstrong Williams, a syndicated columnist who had frequently backed the Bush administration, was revealed to have received $240,000 in federal government funds in a contract organised by Ketchum, the same PR company who were at the heart of the scandal over phoney VNRs. Soon afterwards, two other columnists, Michael McManus and Maggie Gallagher, also admitted taking government money while writing pro-government stories. There was a similar scandal in Australia in 1999, when two of the country's best-known radio presenters were revealed to have been taking cash from PR companies in exchange for favourable comment on various banks, airlines and casino companies; and in the UK, in February 2002, when the conservative columnist Roger Scruton was shown to have been claiming a monthly retainer of £4,500 from a Japanese tobacco company while writing in favour of smoking in the *Financial Times*, the *Daily Telegraph*, the *Independent*, *The Times* and the *Wall Street Journal*.

Only a little further away from the ethical boundary line, it is now common practice for trade magazines to send PR companies 'forward features' lists, outlining the subjects which they plan to cover in the near future and inviting PR material to help them do so. Indeed, some PR companies now offer a special service for reporters to fill their stories with PR material. Response Source, for example, offers journalists a ready-made form to submit their requests: 'You can contact hundreds of PRs at once, saving you hours of research.' Quick and easy, but a highly unreliable route to the truth.

At best, the dependence on press officers means that the same churnalists who complain constantly about dishonesty in government PR, themselves turn to the same PR sources, like babies in a high chair, waiting to be spoon-fed their stories.

Alastair Campbell's deputy, Lance Price, in *The Spin Doctor's Diary*, catches several examples of the ease with which Downing Street manipulated reporters. He says Campbell deliberately told a *News of the World* man that Blair had stayed on the eighth floor of a hotel, just as a test to see whether he would check and find that the hotel was only six storeys high. He didn't. Similarly, when Campbell went to a Britney Spears concert and got her to sign a photo, he bet somebody £200 he could get the *Standard* to splash on a story that Britney supported Labour. He won the bet the same day.

Beyond this, the second contribution by political reporters to the growth of manipulation by government is that, over the years, some of them have behaved with such vicious mendacity that they positively provoked governments into trying to defend themselves by deploying the most insidious tricks known to PR. There is real hypocrisy here.

A British political correspondent described to me a golden moment during the G8 Summit in Okinawa in July 2002 when, short of easy copy, some of the British reporters ran stories complaining about the extravagant spending of the Japanese hosts. Alastair Campbell, at his next press briefing, challenged the reporters to return the handsome collection of freebies which they themselves had been given, including miniature tape recorders, dolls for their daughters, pens, bags and contraceptives. One political correspondent agreed that they should. Another famously replied: 'Nothing should come between the British journalist and his freebie.' And so they kept them.

During the years when the British Labour Party was led by Michael Foot and then Neil Kinnock, its political prospects were ruined by spectacularly malicious coverage, particularly in the *Sun* and the *Daily Mail*, and this treatment clearly persuaded the party of the Blair years that it had to fight back by developing more powerful PR. Predictably, this was one of the few messages which Alastair Campbell never succeeded in injecting into Fleet Street coverage. He did squeeze it into an interview with the *British Journalism Review* in 2000: 'When different advertising agencies were pitching for the Labour Party's election account, apparently the one that won did, as part of their presentation, an analysis of positive and negative coverage of the government in one set of Sunday newspapers. The positive ran to a handful of cuttings. The negative had been copied on one roll of paper, which they rolled out the length of the entire room and beyond.'

He put it more bluntly to the Public Administration Committee of the House of Commons when he gave evidence to them in May 2004 about the behaviour of journalists: 'They write drivel. They write rubbish. They tell lies.'

In other words, if Alastair Campbell had not existed, it would have been necessary to invent him.

Official manipulation of the media has a long pedigree, from the Liberal government of Lloyd George ('The press? What you can't square, you squash. What you can't squash, you square'), to the Conservative government of Anthony Eden, whose press adviser, William Clark, explained in relation to the Suez crisis: 'Public opinion could not be ignored. It had to be fooled. The power of government to deceive is so immense that fooling all of the people some of the time can successfully and easily lead to fooling them all of the time.' This does not mean that all government PR is false or distorted: great chunks of it are perfectly straightforward and frequently dull. I have dealt with Whitehall press officers who have routinely given me reliable information; I've also dealt with some slippery bullies.

Downing Street under Tony Blair certainly took PR to a new level. When embarrassing stories broke, they put out decoys to distract attention. Famously, the tale of then Foreign Secretary Robin Cook's affair with his secretary saw Fleet Street fed variously with the idea that the former Governor of Hong Kong, Chris Patten, was being investigated for spying and that the royal yacht *Britannia* might be saved from the scrapyard. Less famously, an embarrassing gaffe by Peter Mandelson, who announced the wrong details for the new national minimum wage, was decoyed with the tale of the then sports minister, Tony Banks, describing the Leader of the Opposition, William Hague, as a foetus who must have made Tory MPs wish they had not voted against abortion. (The artificial row from enraged anti-abortion groups ran all week.)

When they wanted to promote stories, Labour PR officers offered contrived 'leaks' as exclusives with strings attached: 'You can have this, but only if you guarantee to put it on page 1.' Then they would keep it going, by feeding out new angles day after day. When they wanted to conceal bad stories which they had to release, they slipped them out quietly on a busy news day (it's called 'throwing out the bodies'). When they wanted to suppress bad stories which the press had come up with, they aimed to trade them for good ones (Lance Price's *Diary* records the *Express* being accidentally sent a list of all Downing Street's plans for 'managing the news' by planting selected stories in selected papers; instead of publishing it, the *Express* allowed themselves to be managed even further, by suppressing the story in exchange for a couple of extra scoops). When Labour PR wanted to discredit embarrassing stories which they could not suppress, they would deny a single incorrect detail, or deny a non-existent detail, or lie.

This is what happened, for example, after the BBC radio reporter Andrew Gilligan in May 2003 broadcast his notorious story that Downing Street had ordered that the September 2002 dossier on Iraqi weapons be 'sexed up'. Later that day, Alastair Campbell's office issued a firm denial: 'Not one word of the dossier was not entirely the work of intelligence agencies.' Downing Street could not have known it at the time but, as a result of the death of Gilligan's source, Dr David Kelly, subsequent official inquiries by Lord Hutton and Lord Butler published material which revealed that that was simply not true.

This material included, for example, two messages to the head of the Joint Intelligence Committee: an email from the Downing Street chief of staff, Jonathan Powell, successfully asking for the removal of a sentence which suggested that Iraq would use chemical and biological weapons only if it was attacked; and a memo from Alastair Campbell himself which successfully produced a line saying that the Iraqi military 'are able' to deploy chemical and biological weapons within forty-five minutes of an order to do so, whereas the original draft from the intelligence agencies had said only that they 'may be able' to do so. (In the classic two-step dance between PR and churnalism, this subtle distortion was converted into brazen falsehood: '45 Minutes from Attack' in the *Evening Standard*, 'Brits 45 minutes from Doom' in the *Sun*.)

Downing Street's manipulation of the media over Gilligan's story went much further than this original lie. The evidence suggests that Alastair Campbell used it as a decoy to distract attention from a highly embarrassing story, which was emerging slowly in May and June 2003, that the long-debated Iraqi weapons of mass destruction did not exist. The decoy strategy began to unfold on 25 June, when Campbell was called to give evidence to the Select Committee on Foreign Affairs. There were three key moves.

First, giving his evidence to the committee, Campbell reserved his best sound bites for an outspoken attack on Gilligan's story, stabbing his finger in the air and demanding an apology: 'Until the BBC acknowledges that that is a lie, I will keep banging on.' On the face of it, this was a very odd thing to do. Four weeks had passed since Gilligan broadcast his story. In that time, Campbell had criticised it twice in letters to the BBC, but he had written stronger comments on other BBC stories; he had never asked for an apology for Gilligan's particular story; he had never even referred it to the BBC's complaints department; and, when he had lunch with Gilligan's boss, Richard Sambrook, during this time, he had never mentioned it.

The reality was that Campbell was in a tight corner in front of the select committee, vulnerable to hostile questioning over his role in both of the government's dossiers on Iraqi weapons, in September 2002 and

February 2003, both of whose contents were now surrounded in controversy. Just like Bell Yard in their handling of the NatWest Three, Campbell switched the story, focusing media coverage on Gilligan's broadcast because it was a vulnerable pressure point. While the core of Gilligan's claims were true, the broadcast also contained significant errors. As Campbell recorded in his diary, subsequently disclosed to Lord Hutton: 'Opened a flank on the BBC.' That night, broadcast bulletins ran with Campbell's angle. The next day, all the national paper churnalists picked up on it, some of them using it as the intro for their stories.

Campbell's second step, on the following day, 26 June, was to write a ferocious letter to Gilligan's boss, Richard Sambrook, now suddenly describing the four-week-old story as 'potentially so damaging to the integrity of the Prime Minister, the government and the political process' and demanding a reply that same day. Crucially, he released this letter to the press, creating a pseudo-event which the media duly reported across the board at great length.

Finally, on 27 June, Campbell turned up effectively unannounced in the studio of Channel 4 News and went on air live to deliver an attack on the BBC which was so aggressive that political columnists started to wonder out loud whether the Prime Minister's press secretary might be cracking up under the strain. Be that as it may, this move finally established the decoy story as the main media line. The original questions about the Iraqi weapons of mass destruction were shunted into the sidings. Several political reporters wrote at the time that this looked like a diversionary tactic. Nonetheless, all of them agreed to be diverted. PR works.

This kind of high-impact PR manipulation spread from Downing Street across Whitehall, causing some friction. In September 2004, a memo leaked to the *Sunday Times* caught a little of what went on when the 'communications directors' of government departments gathered for a two-day conference. Among other things, they complained that Downing Street was bullying them. Sian Jarvis, director of communications at the Department of Health, said: 'It's been a hard educational process to explain to my ministers that the reason we are not getting the story across is that we haven't got a policy. This is the Number 10 problem: they are asking for announcements before we have a policy. The people around

Number 10 are fuelling this.' And Julia Simpson, head of the Home Office press office, said: 'Number 10 think they can rugby-tackle you. They have made an announcement before you have thought through the policy. One time, the Prime Minister was making a visit. His people said he needs to make an announcement. The people around him wanted a snappy line.'

Campbell may have set the tone, but the Whitehall press officers showed every sign of being happy to oblige. The same Julia Simpson who complained of being rugby-tackled was in charge of the press office at the Department of Education when David Blunkett was Secretary of State and was responsible for some of the most eye-watering PR distortion. It was during this time that the department repeatedly claimed a fictional increase in its budget, of £19 billion, which was created by double and treble counting parts of its funding – a fiction which was faithfully reported by Fleet Street for eighteen months, despite the fact that within two weeks of its announcement the Treasury Select Committee had rumbled the trick and warned: 'There is no cash bonanza of the type which newspaper headlines might suggest.'

During Julia Simpson's time, the Education Department also produced four separate press releases apparently announcing a total of £244 million to cut the size of infant classes, even though the truth was that there was only £100 million: they were simply announcing the same money in whole or in part four times as though each one were new. At one point, local education authorities were so broke that Blunkett had to find them an extra £154 million to keep them afloat. This was announced by Julia Simpson's office with the following words: 'An increase of £1.8 billion for local education authorities in England was announced by Education and Employment Secretary David Blunkett today.' They managed this by adding in £1.6 billion of funding which, so far from being 'announced today', had been revealed and repeatedly discussed for up to sixteen months.

It is a measure of David Blunkett's respect for the media that when he was made Home Secretary, in May 2001, he took Julia Simpson with him. While she was being rugby-tackled by Downing Street, she had time to infuriate home affairs correspondents by adopting the practice of releasing a mass of different research papers on a single day. At one point, twenty-two home affairs specialists from print and broadcast outlets jointly wrote to her to complain of 'dishonourable tactics'. The following month, the same thing happened again.

So, the picture emerges. Journalists who no longer have the time to go out and find their own stories and to check the material which they are handling, are consistently vulnerable to ingesting and reproducing the packages of information which are provided for them by this PR industry. At the very least, this involves their being directed into accepting stories and angles which have been chosen for them in order to satisfy somebody else's commercial or political interests. At the worst, this embroils them in the dissemination of serious distortion and falsehood.

This is inherently irrational. The news factory selects its stories and its angles and its facts under the pressure of its rules of production, which may or may not deliver what is important and what is true. The PR industry aggravates this irrationality. It uses the most sophisticated mechanisms to monitor the emotions and beliefs of its target audiences and then consciously fabricates news to appeal to those emotions and beliefs, recycling whatever falsehoods and misunderstandings it finds. It is one of the great unspoken ironies of the PR industry that while it may have set out in the United States in the 1920s to control the irrational feelings of the masses, it has succeeded finally in amplifying them. Globally.

And this is inherently conservative in a political sense. By favouring facts and ideas which are safe, especially those which are supported by official sources, the news factory tends to recycle a view of the world which reflects the status quo. PR reinforces this, simply because it is expensive. Three burglars from Brixton are never going to be able to buy the kind of media influence that changed the way the whole of Britain felt about the NatWest Three. Bell Pottinger do not work for the 80% of the world's population who live below the poverty line. Hill & Knowlton are not being hired to run a campaign exposing the one-third of global product which is traded through tax-free offshore accounts.

The result is that all kinds of public debates which should be being settled on the basis of evidence and logic are instead being settled by the power of competing agencies to push their line. In his history of the public relations industry, the American academic Stuart Ewen concluded: 'The customized manufacture of public discourse . . . has become epidemic.'

The conspiracy theorists may be right that some part of this picture involves owners or advertisers abusing their position to distort the work of the media. But that is only a small part of the picture. For those who want to interfere in the flow of news, there is now no need to break in through the proprietor's office or the advertising department, because the front door to the newsroom itself is hanging wide open before them.

As the excellent Daniel Boorstin put it in *The Image*: 'This is the age of contrivance . . . We are deceived and obstructed by the very machines we make to enlarge our vision.'

And there is one other domain of persuasion which remains even more hidden.

6. The Propaganda Puzzle

From the early months of 2002, newspapers and broadcasters started to report the activities of a terrorist named Abu Musab al-Zarqawi. By the time he was killed by an American air strike in Iraq in June 2006, Zarqawi had become the most notorious Islamist fighter in the world, exceeding even Osama bin Laden in the scale of the killing which was attributed to him.

We now know that a high proportion of what was said about Zarqawi was false.

We know this, in part, because the story itself was internally contradictory; in part, because official inquiries and trials have disclosed previously unseen intelligence material; and, in part, because a minority of journalists and academics suspected from the outset that the Zarqawi story was bogus and, unlike the mass of their colleagues, had both the time and the courage to go and check.[*]

The Zarqawi story is important, not just because it is in itself such a striking example of Flat Earth news, but also because of the clues which it yields to a sudden surge in the activity of a key supplier to the news factory – the secretive nexus of intelligence agencies and of military units and government departments which produce what is now officially known as 'strategic communications'.

This nexus is not new. Crude propaganda is a familiar friend of power. But as I tracked back from the Zarqawi story, trying to discover its source, I came across a complex and potentially alarming apparatus,

---

[*]I am thinking particularly of Loretta Napoleoni, author of *Insurgent Iraq*; Jason Burke and Luke Harding of the *Observer*; Jeffrey Gettleman of the *International Herald Tribune*; Nick Fielding, formerly of the *Sunday Times*; and Ahmed Hashim of the US Naval War College. For more on their work, see www.flatearthnews.net.

which had grown rapidly after the terrorist attacks of September 2001 and which was now working busily and generally without public recognition, using the mass media to spread dubious stories on all kinds of subjects, quietly rewriting the rules which once had attempted to restrain it, adding new jeopardy to the function of truth-telling journalism. For the first time in human history, there is a concerted strategy to manipulate global perception. And the weakened mass media are operating as its compliant assistants.

The first mention I can find of Zarqawi in the international media is in a short story filed by the Associated Press from Jordan on 4 April 2001. The signs of distortion are already there. The AP story quoted unnamed Jordanian officials saying that that they had two new suspects for a conspiracy to cause explosions in the United States and Israel on Millennium Eve: one of these suspects was a Jordanian named Abu Musab al-Zarqawi. The evidence suggests that this was, at best, contentious and, at worst, a self-serving fabrication from the Jordanian authorities.

Since December 1999, the Jordanians had been claiming to have foiled a plot to cause explosions on Millennium Eve, but the alleged targets had always been in Jordan, including the Radisson SAS Hotel in Amman, never in the US or Israel. Furthermore, in September 2000 – seven months before this AP story – the Jordanians had tried twenty-eight people for the conspiracy and sentenced six of them to death, but, even though Jordan is heavily implicated in the torture of its prisoners, not once was Zarqawi's name even mentioned.

Why, seven months later, would the Jordanians suddenly throw Zarqawi's name into the public domain and furthermore present him as a threat to the US and Israel? What we now know is that since the late 1980s Zarqawi had been drifting into radical Islamism and had committed himself to using violence to unseat the Jordanian royal family. By June 2000, aged 33, he was in Afghanistan running a small camp whose sole purpose was to prepare for attacks on Jordan. Many of those who were with him were also Jordanians, and it is not surprising that Jordanian intelligence heard about what he was doing. It may or may not be true that he had links to people who had plotted explosions in Jordan on Millennium Eve, but the decision to name him in this way in the AP story, first, gave the Jordanian authorities a means of jailing this hostile opponent if ever he returned to their soil, and second, allowed them to win favour with their American and Israeli allies.

Five months after that story, terrorists attacked New York and Washington DC. Launching their global war on terror, US intelligence agencies contacted allies around the world, calling in raw material. The Jordanians passed them the names of a mass of suspected Islamist fighters, including Zarqawi. So too did the Kurds, who were being attacked by a group of Islamists who had set up camps in northern Iraq, some of whom knew Zarqawi. It was not long before his name started to crop up in the small print of US newspaper reports.

On 10 January 2002, he was named without any amplification in the *San Francisco Chronicle* simply as 'an operational commander' in a long list of Taliban supporters who were still at liberty after the US invasion of Afghanistan. This was attributed to 'US officials'. On 24 March 2002, he turned up in the middle of a substantial story in the *New York Times*, identified for the first time not as a Taliban supporter but as 'a senior al-Qaeda leader' who had fled Afghanistan and taken refuge in Iran. This was attributed to 'senior Israeli and American officials'.

Over the following months, his profile slowly started to rise as he cropped up among numerous other alleged al-Qaeda leaders, in a dozen more stories in major US newspapers. Sometimes, he was linked to Iran, with the Defense Secretary, Donald Rumsfeld, complaining that 'Iran has served as a haven for some terrorists leaving Afghanistan'. Sometimes, he was linked to Syria; and/or to Hizbollah in Lebanon; and/or to Palestinian bombings in Israel; and/or to plots in Germany. In September 2002, in a week when Rumsfeld publicly linked al-Qaeda to the Iraqi regime, Zarqawi was linked to Iraq as well. These stories were always attributed to unnamed 'officials', usually from the CIA and the Pentagon. By this time, the Jordanians had sentenced him *in absentia*, for his alleged role in the Millennium Eve plot, to fifteen years in prison. Still, Zarqawi remained a minor figure, one name among many.

Then, on 7 October 2002, for the first time, somebody referred to him on the record. In a nationally televised speech in Cincinnati, President George Bush spoke of 'high-level contacts' between al-Qaeda and Iraq and said: 'Some al-Qaeda leaders who fled Afghanistan went to Iraq. These include one very senior al-Qaeda leader who received medical treatment in Baghdad this year, and who has been associated with planning for chemical and biological attacks.' This coincided with a crucial vote in Congress in which the President was seeking authority to use military force against Iraq. Bush never named the man he was referring to, but as the *LA Times* among many others soon reported: 'In a speech Monday, Bush referred to a senior member of al-Qaeda who received medical treatment in Iraq. U.S. officials said yesterday that was Abu Musab Zarqawi, a Jordanian, who lost a leg during the U.S. war in Afghanistan.'

By now, a few reporters, notably Robert Collier in the *San Francisco Chronicle* and Dana Milbank in the *Washington Post*, were finding their own contacts in the intelligence community who cast doubt on the emerging story of al-Qaeda's links to Saddam and, within that, of Zarqawi's role. But this trickle of scepticism was overrun by a steady flow of stories in the US media which now placed Zarqawi not only in Iran, Syria and Iraq, but also in Lebanon, Turkey and Georgia, and credited him not only as an Islamist terrorist but as a specialist in the use of poisons, chemical warfare and gas attacks. In December 2002, the Jordanians stepped in again, naming him as the leader of an al-Qaeda cell which had assassinated an American diplomat, Laurence Foley, in Amman two months earlier.

Even now Zarqawi was a footnote, not a headline, but the flow of stories about him finally broke through and flooded the global media on 5 February 2003, when the Secretary of State, Colin Powell, addressed the UN Security Council, arguing that Iraq must be invaded, first, to stop its development of weapons of mass destruction, and second, to break its ties with al-Qaeda. For this second point, Powell relied heavily on the Zarqawi story. He pulled together the previous lines and built a platform on which a mass of future media coverage was built. That platform, we now know, was largely constructed of falsehood.

Powell said that 'Iraq today harbours a deadly terrorist network headed by Abu Musab al-Zarqawi'. He claimed that Saddam Hussein's regime was providing 'safe haven' for this group, identified as Ansar al-Islam. This was false.

Zarqawi almost certainly had taken refuge in the wildlands of northern Iraq where Ansar al-Islam was based, but he was not leading the group and, more important, Saddam was not giving it safe haven. The strongest evidence of this is contained in a report published in September 2006 by the US Senate Intelligence Committee which drew on internal Iraqi paperwork and US intelligence interviews with former Iraqi officials, both of which had become available after the invasion of Iraq in March 2003. These showed that, so far from harbouring Ansar al-Islam, Saddam's government had regarded the group as 'a threat to the regime' and blamed it for two bombings in Baghdad. At one point, the Jordanians had told the Iraqi regime that they wanted Zarqawi and others handed over, and Iraqi intelligence had formed a special committee to organise their capture. Surviving paperwork recorded their fruitless efforts to do so. The Senate report concluded with a CIA assessment that before the war 'the regime did not have a relationship, harbor or turn a blind eye towards Zarqawi and his associates'.

Powell also said that Ansar al-Islam's camp was being used for 'poison and explosive training'. This is directly contradicted by the evidence of Luke Harding of the *Observer*, who succeeded in reaching the camp only three days after Powell's speech and reported: 'The terrorist factory was nothing of the kind – more a dilapidated collection of concrete outbuildings at the foot of a grassy, sloping hill. Behind the barbed wire and a courtyard strewn with broken rocket parts, are a few empty concrete houses. There is a bakery. There is no sign of chemical weapons anywhere.' Having inspected the whole camp, Harding concluded that Powell's allegation was 'clearly little more than cheap hyperbole'. He also explained that the allegation came from the Kurds who were being attacked regularly by Ansar al-Islam and who, therefore, had a clear interest in trying to persuade the Americans to come in and get rid of them. After the invasion, US troops and reporters who went to the site found nothing more than old rat poison in defence of Colin Powell's claim.

Powell said Zarqawi was 'an associate and collaborator of Osama bin Laden and his al Qaeda lieutenants'. This crucial point is also contradicted by the report of the Senate Intelligence Committee, who found that in April 2003 'the CIA learned from a senior al-Qaeda detainee that al-Zarqawi had rebuffed several efforts by bin Laden to recruit him. The detainee claimed that al-Zarqawi had religious differences with bin Laden and disagreed with bin Laden's singular focus against the US.' The same conclusion was reflected in the evidence of Shadi Abdallah, an associate of Zarqawi who was arrested in Germany ten months before Powell's speech and became a prosecution witness. Abdallah said that, so far from being allies, Zarqawi was a rival to al-Qaeda and that on one occasion, he had refused to share with al-Qaeda money which had been raised for both groups by sympathisers in Germany. Loretta Napoleoni, the terrorism expert who has done most to research Zarqawi, considered the claim that he was allied to Osama bin Laden at this time and concluded: 'No evidence of such an alliance has ever been provided.'

As Jason Burke put it in the *Observer* in July 2003: 'Al-Zarqawi was indeed in Iraq but was not, as a thick sheaf of reports of interrogations of his close associates open on my desk make clear, an ally of bin Laden. His group, al-Tawhid, was actually set up in competition to that of the Saudi. To lump them together is either a wilful misrepresentation or reveals profound ignorance about the nature of modern Islamic militancy. Either way, there's no link there. Nor has any evidence for one surfaced since the end of the war.'

Powell said that Zarqawi had 'fought in the Afghan war more than a decade ago'. Reporters who have gone to Zarca in Jordan, where Zarqawi grew up, suggest that this cannot be true, since he did not make his first trip to Afghanistan until the spring of 1989, by which time the Soviet Union, against whom Osama bin Laden and other Islamist groups had been fighting, had already pulled out. Jeffrey Gettleman reported in the *International Herald Tribune* that 'Instead of picking up a gun, Mr Zarqawi picked up a pen. He became a reporter for a small jihadist magazine, *Al Boñian al Marsous*, whose name means "The Strong Wall". He was 22, with a medium build and shiny black eyes, and roamed the countryside interviewing Arab fighters about the glorious battles he had missed.'

Powell said that 'Zarqawi and his network have plotted terrorist actions against countries, including France, Britain, Spain, Italy, Germany and Russia'. There is evidence that Zarqawi had contacts who were raising money for him in Germany, and he may have been involved in plots there. But the rest of Powell's claim is riddled with uncertainty. Powell specifically suggested that Zarqawi was involved in plots to use ricin in attacks in England and France. In England, police had arrested a group of Algerians who were accused of plotting ricin attacks, but there was never any evidence to suggest they were working with Zarqawi, and laboratory tests showed that the 'ricin' was simply castor beans and cherry stones. In France, too, police had arrested suspects and accused them of planning a ricin attack, but there the 'ricin' turned out to be wheatgerm and barley, and they were all released. On the same day as Powell's speech, the Spanish Prime Minister, José Maria Aznar, a close ally of the Americans, told his parliament that police had arrested sixteen suspects linked to Zarqawi and in possession of ricin. No evidence was ever produced that these sixteen had any connection with Zarqawi, and in their case, the 'ricin' turned out to be washing powder.

Powell made two other claims. The first was that the Jordanians had arrested a man for the assassination of the US diplomat Laurence Foley in Amman in October 2002 and that 'the captured assassin says his cell received money and weapons from Zarqawi for that murder'. This was true in the literal sense that the Jordanian suspect had made this allegation. Whether he was telling the truth or simply complying with torture is less clear. It may be significant that the killing had already been claimed by a group calling itself the Honourables of Jordan who later repeated their claim and underlined the point by enclosing shells from the bullets which had been used in the attack.

Powell's final claim was to repeat the allegation, first aired by President Bush four months earlier, that Zarqawi had been in Saddam's Baghdad for an operation. In itself, this has never been finally confirmed or refuted. But it is a fact that US intelligence sources who told the press that Zarqawi had lost a leg before or during this operation were later compelled to admit their information was wrong, when Zarqawi sub-sequently appeared in videos with two perfectly healthy legs.

Somewhere buried beneath all this, there was a reality. Zarqawi was indeed an Islamist radical who had trained in one of the Afghan camps in the early 1990s and then gone back there in 2000 to set up his own camp to train others. He was determined to overthrow the Jordanian government and may well have had a hand in attacks in that country; and he knew others who had travelled to Western Europe where they raised money for his group and may have planned further attacks. He was, in short, a terrorist. But he was not the man portrayed by Colin Powell.

If the Zarqawi story ended there, it would take its place alongside the whole saga of the Iraqi weapons of mass destruction as part of the chain reaction of faulty intelligence, overstated official claims and failed journalism which shaped the build-up to the invasion of Iraq. But the construction of the Zarqawi story moved from the ad hoc teams of neoconservatives in Washington who had wanted to justify the war, into the hands of the new and permanent apparatus of 'strategic communications'. It is not clear whether the people who briefed Colin Powell knew they were misleading him or were themselves the victims of falsehood supplied by the Jordanians and the Kurds and the Iraqi exiles who provided so much misinformation about Iraqi weaponry. But in what followed, the evidence of deliberate fabrication is more and more persuasive.

February 2004, for example, saw a striking sequence of events. It began on the morning of 9 February, with a front-page story in the *New York Times*. The paper's Baghdad correspondent, Dexter Filkins, reported that US officials had obtained a seventeen-page letter, believed to have been written by Zarqawi to the 'inner circle' of al-Qaeda's leadership, urging them to accept that the best way to beat US forces in Iraq was effectively to start a civil war. The letter argued that al-Qaeda, which is a Sunni network, should attack the Shia population of Iraq: 'It is the only way to prolong the duration of the fight between the infidels and us. If we succeed in dragging them into a sectarian war, this will awaken the sleepy Sunnis.' (See www.flatearthnews.net for full text of story and letter.)

That morning, at the regular US press briefing in Baghdad, General Mark Kimmitt dealt with a string of questions about the *New York Times* report: 'We believe the report and the document is credible, and we take the report seriously . . . It is clearly a plan on the part of outsiders to come in this country and spark civil war, create sectarian violence, try to expose fissures in this society.' The story went on to the agency wires and, within twenty-four hours, it was running around the world.

Over the following days, the story was boosted repeatedly: first, on 10 February, when a lethal car bomb in Baghdad was attributed to Zarqawi by US officials; then, on 11 February, when the White House put out a 'global message' citing the letter as 'an effort to spark civil war'; again on 11 February, when General Kimmitt told reporters in Iraq that the reward on Zarqawi's head was being doubled, to $10 million; and once again, on 12 February, when Kimmitt announced a campaign of Zarqawi posters to be displayed around Iraq, and a new 'wild card' putting Zarqawi into the well-publicised pack of fifty-five playing cards showing the most wanted men from the Saddam regime.

The story ran on through the rest of February, given new impetus by public comments by President Bush in a speech in Louisiana on 17 February, and by Donald Rumsfeld at a press conference in Ireland on 23 February, both of them citing the letter as evidence of al-Qaeda's role in leading the insurgency. As the stories flowed around the world, reporters routinely recycled background on Zarqawi which was drawn from Colin Powell's flawed speech to the UN Security Council a year earlier. From March, Zarqawi became the central figure in media coverage of the Iraqi insurgency, repeatedly named as the man behind bombings, kidnappings and beheadings all over the country and as the man who was leading efforts to disrupt stability and the introduction of democracy. 'Every soldier in Iraq is looking for Zarqawi,' General Kimmitt told reporters.

Thanks to the efforts of the *Washington Post*'s military correspondent, Tom Ricks, we now know for sure that all this was the work of US strategic communications. In April 2006, Ricks obtained copies of a slide presentation which had been prepared for US General George Casey, then heading the Multi National Force in Iraq.

The first slide was headed 'Offensive Strategic Communications: Fighting the Negative Insurgency'. Then there was an arrow pointing to Zarqawi's name. The slide then went to a subheading, 'Feb '04 – The Zarqawi Letter', under which there were several bullet points. The first read: 'Selective leak to Dexter Filkins'. The second read: '$10 million reward'. The slide then went to another subheading, 'Mar '04 to Present: Villainize Zarqawi/leverage xenophobia response'. The subsequent bullet points included 'Media operations' and 'PSYOP', which is short for 'psychological operations'.

A second slide was titled 'Result', and it consisted of two paragraphs. The first read: 'Through aggressive Strategic Communications, Abu Musab al-Zarqawi now represents: Terrorism in Iraq; Foreign fighters in Iraq; Suffering of Iraqi people (infrastructure attacks); Denial of Iraqi aspirations (disrupting transfer of sovereignty).' The second paragraph read: 'Effect: Eliminate popular support for a potentially sympathetic insurgency. Deny ability of insurgency to "take root" among the people.'

All this was clearly reflected in the media campaign of February 2004, starting with the fabrication of news via the 'selective leak' of the letter to Dexter Filkins of the *New York Times*. When Tom Ricks exposed this, he spoke to General Mark Kimmitt, who acknowledged his role in the leak: 'We trusted Dexter to write an accurate story, and we gave him a good scoop.' And yet, when Kimmitt had dealt with questions from reporters on the morning of the *New York Times* report, he had spoken as though it were news to him: 'We believe the report and the document is credible, and we take the report seriously.' Two days later, again reflecting the slide presentation, Kimmitt was fabricating more news, telling reporters about the new $10 million-dollar reward on Zarqawi. Reporters simply swallowed and recycled all this and more. Indeed, Tom Ricks obtained another internal US military document in which Kimmitt himself wrote: 'The Zarqawi Psyop program is the most successful information campaign to date.'

This was not simply a matter of agenda-setting: in all of its most important features, the story line in this campaign was false.

It was not true that al-Qaeda was behind the insurgency in Iraq. There is clear evidence that it began in April 2003 when Moqtada al-Sadr led a Shia rebellion in what became known as 'Sadr city' in Baghdad; that, by May 2003, Sunni groups also were fighting the US coalition; and that the fighting then spread and fragmented as different political, ethnic, tribal and criminal groups attacked the coalition and each other.

Ahmed Hashim of the US Naval War College, one of the few academics who has had the courage to go to Iraq, researched the claim that foreign fighters were leading the insurgency and concluded: 'Hard empirical evidence – often from the US military forces – indicates that the foreign element is miniscule.' He discovered that of 8,000 insurgents detained in Iraq, only 127 held foreign passports. He then personally interviewed some of these foreign detainees and found that many were 'unsponsored' by any state or organisation, had no previous involvement in terrorism and had simply taken it upon themselves to go and fight the Americans in Iraq, where they had made contact with Sunni imams who became their 'mentors'. The small group of foreigners who had gone to Iraq on behalf of groups like al-Qaeda had been particularly active but had relied on Iraqi Sunnis to provide them with weaponry and logistical support, he found.

A September 2005 report by the Centre for Strategic and International Studies similarly found that the US had been 'feeding the myth' that foreign fighters were behind the insurgency when, in reality, they accounted for fewer than 10% of those involved. Tom Ricks's story about the Zarqawi media campaign cited a speech by a military intelligence officer, Colonel Derek Harvey, who had served in Iraq and who told an army meeting in the summer of 2005 that foreign fighters were 'a very small part of the actual numbers . . . The long-term threat is not Zarqawi or religious extremists but these former regime types and their friends.'

Furthermore, it was still not true that Zarqawi was working with al-Qaeda, any more than it had been when Colin Powell tried to make the link in his speech in February 2003. The evidence suggests that Zarqawi certainly was involved in violence in Iraq by August 2003 and that he had a small group around him, as he had when he ran a camp in Afghanistan from June 2000. But when the Americans launched their strategic communications plan against him in February 2004, he was still operating as a small, independent rival to Osama bin Laden. His attraction for the Americans appears to have been that he was a foreigner who enabled them to play the xenophobia card with their Iraqi audience; and that, courtesy of Colin Powell's speech to the UN, he was already an established media character.

Finally, there is good reason to suspect that the Zarqawi letter itself was a fake. It specifically claimed responsibility for all the suicide bombings in Iraq – apart from those in the Kurdish-controlled north – even though videos made by some suicide bombers clearly show they were Iraqi. The letter is also inherently suspect, because its contents so clearly served the US agenda. 'Zarqawi' complained that US security was getting stronger every day; that the creation of Iraqi security forces was removing his allies; that ordinary Iraqis would not assist him; and that the introduction of democracy would take away his pretext for fighting. It dealt with those who insisted that Zarqawi was a rival to bin Laden by saying, 'We do not consider ourselves people who compete against you.' It even slipped in a good word for US intelligence agencies: 'Our enemy is growing stronger day after day, and its intelligence information increases. By god, this is suffocation!' As General Kimmitt himself put it to reporters on the day of the *New York Times* story: 'This document does, in fact, demonstrate what we have been assessing all along.'

Beyond that, the letter simply showed no sign of having been written by Zarqawi. The Americans said it had been found on a CD, which naturally had no handwriting which could be compared with samples of Zarqawi's. The letter itself was not signed in anybody's name. And it was written in sophisticated, rhetorical Arabic which ran for seventeen pages – but Zarqawi was almost illiterate. Jeffrey Gettleman from the *International Herald Tribune* interviewed a man who had been in prison with Zarqawi in Jordan in the mid-1990s, who described how Zarqawi had once sent him a threatening note complaining that he was reading *Crime and Punishment*: 'He spelled Dostoyevsky "Doseefski". The note was full of bad Arabic, like a child wrote it.'

Finally, there was an embarrassing confusion about where the letter was supposed to have come from. General Kimmitt and his officials briefed reporters that it had been found on a CD in the possession of a courier named Hassan Ghul, who had been caught on the northern Iraqi border on 22 January, two and a half weeks before it was leaked to Dexter Filkins. However, a check back to the original press briefings on Ghul's capture shows that the Americans had claimed consistently at the time that Ghul was captured as he tried to cross from Iran to get into Iraq – surely the wrong direction of travel if he was supposed to be carrying a message from Zarqawi to bin Laden.

The illustration was very clear. It showed a cross-section of the interior of a mountain containing an enormous man-made cave: cut deep to avoid thermal detection; concrete stairs linking at least ten subterranean floors with dormitories, several floors of offices, a fuel depot and storage areas for weapons, including Stinger missiles; electric lighting, sophisticated ventilation, computer systems and telephones, all powered by the cave's own hydroelectric power generated from mountain streams; with secret exits and a main entrance big enough to take trucks and tanks. This illustration ran in media outlets across the world in November 2001, describing the refuge of Osama bin Laden in the mountains of Tora Bora in north-eastern Afghanistan. The then US Defense Secretary, Donald Rumsfeld, commented on it on the US television programme *Meet the Press*. 'Oh, you bet,' he said. 'This is serious business. And there is not just one of those. There are many.' In truth, there were none. Somebody fabricated that illustration.

The story was very clear. Suicide bombers working with al-Qaeda had attacked targets in Tashkent, the capital of Uzbekistan, killing themselves as well as police officers and innocent bystanders. This story ran around the world in late March 2004, complete with quotes from US and British 'officials' warning of the al-Qaeda threat to the region and naming two Islamist groups who were responsible for the deaths. However, the then British ambassador to Uzbekistan, Craig Murray, visited the site of all the incidents and was struck by the fact that there was no sign of any explosion at all; and the dead 'terrorists', who were said to have been blown up by their own devices, seemed to have been shot. He also read US intelligence transcripts of conversations intercepted at the time from senior al-Qaeda figures asking each other who was behind the attacks. He sent a message to the Foreign

Office in London pointing out that there was no evidence that these incidents had anything to do with al-Qaeda terrorism. He was re-assured to receive a reply from the Cabinet Office's Joint Terrorism Assessment Centre, which agreed with him. Somebody fabricated that story.

The TV interview was very clear. General Peter Pace, vice chairman of the US Joint Chiefs of Staff, told CNN's *Larry King Live* show that Iraqi troops resisting the US invasion in March 2003 had shot US prisoners of war, used civilians as human shields, stored weapons in schools, set up command posts in hospitals and pretended to surrender only to open fire. And in a line which made media stories around the world, he added the chilling tale of an Iraqi woman who, he said, had been hanged simply because she waved to coalition forces. In Washington DC, Sam Gardiner listened to that and strongly suspected that somebody had fabricated it. He added it to the thickening file of media stories which troubled him.

Sam Gardiner is no kind of anti-American radical. He is a former colonel in the US Air Force, who retired to teach strategy at the national war college. Gardiner had started his file just as the invasion began when he heard US officials describing units of Iraqi soldiers as 'terrorist death squads'. That troubled him because he knew it was not true (there is a difference, he said, between army units and terrorist death squads) and because it looked like a politicised attempt to maintain a link between the Iraqi regime and Islamist terrorism.

As the invasion proceeded, his file grew thicker. He spent four months collecting and checking media reports, and then he published a paper, called 'Truth From These Podia', which received almost no media attention (full text on www.flatearthnews.net). He logged stories about the Iraqis using children to fight US forces (he found this was untrue); Iraqi troops waving white flags and then attacking US troops when they stepped out to talk to them (almost certainly untrue); Iraqis wearing US uniforms to commit atrocities which would be blamed on the Americans (untrue); Iraqis ambushing US marines on the road to Baghdad (he found the marines had been attacked repeatedly by a US plane); Iraqis shooting prisoners of war (claimed personally by both George Bush and Tony Blair, later said by Downing Street to 'lack absolute evidence'); Iraqi artillery hitting a Baghdad street market (untrue – Robert Fisk of the *Independent* found chunks of US missile at the scene). In each of these cases, Gardiner tracked back and found that the falsehood had been fed into the media by 'official sources' of one kind or another.

Gardiner recorded stories about the mass surrender of the entire 51st Iraqi mechanised division (untrue); the fall of Umm Qasr (days premature); the fall of Basra (repeatedly, many days premature); the uprising by the people of Basra in support of the coalition (untrue). He followed the stories about Saddam Hussein's secret plans to fly his family to safety (no evidence) and Saddam's personal stash of $3.5 billion in a Libyan bank account (no evidence). That last story hit two targets in one smear, Saddam and the Libyans, and Gardiner tracked the flow of similar doubled-headed stories which attacked unfriendly regimes while delivering messages about Saddam. The Russians, who had failed to back the US invasion, were said to be hiding Saddam in their embassy in Baghdad (untrue). There were stories about the French, who had also refused to support the invasion, supplying missiles to Saddam (no evidence), and holding illegal strains of smallpox (untrue). There were even some triple-headers: the disliked French were using their embassy in the distrusted Syria to give passports to the enemy Iraqi elite to help them escape (all untrue); and both the French and the refusenik Germans were reported to have provided the Iraqis with precision switches for their nuclear weapons (untrue).

Gardiner concluded in his paper: 'It would not be an exaggeration to say that the people of the United States and the United Kingdom can find out more about the contents of a can of soup they buy, than the contents of the can of worms they bought with the 2003 war in the Gulf.' When I visited him in Washington, Gardiner told me that, after his paper was published on the Internet, he received a phone call from a PR officer who had been working for the chairman of the Joint Chiefs of Staff, General Richard Myers, who told him his suspicions were right on just about every story he had cited.

The pattern is clear. From Zarqawi to Saddam, from Afghanistan to Iraq, from Washington DC to Tashkent: there is a steady flow of fabrication. The storyline about Zarqawi is part of a larger storyline about al–Qaeda which is part of a larger storyline about terrorism which, in turn, is part of a global storyline about US foreign policy and its opponents. The notorious misinformation about the weapons of mass destruction in Iraq is simply one element in this pattern.

Not all of this is new. Throughout the cold war, the Americans fabricated media stories to put pressure on the Soviet Union and its allies. One example among many has been exposed by John Stockwell, who was the CIA Chief of Station in Angola during the civil war there in the mid 1970s, when Cuba had sent troops to defend the Marxist MPLA, who eventually formed a government. Stockwell recalled the glib ease with which his staff created storylines about the MPLA and the Cubans and fed them into the media either by putting out press releases through their local political allies or by briefing Reuters.

In a television interview, Stockwell described how one of his staff came up with a particularly successful creation which ran for weeks: 'It was a good story in terms of the CIA's propaganda interests. He had some Cuban soldiers raping some young Angolan girls. Then there was a battle and he had that Cuban unit cut off and captured. Then he had one of the victims identify the rapists. Then there was a trial and they were convicted. Then he had them executed by a firing squad of the women who were supposed to have been violated, with photographs of young African women with weapons shooting down these Cubans. There had never been a rape, there had never been military action, the Cubans had never been captured. It was all a fiction.' It all ran in the media.

In the same way, the US fabricated stories to attack unfriendly groups or nations by associating them with the Soviet Union. During the Reagan administration's campaign against the left-wing Sandinista government in Nicaragua, for example, US media outlets reported that the Russians had sent a freighter of MiG fighters to Nicaragua; that Nicaragua had sent arms and men to support communist guerrillas in Colombia and El Salvador; that the Sandinista government was anti-Semitic (even though the US Embassy in Managua had sent an undisclosed cable to Washington to say that the claim was baseless); that the Nicaraguans were trafficking cocaine into the United States; and that the brother of the Nicaraguan President had a personal stash of $1.5 billion in a Swiss bank account. As the then deputy assistant secretary for the air force, J. Michael Kelly, put it in a 1983 speech to the National Defense University: 'The most critical special operations mission we have . . . today is to persuade the American people that the communists are out to get us.' They did.

That cold-war operation lost funding and power after the collapse of the Soviet Union. But since then, it has rebounded. This started to happen in 1990/1, when the US military ran what it regarded as a successful psychological operations campaign as part of its strategy to oust Saddam Hussein's troops from Kuwait. This involved using the mass media to inflict deception on Saddam's generals, for example by staging a massive landing exercise in an area which was never intended to be part of the assault and 'allowing' reporters to hear about it. They sent leaflets and radio messages which, they believed, led to the mass surrender of Iraqi troops. As US troops crossed into Kuwait, this also involved the most tightly reined and manipulative use of reporters since the Korean War.

In his book *Second Front*, the US journalist John MacArthur describes how reporters on the ground were required to sign contracts, agreeing to be escorted at all times and to have every story and every photo read and approved before being filed; how reporters who tried to break out of these restrictions were obstructed, harassed and even arrested; how the US military filled the resulting news vacuum with carefully crafted appearances by the US commanding general, Norman Schwarzkopf ('a certifiable genius' – AP), video releases of 'smart bombs' hitting their targets (70% of US missiles missed their targets, according to subsequent military estimates) and soft interviews with US pilots and their families. This exercise was overseen by the then Defense Secretary, Dick Cheney, who later explained his view of the media during the war: 'Frankly, I looked on it as a problem to be managed. The information function was extraordinarily important. I did not have a lot of confidence that I could leave that to the press.'

This battlefield media strategy followed a $12 million campaign, orchestrated by PR specialists from Hill & Knowlton, which used misinformation from Kuwaiti exiles to provide a series of fabricated stories, climaxing, as John MacArthur found, in a substantially false presentation to the UN Security Council, in which five of the seven witnesses turned out to be using false names. The high point of this campaign was a notorious incident when Hill & Knowlton presented the story of a fifteen-year-old Kuwaiti girl, Nayirah, who was said to be so frightened of reprisals against her family that she could not give her full name and who described how she had seen Iraqi troops pulling premature babies out of incubators in a hospital in Kuwait City and hurling them to their death. Much later, the story was exposed as a falsehood, and Nayirah was revealed to be the daughter of the Kuwaiti ambassador in Washington DC. By that time, the story had gone around the world along with numerous other accounts of rape and torture. (One photograph which purported to show Kuwaiti civilians being shot by a firing squad of Iraqi soldiers turned out to be a picture of Iraqi soldiers being executed for looting.)

That campaign in 1991 encouraged the US military to expand the use of information as a weapon. But two other factors finally stimulated the creation of the new apparatus of strategic communications, linking military and civilian bodies alongside intelligence agencies and hugely expanding the scale of all their operations: first, the development of the Internet and the globalised news factory, which gave them the capacity to distribute messages rapidly and easily around the planet; second, the attacks of September 2001, which gave them a new kind of war and new political backing. Much of this apparatus is hidden deep in the darkness of government bureaucracy and yet, in addition to the media stories which are provably false, there are other ripples on the surface.

There are websites like Empower Peace (www.empowerpeace.org), which appears to represent a grass-roots campaign for world peace but which is, in fact, the creation of the US State Department, promoting US foreign policy; and the Iraq Crisis Bulletin which claimed to be an independent source of news about the US invasion in March 2003 but which turned out to be a front for Voice of America (www.iraqcrisisbulletin.com, now closed).

There is evidence of a very simple fabrication of media stories at the Operation Tribute to Freedom website where US soldiers returning home can log on and download pre-packaged speeches, including, for example, one specially designed for black servicemen ('I'm honoured to be speaking here at . . . name of event . . . and to have a chance to reflect on the rich heritage of African Americans etc'). Web-surfers will find blogs which claim to be from genuine US troops, attacking media reports on the troubles in Iraq and explaining, for example, that 'The Iraqi people want us here . . . Business is really picking up in the city, they are cleaning the streets, rebuilding the shops, and free enterprise is beginning to catch on.' Or they may find the widely circulated letter to 'Dear Mom' in which a US serviceman explains: 'I strongly believe in what we are doing and wish you were here to see for yourselves the honor and privilege that American soldiers aboard this ship are feeling, knowing that we are going to be a part of something so strong and so meaningful to the safety of our loved ones. Then you would know what this potential war is about. We will stand tall in front of terrorism and defeat it. We as soldiers are not afraid of what may happen. We are only afraid of Americans not being able to understand why we are here.'

And then there are the recurrent stories which precisely fit the template of traditional propaganda, albeit their falsehood has not been proved: the Taliban tearing out the fingernails of Afghan women who were caught wearing nail polish; the Taliban torturer who was said to have told his men, 'I want your unit to find new ways of torture so terrible that the screams will frighten even crows from their nests'; the Taliban leader, Mullah Omar, who was said to suffer brain seizures in which 'he sits in the driving seat of one of his cars, turning the wheel while making the noise of an engine'; and Osama bin Laden using hand grenades to go fishing.

In the same way, at various times, the world has been told about Saddam Hussein putting anthrax into commercially available perfume ('official sources'); the underground training centre for terrorists discovered in the Iraqi desert (US military briefing); the British marine who was hit four times in the helmet and was said to be the luckiest man alive. That last one we know was false: the *Daily Mirror* discovered that the marine's helmet had been shot up by his own mates while it was lying on the ground. That was handed out on the UK Ministry of Defence website.

As the US increased pressure on Iran over its alleged programme to build nuclear weapons, we have had stories about the Iranian President banning mobile-phone texts which make jokes about him (Iranian exile website with a track record of fabrication); Iranian Jews and Christians being forced to wear badges which declare their religions (Iranian exiles); a tanker-load of forged ballot papers being driven from Iran into Iraq for the election (Iraqi Interior Ministry to Dexter Filkins of the *New York Times*); Iranian ayatollahs encouraging sex with animals and girls of only nine (Iranian exiles); Iran's ambassador to the UN being one of the students who made hostages of US Embassy staff in Tehran in 1979 (Iranian exiles); terrorists in Iraq using equipment from the Iranian Revolutionary Guard to kill British soldiers in Iraq (British Foreign Office briefing, later retracted); the Iranian government running training camps for terrorists in Iraq (British military briefing, later retracted).

The ripples on the surface are clear to see. The difficulty is to get beneath the surface to see the hidden apparatus whose work is producing them.

It's very hard to be certain about anything in the world of intelligence, but, on the best evidence available, it appears that for several decades during the cold war, the largest media organisation in the world was the one run covertly by the Central Intelligence Agency of the United States.

That organisation shifted and shrank under the weight of a series of scandalous exposures, as American public opinion recoiled at the scale and nature of the CIA's manipulation of news; parts of it shrank again after the collapse of the Soviet Union.

Now – again, on the best evidence available – it appears that the CIA has been rebuilding its network of influence. And unlike the old cold-war model, the current CIA network is coupled up with the powerful new apparatus of strategic communications in which the US Departments of Defense and State are attempting to link all of their activities in the public domain in order to control the 'information battlespace'. And this, in turn, is flanked by similar intelligence projects which have been launched by US allies in the Middle East and

Western Europe, including Britain. All this has happened with the minimum of public scrutiny.

Although the intelligence operation is being shaped to work in harmony with the new apparatus of strategic communications, it differs from its partners in one key respect. While the military and state departments, as we shall see, are generally injecting their material into the media more or less overtly, through their PR arms, the intelligence agencies are working by subterfuge. In other words, the reporter who takes a 'strategic communications' story may well not realise that it is false, but at least he or she knows its origin. The CIA's hand, however, is usually completely hidden.

We can see this best by looking back at the way the agency ran its propaganda during the cold war. There, at least, we have enough solid information to see the way in which the subterfuge worked. Almost all of this information comes from two 1976 congressional inquiries, chaired by Senator Frank Church and Congressman Otis Pike; and from two defining works of investigative reporting in late 1977, by Carl Bernstein in *Rolling Stone* magazine and by John Crewdson and Joseph Treaster in the *New York Times*.

In sum, this shows the CIA was able to pump disinformation into the media through more than eight hundred different 'assets', scattered through every nation in the world, all of them disguised. More than four hundred of these assets were human: CIA officers posing as reporters; owners, editors and reporters who had signed secret agreements with the agency; freelance stringers who were on its payroll; staff and stringers who were available from time to time if the agency needed them. This list of human assets does not include cooperative reporters who, from time to time, were given briefings by the agency. Beyond this, the CIA used phoney front companies and foundations to take a controlling stake in a global network of newspapers, magazines, radio stations and news agencies. Some of these were existing outlets in which they made disguised investments; others were their own creation. 'We had at least one newspaper in every foreign capital at any given time,' according to one former CIA man talking to the *New York Times*.

The Pike Committee found, from the limited information which it was given, that 29% of the CIA's covert operations were for 'media and propaganda'. An enterprising researcher took that figure, compared it to the total annual CIA budget for all covert operations and concluded that in 1978 the agency had spent at least $265 million on propaganda, which turned out to be as much as the combined budgets of the world's three biggest news agencies – AP, Reuters and UPI – put together. The true picture was probably even bigger: the Pike Committee concluded that the 29% was a serious underestimate.

And this truly involved fabrication. The agency did not simply invent false stories; it also invented the evidence. It 'embellished' quotes from a Soviet defector, Aleksandr Kaznacheyev, and fed them to the *Christian Science Monitor*; it forged the diary of its former agent inside the KGB, Oleg Penkovsky, and published it as a book; it interfered with the content of Argentinian news films to encourage hostility to Fidel Castro; and, in the most notorious case, it dealt with its failure to obtain the full transcript of the famous speech by Khrushchev in 1956, denouncing Stalin at the 20th Communist Party Congress, by concocting its own version of thirty-four missing paragraphs and feeding them into the media through the Italian news agency, ANSA.

In practical terms, the CIA had the power to fabricate news wherever it wanted, without its hand being seen. If there was trouble in Japan, it could feed stories into the *Okinawa Morning Star* (it owned a substantial chunk), or the *Tokyo Evening News* (it owned the whole paper), or the *Japan Times* (it had agents in the paper). Faced with revolutionary movements in South America, it owned the *South Pacific Mail* in Chile; ran agents in the *Caracas Daily Journal* in Venezuela, the *Sun* in Haiti and the *Chronicle* in Guyana; flooded a mass of other South American newspapers through its undisclosed role in news agencies such as Agencia Orbe Latino Americano, LATIN and Editors Press Service; and poured stories into a hundred radio stations through the AIM radio agency (it owned it). In one single operation, to unseat the democratically elected government of Salvador Allende in Chile, the agency spent $12 million on propaganda.

Its most influential agents were tucked into foreign bureaux at AP and UPI, from where they could feed stories to the entire world. The CIA kept no agents in Reuters, simply because it was British-owned, and the CIA recognised that it was MI6 territory. However, when the need arose, the CIA used the MI6 agents in Reuters to place its own stories, and Pike concluded that the agency had done this frequently. 'Because Reuters is British, it is considered fair game,' according to Pike's final report. Alongside these mainstream news agencies, the CIA created its own, Forum World Features, which supplied stories to 140 newspapers around the world.

It had no scruples about spreading disinformation in allied nations. In Western Europe, it owned or invested in *Paris Match* and *Preuves* in France, *Der Monat* in Germany, *Forum* in Austria, *Encounter* in the UK, *Argumenten* in Sweden, the *Rome Daily American* in Italy, the *Brussels Times* in Belgium, an unidentified magazine in Athens, and *Vision* which covered all Europe and Latin America. At various times, it invested particularly heavily in propaganda in France, Italy and Western Germany, attempting to influence the outcome of general elections in which the agency also passed tens of millions of dollars to the political parties it wanted to win.

It had very few scruples about spreading disinformation in the United States, even though the 1948 Smith-Mundt Act clearly prohibits this. It did some of this indirectly, through 'blowback', when stories planted abroad were picked up by US media. One former CIA official told the *New York Times* that this was 'commonplace'. An internal CIA assessment of the campaign against Salvador Allende, for example, noted that fabricated stories had been appearing in the *New York Times* and *Washington Post* and simply commented: 'Propaganda activities continue to generate good coverage of Chile developments along our theme guidance.' In what might be regarded as a piece of cynical sophistry, a 1967 internal CIA directive concluded: 'Fallout in the US from a foreign publication which we support is inevitable and consequently permissible.'

But the agency also fed disinformation directly into US media, through some of the hundreds of human assets which it had hidden in the global media. The CIA attempted to draw a distinction between its foreign assets and its US ones. Asked if the foreign assets were used to plant stories, the then CIA director, William Colby, replied: 'Oh, sure. All the time.' (The *Guardian* in 1991 reported that the corrupt

Bank of Credit and Commerce International had been used by the CIA to make payments to hundreds of people, including ninety British journalists.) But Colby insisted to the Congressional inquiries that, in contrast to these foreign media assets, the fifty or so American journalists who were secretly linked to the CIA were used only to gather intelligence or to provide help on operations, never to run fabricated stories.

This admission in itself was startling, since the CIA network turned out to be concentrated in the most prestigious media outlets in the US: the *New York Times* had provided cover for at least ten CIA agents and had a general policy of cooperation with the agency; CBS Television was also providing cover and allowing the CIA to monitor all reports flowing into its newsrooms in New York and Washington DC; the NBC and ABC networks also worked with the CIA; *Newsweek* had an editor, a foreign editor, its Washington bureau chief, three business managers in its Tokyo bureau and stringers in Rome, South-East Europe and the Far East working at various times for the agency; executives at *Time* were so helpful that one CIA man told Carl Bernstein that 'You don't need to manipulate *Time* magazine, for example, because there are agency people at the management level'; *Reader's Digest* regularly ran CIA material; the *Christian Science Monitor* supplied unused copy to the agency and had a Far East reporter who was also the CIA's political adviser to the head of state about whom he was writing; Copley Press, which owned nine US newspapers and a wire service, harboured no fewer than twenty-three staff with links to the CIA; the London bureau chief of the Hearst news service was on the CIA books; other assets worked in the *Miami Herald*, the *Chicago Tribune*, the *Louisville Courier Journal*, the old *Washington Star*, the *Saturday Evening Post* and the *New York Herald Tribune*.

But the investigations by Carl Bernstein and the *New York Times* suggest that the CIA was covering its back when it denied using these assets for the direct distortion of US news coverage. They found, for example, that Arthur Hays Sulzberger, publisher of the *New York Times*, shifted one of his correspondents, Sydney Gruson, out of Guatemala at the request of the CIA which feared Gruson was about to uncover their plans to topple the democratically elected government there.

They found, too, that Sulzberger's nephew, C. L. Sulzberger, chief of the *New York Times* foreign service, had a briefing paper written specially for him by the CIA, put his byline on the top and ran it verbatim in the paper, on 13 September 1967.

There was a notorious controversy about this system at work after the attempt to kill Pope John Paul II in Rome in May 1981. Over the following two years, global media started to report that the would-be assassin, a Turk named Mehmet Ali Agca, had been working for Bulgarian intelligence and, therefore, ultimately for the Soviet Union. This was a politically powerful story in the context of the US looking for international support in its arms negotiations with the Soviet Union, and of the Pope's identification with the Solidarność rebellion against Soviet influence in Poland. Agca's trial, in March 1986, provided no compelling evidence at all to support this theory, but, by that time, reporters all over the world had repeated it.

It may be significant that it was originally promoted by two writers working together: Claire Sterling, a neoconservative journalist, who had a history of running CIA black propaganda; and Paul Henze, who was a former CIA station chief in Turkey. They published the first detailed account in September 1982, in *Reader's Digest*. The story was then picked up and recycled by several prominent media outlets, including CBS and NBC television, the *New York Times*, and *Newsweek* and *Time* magazines. In the absence of evidence, the story was kept alive by the Italian intelligence agency SISMI, closely allied to the CIA, which leaked an internal report claiming that Agca had been trained in the Soviet Union and then an alleged confession from Agca that he had been working for Bulgarian intelligence. Both were later denounced as fabrications.

Certainly, this concealed apparatus made a plaything of the media, to be taken down from the shelf and used in whatever political game plan suited the administration of the moment. There is a rare confirmed glimpse of the scale of this at work behind a story which appeared in the *Wall Street Journal* on 25 August 1986. The *Journal* told its readers that the Reagan administration was on a collision course with Libya after finding new evidence of its involvement in terrorism. The story was picked up by other US media. Three months later, documents which were leaked to Bob Woodward at the *Washington Post* revealed that this story was fiction and that it was merely one part of a complex strategy of psychological warfare, designed to destabilise the Libyan leader, Colonel Gaddafi.

Woodward revealed that two weeks before the *Wall Street Journal* published its story, the then head of the National Security Council, Admiral John Poindexter, had written to President Reagan to outline the strategy. 'One of the key elements,' Poindexter wrote, 'is that it combines real and illusionary events through a disinformation program, with the basic goal of making Gaddafi *think* that there is a high degree of internal opposition to him within Libya, that his key trusted aides are disloyal, that the US is about to move against him militarily.' The aim was to throw Gaddafi 'off balance', and make him appear ineffective in order to provoke opposition groups in Libya into overthrowing him. As Poindexter wrote: 'Any alternative leadership to Gaddafi would be better for US interests and international order.'

The strategy involved 'foreign media placements' by the CIA, including false stories that the Soviet Union was planning a coup against Gaddafi; high-profile military exercises by US and Egyptian forces on the Libyan border; deliberate incursions into Libyan radar range by US fighter planes; 'deceptive' movements by a US air carrier, designed to look like preparations for an invasion of Libya; 'disinformation' about visits by two senior US diplomats to Europe and North Africa, to make it appear that they were discussing Libyan terrorism; and the fictitious story in the *Wall Street Journal*, whose publication was met by a White House spokesman declaring that it was 'authoritative'.

By contrast, we know almost nothing about what the CIA is doing now. We know it is active again in propaganda. US News and World Report, in April 2005, reported that soon after the terrorist attacks of September 2001, President Bush signed a secret national security directive giving the CIA a free hand in fighting al-Qaeda, specifically including propaganda. By that time, the agency's Strategic Influence Section had been reduced to a staff of only some twenty people, but it created a new Global Information and Influence Team which appears to be spreading its target area beyond al-Qaeda. In February 2005, it ran a conference on strategy for influencing six nations: China, Egypt, France, Indonesia, Nigeria and Venezuela.

We know, too, that other allied intelligence agencies are working in the same way. In January 2005, *Haaretz* reported that the Israelis were reviving their Psychological Warfare Unit as part of 'the battle for consciousness'. In December 1996, *Izvestiya* reported that the Russian Federal Security Service was creating a new department of intelligence operations to influence the reporting of security affairs. In the background, two Italian journalists, Luca Fazzo of *La Republica* and Renato Farina of *Libero*, were suspended from their professional organisation after admitting to working secretly for the Italian SISMI. This emerged after prosecutors raided a flat which turned out to be an off-the-books office for SISMI and which contained files showing routine contacts between the agency and reporters.

In Britain, according to a recently retired officer, MI6 runs an I Ops section, which consists of two Intelligence Branch officers and four support staff. He says this section has particularly close links to the *Daily Telegraph*, the *Sunday Telegraph* and the *Financial Times*. Unlike the US, Britain has no law which prohibits intelligence agencies feeding stories directly into domestic media although, as a matter of tactics, he suggests, MI6 will often opt to work indirectly.

One of the few recent examples of this at work is Operation Mass Appeal. The former UN arms inspector Scott Ritter describes in his book, *Iraq Confidential*, how, in London in June 1998, he was introduced to two 'black propaganda specialists' from MI6. Ritter had been involved in monitoring Iraqi efforts to buy ballistic missile components in Romania. MI6 wanted to use this as part of 'a psychological warfare effort, known as Operation Mass Appeal'. According to Ritter: 'Mass Appeal served as a focal point for passing MI6 intelligence on Iraq to the media, both in the UK and around the world. The goal was to help shape public opinion about Iraq and the threat posed by WMD.' He records the MI6 propaganda specialists declaring that they could spread the material through 'editors and writers who work with us from time to time'.

In an interview for this book, Ritter added more detail. He said that he was first approached to help Mass Appeal in December 1997, when the MI6 station chief in New York asked him to dig out unused intelligence material which MI6 could then feed into the media of nations who were failing to support the programme of weapons inspections in Iraq. Ritter told me that the MI6 man specifically mentioned the French and Polish press.

Ritter said he went off and took his boss, Richard Butler, for a discreet walk down the corridor to explain the MI6 plan and, with Butler's consent, later retrieved two unused reports, both of which had been supplied by Israeli intelligence. One dealt with French chemical processing equipment being sent to Iraq in 1993/4; the other dealt with Polish pesticide equipment that had been sold to Iraq in the late summer of 1995. The significance of both reports was that they were unused because they were unconfirmed and were quite possibly misleading in implying that the French and the Poles had some role in assisting a chemical weapons programme in Iraq. Ritter told me he retyped them so that they could not be traced back and then passed them on to the MI6 station chief in New York.

Ritter said he heard no more until May of the following year, 1998, when he went to a meeting with MI6 at the Travellers Club in London and was taken aside by two of their Middle East specialists, who had clearly received the two reports which Ritter had handed over. He said they told him that France and Poland were no longer appropriate targets but, nevertheless, they wanted more unused material to move public opinion against the Iraqi regime. 'We need some new info. Are you still game?' he recalled one of them saying.

It was in the following month, June 1998, that one of the officers from the Travellers Club took him for lunch with the two MI6 'propaganda specialists', who asked for material on Iraqi activities in Romania. Ritter told me that they planned to target the media in countries where Iraq was winning public support, specifically India. 'But, of course, if they run it over there, they will eventually run it in the UK,' he recalled them saying.

Soon after this, Ritter resigned from his job and says he does not know what Mass Appeal then did, although Seymour Hersh, in the *New Yorker*, has quoted an unnamed US intelligence source claiming that MI6 held a series of meetings with a source from the UN inspection team who passed them dozens of 'crap' intelligence reports which MI6 then 'quietly passed along to newspapers in London and elsewhere'. However, there is one very interesting footnote.

Six months after the US invasion of Iraq, Ritter mentioned Mass Appeal in public at the House of Commons. As a result, Lord Butler's subsequent inquiry into the use of intelligence on Iraq asked MI6 to respond. There is compelling evidence either that Lord Butler completely misunderstood what he was told, or that MI6 lied to him and forged paperwork to support its lies. According to Lord Butler's report, the MI6 paperwork confirms that Ritter did indeed meet 'British government officials' in May and June 1998 but that this was to discuss how to make public the discovery of VX nerve agent on the tips of Iraqi missiles. This information, unlike that which Ritter says was involved, was confirmed to be true. Furthermore, this version of events reduces Mass Appeal to just two meetings, whereas Ritter was clear that it was already running before he was first approached in December 1997. 'Operation Mass Appeal was set up for this specific purpose and did not exist before May 1998,' Lord Butler concluded. The point is that this seems highly unlikely to be true, since the US Army laboratory report which found traces of VX nerve agent on fragments of Iraqi missiles was not even written until 10 June.

There is separate evidence of MI6 feeding misleading information to the press in the case of the *Sunday Telegraph* and Colonel Gaddafi's son. On 26 November 1995, the paper's chief foreign correspondent, Con Coughlin, ran a story describing Gaddafi's son, Saif, as 'an untrustworthy maverick' and accusing him of being involved in an attempt to flood Iran with fake currency. The story described a complex plot and claimed that it had been foiled by Egyptian banking authorities. Saif sued and, after several years of legal argument, the case finally came to trial in April 2002, trailing with it the disclosure that the story had been concocted and provided to the *Sunday Telegraph* by MI6.

Documents filed with the court revealed that Coughlin had obtained the story from a sequence of three lunches and two briefings with MI6 officers. At the final meeting, they had shown him what they claimed were photocopies of banking records which apparently proved that Saif was involved with one of the key players in the fake-currency plot. As a pre-trial judgement in the High Court put it, Coughlin 'became convinced' that the story was true. But it wasn't – after one day's evidence, the *Sunday Telegraph* publicly accepted that its story was wrong and agreed to pay a proportion of Saif Gaddafi's legal costs.

According to the recently retired MI6 officer, there was some heated debate inside MI6 about the way that this incident had discredited a favoured newspaper and revealed MI6's hand in the manipulation of the media. As a result, he says, two memos were circulated. One ruled that all future media stories must be 'grounded in truth'. This caused some cynical comment, first, because the wording was so loose as to permit falsehood, and second, because that had always been the official policy anyway. The second memo required all contacts with journalists to be cleared with and authorised by a section director. The former officer says his colleagues laughed openly at this, since MI6 officers in the field routinely briefed journalists and were not about to start asking for permission to do so.

Since 1992, when MI6 was finally given legal status, its I Ops offi-cers have been regularly briefing chosen correspondents, who routinely pass on those briefings as though they were true. (The BBC security correspondent, Gordon Corera, for example, in November 2006, told his audience that British intelligence had 'confirmed' that they did not know the location of the secret prisons where the CIA was holding and allegedly torturing Islamist suspects and that British agencies did not have direct access to the prisoners. He offered no evidence in support of the MI6 claim.)

In the past, certainly, this kind of briefing was backed up by a network of apparently independent news agencies and a PR agency, all of which belonged to MI6 or its sister organisation, the Information Research Department. Its structure appears to have covered the parts of the globe which were not covered by the CIA's cold-war network, including North Africa and the Middle East (the Arab News Service fed nearly every Arab paper while Sharq al-Adna radio covered the region), India and the Far East (the Near and Far East News Agency) and Pakistan (*Star News*). According to *Britain's Secret Propaganda War*, by Paul Lashmar and James Oliver, this network secretly funded news outlets which distributed stories which were variously true, distorted or entirely false; sometimes procured fabricated evidence to support these stories; and enjoyed particularly close links to the BBC Overseas Service and Reuters.

The scale of this British cold-war operation was reflected perhaps contentiously by the Russian spy and former MI6 officer Kim Philby who claimed that MI6 had penetrated the 'English mass media on a wide scale'. He alleged that MI6 had been running agents in the *Daily Telegraph*, the *Sunday Times*, the *Daily Mirror*, the *Financial Times* and the *Observer*. Less contentiously, the author and former MI6 officer John le Carré once said simply that MI6 had 'controlled large parts of the press'.

The new development, since the attacks of September 2001, is the construction by the US government and its allies, alongside the prop-aganda activity of intelligence agencies, of the new apparatus of what they are calling 'strategic communications'. It is a project of extra-ordinary ambition and yet it has been developed almost unnoticed in the public and political domain, almost without debate about its proper boundaries.

Its chief architect is the Pentagon, which has succeeded in engineering a significant expansion of its own ability to manipulate information as a weapon. It has set out its plans in a series of 'doctrine' papers, some of them published and some of them released under the US Freedom of Information Act. Those papers, together with interviews with some of those involved, show that the Pentagon's key contribution has been to increase its own role in military 'information operations', known as IO, to cover five related areas.

In theory, all five are directed only at enemies in the field: inter-fering with the other side's computer activity, including sabotaging or falsifying websites (Computer Network Operations), while protecting their own (Opsec); jamming or interfering with the other side's commu-nications (Electronic Warfare); misleading the enemy as to their own battlefield intentions (Military Deception); and spreading information to influence the 'emotions, motives, objective reasoning and, ultimately, the behavior' of their target audiences (Psyop). The key question for the global media and its consumers, is whether, in practice, those involved have the ability or the will to prevent the product of their activities spilling beyond their chosen enemies and into the public domain.

It is a measure of the importance which the Pentagon attaches to this new machinery that it has declared information operations to be a new 'core competency', formally designating it as the fifth arm of the military, with the same status as army, navy, air force and special operations. The aim, repeated throughout their published doctrine, is 'to dominate the information battlespace'.

That Pentagon machinery is itself only the core of the wider construct of strategic communications. Sitting alongside it is the empire of Public Diplomacy, most of it run for the US by the State Department, pouring multiple millions of dollars into 'pro democracy' media outlets, think tanks and other front groups with the intention of promoting US interests. And both the military IO and the State Department's Public Diplomacy are linked to their conventional PR efforts, not only in the Pentagon and the State Department, but across 'all elements of national power'. Furthermore, this American machinery is being linked to similar operations among allied countries.

In the language of the Pentagon, in a paper published by the US Joint Chiefs of Staff in February 2006: 'Strategic Communication constitutes focused US Government efforts to understand and engage key audiences in order to create, strengthen, or preserve conditions favorable for the advancement of US Government interests, policies, and objectives through the use of coordinated programs, plans, themes, messages, and products synchronized with the actions of all elements of national power.'

Behind that dull language, there is something very big moving. Along with the intelligence agencies, this apparatus must be a prime suspect as the source for at least some of the fabricated stories which have been flowing through the global media. The official line for all of this is that all information must be true and must be honestly attributed. But is that really the way it works? Or is this new apparatus a channel pouring falsehood and distortion into the media? After several inconclusive trips to Washington, I finally found the best evidence for an answer back in London.

Number 1, Whitehall Place is a grand old Victorian building, all oak panels and marble columns and gilt-framed portraits of worthy white-haired gentlemen in robes. It was here, by the banks of the Thames, towards the end of June 2006, that the secretive world of strategic communications chose to meet behind closed doors for a two-day conference. With only a little difficulty, I spent the two days in among them.

They had flown in from all over the world, several hundred of them, from the South African Information Warfare Department, the Australian Department of Defence, the Belgian armed forces, the French defence ministry. There were Dutch and Scandinavians, delegates from NATO HQ and the EU military staff as well as their counterparts from the British Foreign Office and the Directorate of Targeting and Information Operations in the Ministry of Defence. And the Americans.

Most of them were involved in military information operations, but there were Public Diplomacy people there, too, and government PR types as well. As they gathered in the coffee lounge to collect their lapel badges and their glossy folders full of paperwork, I spotted some of the big beasts of strategic communications.

There was Major General 'Buz' Altshuler, head of the US Army Psychological Operations Command, short and muscular with tight-clipped grey hair. Once, he ran his own printing business in California. Now, he was a key man in the creation of information operations as a fifth arm of the US military. From October of that year, for the first time, every brigade, division and corps in the US military would have its own Psyop element.

There was Colonel Jack Summe, known as 'Hollywood Jack' because he has something of the young Robert Mitchum about him, head of the new Joint Psychological Operations Support Element, JPSE (pronounced like 'gypsy'), which had been officially activated the previous October. After eighteen years as a Psyop man, Summe was now running a unit which had hired civilians from the world of advertising and marketing as well as psychologists and anthropologists to work with army specialists producing slick, high-quality newspaper stories, satellite TV, radio networks, leaflets, email campaigns and websites to be distributed through US infrastructure around the world with one simple aim, 'to persuade foreign audiences to support US objectives'.

And there, too, was the legendary John Rendon, the former political PR man turned 'information warrior' who has been working on contract for the CIA, the Pentagon and the US State Department, massaging public opinion on just about every American military action since they invaded Panama in 1989 to grab General Manuel Noriega. Rendon is short and chubby with glasses and talks a little bit faster than a machine gun. He is the man who began the CIA information campaign against Saddam Hussein in 1992 by conceiving, creating and launching what was arguably the world's most influential AstroTurf group, the Iraqi National Congress, whose exiles were eventually to feed so much disinformation into global media. Now he was working for the British Ministry of Defence, advising on 'product', as well as continuing to work for the US government, for whom, apart from his traditional work, he was now running global focus groups, mapping the output of global media and monitoring the activities of global websites and chatrooms.

I had been researching these people for months and so I already knew that this growing domain of strategic communications was responsible, for example, for the multimillion dollar funding of 'pro democracy' groups in countries including Afghanistan, Bolivia, Cuba, Haiti, Iraq, Iran and Venezuela; the network of radio and television stations broadcasting to millions of people in Cuba, North Korea, Afghanistan and the Middle East; news websites such as the Southeast European Times (www.setimes.com), CubaNet (www.cubanet.org), and Maghreb news for North Africa (www.magharebia.com); the funding of outwardly independent media outlets in Iraq; the creation of phoney websites, masquerading as the output of Islamist radicals; showers of emails and phone texts, carrying threats and promises to their target audiences; the campaign of Iraqi posters, including ones showing Saddam's head on Rita Hayworth's body and Zarqawi being spanked over somebody's knee; and the 1.4 million leaflets which were dropped on Iraq in a single day at the beginning of the invasion in March 2003.

But the big question remained unanswered. This new apparatus represented no significant threat to the media if the information which it was handling was essentially true, and/or if its efforts at deceit were confined to the battlefield. But was this domain of strategic communications really clean?

From my early research, I already knew that they were in some trouble. On trips to Washington DC, I had met people working in this apparatus who were simply aghast at US strategy for dealing with its global problems. (One emailed me: 'Things are so fucked up here, it is depressing every day.') I knew that these particular people were arguing that terrorism would never be defeated by 'kinetic force', which is Pentagon-speak for conventional military might; that they had to deal with underlying causes in Palestine and across the Middle East.

'This is all about the POI,' one of them had told me.

I had looked at him blankly.

'The Pissed Off Iraqi,' he said. 'Your unemployed, hard-up, pissed-off Iraqi. He doesn't want to fight, he wants a decent life for his family. We go in there, shooting up the neighbourhood. What the hell is that about? We kill one of these guys, and we recruit a hundred others to the cause. We have to stop killing people and start dealing with the causes of the problem. And we have to start building bridges.'

I had sat in a junk-food joint at Reagan National Airport with one of those who is directly involved and heard him argue that Western public opinion was completely confused, prepared to accept the use of violence but not willing to accept the use of information. 'They don't understand, this is a new kind of war. We have an enemy targeting all of our people all of the time. We can use the military and law enforcement to buy time. But we can't protect all of our people all of the time. We have to aggressively discredit their organisation, their leaders, their tactics, promote the alternatives. We have to stop them wanting to kill all of us – solve the problems that are causing this to happen, communicate, change the way they think. There's no other way. And we don't have to lie to do this. We mustn't lie. If you lie, you get caught and you lose your credibility. This is about persuasion.'

But I had found that these 'realists' were involved in endless turf wars. On the one hand, there were people in the Pentagon and the State Department who wanted nothing to do with a strategy that might be seen as propaganda. On the other, there were plenty of hard-liners who either refused to give up on conventional 'kinetic' warfare or who wanted to use strategic communications with a ruthless, clumsy indifference to truth. But, in spite of all this earlier research, I had no idea quite how bad things were.

I should say here that, about an hour into that first morning, there was a brief squawk of panic when they suddenly woke up to the fact that I was a journalist. But I'd paid for my seat, I hadn't lied on the application form, and an influential British Army officer spoke up for me, so we agreed terms: I could name the people who were there and I could quote what they said, as long as I didn't identify precisely who it was who had said what.

As the two-day conference unfolded, it soon became clear that there was real agreement among the delegates on only one point, that they were losing their information war. They spoke of the attacks in September 2001 not merely as an act of mass murder, but as a highly successful manoeuvre to seize 'the psychological domain', using the global mass media to send a message of hope and defiance to supporters and a message of intimidation to the West. On that day, they said, there had been no more than five fundamentalist websites in the world; now there were five hundred. Their enemies were not just sending out suicide bombers, they were filming the bombers making their heroic martyrdom statements and then distributing them through their websites and as videos and CDs, often cut with shots of victims of US bombing. Even the Taliban, with their aversion to modern tech-nology, had set themselves up on the Internet.

Against that, they acknowledged their own weakness. I heard a very senior US military officer confess: 'Our product is ill-defined and disjointed, uncoordinated and confusing, slow and cumbersome, not well understood, unclear and suspect.' Planning was weak or non-existent. The wrong messages were sent. The wrong audiences were targeted.

The wrong media were used (videos distributed in an area with no TVs, leaflets for people who couldn't read, emails for people who had no computers, radio broadcasts for people who had no radio sets).

One speaker played a video of a group of Iraqis gathering around a briefcase in the street; the briefcase exploded, and the legless scorched body of a man flew briefly across the screen. 'How are we protecting these people?' he asked. Then he played another video, shot at night, of an Iraqi boy casually setting up a roadside bomb. 'Most fighters in Iraq are paid for hire, they're not religious. In Abu Ghraib, there are kids in there – twelve-year-olds who get paid $20 to put down an explosive device; a thirteen-year-old who gets paid to throw a grenade. Halliburton come in and give a guy $3 and a stick to pick up rubbish. He's far better to take $10 to throw a grenade. We've had 40,000 detainees in a year. They get taken out to an aircraft carrier to be shaken up, then back to Abu Ghraib. It's out of control. What are we doing with these people? Are we even trying to dissuade them?'

Over and over again, they came back to the global opinion polls, which showed American credibility falling through the floor; and to their specialist focus groups which monitored young Muslims saying, as one speaker put it: 'You look at us, but you don't see us. You talk to us, but you don't listen. You believe in democracy inside your own borders, but not outside.' One said this 'credibility deficit' was caused by 'the primacy of domestic politics over foreign policy'. Another told me privately that it was caused, or at least aggravated, by their own clumsy media manipulation. He cited the photographs of prisoners at Guantánamo Bay, kneeling shackled before US soldiers, which were taken and released to send a message of victory to a US audience, without realising it was sending a message of arrogant brutalism to the whole Islamic world.

But their failure was their only consensus. The Americans, the British and the NATO delegates all had different doctrines and different definitions and different vocabulary for every element of their work. They could not even agree on what they meant by 'strategic communications'. Indeed, they could not even agree on using that term at all: there were some who wanted to call it 'perception management' or 'influence warfare' or 'strategic effects'.

Behind all this superficial disagreement, it soon became clear, there was a real operational confusion. Even within the sphere of military information operations, the military delegates could not agree on what they should be doing. There were senior US military officers who wanted to focus on psychological operations and unload all the computer, electronic and military deception activity as somebody else's job. That contradicted the official US doctrine. And it was contradicted by senior British figures who argued that Military Deception and Psyop had to stay together and furthermore be coordinated with stories for the mass media.

The military delegates all insisted that they had to find a way to work with their PR people (Public Affairs, as the Americans call it; Media Operations as the British call it; Public Information as NATO call it). They said they also wanted to find a way to cooperate with the long-term 'hearts and minds' work of public diplomacy. But the hard-line military people were fighting like cats in a bag on both of these fronts.

In private conversations during the conference, the PR people who dealt directly with journalists spoke of their alarm that the military specialists in Information Operations were trying to gatecrash their territory, jeopardising their credibility. They were particularly alarmed that, in Iraq and Afghanistan, US commanders had merged their public affairs spokesmen with their IO specialists into joint units, with the result that IO people were dealing direct with the media, sometimes ignoring the 'agreed talking points' which had been drafted by the PR people. The chairman of the Joint Chiefs of Staff, General Richard Myers, had taken the unusual step, in September 2004, of putting out a memo warning of the dangers of this merger: 'While organizations may be inclined to create physically integrated PA/IO offices, such organizational constructs have the potential to compromise the commander's credibility with the media and the public.' Despite the general's warning, the merger in Iraq had remained in place, though the Afghan units had been separated.

It turned out that a similar move had become the source of a bitter internal dispute at NATO HQ in Brussels. The military committee there had recently produced a draft policy memo, M422/2, which suggested that the military should have the upper hand in deciding what information was provided to the mass media. This had provoked some passionate opposition from NATO public information officers who were insisting that the military must remain subordinate to the political leadership of NATO and must not jeopardise NATO credibility by misleading the media. One delegate referred to the damaging incident in the NATO campaign in Kosovo when NATO warplanes bombed a civilian convoy, and NATO told the media: first, that it had not happened; second, that it had happened, but it wasn't a NATO plane that was responsible; third, that it could have been a NATO plane, but there was a Serbian tank in the convoy; fourth, that it was NATO, but the Serbs had done worse on other occasions; and finally, that NATO had screwed up and was deeply sorry for the loss of life. The conference was told that this fundamental policy dispute at NATO remained unresolved.

The hard-line military types, on the other hand, made no secret of their disdain for some of their PR colleagues. They were convinced that it was the Pentagon public affairs department which had leaked to reporters, in February 2002, their plans to set up an Office of Strategic Influence, to coordinate their IO activities. The leak led to the office being closed within days amid a national outcry against the use of propaganda. The hardliners insisted this was all media distortion and that the OSI was always going to stick to the truth. However, an account of OSI, written by its head, General 'Pete' Worden and later quoted in the *Columbia Journalism Review*, showed that the real doctrine was not so clear. Worden argued strongly for the truth as a matter of routine, but added: 'There is little doubt that disinformation and lies can be initially effective and that outright lies can be effective, particularly when the promulgator has a long history of apparent truth-telling. This suggests that outright disinformation in the case of the US is somewhat like an information warfare analog to using nuclear weapons.'

In the same way, the hardliners also blamed their PR colleagues for leaking details of the work of the Lincoln Group in the previous December. This revealed that Lincoln had been hired by the Pentagon to pay Iraqi newspapers up to $2,000 a time to run favourable stories which been written by the US military. ('Through diligent patrols, organized raids and searches, vehicle checkpoints and interaction with the Iraqi people, Iraqi army units have taken down terror cells and removed dangerous criminals from Iraq's streets . . .') This provoked another outcry about propaganda, with former Lincoln employees claiming that they had been planting a dozen stories a week, some of them very heavily slanted and containing fabricated quotes from non-existent Iraqi civilians.

And there were clashes, too, between some of the military and the public diplomacy specialists. Privately, hardliners derided the output of Charlotte Beers, the former advertising director who was appointed by President Bush to be Under Secretary for Public Diplomacy at the State Department, and who was responsible for a series of glossy advertisements for Iraqi TV about the lives of Muslims in the United States. And, against these hardliners, the public diplomacy specialists complained of persistent efforts by the Pentagon to muscle in on their activities, citing the Sarajevo Film Festival as a clean example of public diplomacy into which the new Psyop unit, JPSE, was trying to inject its own funding. In the background, in Washington DC, I had spoken to former CIA officers who had nothing but contempt for the whole range of military IO. One told me: 'There is a long history in the US, more than thirty years, of the Department of Defense clumsily getting into the realm of covert action, and they always fuck it up.'

Beyond this internal squabbling, there were striking examples of their shortage of skill. The Belgians distributed Psyop leaflets which they had produced for the Congo, which would have failed the grade as a first-year student magazine – badly laid out with long slabs of text; badly written with long, wordy intros which failed to make their point. In a workshop session, when a group was given the task of dealing with a media scandal around abusive behaviour by US troops, they showed a deep suspicion and dislike of journalists and no idea at all of how to handle them. I heard a very senior US military specialist, whose responsibilities included Computer Network Activity, confess that he'd 'never really understood that word "blog"'.

One speaker described a British Tactical Psyops team which had been working in Iraq. Its staff consisted of a builder, a fashion photographer, a telecoms engineer, a nursing graduate, several snipers and a mortar platoon on transfer to make up their numbers. It was headed by a reservist who had been working as the head of English at a girls' private school in Surrey. This highly unlikely team had done their best to persuade local people to accept British troops. They had produced a newsletter, but they had had trouble distributing it because they had no transport and, anyway, they realised most of their audience could not read. They had placed advertisements in the local paper, although they recognised that this was a waste of money, because the paper was a luxury item which very few people could afford. They had put out radio broadcasts and handed out colouring books and sweets and felt they were doing quite well until a Danish newspaper published cartoons of the Prophet Muhammad, and their popularity fell through the floor. Their most successful move was a piece of military deception, when they increased the security of their base by hoisting onto the roof a broken washing machine with an old satellite dish on top.

There were some signs of skill from the British Directorate of Targeting and Information Operations, which uses an 'at-a-glance' guide to controlling media messages, written for them by Alastair Campbell (in the colours of Burnley football club, which Campbell supports). They have hired anthropologists and psychologists to try to understand the people they are attempting to influence, although one senior British source told me that their best information on the tribes of northern Pakistan and southern Afghanistan remains the British East India gazetteers of the late nineteenth century.

And Colonel Summe's new Joint Psychological Operations Support Element – which had been deeply embarrassed by holding a contract with the Lincoln Group – was clearly using some highly competent civilian specialists. But even JPSE, the bright, shining new creation of American Psyop, was suffering: it needed a staff of 115; it had been funded for only eighty-eight; it had succeeded in recruiting only fifty-six, including civilians.

The general lack of skill was matched by a lack of coordination. One senior source in US Army Psyop, who was asked about some of the clumsier messages which had been put out in Iraq, said frankly: 'It was not Psyop professionals doing it. Senior officers paint themselves as information professionals but they lack knowledge of policy and rules; or they know them and ignore them out of expediency.' Another, heavily involved in front-line information operations around Iraq, told me: 'It's uncoordinated. It's not controlled. There is no main thrust. It's like having artillery units firing independently in different directions with no command.' He added that misinformation was being put out by uncontrolled units and was then being absorbed and recycled by other units in the US operation who did not realise that it was false. Some misinformation, he claimed, was even being recycled in intelligence reports.

But, ultimately, what was most striking was the absence of any kind of consistent agreement about the proper boundaries of what they were doing.

Should they always declare themselves as the source of information which they put out? JPSE had just produced a new draft policy and found itself caught in the middle of a dispute. On the one hand, a powerful lobby from the Office of the Secretary for Defense was calling for honest attribution. On the other hand, Centcom, which runs the US military operation in the Middle East, was warning that anything that was attributed to a US source lacked credibility. JPSE's legal advice was that they could get away with false attribution, but JPSE's own policy was to be transparent. Finally, they had produced a policy which attempted to straddle the gap with a dual system: 'active attribution' for some material, which would declare its US origin; and 'passive attribution' for other material, which would disguise its origin, unless there was a challenge, in which case they would admit they had produced it. That immediately ran into trouble with some delegates, who argued privately that passive attribution was a guaranteed device for destroying credibility. 'If you're going to lie, stick with the lie.'

Should they allow their material to reach the US domestic audience? They were completely split. Almost all of them were aware of the 1948 Smith-Mundt Act which forbids the dissemination in the US of information campaigns designed for foreign audiences. The Americans showed real concern to protect US media consumers (although they showed no interest at all in protecting European or allied audiences). Equally, almost all of them declared that with globalised mass media, it was simply not possible to prevent their product seeping back home. The official compromise, spelled out in the Pentagon's 2003 'Information Operations Roadmap', is that 'the distinction between foreign and domestic audiences becomes a question of intent rather than information dissemination practices'. A couple of Europeans pointed out privately that that left the barn door swinging wide open to feeding misinformation into the US.

Finally and most critically, should they tell the truth? This was where the fighting was most intense. The British argued for telling the truth and giving the same message to all audiences, and then in private they acknowledged that at that precise moment they were bending that rule by telling the UK domestic audience that their troops in Afghanistan would eradicate the production of heroin, while taking great care not to say any such thing to the Afghan farmers, whose support they needed and whose livelihood depends on the cultivation of opium poppies.

One of them described a UK Psyop leaflet in Afghanistan which had shown Osama bin Laden in a Western suit. This was a fabrication, albeit not on the most serious scale, and there had been an internal row, which had ended with the disclosure that this had been produced not by their military specialists, fifteen UK Psyops, who are based at the Defence Intelligence and Security School at Chicksands, Bedfordshire, but by MI6, who are not covered by military doctrine.

In open session, the Americans also held out for a policy of truthfulness, and there were several clear statements of intent that all JPSE products would be 'white propaganda' (i.e. attributed and true). In private, however, the American ranks were divided.

I talked to Americans who were deeply embarrassed by some of the misinformation which had been fed into the media by their colleagues. They cited the case of Private Jessica Lynch, who was captured in Iraq after fighting bravely against Iraqi troops (the truth was that her convoy had simply driven into the wrong place, and she had been taken prisoner), and who was raped and tortured in Iraqi custody (simply not true), and who was freed in a firefight at an Iraqi hospital (hospital staff had already tried to hand her over to the Americans and been shot at, and there is real doubt about whether there was an armed Iraqi anywhere near the hospital). But I spoke to others who denied that a single word of misinformation had ever been released about Jessica Lynch: the distortion came entirely from the press, they said. And I had several heated conversations with mid-ranking US military officers who insisted bluntly on their right to lie to the media.

I heard complaints about US military press releases which attributed the same verbatim quotes to supposedly different Iraqi civilians; about a US Psyop unit which had publicly burned the bodies of dead Afghans while broadcasting a message accusing the Taliban of cowardice; about the possibility that the notorious photographs of naked Iraqis being humiliated in Abu Ghraib prison were originally taken as part of a US Psyop operation; and about the death of twenty-four Iraqi civilians in Haditha who, according to leaked versions of an official inquiry the previous month, had been massacred by US marines even though US military spokesmen at the time of their deaths, in November 2005, had told the media that they had been killed by a roadside bomb.

I spoke to senior British sources who said they believed that the discovery of Mohammed Atta's passport in the rubble of the Twin Towers in September 2001 had been 'a throwdown', i.e. it was placed there by somebody official. Similarly, they said, they did not believe that Atta's will, which had allegedly been found in a suitcase which had accidentally failed to make it on to his plane, was anything other than misinformation. They conceded that they could not prove this.

After the conference, I looked at British involvement at the softest end of the spectrum – international news provided by the Foreign Office as part of its £600 million a year programme of public diplomacy. This pays, for example, for British Satellite News, which sends fifteen minutes of free news bulletins via Reuters satellites to 460 broadcasters, most of them in the Middle East and North Africa. Former BSN staff told me that one of their executives meets every Friday with the Foreign Office to discuss storylines, and that Foreign officials phone in with stories to be covered. They complained that scripts were cut or rewritten for political reasons.

I saw draft scripts which appeared to have been edited to placate allied governments. In a piece about Saudi Arabia, a line about the lack of universal suffrage there was cut. An item about a forum at Chatham House referred to a member of the audience asking the Egyptian Prime Minister, Dr Ahmed Nazif, about torture in his country; that was rewritten so that the member of the audience was said to have asked about 'human rights and fighting terrorism'. In a story about a speech by the UN Special Adviser on Displacement, Dennis McNamara, a section had been removed in which he said: 'Who's providing the arms to Africa? We are. The Western countries. Africa is awash with arms, and they're still selling millions of dollars every year.'

The apparatus of strategic communications is still under construction. It was clear from this conference that those involved had failed to answer fundamental questions about how it should be run. It was equally clear that, in the absence of agreed answers – and in the absence of any kind of effective oversight or regulation – a significant number of its practitioners had broken open the door that is supposed to separate them from the mass media and were pouring their product into the public domain.

Fallujah had it all – all the arts of the hidden persuaders. As US General Tom Metz prepared for the battle to take the Sunni town in November 2004, he looked back at the US marines' earlier attempt, in April of that year, and he saw a special kind of disaster, a military defeat inflicted not by the enemy's superior force but by the mass media.

Put simply, the marines' April assault had been stopped in its tracks by a barrage of protest from the interim Iraqi government and world public opinion. Both had seen the operation, as Metz himself later put it, in an article in *Military Review* in June 2006, as 'indiscriminate, disproportionate and in violation of the rules of war'. But in November, as he explained in that article, he set out 'to prevent the worldwide media clamor and international public condemnation that would negatively impact operations'.

Looking back, he described what he then did as 'a textbook case' of the use of information as a weapon and he claimed to have found an answer to the central question of strategic communications, 'to bridge the doctrinal firewall separating Information Operations and

Public Affairs without violating the rules governing both'. The assault on Fallujah did indeed use just about every tool in the information warrior's kit but – whether General Metz intended it or not – it also broke just about every rule in the book.

Metz used traditional military deception, for example by 'aggressive patrolling and feints' in the south of the city, to make it appear that that was where he would launch his attack, even though he always planned to go in from the north. That broke no rules. The same cannot be said for the interview given by a US military public affairs officer to CNN, on 14 October, which clearly suggested that the assault on the city had begun. The reality was that the assault was still three weeks away, but CNN's misleading story was broadcast all over the world and bounced back into Fallujah, where the insurgents reacted by coming out of their hideouts to take up their defensive positions, thus allowing US intelligence to map the lot of them.

Metz used conventional PR to put his angle on the story. Some of this was dreamed up by the Lincoln Group, whose work for the Pentagon was to prove so controversial. A leaked briefing paper from Lincoln was headed 'The Making of Heroes – Lincoln Group and the Fight for Fallujah'. In a section headed 'Concept', it proposed to promote 'the strength, integrity, and reliability of Iraqi forces during the fight for Fallujah'. This was highly contentious if not entirely misleading, since the US Congress had just released figures which showed that up to 82% of Iraqi recruits were deserting their units.

Lincoln, however, fed a classic pseudo-incident to the media by staging a press call in which the interim Prime Minister, Iyad Allawi, reviewed Iraqi soldiers outside Fallujah and delivered a neatly turned sound bite: 'The people of Fallujah have been taken hostage – and you need to free them.' Without recourse to a script, the soldiers cried back in unison: 'May they go to Hell!' To which the equally unscripted Allawi replied: 'To Hell they will go!' And the reporters went away with their story.

Metz understood the business of fabricating news and set up his men to perform manoeuvres whose sole purpose was to generate useful media coverage. As he recalled in *Military Review*, he issued guidance to all levels of his force 'to be prepared to execute actions specifically tailored to capture photographic documentation of insurgent activities'. He added: 'Specific guidance was handed down to key elements to develop bite-sized vignettes with graphics and clear storylines.'

With his men primed to stage events for the cameras, Metz used more than eighty embedded reporters to tell his tale. In the April defeat, Metz believed, the insurgents had used the main Fallujah hospital to generate hostile media coverage of dead and injured civilians. In November, he not only sent troops to grab the hospital at an early stage of the battle, he followed the Lincoln PR line by using a unit of Iraqi troops to do so and sent an embedded reporter, Kirk Spitzer from the CBS network, to cover 'the making of the heroes'. 'Although this small attack garnered only a footnote in history,' Metz recalled, 'it was decisive to winning the Information Operations battle: without this portal, the enemy had a much weaker voice.'

Metz urged his men to deliver what he called 'packaged product' for reporters, i.e. Video News Releases. 'This small component of the battle enabled the coalition to get its story out first and thereby dominate the information domain,' he said. This included an oven-ready story about insurgent atrocities and, as Metz described in *Military Review*, items about the devious behaviour of insurgents. He cited the case of a sniper using a mosque as cover: US troops were entitled to attack the mosque to get the sniper, he said, but 'as a main gun round moves downrange to destroy a sniper position, simultaneously the digital image of the sniper violating the rules of war, plus the necessary information to create the packaged produce, can be transmitted for dissemination to the news media'.

Metz's electronic warfare specialists reinforced their grip on 'the information battlespace' by jamming insurgents' communications to restrict their access to the media. This failed notably only once, when an embedded cameraman from NBC, Kevin Sites, filmed a US marine shooting dead an injured and apparently unarmed insurgent on the floor of a mosque. (After the film was broadcast, Sites was exposed to the full ferocity of the electric fence, and the marine escaped prosecution on the grounds that the insurgent was a threat.) Media control in the city did, however, succeed in suppressing news of the fact that US troops were firing white phosphorus at insurgents in what was later widely regarded as an illegal use of chemical weapons.

And then there were the signs of pure fabrication, picking up on the established theme that the insurgency was being run by foreign fighters linked to al-Qaeda. Once again, this involved the Zarqawi story. And once again, we cannot be sure who was orchestrating it. One of those close to the operation suggested to me that it was a classic example of the untrained military firing off uncoordinated messages, without anybody actually organising it. Against that, it may be significant that throughout the assault, all media contacts were handled by a 'special operations division' of the new Office of Strategic Communications: this was the precise structure, merging public affairs officers with Information Operations specialists, which had provoked the chairman of the Joint Chiefs of Staff, General Richard Myers, only two months earlier, to warn of the risk which this presented to US credibility.

All through the summer and early autumn, US planes had bombed 'precision targets' in Fallujah. Over and over again, doctors and Iraqi police in the city said the victims were women and children, claims which were sometimes backed by videos shot in the hospital; over and over again, the US insisted there had been no civilian casualties and that the target had been a Zarqawi safe house. By this time, Zarqawi was being credited with numerous attacks inside Iraq as well as the bombings in Casablanca, Istanbul and Madrid (for none of which was any evidence of a link ever produced). His arrest years earlier as a youth in Jordan for a crime of violence had been converted, via an AP wire story, into an arrest for sex offences. The US had released new photographs of him and raised the reward on his head to $25 million. A video of uncertain origin had been passed to an Iraqi television station, showing a group of masked 'Iraqi resistance fighters' denouncing Zarqawi. A website of uncertain origin had posted a video of the beheading of the US hostage Nick Berg, with a printed title claiming that this was the work of Zarqawi, even though Arab linguists pointed out that the executioner did not have a Jordanian accent; and others observed that it was strange that if Zarqawi was willing to announce himself as the executioner, he had worn a mask over his face for the video.

During the autumn, newspapers reported 'a leaked Iraqi intelligence document' which revealed that Zarqawi had a force of 1,500 fighters, 500 of whom were in Fallujah. Later, 'US officials' estimated there were 6,000 foreign fighters in the city. In the event, US forces captured some 1,000 men in Fallujah, fewer than 2% of whom proved to be foreign.

As General Metz's men finally moved into the city, a torrent of eye-catching stories flowed through the global media. One, which was widely used, scored an important point for the legitimacy of the assault by reporting that US troops had found Zarqawi's headquarters in Fallujah. This was described as 'an imposing building with concrete columns and a large sign in Arabic on the wall reading "Al-Qaeda Organisation"'. Most reporters simply failed to comment on the profoundly surprising idea that the most hunted terrorist group in the world would advertise its presence as though it were a branch of Woolworths (and the worrying fact that, in spite of this open declaration of its whereabouts, this imposing building had failed to be targeted by any of the US Air Force's 'precision strikes').

Other notable stories reported Iraqi troops finding a torture house full of DVDs of hostages being beheaded; up to twenty other torture houses; a surviving Iraqi hostage found chained to the wall, where he had been beaten with an electric cable; a germ warfare factory; insurgents waving white flags and then attacking US troops when they stepped out to talk to them; Iraqi insurgents shooting foreign fighters who were too cowardly to fight US troops; an audio tape on a website of uncertain origin which claimed to record Zarqawi urging on his fighters in Fallujah; and the mutilated corpse of a Western woman hostage found abandoned in the street (there were only two Western women held hostage at that time: Teresa Borcz Khalifa, from Poland, who turned up alive six days later; and the British aid worker, Margaret Hassan, who was shot to death at the end of November).

Fallujah tells it all, not just about the new aggression of the hidden persuaders, but also about the new weakness of the global media whom they manipulate. It is impossible to be certain that all of the eye-catching stories in that last torrent from Fallujah were untrue. But it is certain that not one of them should have been published or broadcast: each of them screamed the possibility of its falsehood; each of them needed to be checked; and if there was no evidence to support them, then each of them should have been chucked. Yet, all of them ran. Reporting like that would have led the cheers for Pontius Pilate.

Unlike some of his colleagues, Metz had studied 'information operations' and understood the built-in bias in the rules of production in the news factory. 'We must recognize,' he wrote in *Military Review*, 'that the current global media gravitates toward information that is packaged for ease of dissemination and consumption: the media will favor a timely, complete story.' So, he packaged it. In theory, the media were free to reject his packages. In practice, they accepted all of them.

There were stories coming out of Fallujah – from the Office of Strategic Communications or from the hidden hand of intelligence agencies – which were untrue, falsely attributed and deliberately aimed not only at the insurgents inside the city but at global media consumers including those in the United States and allied countries. As General Metz observed in *Military Review*: 'The capabilities to move information not only around the battlefield but also around the world have grown exponentially. Information Operations' importance grows daily.'

It is this ability to reach into the news factory, to plant stories at will and then to watch them circulate the planet, which links the two domains of the hidden persuaders: the burgeoning industry of public relations, and the newly expanded apparatus of propaganda. Both of these domains have a history which reaches back before the point at which corporate owners took over the media and undermined their ability to gather and check facts. Both of them have become immeasurably more powerful as a result of that takeover and its reduction of the work of so many reporters to the passive processing of easy information.

Ultimately, the US has run into trouble with its strategic communications in Iraq, particularly with its use of the Zarqawi story. After February 2004, the Americans continued to give the media alleged letters to and from the terrorist mastermind. One of them, released in October 2005 and said to have been written to him by Osama bin Laden's deputy, Ayman al-Zawahiri, was so full of inconsistencies and improbabilities that Neil Quilliam, an Arabist working for the Control Risks security group, told me that at one point, he laughed out loud as he read it. Zarqawi put out a public statement saying that the letter was a fake. In May 2006, when yet another of these alleged letters was handed out to reporters in the Combined Press Information Centre in Baghdad, finally it was widely regarded as suspect and ignored by just about every single media outlet.

Arguably even worse than this loss of credibility, according to British defence sources, the US campaign on Zarqawi eventually succeeded in creating its own reality. By elevating him from his position as one fighter among a mass of conflicting groups and thus scoring political points with its domestic political audience, the US campaign to 'villainize Zarqawi' glamorised him with its enemy audience, making it easier for him to raise funds, to attract 'unsponsored' foreign fighters, to make alliances with Sunni Iraqis and to score huge impact with his own media manoeuvres. Finally, in December 2004, Osama bin Laden gave in to this constructed reality, buried his differences with the Jordanian and declared him the leader of al-Qaeda's resistance to the American occupation.

However, the most important problems are not those of the US military but of the global population of media consumers who continue to turn to newspapers and broadcast outlets as though they were sources of truth. Sometimes, they may be. It is worth repeating that there are still reporters out there who have the time and skill and courage to do their work effectively. But, for the most part, falsehood, distortion and propaganda flow freely through the hands of churnalists, who simply have no option but to package it rapidly and pass it on.

Sometimes – perhaps Colin Powell's deeply flawed remarks about Zarqawi at the UN Security Council are an example – the process is as simple as the one that was involved in the global tale of the millennium bug: born out of genuine uncertainty, 'cranked up' by those who think it might be true, and then exaggerated remorselessly by those who have a vested interest in it and then again by those who simply have no idea what they are talking about. Pure ignorance usurping knowledge.

More often, the rules of production of the news factory themselves impose their own demands as media outlets pick easy stories with safe facts and safe ideas, clustering around official sources for protection, reducing everything they touch to simplicity without understanding, recycling consensus facts and ideas regardless of their validity because that is what the punters expect, joining any passing moral panic, obsessively covering the same stories as their competitors. Arbitrary, unreliable and conservative.

Most worrying, however, this flow of falsehood and distortion through the news factory is clearly being manipulated, by the overt world of PR and the covert world of intelligence and strategic communications.

It is particularly striking that, during the 1950s, as both the PR industry and the cold-war apparatus of propaganda took off in the United States, there was a loud chorus of concern. This is when Vance Packard published *The Hidden Persuaders*, warning that 'Americans have become the most manipulated people outside the Iron Curtain'. This is when Daniel Boorstin was researching *The Image*, warning that 'the making of the illusions which flood our experience has become the business of America'.

Those warnings went unheeded. The boundaries of acceptability have slowly slipped backwards; what was America's problem is now the world's; what was scandalous is now merely normal. Somewhere out there, the truth is dying.

Part Four
Inside Stories

'If the public knew the truth about the way certain sections
of the media operate, they would be absolutely horrified.'

Alastair Campbell

7. The Dark Arts

It was a shocking morning in Orchard Grove. The neighbours with the neat lawns and the detached houses were thoroughly ruffled to see clear signs of some kind of official raid going on in their street. Steve Whittamore was positively gutted, as he later put it, to find out that it was his house which was the object of the raid. And then the raiding party itself were shocked, at the sheer scale of what they found. It was the morning of 8 March 2003. The lid was coming off the top of Fleet Street.

Inside number 3 Orchard Grove, the officers from the Information Commission, which polices the security of confidential databases, went to work in Steve Whittamore's office. They knew he was a private investigator. They knew he had been working for Fleet Street newspapers. What they never suspected was that he had kept a more or less complete record of every job he had done for every newspaper for the past six or seven years.

The raid that morning in Orchard Grove, New Milton, down on the Hampshire coast, yielded up boxloads of workbooks, ledgers and invoices as well as the handwritten notes which Whittamore had kept of every conversation with every reporter who had called him. There they all were, Fleet Street's finest, calling up their dealer to order their illegal supplies – criminal records, ex-directory telephone numbers, itemised telephone billing, mobile-phone records, lists of 'friends & family' telephone numbers, credit-card statements, bank statements, driving licence details.

When its officers had finally amassed and analysed all the paperwork, the Information Commission found that, in the last three years alone, 305 different journalists had asked Steve Whittamore for a total of 13,343 different items of information. Some of these journalists worked for magazines. But the overwhelming majority worked for Fleet Street titles – eight national dailies and ten national Sundays.

And this was not only red-top tabloids, but also the *Evening Standard*, the *Observer*, the *Sunday Times*, *The Times* and the *Daily Mail*. Indeed, it was the *Daily Mail* which was the most active single buyer – sixty-three *Mail* journalists had made a total of 985 requests (an average of at least one every single working day over the three years).

And, overwhelmingly, the requests which had been made of Whittamore involved breaking the law. When the Information Commission analysed the 13,343 requests, it found that Whittamore's records for 1,998 of them were too vague to allow any definite conclusion, but the remaining 11,345 were all classified as being either certainly or very probably in breach of the Data Protection Act, which forbids access to confidential databases. In their attempts to persuade Whittamore to break the law for them, Fleet Street journalists had handed over huge amounts of money. Analysing the requests from the ten most active journalists, the Information Commission found that between them they had paid Whittamore to obtain 3,291 pieces of information which were certainly or probably illegal, costing them an estimated £164,537.50. The total price tag for all of the requests over the previous three years had to be well over half a million pounds.

For the investigators, the shock was not just the scale of the demand from newspapers for illegal access to information, but also the number of different people who seemed to be involved in supplying it. Over the next few months, they followed up the leads in Steve Whittamore's paperwork and exposed a cluster of loose networks which had been working together sucking information out of confidential databases and trading it to Fleet Street. They found the networks had two techniques – sometimes they conned the information out of unwitting workers ('blagging', as they called it); sometimes they simply bribed. The investigators followed the leads.

Down on the Sussex coast they found a Hell's Angel – a former soldier who had long hair, a long beard and a well-honed ability to call up the offices of British Telecom, posing as a BT engineer or accounts worker, to blag them into providing supposedly secret information. He specialised in finding ex-directory numbers for famous people and converting phone numbers into home addresses, so that reporters could turn up on the doorsteps of their targets. They raided him.

In south London, police working on Information Commission leads found their way to a civilian police worker called Paul Marshall, then aged thirty-nine, who admitted that he had been using his job in the control room at Wandsworth police station to dabble his fingers in Scotland Yard's computer databases in search of saleable titbits about celebrities who had been the victims or witnesses or even the perpetrators of crime. Police also found he had stolen a truncheon, handcuffs and other police equipment to use in sex games with his partner, an unexpected discovery which proved to be very important. He was arrested.

In Sidcup, Kent, the Information Commission traced two men who worked in the regional office of the DVLA, the Driver and Vehicle Licensing Agency, who had apparently been selling the home addresses of celebrities and public figures who had registered their cars, as the law requires, without realising that that exposed them to Fleet Street's intrusion. The investigators searched the two men's desks and found a diary which listed Steve Whittamore as a contact. Both men were suspended from work.

In Devon, police who were independently pursuing members of the same cluster of networks arrested two police officers and a civil servant from the Department of Work and Pensions and charged all three of them with selling confidential information.

These sources, scattered across some of the state's biggest databases, appeared to be peddling their information through at least ten different private investigators, former police officers and petty criminals, who knew each other and worked with each other, swapping contacts and making deals together in their corner of the information black market. All of them were traced and raided and questioned by the Information Commission or police, who found yet more paperwork.

Armed with this evidence, the Information Commission and police in London and Devon prepared a sequence of four different court cases. This was the most powerful attack ever mounted on the infor- mation black market in Britain. It threatened to knock a hole in its operations, not simply by exposing the way it worked but also by subjecting its members to the kind of fines which would wipe out their profits. Beyond that, it threatened to expose the role of Fleet

Street, the reporters and editors and owners who were commissioning these offences. It was a nervous time for newspapers.

They need not have worried.

It was two years before Steve Whittamore finally found himself in the dock. At Blackfriars Crown Court, in south London, on 15 April 2005, Whittamore sat in his best dark suit alongside the civilian police worker Paul Marshall, a recently retired police officer who had worked with Marshall named Alan King, and an old friend of Whittamore's called John Boyall who is also a private investigator. This, the most serious of the four cases, focused on the procuring of information from police computer systems. All four men admitted that they had broken the law. The sole object of the hearing was to decide how they should be punished.

A prosecution lawyer, Riel Karmy-Jones, stood and outlined the case against them, explaining how Paul Marshall had trawled Scotland Yard's computer databases in search of 'very personal and confidential details' on well-known people including among others: the Mayor of London, Ken Livingstone, and his partner, Emma Beal; two actresses from *EastEnders*; the family of Ricky Tomlinson, who stars in the BBC comedy *The Royle Family*; a leading trade unionist, Bob Crow of the Rail Maritime and Transport Union; and a former occupant of the Big Brother house on Channel 4. The police computers were linked to those of other organisations so that, apart from criminal records, Marshall had been able also to search the secret list of ex-directory phone numbers and the supposedly confidential database listing the names and private addresses of car owners. He had sold whatever he found onwards through the other three men in the dock, often exposing the private problems not only of the targets but of their friends or family.

The prosecutor was just explaining how the ultimate paymasters for all this activity were journalists, how the prosecution had traced nineteen separate occasions on which this group of men had been paid to obtain police information by Fleet Street newspapers including the *Sunday Mirror*, the *Mail on Sunday* and the *News of the World*, when the judge, John Samuels QC, interrupted and asked a highly relevant question. Where were the journalists? Everybody else was in the dock. Where were the paymasters, the people who had commissioned this illegal activity?

The prosecutor could not explain.

As to the four men who had been placed in the dock, if the police who had brought this case believed that at least these defendants faced some serious punishment, they were badly mistaken. In theory, the law allowed the men to be given an unlimited fine and/or imprisonment for up to six months. The judge talked of severe penalties: 'A message has to go out to others who are tempted to act in a similar way. It will, in appropriate circumstances, result in immediate custodial sentences.'

However, the judge went on to explain that Paul Marshall had already been dealt with in an earlier trial, for stealing police equipment for his sex games. The judge in that case had been told that Marshall was seriously ill and about to die and, therefore, had decided to give him a conditional discharge, even though stealing from an employer and then denying it in court could easily have earned him a prison sentence. Now, this judge explained, he found himself boxed into a corner – selling information was a less serious offence than theft, and so he could not impose a more severe punishment than the one which had been imposed on Marshall at the earlier trial. With clear reluctance, he gave Marshall another conditional discharge. And since the other three men in the dock were no more guilty than Marshall, the judge was compelled to give them the same.

Steve Whittamore and his three co-defendants contained their feelings just long enough to leave the court, walk down the road and stumble through the door of the nearest pub before allowing themselves to punch the air and whoop for joy.

In theory, Whittamore was still in trouble. He faced a new trial, brought by the Information Commission, for his work with another of the networks which had been trading information. This group had drawn on the work of the Hell's Angel who blagged British Telecom and of the two men who had been suspended from their jobs with the DVLA in Sidcup. One of those men had died, but the Hell's Angel and the other DVLA worker had been charged along with Whittamore. Those three were joined on the charge sheet by two more of Whittamore's private-investigator friends and also by an associate from south London. The Information Commission had been building the case for more than two years. It soon fell apart.

The commission was worried about the cost of the trial. There were six defendants with their solicitors. If the defendants instructed barristers, the Information Commissioner would have to do the same. A trial could run for two or three weeks. The final costs to the public purse would run into hundreds of thousands of pounds and at the end of it, even if they were all found guilty, the six men's lawyers certainly would argue that any sentences would have to fall into line with the earlier case at Blackfriars Crown Court – so they would all walk out with conditional discharges.

In June 2005, two months after the Blackfriars hearing, the Information Commission decided that it just wasn't worth it and dropped all the charges against Whittamore and the five other defendants. It should be said on their behalf that since the evidence against them was never tested in court, there is no basis for saying that any of Whittamore's co-defendants in this case actually broke the law.

The following spring, in March 2006, Devon police went to Gloucester Crown Court to try the two police officers and the civil servant from the Department of Work and Pensions whom they had investigated and who, they believed, had been selling information. In the dock beside them were three other men who were said to have helped them sell their product, including one of Steve Whittamore's private-investigator friends who had just had charges dropped by the Information Commissioner. This case had been in the pipeline for nearly four years. It too fell apart when the defence lawyers put forward legal arguments, and the judge accepted that there was insufficient evidence to prove any offence.

In one remaining case, another of Whittamore's private-investigator friends who had seen the Information Commission drop charges, John Gunning, was caught personally blagging information out of British Telecom. A BT worker who dealt with his calls had become suspicious, and Gunning was traced, charged and convicted at Salisbury Magistrates' Court on 27 March 2006. He was fined just £600.

Four cases; a total of fourteen defendants, several of whom had been charged in more than one case: final result, just about nothing. And what about Fleet Street?

The *Guardian* ran a story about the end of the Blackfriars case on its website. No other national newspaper mentioned a word about any of the cases.

And, in particular, nobody pursued the question which the Blackfriars judge had posed. Why weren't the journalists in the dock too? All that paperwork which they had found in Steve Whittamore's office left no doubt at all that newspapers had been paying for this information. It named the reporters who had commissioned the work; it identified the news editors who had approved the work; helpfully, some of the invoices explicitly identified the goods that had been traded as 'confidential information'. The investigators had even found copies of itemised invoices which named the commissioning journalists and, for example, quoted the particular car number plate which had been converted into an address via the contacts at the DVLA in Sidcup.

The problem was money. The Information Commission feared that Fleet Street newspapers would defend themselves by hiring expensive QCs which, in turn, would mean that they would have to hire their own QC; that the newspapers would then embroil them in a long series of preliminary hearings to test the law and the evidence, all of which would break the limited legal budget which was available to them. Fleet Street was just too big a beast.

It was as if no journalist had ever done anything wrong.

Many journalists will protest that there is nothing wrong with any of this. They will say that their job is to obtain information; that the state has no business deciding what should and should not be published; that this is simply the free press at work. Most of all, they will say that they are working in the public interest.

They may prefer not to acknowledge that buying their way into confidential databases involves no skill and no professional satisfaction and is really no better than a fisherman who can't be bothered with a rod and line and just chucks some explosives into the lake instead.

Certainly, they would deny that they could, in truth, be doing most of this blagging and bribing themselves and that a big attraction of hiring private investigators like Steve Whittamore is that, for the most part, it is they and not the journalists who will end up in the dock.

Some may even claim that they don't believe in privacy, that if you have nothing to hide, you have nothing to fear, although it is a strict rule in every office of every media organisation that they will not give out home addresses for journalists; and most journalists have ex-directory phone numbers; and just about none of them has ever published his or her own bank statements or credit-card printouts or tax returns.

But what is most important is that, if they choose to defend this kind of activity, they will be defending the behaviour of the organisations for which they work, which demand scoops but which will not pay for the staff to deliver them by lawful means. If falsehood and distortion are now the routine products of the corporate news factory, corruption is its most dangerous by-product.

It's never easy to look back from the midst of the epidemic and see how the germ first started to spread. There has always been a little dirty play, a little illegal stuff going on in the shadows of Fleet Street.

In the old days, it was the crime reporters who were most likely to cut a dodgy deal, not so much with the villains they wrote about (although one or two of them were a touch too friendly with the Kray gang) but with the detectives from whom they wanted stories. Crime reporters regularly bunged cash bribes to serving police officers in order to procure information.

In the early 1970s, two of them were hauled into court for it. Tommy Bryant, who ran a news agency which specialised in crime, was charged with stealing six police photographs and with more than forty counts of dishonestly handling police material. The court heard about his diary, in which he listed the birthdays and wedding anniversaries of police officers and their wives and children so that he could send them a little gift as required. Then John Ponder, the chief crime correspondent of the *Evening Standard*, was charged with inducing a police officer to commit a breach of discipline. Both men ended up being acquitted of all charges, but Ponder suffered badly. Before his trial, he became so depressed that he shot himself, although he survived with a ruined spleen, and then the *Evening Standard* sacked him.

At the time, the two trials caused intense bad feeling. The other crime reporters complained bitterly that it was hypocritical of the police to prosecute reporters for malpractice from which so many officers had been content to profit; and perhaps even more hypocritical of the *Evening*

Standard to sack a man for breaking the law on their behalf and, the other reporters suspected, with their knowledge.

What was really happening was that the new commissioner at Scotland Yard, Robert Mark, had encountered a force so bent that, as he put it, 'I had never experienced institutionalised wrongdoing, blindness, arrogance and prejudice on anything like the scale accepted as routine.' He sacked, ousted or jailed numerous gangs of bent officers, sweeping away with them the whole business of hacks bribing cops for information. Mark was happy enough for that to happen, describing the 'questionable relationship' between crime reporters and police officers as 'one of the most long-lasting and successful hypocrisies ever to influence public opinion'. So things changed. In shape but not in kind.

In Fleet Street now they talk about 'the dark arts'. Well, they talk about it in private, but they won't tell the truth about it in public. The truth is that soon after Robert Mark crushed the old corruption in the mid 1970s, national newspapers found new ways to operate, by using other people to do their dirty work for them. It's impossible to pinpoint the moment when that started, but certainly by the early 1980s, the dark arts were beginning to spread through Fleet Street, with private investigators as their vehicle. Once again, it started with the bribery of serving police officers.

One of the key figures in this darkly shadowed history is a man who, for legal reasons, I can't name. Let's just call him Z.

Z is happy to describe himself as a journalist, and it's true that he earns a living by selling stories to national newspapers. Z is also happy to describe himself as a former detective. The simple reality is that Z is bent. He was bent in the police and he went on to be bent in Fleet Street.

As a detective, he was the target of a lengthy inquiry during the early 1980s, which concluded that he had been taking cash from professional criminals in exchange for burying damaging evidence. With some deft footwork, Z managed to avoid a conviction, but he was kicked straight out of the police. Within months, he was earning a new living (and taking sweet revenge on his former employers) by acting as a conduit for corruption, linking Fleet Street's money with police officers on the take. As a senior figure in Z's former force put it to me: 'He was a corrupt officer. He knew a lot of other corrupt officers. And he acted as a go-between.'

Journalists who have worked with Z agree that they have used him as a middleman to carry cash bribes from their newspapers to serving police officers, in exchange for which those officers have supplied confidential information about crimes and victims of crime as well as pulling background information off the computer networks to which police have access. Senior police officers believe whole inquiries have had to be abandoned as a result of leaks sold through Z. In one high-profile murder inquiry, a detective who was a close friend of Z was taken off the investigation after being accused of selling information to the press.

In some cases, the reporters have come to know the serving officers who are on the receiving end of their bribes. One of those officers was stashing his Fleet Street cash in a safety deposit box, only to be caught out when, for entirely separate reasons, Scotland Yard got a search warrant to open the boxes of several serving detectives; the officer claimed that he was simply keeping the cash there for personal reasons and survived to sell again. Another officer who was taking bribes to supply the press via Z got fed up with Z skimming a fat commission off the top of the payment and started selling direct to reporters. Somebody grassed him, and he found himself on the wrong end of a corruption inquiry. He blamed Z for pointing the finger at him, suffered a nervous breakdown and retired on grounds of ill health.

Several private investigators soon started to play the same game, particularly after 1987 when British Telecom introduced itemised phone bills, which rapidly became a target for PIs who obtained copies of the bills, initially by bribing BT staff and then later by developing the techniques of blagging. Ian Withers, for example, became a key source for Barrie Penrose, a famously slippery investigative reporter at the *Sunday Times*. I have no evidence that Withers broke the law on his behalf although, by the time he started working with him, Withers had already picked up convictions for organising a plot to snatch a two-year-old girl from her mother, using illegal bugging equipment, and illegally obtaining confidential information from police, Inland Revenue, banks and building societies (although this last conviction was overturned on appeal by the House of Lords).

Withers was the personal contact of Barrie Penrose. The man who started to supply a regular service to the Murdoch papers generally was a garrulous northerner called Jonathon Rees. He had never been a police officer himself, but he ran a security business in south London, called Southern Investigations, which hired serving officers who went moonlighting from their work at Scotland Yard to do jobs for him. This gave him a highly effective network of contacts.

Rees soon became a prolific source of leaked information, especially for the *News of the World*, for whom he provided a steady series of leaks from active police inquiries and sensitive data from Yard records. By the late 1980s, the paper was the main client for Rees's security business. According to one of those involved, a *News of the World* executive became involved in a corrupt relationship with him, paying Rees over the top for the work he did for the paper while Rees handed him back enough cash to pay off his credit-card debts and to cover private school fees for one of his children.

Rees picked up other media clients, including the *Daily Mirror*, the *Sunday Mirror* and the *Sunday Times*. By the late 1990s, Scotland Yard was so alarmed by his activities that, in May 1999, they placed a bug in his office in south London and recorded some of his business. Among his sources, they found, were Tom Kingston, a detective constable in the south-east regional crime squad who eventually ended up in jail for selling drugs; Duncan Hanrahan, who left the force to set up his own security agency and ended up in jail for corruption; Martin King, who had left the force and was working with Hanrahan and ended up in jail for conspiracy to corrupt; Austin Warnes, a detective constable and heavy user of cocaine, who ended up in jail for conspiracy to pervert the course of justice; and an officer from the Royal Protection Squad who was on a retainer of £150 a month to provide information about the royal family and other VIPs. An internal Scotland Yard report concluded that Rees and his colleagues 'have for a number of years been involved in the long-term penetration of police intelligence sources . . . Their thirst for knowledge is driven by profit to be accrued from the media.'

Scotland Yard's bug recorded Rees earning multiple thousands of pounds from news desks. Sometimes, he was selling trivia – the Buckingham Place police officer who had been having an affair with a female member of staff; the neo-Nazi bomber David Copeland hearing the voice of God in prison. Sometimes, he was selling material which clearly threatened important police operations, including a Special Branch bulletin summarising police knowledge of Albanian crime gangs in London, which turned up in the *News of the World* in August 1999. Journalists were prepared to use Rees to buy leaks from the inquiry into the murder of their BBC colleague, Jill Dando, even if that did make it more difficult to catch her killer; and to disclose the source of intelligence which had led to the capture of the gangster and murderer, Kenneth Noye, even if that did jeopardise the future use of the intelligence source.

One journalist, Doug Kempster from the *Sunday Mirror*, was in regular contact with Rees, buying information about active police operations. Kempster was caught by the bug sharing his opinion that 'Asians look better dead' and having a laugh with Rees about a 'one-legged nigger'. Kempster was subsequently arrested and questioned about suspected offences under the Prevention of Corruption Act. While police were searching his home, a postman arrived with an envelope containing a copy of the confidential *Police Gazette*, which contains details of active police inquiries, and a note signed with the initials JR. The Crown Prosecution Service decided not to prosecute Kempster on the grounds that although he had clearly been paying Rees for police information, it was not clear that he knew Rees was acquiring the information by corrupt means.

Newspapers also used Rees's police sources to buy information from confidential databases. On 29 July 1999, the bug caught Doug Kempster casually chatting to Rees about getting access to the bank accounts of Prince Edward and his wife, the Countess of Wessex, not because some powerful public interest justified it but simply so that the *Sunday Mirror* could find out whether the Countess had been paid for appearing in *Hello!* magazine. Rees was happy to oblige: he had two particularly good contacts who worked for one of the main high street banks. One of them, whose first name is Robert, was known as Rob the Bank; the other, who specialised in handling 'high value' accounts was known simply as Fat Bob. The bug also recorded Rees 'monitoring phone lines', obtaining telephone records and penetrating the DVLA database. (On one occasion, he was asked to find out about the owner of a Porsche and, within precisely thirty-four minutes of being given the car's details, he had the owner's name and home address from the

DVLA as well as his criminal record from the police national computer.)
All this was illegal. Indeed, even when he gained access to open records,
Rees managed to find an illegal way to do it. When he used Cameo,
an online version of the electoral roll, he did so by using the account
of the *Sunday Times*, whose password had been slipped to him by his
corrupt executive friend at the *News of the World*. 'We're stealing this,'
Rees chuckled as he showed off his access to a colleague.

Rees was so useful that News International were put off him neither
when he was arrested on suspicion of murdering his business partner
(and released without charge), nor when his more recent business
partner, former Scotland Yard detective sergeant Sid Fillery, was
convicted of possessing child pornography, nor when he was arrested
for plotting to plant cocaine on the estranged wife of a client who
hoped it would help him get custody of his child (for which Rees
was sentenced to seven years in prison). News International records
show that, even after he emerged from this prison sentence, he was
still routinely selling them information, including telephone records,
and had his own account with them (number 583266).

Z and Jonathon Rees were merely the brand leaders. By the mid
1990s, Fleet Street was employing several dozen different agents to
break the law on its behalf. Most were PIs. A few were ordinary civilians who developed the knack of 'blagging' confidential information
out of banks and phone companies. A middle-aged mother from Ruislip,
Rachel Barry, was regularly conning ex-directory numbers and itemised
phone bills out of BT on behalf of various newspapers until she was
caught and convicted in October 1997.

At first, they worked almost entirely for the tabloids. Over the years,
they helped red-top reporters to pull off some highly successful stunts:
the electronic bug which Ray Levene from the *Sunday People* used to
catch the Conservative minister David Mellor visiting his girlfriend's
flat; the attempts by various hacks to intercept the phone calls and
messages of Richard Kay, then the *Daily Mail*'s royal correspondent,
because they thought he must be having an affair with Princess Diana;
the tap on the phone line of the television presenter Angus Deayton
when he was being pursued over his sex life. Maybe it did mean
breaking the law. But it sold papers.

Every so often, one of these stunts would break out into the public domain. The tabloids would deny everything, and the posh papers would look straight down their noses and write slightly smug, slightly amused pieces about those wild and whacky red-top chaps and their dodgy ways, as if this sort of activity was something entirely alien to them. The truth is that, by the mid 1990s, the posh papers were bang at it too – because they were suffering from exactly the same commercial pressures which had corrupted their tabloid colleagues. In the world of profit-seeking journalism, ethics were sidelined along with real journalism.

Z continued to buy bent officers for the red-tops but opened up a particularly lucrative line of business with the *Daily Mail*, which seemed to suffer no anxiety at all about the fact that they were privately commissioning police corruption at the same time as they were publicly demanding law and order and claiming to support the police.

Reporters who have worked at the *Mail* talk of handing over envelopes containing up to £3,000 in cash. Some of these were for Z to pass on to serving officers as bribes. Some were passed direct to the officers. Some were passed through other private investigators. *Mail* reporters say they often drank with corrupt officers at the Wine Press in Fleet Street. One night a group of them, emboldened by much alcohol, decided to go off and burgle the home of a senior official in the criminal justice system whose son, they had heard, was growing cannabis. They enlisted the help of a specialist officer who had been trained in the art of burglary so that he could place bugs in the homes of criminals. According to another reporter who was in the Wine Press with them, a *Daily Mail* reporter led this group off to the senior official's home in north London and finally failed to break in only because a senior detective in the robbery squad heard what was happening, contacted them by phone and warned them that their target was so senior that they would be caught by the sophisticated alarm systems which had been installed in the house to stop terrorists.

At one point, the then commissioner of the Metropolitan Police, Paul Condon, was so worried about reporters corrupting his officers that, like Robert Mark before him, he ordered an inquiry. But the corruption beat him. One *Mail* reporter recalls taking a phone call from a friendly officer who wanted to warn him that they had been running undercover video surveillance on the Wine Press and had caught on camera an officer talking to a reporter who fitted his description. Forewarned was forearmed, and Condon's inquiry failed to expose any of the newspapers. (Indeed, the bug in Jonathon Rees's office recorded him cursing Condon and planning a newspaper story to embarrass the commissioner and a senior officer in the anti-corruption squad. 'It's only worth doing if it hurts them,' he said.)

Reporters from the *Daily Mail* to whom I spoke independently agreed that they have bribed not only police officers but also civil servants. For example, they targeted officials who had access to the massive database of the social security system, which registers the personal details of every British citizen with a national insurance number and every foreign national with a right to work in Britain – some 72 million private citizens. One reporter who has now left the *Mail* recalled: 'We used to use the social security computer as if it was an extension of the *Daily Mail* library. You phone your contact, have a chat, say you're looking for such-and-such a guy, this age, rough location – is there any chance? Keep chatting. He says, "Oh, we've got five people of that name." You say, "Well, give me all five". You get home addresses, phone numbers, maybe workplace too. They get you information off the database, and you reward them with a dirty great meal or an envelope.'

Mail reporters soon discovered that if they had one source with access to a government database, that same source was probably linked to other confidential databases in other departments. At one point, according to one *Mail* source, a reporter in the newsroom was bribing a Ministry of Defence police officer who could access several databases including Scotland Yard's. *Mail* reporters separately claim that they also had regular access to what is arguably the most sensitive of all confidential information, the health records of some of their targets. They recall one particular reporter in the newsroom who specialised in this. In sum, as one *Mail* veteran put it to me: 'If the *Mail* go for you, they get every phone number you have dialled, every schoolmate, everything on your credit card, every call from your phone and from your mobile. Everything.' Even if it is against the law.

While Z spread the dark arts to the *Daily Mail*, his rival Jonathon Rees, whose main source for funding police corruption has always been

Rupert Murdoch's papers, was doing bits of business for the *Sunday Times* as well as for the *News of the World*. But Rees was only one small item in the gallery of dark arts at the *Sunday Times*. By the mid 1990s, the paper was up to its elbows in illegal news gathering.

Sunday Times reporters, like their colleagues on the *Mail*, speak of the routine payment of cash bribes to civil servants and police officers. One recalls, as a young trainee, being sent off to the Charing Cross Hotel to hand over £2,000 in cash to a man he understood to be a civil servant. 'There was enormous pressure to deliver stories, and we were not allowed to come back empty-handed,' according to another, long-serving *Sunday Times* man.

Like the *Mail*, the *Sunday Times* has used private investigators routinely to breach the privacy of its targets. I spoke to one expert blagger, on condition of anonymity, who described how he had started working for the paper while he was on the staff of a security agency, where he specialised in penetrating social security records and private bank accounts. Later, he went independent and worked directly for senior *Sunday Times* reporters.

One investigator described being hired by the *Sunday Times* to target Asif Zardari, the husband of the then Prime Minister of Pakistan, Benazir Bhutto, whose credit-card statement he supplied so that *Sunday Times* reporters could find out where he had been staying and what he had been spending his money on. Yet another private investigator worked first for the *News of the World* and then for the *Sunday Times* in a bizarre and ultimately unsuccessful attempt to prove that Prince Harry was not really the son of Prince Charles: this involved trying to follow the Prince around in order to seize a drinking glass or a used tissue to test his DNA.

But the *Sunday Times* went one step further and, in addition to using private investigators, directly hired their own blaggers. The most successful of these was a former actor from Somerset named John Ford, who used the skills of his former profession as well as a natural gift for mimicry to blag his way into confidential databases, particularly those of British Telecom, building societies, credit-card companies and banks. Ford's work for the paper was an open secret: he was used widely by different reporters and was paid through the news desk. When I spoke to him, Ford claimed he had now stopped for ethical reasons. Reporters also describe using an actress as a blagger. In addition, the paper directly hired an accountant named Barry Beardall, who set up a front company in order to blag for them. (Chapter 8, which deals with the history of the *Sunday Times*'s Insight team, includes tape recordings of Beardall blagging information about the future Prime Minister, Gordon Brown, from Brown's solicitors.)

As the *Sunday Times* became more embroiled in corruption, so, too, its leading lights became more anxious about being caught. This reached the point where, in July 2003, they approached an experienced former *Sunday Times* reporter called David Connett and offered him a bizarre deal: they would bring him back into the London office as a full-time senior member of the Insight team, which specialised in investigations, but they would disguise their link to him. Instead of putting him on the staff, they would pay him as a freelance. He would work in their office alongside staff reporters, he would act as deputy editor of Insight and attend conferences with senior executives, but he would have no staff contract, no *Sunday Times* email address, no internal phone number. The object was for him to handle the dark arts for Insight and, just in case he got caught doing something illegal, they could deny their connection to him.

This secret arrangement emerged only because two years later, in July 2005, the *Sunday Times* closed the Insight team and made David Connett redundant without recognising his rights as a staff reporter. He appealed to an employment tribunal. In a hearing in Stratford, east London, in April 2006, which was widely ignored by Fleet Street, David Connett blew the whistle on the *Sunday Times*.

He told the tribunal: 'The *Sunday Times* had developed a taste for a number of reporting techniques which were known in the news room as "the dark arts", ranging from sleight of hand to others which are unlawful. These techniques were not exclusive to Insight, as others in the *Sunday Times* carried out similar procedures. Insight was at the heart of most of it.' He explained that he had been hired 'off the books' because Dean Nelson, who had been appointed editor of Insight, was a Christian who found it morally difficult to be involved in the dark arts, even though senior executives insisted on using them: 'The point was that in the event of problems arising over difficulties – sensitive stories – if it came out we had purchased stolen goods, stolen documents, the purpose of this arrangement was for Dean to be able to say it wasn't the *Sunday Times*, it was a freelance . . . I would work off the books so Dean could say it was nothing to do with the Insight team and that he had merely commissioned the story from a freelance in good faith.'

Connett told the tribunal of repeated pressure from senior executives on the paper to use the dark arts and suggested that the managing editor Richard Caseby, the managing editor for news Mark Skipworth and the news editor Charles Hymas had all approved his employment arrangement. The tribunal heard that some executives used to make a joke of it, pretending to be unable to hear Connett's remarks in discussions 'because you're not here, mate, are you?' The tribunal considered an email from one of Connett's former colleagues on the Insight team, Edin Hamzik, which recalled: 'It was better for the team to keep him off the books in case we got rumbled on one of the projects . . . so we could have a get-out clause if we got caught.'

The *Sunday Times*, in evidence to the tribunal, denied Connett's story and said he was hired on a freelance basis simply because he was a freelance. However, the tribunal agreed that, although Connett might not have been entitled to all the benefits of a staff member, he was clearly more than a casual employee. They awarded him £30,000 for unfair dismissal.

By the late 1990s, according to one of those who was involved in the networks around Steve Whittamore, some twenty private investigators were specialising in servicing Fleet Street's demand for illegal access to private information. Both Scotland Yard and the Inland Revenue caught staff trawling sensitive databases in search of saleable stories. Led by the *Daily Mail* and the *Sunday Times*, other quality newspapers joined the red-tops in corrupt practice.

The *Sunday Telegraph*, which might compete with the *Daily Mail* for its place on the moral high ground demanding law and order and ethically correct behaviour, has done it. At one stage, reporters there were allowed to commission the dark arts themselves, but the costs started running out of control so the paper imposed a rule that all such work must be commissioned through a news executive. Go back, for example, to the day when Thames Valley police discovered the dead body of David

Kelly, the Ministry of Defence weapons specialist who had been swept into the caustic row about the BBC's reporting of the invasion of Iraq.

His body was found at about 8.30 on the morning of Friday 18 July 2003. At 11 a.m., the police announced the discovery in a press release. Less than five hours later, the *Sunday Telegraph* had procured a printout of the contents of the dead man's itemised phone bill. The information was sent by fax, timed at 15.38 that afternoon. It listed every phone number that had been called from David Kelly's home between 1 March and 23 April, including the list of those which were recorded as belonging to 'friends & family'. There was no great 'public interest' reason for this swift invasion of the dead man's private life: this was nothing to do with uncovering the truth about Iraqi weapons or government policy. This was simply a device for the *Sunday Telegraph* to buy itself a lead over its competitors in finding people who would give them background about David Kelly's life. The *Sunday Telegraph* may or may not have known that the source who sold them Kelly's phone bill had already sold the same bill to the *Sunday Times*.

The Times, too, has enjoyed the dark arts. One of its reporters used Steve Whittamore. And according to the former Conservative treasurer, Lord Ashcroft, *The Times* used a private investigator called Gavin Singfield to obtain confidential information about his donations to the Conservative Party. In his book *Dirty Politics, Dirty Times*, published in 2005, Lord Ashcroft wrote: 'Gavin Singfield is not a sophisticated computer hacker and he did *The Times*' dirty work, not by a technical breach of computer security, but by out-and-out con-artistry . . . Singfield "blagged" his way into the Conservative Party's banking records held by the Drummonds branch of the Royal Bank of Scotland.' Lord Ashcroft suggests that, in order to disguise the source of the information which *The Times* obtained in this way, one of its reporters, Tom Baldwin, shared the story with journalists on two rival papers, the *Guardian* and the *Independent*, with all of them publishing on the same day. Lord Ashcroft's lawyers later wrote to Singfield, telling him that they had 'information and evidence' of his role, believed to be a reference to a copy of a *Times* invoice making a payment to Singfield. Singfield, however, insisted that he was not involved.

Lord Ashcroft and another peer, Lord Levy, both had their tax records blagged by somebody who appears to have been working for the *Sunday*

Times. An inquiry by the Inland Revenue and the Information Commission found that, in the week before the *Sunday Times* wrote about Lord Ashcroft's tax affairs in February 2001, somebody posing as him had made five phone calls to the tax office in Bootle which was dealing with his file. Two similar bogus calls were made to the Inland Revenue by somebody posing as Lord Levy before the *Sunday Times* wrote about his tax payments in June 2000, quoting 'information passed to the *Sunday Times*'. Gavin Singfield has denied being responsible for these calls.

Now the reach of the dark arts is expanding, as reporters discover new technological aids. A few have started using 'Trojan horse' emails which can be sent to a target, who will open an attachment without realising that this also opens spyware which copies all the data on the target's hard disk and relays it to an email account which cannot be traced back to the reporter. One journalist on a quality newspaper told me he had used this kind of technology on a senior government adviser, the contents of whose laptop were copied, and on a prominent business figure who was targeted via the computer of a secretary in the office of a close associate (the reporter also claims to have procured itemised phone bills for every adult member of this man's family). When the *News of the World*, in the summer of 2006, was trying to track down Freddy Scappaticci, the former IRA man who had been exposed as an MI6 informer code-named Stakeknife, the paper paid Jonathon Rees to obtain his phone records and, according to one source, to use a Trojan horse to try to steal information off the hard disk of a former member of British special forces in Northern Ireland, known as Martin Ingram, who had written a book about him.

In the same way, private investigators will install a 'mirror wall' into a target's computer so that all email traffic is copied and relayed to an untraceable account where it can be read. It was this technology which allowed *The Times* and the BBC Radio 4 *Today* programme in June 2003 to prove that Dame Shirley Porter was hiding millions of pounds in an account in the British Virgin Islands while she claimed to have no significant assets with which to pay the surcharge imposed on her for her 'disgraceful, unlawful and improper' behaviour as leader of Westminster City Council. However, in that case, it was not journalists but a business rival of her son, John, who commissioned the spying and passed the results on to the media. In spite of the apparently strong public interest in the story, the businessman Cliff Stanford was fined £20,000 for unlawfully intercepting an electronic communication.

Reporters now have also started using software which was developed by the National Criminal Intelligence Service to sort through the phone numbers which are acquired by private investigators. One says he has also used an electronic device which blocked all landlines in the target property, so that the occupant was forced to use a mobile phone whose records, in turn, could be searched via a private investigator.

And just a quick word about dustbins. There is something temptingly symbolic about the modern reporter using nauseating rubbish for raw material and then producing the same in garbage stories. Of course, it isn't just symbolic.

One of the few examples of Fleet Street at least beginning to tell the story of its own operational corruption concerns the bizarre and bountiful career of Benjamin Pell, known to all who used his services as Benji the Binman – a professional scavenger who made it his business to raid multiple thousands of dustbins in search of titbits to sell to reporters. The story spilled over into the public domain in part because there was so much of it that it really couldn't be contained; and, in part, because a freelance journalist called Mark Watts, formerly of Granada Television's *World In Action* programme, wrote a book about it called *The Fleet Street Sewer Rat*.

By all accounts, Benjamin Pell is a highly intelligent and highly neurotic figure who once said that he would be the first person to describe himself as mad. For three years, starting in early 1998, Benji was in and out of just about every office in Fleet Street apart from the *Financial Times*. He started with tat about show-business celebrities – the Spice Girls, Robbie Williams, All Saints and Oasis – which he had filched from the bins of law firms and management companies who worked with them. He caused chaos in the relationship between Elton John and his manager, John Reid, by repeatedly selling stories from Reid's bin which led the singer to suspect that either Reid or somebody in his office must be deliberately betraying him to the press.

While reporters slept comfortably, Benji was out on the streets of

London, six nights a week, driving his little van from bin to bin, sometimes collecting a hundred bags of rubbish in a night and then spending
half the following day panhandling the filth in search of treasure for
the tabloids. Then, in the summer of 1998, working through a lawyer's
trash, he came across a bundle of legal documents which were to lift
him into a new league.

What he found among the fag ash and dirty tissues was highly confidential paperwork about a legal dispute between the heir to the throne
of Saudi Arabia, Prince Mohammed, and one of his closest associates,
Said Ayas. What made this so important was that these two men were
at the heart of the corruption scandal surrounding Jonathan Aitken, the
former defence minister who had sued the *Guardian* and *World In Action*
for suggesting he had an improper relationship with powerful Saudis.

The journalists who had investigated Aitken had always suspected that
he was using his position at the Ministry of Defence to set up arms
deals, from which he personally could skim a healthy 'commission', i.e.
a bribe. This was the real reason for investigating Aitken, but the entire
project had been diverted into a fight about whether or not Aitken had
allowed his Saudi associates to pay his bill at the Ritz Hotel in Paris one
weekend in 1993. The journalists who were involved suspected that that
hotel bill was simply one tiny loose end from a vast bundle of corruption, but they had never been able to prove it.

Now, Benji had stumbled onto a binful of leads. The first document
he found was part of a scam by Aitken to get himself out of trouble by
pretending that all of his dealings with the Saudis were, in fact, part of
a British intelligence operation in which he was a conduit between MI6
and the Saudi royal family. Benji offered the document to the *Independent*,
who took it but ran no story, so he approached the *Guardian* where he
was put on to the veteran investigative reporter who had led the way
on the Aitken story, David Leigh.

Leigh embodies the maxim, coined by the admired former *Sunday
Times* reporter Nicholas Tomalin, that all any reporter needs is 'a plau-
sible manner, a little literary ability and ratlike cunning'. Leigh was
extremely interested in Benji's access to paperwork about Aitken, but he
knew two things: first, that out of a combination of principle and poverty,
the *Guardian* would never pay Benji for this sort information; second,

that since the *Guardian* were still fighting Aitken in the courts, trying to get him to pay costs for his failed libel action, it could be fatal to the *Guardian*'s cause if they tainted potential evidence with payment.

But, with an excess of natural cunning, David Leigh can spot a loophole at a hundred yards. He offered Benji a deal: if the scavenger would keep him up to date with any further discovery of interesting paperwork on Aitken, he would pay him a small finder's fee of £100 for this particular document but also he would introduce him to a freelance journalist who would assist him in finding the right stories and selling them to the right takers at the right price. Benji, who had already discovered that he was likely to be ripped off by Fleet Street news desks, agreed. In this way, Leigh kept the door open to Benji's gold mine while neatly sidestepping the mucky business of paying him, simply by arranging for others to pay him instead.

The freelance whom Leigh brought in to act as Benji's guide was Mark Hollingsworth, an old friend of Leigh's who specialised in long, difficult inquiries into the rich and powerful. He had written aggressive books on Margaret Thatcher's son, Mark, and her PR adviser, Tim Bell. Hollingsworth was soon steering Benji to dig out information which was far more politically sensitive than the showbiz tat with which he had started; and together the two of them sold the results, most often to the *Mail on Sunday* and the *Sunday Times*. In the process, they finally struck real journalistic gold in the search for the truth about Jonathan Aitken.

Digging around in the bins outside the offices of Aitken's solicitors, Benji unearthed documents which showed that the former Minister had indeed been setting up a sequence of huge arms deals between British companies and the Saudis, with the assistance of Prince Mohammed; that one of the go-betweens in these deals was Said Ayas, who worked for the Prince and who was now embroiled in a legal dispute with him; and that Said Ayas had arranged that, if the deals went through, commissions worth hundreds of millions of dollars would be paid through account number 556.862 at the Union Banque Suisse in Geneva – money which he could then share with his old friend and business partner, Jonathan Aitken. As the *Guardian* put it when they eventually published all this: 'If there is a more serious act of corruption in post-war British politics, we would be interested to know of it.'

The *Guardian's* stories about Aitken's plans were written without revealing the source of their information. Under Mark Hollingsworth's guidance, Benji continued to target the bins of senior politicians including Lady Thatcher, PR companies who work for governments and corporations including Burson-Marsteller and Freud Communications, political lobbyists including Tim Bell, high-powered solicitors, and the headquarters of the Labour and Conservative parties. At one point, Benji claimed to be targeting the bins at 115 different addresses.

Some produced nothing but rubbish, but others produced little gems such as the sequence of memos between Tony Blair and his pollster, Philip Gould, which were published by the *Sunday Times*, *The Times* and the *Sun* in mid 2000, all of which came with Benji's grubby fingerprints. While he was about it, Benji continued to sell to the tabloids, reaching a peak when he robbed the dustbins outside the *Daily Mirror* and sold to *Punch* magazine printouts of emails from the then *Mirror* editor, Piers Morgan, himself a front-runner in the invasion of privacy.

By 2000, Benji found himself struggling under an avalanche of injunctions, and a court order to search his home. Eventually, he was convicted of theft, with the court confirming that, although he was taking material which had been thrown out, what he was doing was still an offence in the eyes of the law. In the familiar pattern, none of the newspapers which had paid him to commit these thousands of thefts was even questioned by police, let alone prosecuted. As trouble closed in around him, the newspapers which had used him rapidly dumped him. Several of them, however, including the *Sunday Times*, were reluctant to stop binning and proceeded to set up their own operations, once more using private investigators to take their risks for them. According to one source, those investigators attempted to protect themselves from prosecution by taking their target's rubbish, copying anything important and then carefully replacing it (although one quality paper did steal some old knickers of a prominent politician's daughter as a newsroom souvenir).

Over all this illegal activity by journalists, there hangs a tricky question. When would any of it be allowed in the public interest? The Data Protection Act and the journalists' codes of conduct all recognise that a breach of privacy could be justified if it were to reveal information which the public genuinely needed to know. But the line is ill-defined. Even the Press Complaints Commission is unclear about where it lies. Its chairman, Sir Christopher Meyer, told the Culture and Media Select Committee in March 2007: 'The animated debates that we have every month when the board of commissioners meets at the PCC to adjudicate on cases, very often rotate around an issue of where is the line between what is properly private and what is genuinely in the public interest, and this can be very contentious and very difficult.'

And even when there is some agreement that a particular story needs to be told in the public interest, there is more confusion about what journalists are allowed to do if they start off with nothing more than a suspicion and then, having breached the privacy of their target, discover that their suspicion was unfounded. If that is permitted, it opens the door to a mass of breaches. If that is forbidden, it may lock the door to the genuinely important story.

As it is, the head of the Information Commission, Richard Thomas, told the Culture and Media Select Committee that, having analysed the activities of all the PIs and blaggers they had prosecuted – including all 13,343 media requests to Steve Whittamore – they had never yet seen 'a whiff of public interest'. And he pointed out that, when they had come to trial, Whittamore and his co-defendants had not even attempted to claim that they had a public interest defence for the work they had been doing for the press.

However, the reality at the moment is that, for the newspapers who are involved in this, the question of public interest seldom needs to be answered since the law and the codes of conduct are scarcely being applied to Fleet Street.

Scotland Yard has tried to bust Z not only to protect its confidential databases but more importantly, to stop him jeopardising the course of current investigations. They believe he has sold information on active counter-terrorism operations as well as on inquiries into organised crime groups in London: as soon as these stories appear in print, the targets are effectively tipped off about the police activity around them and can lie low. There are also examples of individuals refusing to cooperate with police after Z sold their stories. In one case, a celebrity had complained of vicious threats and was highly anxious about what would happen if those who were making the threats discovered that he had reported them to the police: Z sold the story; Fleet Street published it; the celebrity withdrew his complaints and went into hiding; the aggressors got away with it.

As a result, there have been occasions in the recent past when police have used undercover surveillance units to follow Z. I know they have photographs of him meeting with a serving detective and swapping envelopes with him. But they have never been able to prove beyond reasonable doubt that Z is breaking the law.

In the same way, in July 2002, police were called in to investigate after a listening device was found in a BT junction box near the home of Angus Deayton, the television presenter who was being pursued by some Fleet Street papers over his private life. The police arrested a BT engineer, who admitted placing the bug. But he was never prosecuted, and nor was any charge brought against the paper which had hired him. The engineer was disciplined within BT and allowed to carry on working.

The law, as we have seen in the string of cases around Steve Whittamore, is weak in the face of Fleet Street's funding. The voluntary codes of practice which frame the work of journalists are even weaker. The National Union of Journalists asks its members to work 'only by straightforward means' unless there are 'overriding considerations of the public interest'. But the union has no means of enforcing its code over the use of the dark arts and no significant history of doing so. The Press Complaints Commission, which is supposed to regulate the work of all journalists, did not even address the issue of breaching the Data Protection Act until the Information Commissioner, Richard Thomas, approached them, in November 2003, in the wake of the raid on Steve Whittamore. The PCC then showed a marked reluctance to take a strong line. The PCC denies this but, courtesy of the Freedom of Information Act, we know that its denial is more than a little misleading.

The journalist Mark Watts, who wrote the book about Benji the Binman, used the act to obtain copies of correspondence between the Information Commission and the PCC. This showed the commission pushing the PCC to issue 'a clear public statement warning journalists and editors of the very real risks of committing criminal offences'; and Tim Toulmin, the director of the PCC, which was founded and is overseen by the newspaper industry, replying: 'I will have to strike a balance between urging caution and sounding too restrictive – something the newspaper people involved have been concerned about.'

This soon boiled down to a debate about the meaning of 'public interest'. The PCC produced draft guidance which clearly fell short of what the Information Commission was looking for. 'We don't, in any sense, endorse it as we think that they could and should take a stronger line,' one senior official from the Information Commission wrote in an internal email. Richard Thomas had a lunch with the head of the PCC, Sir Christopher Meyer, and then wrote Sir Christopher a strongly worded letter, warning of the 'real risk' that journalists would continue to pay for access to confidential information, wrongly thinking that they had the public interest on their side.

He continued: 'I fear that it might be assumed that simply because a journalist subjectively considers a particular story to be in the public interest, the prohibitions on obtaining personal information without consent can safely be ignored. I am satisfied that the courts would not accept this defence lightly. In other words, they would consider that the public interest in the obtaining (and presumably subsequent publication) of the information in question would have to be extremely strong to justify obtaining the information dishonestly.'

Three months later, in March 2005, the PCC issued its guidance without the stronger wording which the Information Commission had been requesting. In March 2007, at the Culture and Media Select Committee, Richard Thomas publicly declared, in front of Sir Christopher, that he was 'a little disappointed that there was not a more strident denunciation of the activity, by the Press Complaints Commission'.

In the meantime, the whole issue had surfaced again in August 2006, when the royal editor of the *News of the World*, Clive Goodman, and a private investigator, Glenn Mulcaire, were arrested for intercepting voice-mail messages on mobile phones involving Prince William, the publicist Max Clifford, the model Elle Macpherson, the Liberal MP Simon Hughes and several figures from the world of football. With absolutely no sign of any public interest in their favour, Goodman and Mulcaire pleaded guilty to offences against the Regulation of Investigatory Powers Act, which regulates phone tapping, and were jailed, in January 2007, for four months and six months respectively. The editor of the *News of the World*, Andy Coulson, resigned; Clive Goodman lost his job.

The PCC reacted by announcing an inquiry, which turned out to be extremely limited in its scope. Evidence presented in court had shown that Mulcaire had been working for the paper since 1997; that, in July 2005, he had been given a contract worth £105,000 a year; and that other 'research companies' had been hired by the paper for even more. And yet the PCC chose to limit its investigation to the *News of the World's* interception of voicemail messages; it showed no interest in asking the paper about any other kind of activity for which it had paid private investigators, and it declined even to question Andy Coulson on the grounds that he had resigned and was, therefore, no longer within its scope. The Goodman case had produced a cluster of stories indicating that the use of private investigators was widespread in Fleet Street. And yet the PCC declared no intent to investigate any activity, even the interception of voicemail messages, by any other paper. Instead, it decided simply to ask them what internal guidance they had in place.

The truth is that what was once the occasional indulgence of a few shifty crime correspondents has become the regular habit of most news organisations. The hypocrisy is wonderful to behold. These organisations exist to tell the truth and yet routinely they lie about themselves. Many of these organisations have been the loudest voices in the law-and-order lobby, calling for tougher penalties against villains, tougher action against antisocial behaviour, even while they themselves indulge in bribery, corruption and the theft of confidential information.

One footnote. I went and found a key figure who was involved in the cluster of networks around Steve Whittamore. He agreed to speak, but the conversation was off the record, so I can't name him. I can tell you what he said, though: it's back to business as usual. He says they won't touch the Police National Computer any more, because that is what brought in the police in addition to the Information Commission, but they are busy once again, taking calls from Fleet Street newspapers who want them to break the law for them.

The dark arts are free to flourish.

8. Insight into the *Sunday Times*

By January 1967, there were several things that everybody knew about Kim Philby – that he had worked as a journalist and as a low-ranking diplomat in the Foreign Office and, more important, that he had also been a low-ranking spy for the Russians before defecting to Moscow in 1963. These things had emerged slowly through a great many news stories since 1951 when two of Philby's friends and fellow diplomats had defected to the Soviet Union, the much more senior Donald Maclean and the brilliant but erratic Guy Burgess.

The Philby story had the smell of official deceit around it, because the government had spent years dishonestly denying that Philby was 'the third man' whose warning had allowed Maclean and Burgess to evade capture. But Philby himself was clearly the small player caught in the spotlight of the great drama about his two more important friends. This essentially is what was known about Kim Philby in January 1967 when the newly appointed editor of the *Sunday Times*, Harold Evans, happened to have lunch with Jeremy Isaacs, then head of current affairs at Thames Television.

Isaacs said something which caught Evans' attention. He simply pointed out that it was interesting that all three of these diplomatic defectors had been at Cambridge University together in the 1930s. Evans went back to the *Sunday Times* office in Gray's Inn Road with the idea that perhaps they could trace the careers of these three men right back to Cambridge and possibly find out who had recruited them. To handle the job, Evans turned to a group of reporters whom he had just put together, to be known as the Insight team.

There had been an Insight team on the paper for several years, working on background features and off-the-beaten-track ideas, but now Evans had rearranged the group and tasked them to focus on long-term, complex investigations. He had chosen three reporters and put the cerebral Australian Bruce Page at their head.

Insight's investigation was to run for eight months, a very long time in the life of a newspaper. For the final six months, it absorbed all four Insight reporters full-time as well as the efforts of various other *Sunday Times* reporters, researchers and freelance stringers. At one point, there were eighteen journalists on the story, in Britain, the United States, the Soviet Union, Germany, Austria, Spain and the Middle East. The story threw the paper into a head–on confrontation with the British government and its intelligence agencies, who did their best to manipulate and intimidate Evans and his team.

By the time they had finished, Insight had exposed an enormous scandal, which for sixteen years had lain buried beneath a slab of official secrecy and lies, a scandal which had remained almost entirely untouched by the numerous stories produced in that time by other newspapers. They had also set a new standard for British journalism and established the Insight team in the vanguard of a new movement of investigative reporting which was willing and able to challenge secrecy and abuse no matter how powerful the opposition.

The Insight team is dead now. It was finally killed off in the summer of 2005, though the label is still used as a kind of brand name on some *Sunday Times* stories. It died slowly and its demise is worth studying because Insight was infected and brought down by the same germs which spread through the whole body of British journalism during that period. Indeed, the *Sunday Times* as a whole was arguably the first and also the most striking victim of the commercial infection which changed Fleet Street.

Back in January 1967, the Insight team started their Philby inquiry with very few leads. They knew the three defectors had been at Cambridge, so one of the four reporters, David Leitch, went in search of their contemporaries. They knew all three had been diplomats, so they went to the published Diplomatic List in search of those who had worked alongside them.

They had heard, too, that Philby might have done some work for the secret intelligence service, MI6. From a reporter's point of view, this was deeply difficult territory: the government at that time refused even to acknowledge the existence of MI6 and had tried to fence off its personnel and activities behind the screen of the Official Secrets Act. However, Insight began to find openings.

They wrote to the former chief of MI6, Sir Stewart Menzies, who had retired to Wiltshire. Courteously, he declined to see them, but his letter in reply accidentally encouraged them, by failing to insist that Philby had never been involved with MI6, and by adding that Philby was 'a blackguard'.

Bruce Page then noticed that some of those who were said to have been colleagues of Philby's were listed in *Who's Who* as 'attached Foreign Office' and yet they did not show up in the Diplomatic List. He guessed that this could mean that, in truth, they had been working for MI6. Another of the reporters, Phillip Knightley, started to track them down.

David Leitch found more MI6 openings when he went to see the author and critic Cyril Connolly, who had known Maclean and Burgess as friends and had published a book, *The Missing Diplomats*, two years after their defection. Connolly was now a *Sunday Times* book reviewer, happy to share his memories with a colleague and then, unexpectedly, to go to a glass cabinet, pull out a copy of his book and toss it to Leitch, who opened it to find that the margins were full of pencilled references to the sources of all Connolly's information. A reporter's gold mine.

Now they had real leads to follow. They realised that, far from being a 'low-ranking diplomat', Philby had spent at least part of his career as a fully-fledged MI6 officer and, therefore, that he was a somewhat more important spy than they had been led to believe, but Phillip Knightley feared that the former officers they were approaching were being encouraged by MI6 to talk to them, not in order to disclose the truth but merely in order to keep track of what Insight were doing. Still, there were fragments.

Professor Hugh Trevor-Roper, who had worked in intelligence during the war and was now, like Cyril Connolly, a regular *Sunday Times* contributor, gave them an informal tutorial on the world of intelligence and its weakness and then recalled the moment years earlier when he had met a drunken Kim Philby who had suddenly let slip that he admired the writing of Karl Marx in *The Eighteenth Brumaire of Louis Bonaparte*, his account of the Paris uprisings of 1848. Had Philby, this MI6 officer, been a Marxist? And, if so, for how long? The fourth member of the Insight team, John Barry, found a retired Foreign Office man who drew their attention to the careful wording of an official statement in 1963 which, they now saw, subtly allowed the possibility that Philby might have been working for the Russians for many years.

Following the Cambridge connections, Leitch pulled together these loose ends by discovering that Philby had indeed been an enthusiastic Marxist in his student days and furthermore that, after graduating, he had gone to Vienna, at a time when the city was a stage for running battles between fascists and the left. Bruce Page contacted a freelance reporter called Eric Gedye who had been working in Vienna at the time. Gedye remembered Philby as a committed left-winger who had not only helped to smuggle comrades out of Austria to protect them from the fascists but who had also married a member of the Communist Party called Litzi Friedman.

And yet, they found, Philby had returned from Vienna to London and, instead of pursuing the life of a Marxist campaigner, he had taken on a right-wing persona. He had joined the Anglo–German Fellowship, a group of aristocratic Nazi sympathisers. Then he had gone to Spain, where socialists of every kind were gathering to fight the fascists led by General Francisco Franco. But Philby had steered clear of this International Brigade and latched on to Franco's side, picking up work as a stringer for *The Times*. Bruce Page wrote every fragment into a growing 'state of knowledge' memo.

It was now, just as the investigation was taking off, just as the Insight team dropped all other stories in pursuit of the man who had been a Marxist inside MI6, that Bruce Page and David Leitch went to see a former colleague, Alun Gwynne Jones, who had been the defence correspondent of *The Times* but was now Lord Chalfont, a Foreign Office minister. Chalfont was the first official voice to tell them to back off. Their work could aid the enemy, he said. It was essential for national security, he said, that the *Sunday Times* should learn nothing of this or, if they did learn something, that they should not publish it. The Insight team could see no reason to comply: their intention was to write about a man who had defected to the enemy and who, it could reliably be assumed, had spilled every bean in his pot to the enemy's intelligence service.

In the background, however, the Foreign Office was soon playing a more devious game. When Harry Evans was told about Lord Chalfont's warning, he mentioned it to his editor-in-chief, Denis Hamilton, a decent, solid man with a military background who knew his way around the corridors of power. Hamilton quietly arranged to see the Prime Minister, Harold Wilson, and the head of MI6, Sir Dick White. Whether from genuine concern for national security or from a selfish desire to smother a potential scandal, both men insisted that the *Sunday Times* was potentially jeopardising the nation's safety. Hamilton was no coward and was perfectly capable of ignoring pressure from government but also, as he subsequently reported to Harry Evans, he was concerned that the paper might accidentally do something which did cause real damage.

He persuaded Evans to accept a highly controversial deal, to provide an early draft of any story concerning Philby so that the Foreign Office or MI6 could warn them if they were writing something dangerous. Furthermore, Evans agreed to meet Lord Chalfont at the Garrick Club to listen to official concerns and then to do the same with Sir Dennis Greenhill, who was responsible for liaison between the Foreign Office and MI6. Evans held a series of meetings with Sir Dennis at his club, the Travellers, at which the Foreign Office man repeatedly and sternly insisted that the Insight team must stop their work. And all of this was done without the knowledge or approval of the reporters working on the story.

The Foreign Office may well have thought that they had slipped a leash around Insight's neck. And certainly, this activity did give them a straightforward way of finding out what Insight were doing. However, the reality was more helpful to the *Sunday Times*. Evans had retained the right to ignore any request that was made to him. By agreeing to submit a first draft and to listen to Greenhill, he was giving himself a chance to make any changes that genuinely might need to be made while neutralising the official line of attack on the story. As it was, Sir Dennis Greenhill played a poor hand by making it clear that his real worry was not that the story would disclose secrets to the Russians but simply that it would embarrass MI6 in the eyes of the Americans. Insight pushed on. Evans diverted more reporters to help them.

Bruce Page's 'state of knowledge' memo was growing quickly now. They were piecing together Kim Philby's career in MI6 – the firearms course he attended in Hampshire, the spell he served in Istanbul. In Spain, they found the date of issue of the British passport which was supplied to his first wife, Litzi Friedman, when she went to Spain from Austria in 1935. That, in turn, helped them to find the date of her marriage to Philby and of her earlier marriage to a man who now lived in Israel whom they tracked down: he confirmed her membership of the Communist Party and helped them to trace her to her home in East Berlin, where they went to interview her.

They had a couple of breakthroughs. One was merely intriguing. Evans was approached by a man called John Sackur, who said he worked for the Foreign Office but wanted to leave to become a reporter. Evans got him talking, raised the subject of Philby and was excited to be told that Sackur had himself written one of the internal damage-assessment reports on Philby's spying. 'Philby was a copper-bottomed bastard,' said Sackur, although he declined to give much detail. Evans was tempted to hire him in the hope that he might open up. However, his deputy, Frank Giles, who had worked in the Foreign Office, established that Sackur had been employed not by the Foreign Office but by MI6 and was worried that he might still be on their books. Was this an attempt by MI6 to get inside their inquiry? Was it perhaps even an attempt by some faction in MI6 to help them with the inquiry? Or was Sackur simply looking for a new career? Whatever the truth, Sackur served to spur them on, although Evans reluctantly decided not to give him a job.

The other breakthrough was spine-tingling. Phillip Knightley had come across a rather dull book about spying called *British Agent*, written under the pseudonym of John Whitwell who was said to have spent thirty-five years in MI6. Knightley managed to discover the author's real name, which was Leslie Nicholson, and found him living in a seedy room over a café in the East End where he was dying of cancer. He invited him out for a decent lunch. Knightley has often argued that one of the first skills of reporting is a strong head for alcohol as the key to instant friendship. With this skill to the fore, he persuaded Nicholson to talk, and, on his fourth brandy, Nicholson disclosed that Kim Philby had not been a low-ranking diplomat, nor even a low-ranking MI6 officer, but from 1945 had been nothing less than the chief of the new anti-Soviet section of MI6.

This was now a huge story. This wasn't about some misguided bureaucrat who had got into trouble by helping his two important friends. This was about British intelligence setting up a whole new section of their organisation to fight the threat from Soviet spies – and putting a Soviet spy in charge of it. Just how many secrets had been spilled, how many operations had been blown, how many lives had been lost? And it had all been concealed under a blanket of lies. No wonder the authorities were trying to stop them.

Now, Insight started to pick up great chunks of extraordinary information: this KGB agent had been sent by MI6 to Washington to liaise with the CIA and the FBI, both of whom had shared their secrets with him; he had betrayed a US paramilitary operation in the Soviet satellite state of Albania, causing the loss of some three hundred lives; MI5 had been sure of Philby's guilt but MI6 had protected him and carried on using him as an agent right up to the time of his defection. The reporters also discovered that the secrets which Donald Maclean had passed to the Soviet Union involved not merely diplomacy but highly sensitive material from the US nuclear weapons programme.

As the Insight team closed in on their quarry, the government increased the pressure to back off. Phillip Knightley believes that, armed with the claim that Insight was threatening national security, MI6 certainly was tapping their telephones. George Wigg, who was the Prime Minister's specialist on intelligence, lent his rude voice to that of Sir Dennis Greenhill, demanding the suppression of the story and insinuating to Evans that Bruce Page must be a communist. Sir Dennis, for his part, said they should be writing about the KGB not MI6 and, a few days later, a plain brown envelope arrived at the *Sunday Times* enclosing the entire KGB 'order of battle'. This was apparently an attempt to divert the paper into a new story; it also looked like the clearest possible breach of the Official Secrets Act since the document betrayed precisely what MI6 did and did not know about their enemy.

Then Evans and every other editor in Fleet Street was sent a warning from the 'D Notice Committee' asking them not to discuss past or present activities of British intelligence nor even to name the agencies.

But Insight were in the final stretch. David Leitch had the simple idea of looking up Philby in the phone book, and found that he had a son, John, living in north London. It turned out that he wanted to be a photographer, and he accepted a commission from the *Sunday Times* to travel to Moscow, where he took a remarkable picture of his exiled father standing in Red Square.

On Saturday evening, 30 September, the *Sunday Times* was forced to publish at short notice when the *Observer*'s first edition splashed on an extract from a book by Philby's third wife, Eleanor, co-authored by the *Observer*'s Patrick Seale. Evans raced to convert Bruce Page's latest 'state of knowledge' memo into a front-page lead headed by the photograph of Philby in Red Square.

In the row that followed, the former head of MI6, Sir Stewart Menzies, continued to pretend that Philby had never been important in the organisation; George Wigg accused the *Sunday Times* of trying to discredit British intelligence; and the Foreign Secretary, George Brown, said Evans was a traitor and threatened to strip the *Sunday Times*'s owner, Lord Thomson, of his peerage. All of which was answered the following Sunday when Insight published an interview with a former diplomat named John Reed who had contacted them that week to reveal more evidence of the damage done by Philby. Reed described how, as a diplomat in Istanbul in 1945, he had seen the trusted MI6 officer Kim Philby sabotage an attempt to defect by a Russian intelligence officer called Konstantin Volkov, who had disappeared and was last been seen being bundled into a Russian military aircraft and being flown away to a dark and lonely end in Moscow.

The Philby story launched Insight into a succession of extraordinary investigations, notably the campaign to secure just compensation for the 430 British children who had been born without limbs as a result of their mothers taking a sedative, thalidomide, during pregnancy. These children had already been waiting for compensation for up to thirteen years by September 1972, when Evans started publishing Insight stories on the case. These were soon blocked in the courts by the pill's producer, Distillers, and also by the government, embroiling the *Sunday Times* in a battle which it won finally only six years later in the European Court of Human Rights.

Similarly, in the aftermath of the crash of a DC10 plane in Paris in March 1974, Insight embarked on a long and expensive campaign to prove that the plane had been suffering from a structural fault which was known to its manufacturers before the Paris disaster killed 346 men, women and children.

Looking back at the Philby story, Harry Evans later wrote: 'The press shouted a lot over the missing diplomats at the time, but the shouts were ineffective, because nobody did the work of inquiry on the three traitors which alone was capable of making the Government sit up. Our inquiries were admittedly beset with frustration and they were costly. Yet, if the press will not do this work, who else can?'

What Insight did in the Philby inquiry was good, persistent, imaginative reporting but in principle they did nothing that could not have been done years earlier by any other competent reporter on any other newspaper at any time in the sixteen years since Maclean and Burgess had defected. The secret of the *Sunday Times's* success lay, first, in the finance.

The paper in those days made a healthy profit, and, with the support of Lord Thomson's managers, much of that money was recycled back onto the editorial floor. Harry Evans was able to hire talented reporters as he saw fit. Some of these staff went weeks without getting anything into print or indeed even being seen in the office. But the impact on the paper's journalism generally was powerfully good: reporters filed far more stories than were needed so that the 'space barons' who edited the various pages could pick the best; and Evans was able to put together ad hoc teams not only for hard-nosed investigations but for all kinds of special projects. *Sunday Times* reporters could spend whatever time and money they needed in order to get their story.

But there was a second factor behind the paper's ability to land a story which had been sitting waiting to be caught for so many years – their attitude to government. This was embodied in two men, the owner, Lord Thomson, and the editor, Harry Evans. Neither of them considered it his business to make the government feel happy. Nor indeed were they interested in the government making them feel happy. They were there for the journalism. When, at the height of the official pressure on them to suppress the Philby story, government ministers publicly denounced Harry Evans and accused the *Sunday Times* of undermining British intelligence, Lord Thomson – at whatever risk to his peerage – answered quite simply: 'Bunk.'

In January 1981, the *Sunday Times* and its daily sister paper, *The Times*, were sold to Rupert Murdoch. Two senior journalists subsequently recorded scenes of striking similarity.

Hugo Young, who had been a political columnist on the *Sunday Times*, recalled: 'During their first visits to the building, Murdoch and his associates made clear their hostility to *Sunday Times* journalism and their contempt for those who practised it. The journalists collectively were stigmatised as lead-swinging, expense-padding, layabout Trotskyites. Each of these epithets was uttered in my hearing by senior Murdoch executives. The political label was especially emphatic, wholly removed though it was from reality.'

And Frank Giles, who was made editor of the *Sunday Times* by Murdoch, described the scene at the farewell party for Harry Evans, who was leaving to become editor of *The Times*, when Murdoch was joined by his managing director, Gerald Long: 'I recall the pair of them hovering on the edge of the crowd, engaged in muttered conversations, their faces, as they surveyed the roistering company, framed in a scowl which seemed to stop not far short of malevolence.'

Great change was coming. Come forward five years and consider the case of Mordechai Vanunu.

This was the sort of story that keeps reporters happy – a big scoop, which would rattle governments around the world. But it had one great danger attached to it. The source was deeply vulnerable. Mordechai Vanunu had spent eight years at a special installation in Dimona in southern Israel, working on Israel's undeclared and illegal development of nuclear weapons. Now he was offering the *Sunday Times's* Insight team detailed inside information and even photographs to expose the Israeli secret. If the paper were to do the story, they had to protect

Vanunu. There was a clear risk that the Israelis would intervene in some
way to try to stop him, by applying pressure on him through the courts
or through the British government, or simply by confronting and threatening him. Vanunu needed secrecy and security. The Murdoch *Sunday
Times* gave him neither.

Vanunu first surfaced in Sydney late in August 1986, where he told
his tale to an eccentric Colombian named Oscar Guerrero, who saw
a chance to make some money and contacted the *Sunday Times*. Peter
Hounam, a senior reporter on the Insight team, flew out to Sydney,
physically ejected the troublesome Guerrero from his hotel room and,
on 11 September, flew back to London with Vanunu. Unknown to
either of them, the *Sunday Times* had already blown their cover.

The acting head of Insight, Robin Morgan, had sent a reporter to
Israel to try to check Vanunu's credentials – discreetly. This was an
extremely difficult thing to do, particularly in a society like Israel which
is small and highly alert. And Morgan had sent a reporter, Max Prangnell,
who was young and inexperienced and who, we now know, unwittingly triggered an Israeli journalist into going straight to Shin Bet, the
Israeli internal security agency, to tell all.

When Hounam arrived in London with Vanunu, he was astonished
to discover that the *Sunday Times* had booked their secret whistleblower
into the Tower Hotel, just around the corner from the paper's office.
Hounam protested that this made him far too easy to trace, and Vanunu
was moved to a hotel in Hertfordshire, which was chosen not because
it offered better security but because a *Sunday Times* executive was having
an affair with a woman who lived near the hotel and he wanted to
meet her there while telling his wife that he was dealing with Vanunu.

While Hounam and other reporters tried to check out the story,
Vanunu became bored and restless in the Hertfordshire hotel, and so
the *Sunday Times* moved him again – right back to the Tower Hotel
around the corner from their Wapping office. Realising their error,
they moved him again, into the flat of the young reporter Max
Prangnell, whom Vanunu did not like. So he was moved yet again to
a hotel in Covent Garden in the centre of London, from where he
proceeded to wander the streets, usually alone and entirely unsuper-
vised by the *Sunday Times*.

The editor of the paper, Andrew Neil, who had been in post since 1983, then made matters worse by failing to sign the promised contract with Vanunu. This not only upset Vanunu, who became restless and truculent, but also hindered Peter Hounam, who needed the contract to give him some kind of control over the increasingly wayward source.

Aware of the need to protect him, the *Sunday Times* had smuggled Vanunu in and out of their office in the boot of reporters' cars – and then ruined the impact by allowing Vanunu on other occasions to cruise in and out in taxis, from which he was entirely visible. This became a significant problem during Vanunu's second week in London, when Hounam spotted a film crew on the pavement and strongly suspected they were Israeli security. By the time he moved to the Covent Garden hotel, we now know, Vanunu certainly was being tracked by the Israelis.

A situation that was already dangerous became farcical when Oscar Guerrero turned up in London, looking for his slice of whatever Vanunu stood to earn from the *Sunday Times*. He made a series of phone calls to their office, failed to hear what he wanted and told Robin Morgan that he wanted his story back. Morgan, instead of meeting him and attempting to bring him under control, told him to stop being silly and arranged for a trainee reporter, who was in the *Sunday Times* office on work experience, to meet him three days later to find out what he was up to. By that time, Guerrero had already made his move, taking the whole tale to the tabloid *Sunday Mirror*. Their reporters proceeded to fall out with Guerrero, deciding he was a con man, searching his hotel room while he was downstairs in the bar and then physically scrapping with him when they tried to grab his briefcase and he tried to run away.

Any doubts which the Israelis may have harboured about precisely what the *Sunday Times* was doing, were extinguished when the paper, on Tuesday 23 September, made the highly controversial decision to approach the Israeli Embassy in London with a long and detailed account of the story which they were planning, including the fact that they had the personal testimony and photographs of a source who had spent more than eight years working as a technician at the Dimona plant. Andrew Neil later defended this move by saying that 'we were following proper journalistic practice'. In truth, it was unnecessary and entirely self-serving. The fact is that the *Sunday Times* were confronted with a choice between two problems: on the one hand, they could go to the Israeli Embassy for a comment, with the risk that the Israelis would then strike out against their story or their source; or they could try to maintain some kind of security, with the risk that they would find it harder to check their story. And it was this latter problem which they chose to avoid, at enormous risk to their source.

Events tumbled forwards into chaos. The Israeli Embassy lied about the story and told Hounam it had 'no basis whatsoever in reality'. Andrew Neil dithered, worried that the whole thing might be a hoax, and said they should wait to see how the *Sunday Mirror* handled it while they made more checks. One of these checks involved consulting a senior Israeli military analyst, regardless of whether or not he might become yet another conduit of information back to Israeli intelligence.

Vanunu started to rebel. Neil had still not signed his contract. Vanunu complained that he was being given no spending money, he became suspicious and irritated, and he started talking about forgetting the story and going on a trip. So bad was the communication within the *Sunday Times* that nobody even told Peter Hounam of Vanunu's threat. Nor did anybody tell him that on the day after they had approached the Israeli Embassy, on Wednesday 24 September, Vanunu had met a blonde woman in the street near his Covent Garden hotel. She said her name was Cindy. Vanunu liked her, fancied her, trusted her. She was, in truth, an Israeli agent.

The *Sunday Times* had no plan at all to protect Vanunu. They had discussed where he would live after the story, since he would be unable to return to Israel, but nothing had been decided or organised. Now, knowing that they had disclosed their plans to the Israelis in London, one senior figure at the paper came up with the bizarre idea that Vanunu would be safest if he went on a Wallace Arnold coach tour of Scotland. Peter Hounam is sure that it was Robin Morgan who came up with this master plan, although Andrew Neil claims it for himself.

That Sunday, 28 September, the *Sunday Mirror* ran its story, headlined 'THE STRANGE CASE OF ISRAEL AND THE NUCLEAR CONMAN', denouncing Oscar Guerrero and implying that Vanunu's story might well be false. This angle may or may not have been suggested by the paper's then owner, Robert Maxwell, who may or may not have been working for the Israeli government, who may or may not have engineered this story in an attempt to deflect the dithering *Sunday Times*. For Vanunu, what really mattered was that the *Sunday Mirror* had run his picture, so that he was now an open target for anybody who wanted to object to what he was doing – and yet the *Sunday Times* took a deliberate decision not to let him know that the *Sunday Mirror* had published.

On the following day, Hounam was finally told that Vanunu was spending his spare time with the mysterious Cindy. He warned Vanunu that she might be a plant. Vanunu ignored him. The next day, 30 September, Vanunu agreed to fly with Cindy to Rome, where, she said, she would feel more relaxed staying in her sister's flat and, therefore, would be more likely to want to have sex with him. As they arrived at the flat in Rome, Vanunu was attacked by two men who drugged him and tied him up.

The following Sunday, 5 October, the *Sunday Times* finally ran their story – 'REVEALED: SECRETS OF ISRAEL'S NUCLEAR ARSENAL' – with quotes, graphics, photographs and 6,000 words of copy filling half the front page and two whole pages inside. As that was published, the whistleblower who had trusted them with his safety was lying drugged, bound and blindfolded on a cargo boat en route from Italy to Israel. Mordechai Vanunu spent the next eighteen years in prison, eleven of them in solitary confinement.

Peter Hounam has since described the *Sunday Times*'s performance variously as inept, lax and inexplicable, and he has apologised publicly to Vanunu. 'I'm sorry I ever led you into trusting us with your welfare,' he told him.

It is a revealing coincidence that, during the Philby saga, Russian intelligence abducted a would-be defector in Turkey and flew him away to an uncertain fate, and it was Philby who allowed it to happen, while, during the Vanunu saga, Israeli intelligence abducted a would-be whistleblower, but this time, it was the newspaper itself which allowed it to happen.

Here, indeed, was a great change in the *Sunday Times* – simply, a collapse of competence. As an editor, Andrew Neil was highly knowledgeable in the fields of politics and economics, but he had nothing like Harry Evans' track record in running tricky investigations. As a section editor, Robin Morgan knew a lot about handling copy but he had been thrown into the job of acting Insight editor without the experience or the sheer brainpower of Bruce Page. And while Peter Hounam certainly understood his job, the investigation at crucial moments was put into the hands of young reporters who, with the best will in the world, were not equipped to carry the load.

The collapse of competence, in turn, reflected other changes. There had been a flight of experienced reporters, fleeing first from Murdoch and his clear disdain for their history, then from Andrew Neil, an abrasive character who watched the old guard heading for the door and took gleeful delight in handing them their hats and waving them goodbye, and then finally from the angry pickets and the moral worries of Wapping, where Murdoch moved the papers to escape the print unions in January 1986.

Beyond this exodus, there was something even more important – the basic priorities had changed. This was first and most dramatically captured in April 1983 when Rupert Murdoch suddenly informed the *Sunday Times* that they would be serialising Adolf Hitler's diaries. When their expert consultant, Lord Dacre, started to express doubts about the authenticity of the diaries, Murdoch famously declared, 'Fuck Dacre. Publish.' Frank Giles, who was still editor at the time, immediately saw the real danger: 'The imperatives of a journalistic scoop had been allowed to take precedence over the need for proper tests to establish historical truth.'

A scoop that is not true offends real journalists. It does not necessarily offend a corporation whose defining motive is to make money and for whom journalism is primarily a source of income. Where Lord Thomson provided healthy finance and required good reporting, Rupert Murdoch cut one budget after another. When Andrew Neil finally left the paper in 1994, Murdoch made a speech at his farewell party at which, according to guests who were there, he singled out Neil's greatest achievement: that he was producing a paper that was three times as big as Harry Evans' but with the same number of staff. Neither Murdoch nor Neil saw anything wrong with that at all. The result for Insight by that time was that it had ended up so short of resources that it had been reduced to following up stories instead of breaking them and had become known in the office as the Hindsight Team.

The former editor of the *Guardian*, C. P. Scott, famously advised that 'Editor and business manager should march hand in hand, the first, be it well understood, just an inch or two in advance.' Historians of the future may well look back and identify Andrew Neil as a key figure in the demise of Fleet Street, the first editor who functioned primarily as a businessman.

Not enough staff, not enough experience, not enough time. But there was something else.

Hugo Young wrote his vivid portrait of the contempt of Murdoch's men for his colleagues, quoted above, in an essay in *Political Quarterly* in October 1984, three years after Murdoch took over. He went on to analyse what he saw as the most worrying weakness of the new *Sunday Times*. He highlighted the fact that the paper had always been impartial, refusing to allow itself to be identified with any political creed or party: 'The driving force of the *Sunday Times* was the belief that governments, unless properly invigilated, were always in danger of becoming agents of power without responsibility . . . Preserving the *Sunday Times* as a genuinely non-party paper was an essential prop to the credibility of all its journalism.' Within this context, he wrote, the Insight team 'exhibited the paper's own most characteristic instinct: a preference for evidence over propaganda, and for asking questions rather than supplying a pattern of answers linked to an editorial line'.

Now, he argued, this had changed. He cited Andrew Neil's coverage of the protests of the Campaign for Nuclear Disarmament against the stationing of US cruise missiles in the UK, with one particularly large demonstration in London being greeted by the *Sunday Times* with the headline 'SUNSET FOR CND'; and the coverage of the 1984 miners' strike, in which the government's line had been reproduced with such force that 'after a few weeks, even the dullest reader could have been excused for wondering whether he was being got at'.

What Hugo Young was seeing was the outcome of Rupert Murdoch's standard behaviour: for the sake of his business interests, he had forged an alliance with Margaret Thatcher; and in order to maintain that alliance, he imposed a right-wing framework on the paper, a framework which well suited the personal politics of the editor whom he then appointed, Andrew Neil.

Hugo Young concluded with a thought which went to the heart of the change: 'Whereas the old *Sunday Times*, if functioning properly, would have stood back and asked difficult questions of both sides, the new *Sunday Times* became the accomplice of one side only . . . The investigative tradition, which depends on detachment and irreverence as well as professional competence, has been all but abandoned.'

It all began with a burst of official misinformation. At 4.45 in the afternoon, on Sunday 6 March 1988, the Ministry of Defence in London released a statement to the press about a shooting incident in Gibraltar, the British territory on the southern tip of Spain. Three suspected IRA terrorists had been shot dead by security forces and, according to the statement, 'a suspected bomb' had been found.

Reporters started to call the MoD press office, where they were provided with off-the-record guidance. That evening, the BBC television news at nine o'clock led on the shootings and explained that a 500lb bomb had been found inside a Renault 5 car and defused. The main ITN news also reported that a bomb had been defused and added that the terrorists had exchanged fire with the security personnel who killed them: 'The authorities came desperately close to disaster, with a bomb being left in a crowded street and a shoot-out when innocent civilians were in the area.' While these bulletins were going out, the MoD issued a further statement that 'military personnel dealt with a suspected bomb' and, on the following morning, with all the daily papers rehearsing the same script, the minister for the armed forces went live on BBC radio to repeat the story, explaining that the bomb had been timed to explode during a military parade on the following Tuesday.

The truth was that the three IRA terrorists – two men and a woman – had been shot dead by SAS special forces in Gibraltar at 3.47 that Sunday afternoon. But there had not been any exchange of fire because – as the security forces knew within minutes of the shooting – none of the terrorists was carrying any weapon. Furthermore, by 7.30 that evening, at the very latest, the security forces also knew that there was no bomb, and so there never had been any defusing. The MoD guidance had been accurate on the point that a Renault 5 car had been parked by one of the terrorists, but the 500lb bomb was pure invention. After almost exactly twenty-four hours of misinformation, the facts were finally conceded at 3.30 on the Monday afternoon, when the then Foreign Secretary, Sir Geoffrey Howe, made a statement in the House of Commons.

This was a perfect story for a Sunday newspaper. The dailies would climb all over it, but a Sunday paper could spend the whole week digging. And there was no shortage of angles. There was the misinformation from the MoD. There was the IRA operation which was certainly building up to something lethal: on the Tuesday, Spanish police in Marbella, forty miles from Gibraltar, found explosives in a car which had been rented by one of the IRA terrorists, and the IRA themselves admitted that the three dead activists had been involved in a bombing mission. There was the official inquiry into the shooting in Gibraltar where, it rapidly became apparent, the local police were investigating an operation in which they themselves had played a leading role and, oddly, had allowed the SAS men to leave Gibraltar without even being interviewed. And there was the question of whether the SAS should have shot dead two men and a woman when they were unarmed.

This last angle was picked up during the week by the *Daily Telegraph* which generally supported the government but which published a leader warning: 'Unless it wishes Britain's enemies to enjoy a propaganda bonanza, the government should explain why it was necessary to shoot dead all three terrorists on the street rather than apprehend them with the considerable force of police and SAS which appears to have been deployed in the locality . . . It is an essential aspect of any successful anti-terrorist policy to maintain the principles of civilised restraint which obtain in a democratic society.'

Despite the opportunities for investigation, the *Sunday Times* chose to go back to the same official sources which had been responsible for the early bout of misinformation and to rely on them to produce a news story headlined 'SAS: WHY WE FIRED AT IRA GANG'. They also ran an Insight feature which declared immediately that this was 'another victory for Britain's security services'. They reproduced as fact several passages of highly contentious MoD briefing.

For example, the Spanish police and interior ministry had already given reporters a detailed account of how they had followed the IRA terrorists all the way from Marbella to the frontier with Gibraltar. But that caused a problem for the British government who were unable to explain why, if they really believed these terrorists were armed and in possession of a live bomb, they had not grabbed them at the frontier instead of allowing them to cruise into the crowded streets of Gibraltar on a sunny Sunday afternoon. Faced with this conflict between the Spanish providing a detailed account of their following the IRA, and the MoD denying that the Spanish had done anything of the kind, what should a newspaper do? The *Sunday Times's* solution was simple: they followed their briefing from the MoD and simply stated as though it were a fact that the Spanish police had 'lost touch with the terrorists' hours earlier and did not tell their readers anything at all of what the Spanish authorities were saying.

In the same way, they reported as fact that the SAS believed a car bomb had been planted in Gibraltar that Sunday; that one of the terrorists 'appeared to fiddle with something' in the car before leaving it; that an officer 'saw something that suggested the Renault contained a bomb'. All of this might have been true, but all of this was highly contentious, entirely unsubstantiated and based simply on what the MoD had told the paper. Other newspapers during the previous week had found an eyewitness who said she had seen the SAS walk up behind one terrorist and shoot him in the back without any kind of warning. The *Sunday Times* buried the quote from her in the tenth paragraph of a secondary story on page 13.

And by now the paper was making no secret of its allegiance. It was an enthusiastic cheerleader for Margaret Thatcher's government. In his memoir, *Full Disclosure*, Neil later declared with evident pride: 'On many of the biggest struggles of her decade in power, the *Sunday Times* stood shoulder to shoulder with her . . . Thatcher's battles were our battles.' Instead of looking at the evidence, Neil's paper had simply supplied a pattern of answers linked to their editorial line.

There Insight's coverage might have rested, second-rate but no worse than the right-wing tabloids who also had piled into reporting the official line, if it had not been for a forty-five-minute programme called *Death on the Rock*, which was put out by Thames Television's *This Week* team nearly seven weeks later, on Thursday 28 April 1988. This presented four key witnesses who variously cast doubt on two central official claims: first, that the terrorists had made suspicious hand movements which persuaded the SAS they were a threat; and second, that the SAS had shouted warnings before opening fire. The government tried hard to stop the broadcast, but the Independent Broadcasting Authority resisted them.

The reaction in the *Sunday Times* office was immediate. Robin Morgan, now features editor, had previously fallen out with Thames TV over a programme about Czech dissidents which Morgan had accused of dishonesty. Now he went straight in to tell the editor that he did not trust their work on Gibraltar. Andrew Neil was wide open to the suggestion. He was deeply opposed to anything left-wing or liberal, including apparently left-wing or liberal journalism, and, as a former member and employee of the Conservative and Unionist party, he was even more opposed to Irish republicanism.

Two Insight reporters were dispatched to Gibraltar with a video of the programme and instructions to show it to the four witnesses and to ask if they had any complaints about it. That Sunday, the paper published a lacerating attack on Thames headlined 'Gibraltar killings row: SAS "will be vindicated"'. Once again, it relied heavily on official guidance, but this time an internal war had broken out as Insight's reporters on the ground complained bitterly that their work was being distorted.

They complained to Robin Morgan, who had 'written through' their material. Morgan rejected their criticisms. The reporters accused him of becoming hysterical, and Morgan rejected this too in a memo which accused the reporters variously of being 'arrogant and high and mighty . . . rude . . . pompous . . . petulant, unprofessional . . . disgraceful . . . self-important . . . stupid . . . idiotic . . . spoilt brat'.

At first, the fight was a straight two-way clash between Robin Morgan and one of the Insight reporters, Rosie Waterhouse, who had tracked down two of the Thames TV witnesses and shown them the video. One witness was a man named Stephen Bullock who had been walking through Gibraltar with his wife and young child when the SAS had shot the three terrorists in the street.

In her copy (which has survived in its original hand-scrawled form), Waterhouse opened by saying: 'Stephen Bullock, a barrister now living in Jimena, Cadiz, on mainland Spain, does believe the shootings were "an execution".' That simply never made it into Sunday's story.

Waterhouse went on to deal with the vexed question of whether Stephen Bullock's account of the shooting of one of the terrorists, Danny McCann, clashed with that of Thames's most outspoken witness, Carmen Proetta, who clearly told the programme that McCann had raised his hands in surrender before being shot. In the copy which she filed from Spain, Waterhouse explained that Bullock simply could not be sure: 'Bullock only saw the scene from the point McCann was falling backwards after the first shots were fired. However, he said what Proetta said on film was not inconsistent with what he saw.' By the time this arrived in the paper, it read: 'Insight has established that her [Carmen Proetta's] evidence is inaccurate . . . Stephen Bullock, a barrister, is emphatic that the terrorists' arms were raised in defence, not in surrender.'

Then Waterhouse filed the two key points from her interview with a second Thames witness, Josie Celecia. The first was that Mrs Celecia, like Carmen Proetta, was 'adamant' that the SAS had not shouted any warning before firing. That simply never made it into the story. However, the story did add the entirely unsubstantiated claim that Mrs Celecia was too far away to hear whether any warning had been shouted.

Rosie Waterhouse's copy then added that Mrs Celecia and her husband did disagree with one detail of Carmen Proetta's account. Proetta had said that two of the terrorists who were about to die had looked back over their shoulders towards a police car whose siren was wailing. This could not be right, the Celecias said, because the police car had come towards the two terrorists, so they would have had no need to look backwards. That detail of Carmen Proetta's account was 'ridiculous', they said. By the time this reached the front page of the *Sunday Times*, the copy read: 'Josie Celecia said that the evidence of another witness, Carmen Proetta, who claimed that the terrorists had tried to surrender, was "ridiculous".'

On the following Tuesday, when staff went back into their office, Waterhouse confronted Morgan. As she recalled in a subsequent memo to him: 'I said the story left the *ST* wide open to accusations that we had set out to prove one point of view and misrepresented and misquoted interviews to fit – the very accusation we were levelling at Thames . . . You apparently interpreted this as me having "an attitude problem".'

Waterhouse was particularly concerned that the paper once again had recycled MoD guidance as though it were fact. For example, there was a great dispute about the precise time at which a police car's siren had started wailing. Thames's most damaging witness, Carmen Proetta, said she had heard the siren and then looked out of her window and seen the whole incident. But the British government wanted to claim that the siren had sounded only after the shooting had started, so that by the time Carmen Proetta looked out of her window, it would have been too late for her to see whether the SAS men had shouted a warning and whether the terrorists had raised their hands in surrender. The *Sunday Times* had no doubt. 'Insight has established that the police siren sounded after the first shots were fired,' they declared. Their sole evidence for this? An unidentified 'senior defence source' had 'confirmed' that the evidence to be submitted to the inquest would 'quite definitely' prove this. (It didn't.)

In her memo to Morgan, Waterhouse listed nine points of detail about which she had complained and she recorded the reaction to the story from those she had interviewed: 'The Celecias deny they said all Proetta's evidence was ridiculous, and Bullock is furious. He says his evidence was misinterpreted and completely misrepresented in places and wrongly used to contradict Proetta's account.' Bullock had written a letter of complaint to the *Sunday Times* and also sent a detailed account of his experience with the paper to Thames.

The following week, it got worse. Rosie Waterhouse was sent back to Gibraltar, with a second Insight reporter, David Connett. As the week unfolded, both spoke to Robin Morgan in London and both became worried that he seemed intent on supporting the official government line and unwilling to listen to any point which contradicted it. Connett made him promise to check with the two of them before he tried to write the story and to read it to them before 'putting it to bed', i.e. before sending it off to be printed. In the event, they engaged in a telephonic game of three-way hide-and-seek, with the result, first, that Morgan wrote the story without talking to them; and, then, that he put it to bed for the first edition without reading it to them, with the further result that, when the reporters finally heard the contents of the story, both of them ended up having arguments with him, as they recorded in memos which they swapped with each other during the following week.

Rosie Waterhouse wrote to Morgan: 'I now find myself in the untenable position that if I was asked to stand by certain parts of both stories, of May 1 and May 8, which involved my research, I could not.' Morgan wrote back to her and David Connett: 'Rosie was rude and tried to teach me my job. I had been subjected to this pompous lecturing all week long and I was frankly tired of listening to it.' Waterhouse replied: 'Every time I tried to question the official line or play Devil's advocate or clarify exactly what the Celecias and Bullock had or had not said, you took it as a personal insult. Surely Insight's role is to investigate the truth.'

Connett wrote to Morgan to complain about 'serious inaccuracies and omissions' in their coverage. He was particularly concerned that the story had done nothing to correct the previous week's 'official guidance' that 'Insight has established that the police siren sounded after the first shots were fired'. Connett had interviewed the attorney general of Gibraltar and a senior police officer, both of whom were clear that this was wrong. Yet no word of this had appeared in the paper. Connett added: 'It appears to me that we have confused guidance with hard evidence. Of the former, there is much. Of the latter, very little.'

A third reporter, Barrie Penrose, who had worked on the story from the London office, also complained, writing to Morgan about the Gibraltar stories: 'In recent weeks, I have expressed strong reservations about our coverage. In a nutshell, I have seen how facts and witnesses are misused to launch the attack against *This Week*. Last week, I urged you to be more sceptical and to listen to what reporters were saying on the ground. To no avail.'

Morgan remained unrepentant, insisting that he had done no more than to pull together the raw material he had received from different reporters. The *Sunday Times* too refused to back down and continued to rehearse their attacks on Thames without ever telling their readers that their stories had been disowned by their own reporters.

Over the following months, some staff tried to fight back. Peter Hounam, who had left Insight after the mishandling of Mordechai Vanunu but stayed on the paper, managed to run a news story casting some doubt on the Ministry of Defence version of events. He was backed in this by the managing editor for news, Roy Greenslade, who was provoked into one particularly bizarre manoeuvre in his efforts to let some light into the story. Greenslade believed in the Irish republican cause and occasionally wrote for the Sinn Fein paper, *An Phoblacht*, but discreetly hid his work behind the pseudonym George King (i.e. the opposite of King George). When Greenslade's Sinn Fein contacts gave him some useful information about the Gibraltar shootings, he felt unable to pass it on openly, fearing that it would be rejected simply because of its republican source. Instead, he resorted to the unusual tactic of making a series of phone calls to Peter Hounam in which he faked an Irish accent and posed as the friend of an airline pilot who had overheard the SAS talking.

It was more than nine months after the shootings when the *Sunday Times* was finally forced to retract. The paper's version of events was undermined from two directions: from detailed evidence at the inquest in Gibraltar, although the jury did conclude that the shooting of the terrorists was lawful; and from the report of an inquiry into the Thames TV programme, produced by a Conservative peer and former Northern Ireland minister, Lord Windlesham.

In an unsigned article in January 1989, the paper conceded that there had been errors in their stories. Although this concession was placed inside a story which claimed that their coverage had been a matter of scoops, revelations and leading the way, they acknowledged that they had been wrong to claim that the evidence of Carmen Proetta was undermined by that of the two witnesses who had been interviewed by Rosie Waterhouse; that they had been wrong to pretend that one of these witnesses had dismissed all of Carmen Proetta's evidence as 'ridiculous'; that they had been wrong to claim that the same witnesses could not have heard whether or not the SAS shouted

a warning; that they had been wrong to claim that they had established that the police car's siren had sounded only after the shooting
had started. Still, they did not tell their readers that these and other
criticisms had been laid in front of them by their own reporters many
months earlier. Nor did they explain to their readers that the underlying error in their stories flowed from their willingness to recyle
untested claims made by a government which, from the earliest stage
of the story, had dealt in official misinformation.

You can see a toxic chemistry at work here. For all that Rupert Murdoch
is a corporate owner who cares far more about profit than propaganda,
he had nevertheless installed an editor, Andrew Neil, who had strong
political views which helped him to maintain his alliance with Margaret
Thatcher. These included a deep hostility to the ambitions of Irish
republicans. It is clear that political partisanship was part of the problem
when the *Sunday Times* came to cover the Gibraltar shooting. But
equally clearly you can see the now familiar stream of churnalism,
running beneath the paper's handling of both Mordechai Vanunu and
Death on the Rock, eroding truth-telling journalism: the lack of staff and
experience and time, importing incompetence; the safe and easy recourse
to official sources, at the Israeli Embassy or the Ministry of Defence;
the succumbing to moral panic over terrorism; the willingness to stay
on the right side of the electric fence which was being used to punish
Thames TV with a ferocity that was not seen again until the Blair
government turned on the BBC after the invasion of Iraq. Some of
those involved in the Gibraltar story also believe that the paper was
the victim of the intelligence agencies, feeding a propaganda line to
them through the press office of the Ministry of Defence.

So much had changed.

Frank Giles, who succeeded Harry Evans as editor of the *Sunday
Times*, looked back at his predecessor's time in charge and said: 'Harry's
career provided a living negation of the theory that, to be a successful
leader, you have to be a bit of a shit.' Nobody has ever said that about
Andrew Neil. There are some journalists who would rather inhale vomit
than work for Andrew Neil. And yet, journalists who stuck with him
have some respect for the man.

They say he genuinely did want great stories, even if Murdoch's organisation made it difficult to deliver them. And, despite his high-profile failures, he was sometimes willing to stand up against power. Famously, he fought the Thatcher government through the courts to publish the memoirs of the former MI5 officer, Peter Wright. He was also willing to break away from the Fleet Street herd, although it did not always work out well. Notoriously, he refused to accept the consensus view of Aids, promoting the idea that this was a disease of gay men and drug addicts, attacking official advice that heterosexuals too were at risk. Real journalism took a terrible battering during his reign at the *Sunday Times*, but it was not yet dead. Not yet.

It was just after lunchtime when the Lesbian Avengers arrived. The reporters were in the newsroom, which in those days was in a converted warehouse near the main entrance at Wapping, when a couple of dozen women burst in with whistles and megaphones and started handcuffing themselves to the desks.

The immediate threat was to Maurice Chittenden, formerly of the *News of the World*, who had written the *Sunday Times* story which had angered the women by caricaturing them as troublemakers in Doc Martens boots. He happened to be standing there as the avengers came in.

'Where's Maurice Chittenden?' said one.

'Maurice Chittenden?' said Chittenden. 'I think he might be in the library – I'll go and get him.'

The new editor of the paper, John Witherow, came out and scowled at the women and arranged for the police to be called and, soon enough, the invaders were removed, and – apart from the *News of the World* story the next day which linked Witherow with lesbians and handcuffs – the threat might have gone no further. But then Richard Ellis had A Great Idea.

Ellis, formerly of the *Sun*, was managing editor responsible for news and he really didn't like what the lesbian avengers had done, so he put his head together with a couple of other executives and decided that what was needed here was a bit of infiltration: they would put an undercover reporter in among these women and expose their evil ways. And no sooner was the idea agreed than the reporter was chosen. Ciaran Byrne would go in undercover. This was an odd choice because Ciaran Byrne was a trainee with little experience of reporting and none at all of working undercover, which is always demanding and sometimes dangerous. Furthermore, Ciaran Byrne is a man. That caused a little trouble.

Byrne didn't want to do it. The women would spot him immediately, as soon as he started to speak, he complained. No problem, said the executives: they'd get him a voice coach to teach him to sound like a woman. And they would get a clothing coach to teach him how to dress like a woman. Byrne protested that he still wouldn't look like a woman. But that was the point, explained the executives: 'They're all so bloody ugly, they look like men!' Byrne started to feel desperate: he was only twenty-three and he had made it onto the *Sunday Times* – the paper of Harry Evans and Insight – and it turned out to be more like the *Sunday Sport*. If he did as he was told, he'd be humiliated. And the executives were making it very clear that they were not going to let him say no.

Luckily for Byrne, several senior journalists heard what was happening and stepped in to persuade Richard Ellis and the other executives that this was not such A Great Idea. Reluctantly, they let Byrne off the hook. But he was not allowed to get away with his insolence. For months he found himself pushed into a professional black hole – given crap stories to work on, his own story ideas given to other reporters, his byline dropped off stories he did manage to write.

It was January 1995. Andrew Neil had finally fallen out with Murdoch and been replaced by John Witherow. Neil's era had seen a collapse of competence as experienced staff fled and an erosion of honesty as political prejudice began to infiltrate the news process. Now the new era under John Witherow saw something different, a regime of pure pragmatism. 'There were no rules,' according to one reporter who worked there at the time. 'There were no boundaries,' according to another, speaking separately. The commercial imperative had taken over.

Where Harry Evans had worked with an owner who gave him huge resources and encouraged him to find great stories, Murdoch's men cut the staff and cut the budget and simply demanded scoops. Reporters who have worked under this regime talk about a relentless pressure to deliver stories even if that did mean distorting the truth, even if that did mean inventing a quote or inventing a whole story or breaking the law (or pretending to be a woman) along the way. As one experienced reporter put it: 'The *Sunday Times* want something for nothing. And they want it fast.'

Looking back, you can see this pragmatism beginning to take hold during Andrew Neil's time. Where Harry Evans was an enthusiastic hirer of talent, Andrew Neil was a delirious sacker. He dumped so many people for being leftish that the reporters discreetly conducted a poll and found that at least half of the newsroom were Tories. The most ruthless dumping involved Simon Freeman, an engagingly shifty individual who had worked alongside Barrie Penrose on investigations.

In his autobiography, Neil trumpets Simon Freeman's success in exposing the mutual dislike which was troubling relations between the Queen and the Prime Minister, Margaret Thatcher. The story caused a huge fuss as both the Palace and Downing Street attempted to deny it without any great success, and Neil cites this as a prime example of his willingness as an editor to take on the establishment, no matter how much pressure was put on him. In the process, he repeated the Vanunu error, effectively exposing the Queen's press secretary, Michael Shea, as Freeman's supposedly anonymous source, but Neil was triumphant.

He celebrated Freeman's success by holding a party in his honour at his flat. One guest recalls Neil strutting over to his stereo system and declaring to the room at large that he was going to get this party going: he put on the album of *Flashdance*, turned up the volume, stripped off the jacket of his suit, stripped off his shirt to reveal a slashed-back vest with the word 'Flashdance' across its front, and then broke into an enthusiastic solo disco dance, his well-moistened armpits flashing at his guests. Then Freeman was dumped.

One minute, Freeman was being rewarded with a transfer to the United States to run the Washington bureau; the next, he was told the US job was going to somebody else, and there was nothing much for him in London. The weakened remains of the journalists' union in the office passed a resolution deploring Freeman's treatment. It made no difference. Somehow or other – whether it was pressure from Downing Street or from the Palace or from the proprietor or from the circulation department, or simply the editor's arbitrary whim – Andrew Neil was dancing to a different tune. Freeman the hero was out.

Along the way, Murdoch's men had hired several executives out of the tabloid press in the belief that they were hard-arsed, no-nonsense story-getters who would deliver the headlines which would sell the paper. Some of them did know how to deliver a story. They also knew the tricks the tabloids used to do so: the private investigators, the blaggers, the stories stretched to breaking point. Several reporters use the same expression to describe the atmosphere in the newsroom – 'a climate of fear'.

They talk about a wallchart which listed each reporter's success in landing page leads and front-page stories; about reporters being reduced to tears by bullying, two of them at one particularly unjolly Christmas party; and about young reporters being pushed into situations they could not handle.

At around the same time that Ciaran Byrne was being pressurised to pose as a lesbian, the *Sunday Times* was working on a big story which had been given to them by a man who was extraordinarily obsessed with sex, leering at women in bars, leaning out of car windows to yell comments at women in the street. He was also highly aggressive. In order to make sure that this man spoke to no other newspaper, the *Sunday Times* had to send somebody to stay with him in his hotel (it's known as 'babysitting') and, whether from stupidity or cruelty, they chose a young, female trainee. She soon found herself on the wrong end of the man's sexual aggression: colleagues say she had to barricade herself into her room to get away from him. And when she complained to the office, she was ordered to carry on looking after him.

This climate produced ruinous results. The *Sunday Times*'s chances of restoring its reservoir of skills were frustrated by the steady drain of talented reporters who escaped at the first opportunity. And since those who remained sometimes lacked the skills and usually lacked the time to do their job properly, the executives who were themselves under relentless pressure to produce scoops had no alternative but to persist with that pressure. So the paper was trapped. But as long as the scoops were being delivered, the paper was selling; Murdoch's people were happy.

In the spring of 1996, an unhappy accountant phoned the newsroom at the *Sunday Times*. He explained that he had been doing some work for Jeffrey Archer, they had fallen out, and Archer was refusing to pay him. Now, he wanted to publicise the fact that Archer had managed to lose £375,000 on an obviously daft investment to which he was attracted only by his unfathomable greed for easy money. The accountant was put onto the paper's leading investigative reporter, David Leppard, who ran the story. And thus began an extraordinary partnership.

Those who have worked with David Leppard are deeply divided about him. Some will say he is a brilliant reporter with a unique range of contacts and an endless source of leads. Others dismiss him as a ruthless charlatan who cheats his sources and makes up stories. All agree that, for better or worse, he is the heart of the *Sunday Times's* newsroom.

In the unhappy accountant, Leppard found a man of equally ambiguous character. Barry Beardall, who was fifty when he first contacted the paper, has a high-performance brain inside a low-performance body. While his thinking is shrewd and as fast as a ferret, his body is hugely weighed down with obesity, and he wheezes while he walks. He is particularly good in business meetings, juggling offshore funds and bottom-line figures, and yet he is not qualified as a chartered accountant and eventually ended up in prison for fraud.

Barry Beardall became a frontman for the *Sunday Times*. Working with David Leppard, he used his accounting skills to set up phoney companies with phoney accounts and phoney histories and then conducted investigations which were at best highly unorthodox and at worst exercises in pure entrapment.

One of his first ventures for David Leppard was an abortive attempt to trick confidential information out of financial advisers who were working for the then Labour leader, Tony Blair. The *Sunday Times* sponsored this exercise just as Blair was preparing to fight the May 1997 election, which saw him become Prime Minister.

To penetrate the Labour leader's finances, Beardall created a company called Dealson Management (as in 'the deal is on'). He concealed his own links with it by registering it in the Irish Republic with shares held by three other front companies, which in turn were registered in the Irish Republic, the Isle of Man and London. Posing as Dealson's financial adviser, Beardall then approached Blair's accountants in London to ask for advice about how best to set up an offshore trust fund. Those accountants recommended a managing agent in Jersey. Beardall and a business friend, Sam Lord (who also was eventually jailed for fraud) then flew together to Jersey at the *Sunday Times*'s expense and attempted to sucker information out of the agents by pretending that they were setting up trust funds for Labour MPs. They got nothing.

A less pragmatic newspaper would not have run the inquiry. It involved deception and breach of privacy – and no evidence of the kind of wrongdoing that would justify it in the public interest. It is hard to see it as anything other than a fishing trip. In the background, Blair had declared publicly that his office was being funded from a 'blind trust', which was constructed so that Blair himself had no idea who the donors were and, therefore, could not be accused of giving them political favours. A Conservative MP, David Shaw, was alleging without evidence that this was all a lie, that Blair was dealing direct with the donors, and the *Sunday Times* ran an aggressive leader comment in support of him. Eventually, the parliamentary commissioner for standards, Sir Gordon Downey, publicly criticised both the Conservative MP and the *Sunday Times* for their pursuit of 'hearsay reports'.

Undaunted, the paper continued to use Beardall as a front, often targeting leading figures in the Labour movement. One such operation was pure entrapment.

In the run-up to the first election for a mayor of London, in May 2000, Beardall approached aides to the Labour candidate, Frank Dobson, posing as a property developer, and then spent three months trying to con them into giving him a political concession in exchange for a £10,000 donation to the Dobson campaign. If he had succeeded, David Leppard would have been able to blow Dobson out of the water.

Tape recordings of these meetings, which have survived, show that Beardall pretended to be an executive with Dealson Property

Management which was, in turn, he claimed, a subsidiary of Dealson Investment, which he described falsely as 'a substantial and very rich and very large company'. He opened his campaign with a meeting at the Lanesborough Hotel in Knightsbridge, central London, in November 1999, with Terry Ashton and Baroness Mary Goudie, both senior figures in Dobson's campaign. Beardall offered to give the campaign £10,000 but explained that he wanted them to rewrite the manifesto on their website to include a specific endorsement for business investment in the City and also to state their opposition to a European plan to tax investment. The trap was set.

The two officials hesitated and said they would need to explore all this. Over the next three months, they asked Beardall for accounts for his property company. He prepared and supplied fictitious paperwork. Baroness Goudie then told him that they would be happy to accept the donation but that she could not give him the change to the manifesto which he wanted. 'I can't get changes,' she said in a call taped by Beardall. 'You know what I mean?' But she left the trap open by suggesting that if he wanted to pursue this, he should speak again to Terry Ashton.

Beardall then phoned Ashton and told him that Dealson had been accepted as donors and then claimed entirely falsely: '[Baroness Goudie] just wanted me to have a quick check with you to confirm that the change to the website that we agreed at the Lanesborough Hotel was certainly within your remit and that you were happy to encompass business and investment in the city into the website.' Adding incentive to his lie, Beardall said that if that was all right, he would put an opening payment of £2,500 in the post. (Leppard, mindful of Murdoch's cash, was refusing to release the full £10,000.)

Ashton, however, stalled and then, on 31 January 2000, wrote a formal letter to Beardall declining to accept the donation. Beardall phoned him to apply more pressure. He was shocked and confused, he said (again falsely), because Mary Goudie had told him there was no problem.

Ashton stood his ground: 'The situation is quite simple really, Barry. I'm sorry we have kept each other hanging on this long. What we can't do is – what we won't do is – to accept a donation, much as we would like to, for obvious reasons, in exchange for policy influence, however innocuous that may seem to be.'

Beardall interrupted: 'Is there a way that we can overcome this?' Dangling his incentive again, he said: 'The board have set aside certain funds that they wish to donate.'

When Ashton continued to decline, Beardall then added weight to the incentive, claiming that his fictitious company had eight fictitious buildings to sell, worth a total of £7.5 million which they might invest in London. 'There's nothing suspicious about this,' he said. 'This is a plain, simple situation.'

As Ashton continued to resist, Beardall piled on the pressure, saying that 'I can't accept this'; that he was not even asking Dobson to vary his policy, just to clarify it; that 'I find it extraordinary that you are not prepared to accept a donation'; that 'I find it insulting, and so do the directors of the company, and we will be writing accordingly'; and that he simply couldn't understand Ashton's reasoning. Ashton apologised. 'The answer is still No,' he said.

It was open to David Leppard to run a story about all this, revealing the incorruptible character of the Dobson campaign. He didn't. No story appeared. It is quite possible that Leppard did not know the lengths to which his frontman was prepared to go in his efforts to deliver a story, although he can have had no doubt that Beardall's activities were essentially deceitful.

Beardall set up stings for the *Sunday Times* for about five years. By the time he targeted Frank Dobson, he had already been arrested for conspiring to cheat the VATman of some £7 million by importing 700,000 bottles of spirits without paying duty. While he was awaiting his trial, in January 2000, he went on to con a firm of London solicitors, Allen & Overy, on behalf of the *Sunday Times*. His target was confidential information about the private flat which the future Prime Minister, Gordon Brown, had bought for himself in central London in 1992.

Posing as an accountant 'for the Dealson group of companies', Beardall phoned Allen & Overy and told them that his company was thinking of buying this flat. A tape recording of his calls reveals Beardall effortlessly persuading first one secretary and then another to cooperate with him by calling up Gordon Brown's property deeds from the archive and then reading out the details of the sale. Having captured his information, the tape shows, Beardall put down his phone and said to somebody in the room: 'Ring David now.'

This operation, like the attempted raid on Tony Blair's accountants, was based on nothing more than hearsay. Gordon Brown's flat had once belonged to the late and corrupt millionaire Robert Maxwell, via one of his companies which went bust after his death in November 1991. The busted company was linked to Gordon Brown's Labour Party colleague, Geoffrey Robinson, who had been a director of its parent company. The speculation was that Brown and Robinson had put their heads together and arranged for the flat to be sold to Brown at a below-market rate. That would have been highly controversial, if not downright unlawful, because it would effectively have defrauded the company's creditors of money to which they were entitled. That would have given the *Sunday Times* the kind of public interest to justify getting access to confidential information from Brown's legal file. But it was not true. And nothing that Barry Beardall or David Leppard turned up gave them the evidence to stand up their theory. It was another fishing trip.

This time, Leppard and three colleagues did write a story, on the front page, running to just over a thousand words. It was a classic of its kind. They used the balance rule to lay out their theory and then, to make it legally safe, they included other material which contradicted it. They suggested that Brown had obtained the flat at 'a bargain price'; but, lower down, they acknowledged that repossessed properties usually sell cheap. They said that Geoffrey Robinson had been a director of the Maxwell company which had owned the flat; but, lower down, they acknowledged that he had been a director only of the parent company and that he had resigned from its board two years before the sale was made. They left the implication that Brown had made the purchase with Robinson's help; but, lower down, they included a statement from Brown that 'I never discussed it with Geoffrey Robinson'. They implied that there was something suspicious or unusual about the deal; but, lower down, they included Brown's statement that he had bought the flat in the normal way, through an estate agent on the open market. They said Brown would be embarrassed by the disclosure; but they quoted his saying that there was no impropriety involved. This was not the way that the *Sunday Times* once nailed Kim Philby.

Insight into the Sunday Times

In April 2001, Barry Beardall's career as the *Sunday Times*'s con man ended when he was jailed for fraud at Southampton Crown Court for six and a half years.

In a sense, Witherow was unlucky in that soon after he formally took over as editor, the beleaguered Insight team produced a genuine scoop when they caught two MPs taking cash to put down parliamentary questions. This was a project which had been started by Andrew Neil, who had lost faith in the Conservative government of John Major and declared in January 1994 that he wanted the head of a government minister. Six months later, Jonathan Calvert of the Insight team targeted ten Labour MPs and ten Tories, for whom he posed as a businessman offering £1,000 if they would table helpful questions involving either a company called Githins or a drug called Sigthin. None of them seemed to spot the anagrams of Insight. There were no takers among the Labour MPs, but two of the Tories went for it.

This was work which was close to the ethical borderline, and a select committee subsequently complained that it 'fell substantially below the standard to be expected of legitimate investigative journalism'. But, to most reporters this criticism looked like a collective tantrum from ruffled politicians attacking a story which had been exclusive and accurate. Calvert had simply held out a carrot to see who would take it, whereas Barry Beardall had done his best to force the carrot down his targets' throats and then complained bitterly when they spat it out.

This success may well have misled Witherow into believing that he was running a healthy newspaper, and not one which was structurally weakened by lack of skill, lack of resources and political interference. The paper struggled like a trapped beast.

Sometimes, they were reduced to running stories of alarming weakness, like the front-page investigations into the National Health Service losing water from dripping taps and the one about the Ku Klux Klan supposedly moving into the UK. They tried hard to procure another Great Scoop accusing John Major's Cabinet ministers of using inside information to pay their domestic gas bills before they announced that they were imposing VAT on gas. This last story ended badly, first, because there was no evidence that even one minister had bothered to risk his or her career in order to save ten or twenty quid on a gas bill, and then because there was a full-scale diplomatic row when an Insight reporter, frustrated at the then environment minister John Gummer's refusal to answer questions about his gas consumption, conned one of Gummer's children into allowing him into the minister's family home one Saturday morning, leading rapidly to his being ejected to the sound of Mr Gummer's red-hot rage and Mrs Gummer's tears.

Weak stories were hyped. Reporters say their copy was frequently rewritten in order to sharpen an angle, even if that meant distorting or inventing the truth. 'Everything had to have a sensational intro . . . Even bog-standard page leads were being rewritten.' Sometimes, the rewriting might be quite small. One news-desk source remembers them sending a reporter out on a story about plans to erect a statue of the Duke of Cumberland on the battlefield of Culloden where the duke had ordered the torture and slaughter of hundreds of Scots. The news desk told the reporter that this was outrageous, like erecting a statue of Hitler at the Belsen concentration camp. The reporter duly went and researched his story and filed his copy – and an executive then rewrote it claiming that opponents of the statue 'liken the move to erecting a memorial to Hitler at Belsen'. Which was fiction.

At other times, entire stories were shaped to fit a pre-assigned agenda. When the Insight team were tasked to look at immigration and asylum, they found that it was true, as right-wingers had alleged, that the asylum process was in chaos; but they also found impressive evidence that immigration was good for the country. They were allowed to write only the first part of the story.

When the Insight team were told to balance the cash-for-questions scoop by finding some Labour sleaze, they eventually ran an extraordinarily weak story which declared that they had 'uncovered a coordinated strategy by Labour councillors in Birmingham to influence the way people voted in May's local government election'. Apart from revealing exclusively that the councillors had been trying to persuade people to vote for them, the story went on to claim that they had spent £7 million on improvements which were specifically targeted at marginal wards. However, they were unable to identify even one ward to support their claim. The audit commission subsequently checked the story and found there was nothing in it.

The desperate quest for suitable scoops without suitable resources also produced a string of stories which were simply fictitious. There was a joke in the office: 'Our stories are more manufactured than retail.' Journalists on other newspapers who were used to following up *Sunday Times* exclusives simply stopped bothering. It became a Fleet Street cliché to talk about the stories on the *Sunday Times* which 'stood up on Sunday and fell down by Monday'. I know Whitehall press officers now who rank the paper above even the cheapest red-top tabloid as a source of fabricated stories.

For example, in July 1994, within weeks of the cash-for-questions story, David Leppard wrote about a car bomb which had exploded outside the Israeli Embassy in London. The female bomber had been identified, he told his readers. And the source of the car which she used in the attack had been traced. The bomber, he said, had turned to terrorism when her son and husband were killed by Israeli forces in southern Lebanon in 1990; she was aged between fifty-five and sixty; and she was a member of Hizbollah. If David Leppard was right, he was well ahead of the security services. Although Leppard stated as a fact that she had been identified, such a woman has never been arrested for the crime. A woman was arrested. But she had two sons and a husband, all alive; was aged forty-eight; and was not a member of Hizbollah. She was also acquitted. As to the car, Leppard declared that it had been bought on the second-hand market in London in July 1994; it turned out to have been bought at an auction in Milton Keynes in June.

Eight months later, David Leppard produced the most spectacular fiction of this period with the story of Agent Boot, a major *Sunday Times* exclusive which never even made it to Monday morning before falling down. John Witherow himself collapsed it by Sunday lunchtime.

The story, published in February 1995, some eight months after the cash-for-questions scoop, claimed that the former leader of the Labour Party, Michael Foot, had been a KGB agent of influence, known as Agent Boot. The story was riddled with silliness – the giveaway code name for the supposedly secret agent, the supposedly secret meetings

with Foot which turned out to be in a Soho restaurant full of journalists and politicians, Foot's KGB controller who was supposed to
have 'deep cover' which turned out to mean he was the entirely overt
press attaché at the Soviet Embassy in London. On the day before it
was published, a nosy reporter in the *Sunday Times* newsroom managed
to hack into the part of the computer system where the story was
being prepared: the reporters who gathered around his desk rapidly
concluded that the story was daft. But that didn't stop the pragmatic
newspaper from publishing it on its front page with two more pages
inside.

As soon as the story came out, it was ridiculed by Labour MPs,
Tory MPs, the former Prime Minister Edward Heath who had had
access to intelligence material, the KGB officer who was supposed to
have been Foot's controller and by Foot himself. That Sunday lunchtime,
John Witherow gave a live interview to BBC Radio 4 in which he
was pinned down by the falsity of the story, wriggled desperately and
ended up declaring that his paper had never meant to suggest that
Foot really was an agent of influence, merely that it was interesting
that the KGB mistakenly seemed to have thought that he was.

Life got no easier for the *Sunday Times* when they tried to fight off
a libel action by Foot with a tape recording of Leppard's interview
with a former KGB man, which turned out to be missing the key
passage in which he was supposed to have confirmed the story. Five
months later, the paper threw in its hand and paid Michael Foot
substantial damages and costs.

With its inviting comparison with the old *Sunday Times*'s skill in
exposing Kim Philby as a KGB agent, the Agent Boot story was deeply
damaging to the paper's standing. It also publicly shredded the reputation of the star reporter, David Leppard. Now, colleagues would see
stories in production and say with heavy irony: 'Leppard is doing it,
so it must be true.'

And in the background, the climate of fear was pushing reporters
into the chaotic and the corrupt. As we saw in Chapter 7, their use of
private investigators and blaggers was voracious. Now the reporters
themselves began copying their techniques. When the neuroses of Benji
the Binman made him simply too dangerous to deal with, they set up

their own internal Bin Unit which started systematically borrowing the garbage of their targets.

A young reporter who was told to track down one of two Kurdish associates of Jeffrey Archer, known in the office as Lemon Kurd and Bean Kurd, was put under such pressure to find his man that he ended up climbing into giant cylindrical metal dustbins outside an apartment block, splitting bin bags and sifting filth in search of a clue to which flat the Kurd lived in.

An Insight team tried to investigate some City brokers who were allegedly pimping young women, by booking an expensive hotel room and phoning for a couple of random prostitutes in the vague hope that they would disclose something useful. The reporters rapidly lost control of the situation when the women arrived and instantly realised that they were not real punters and proceeded to con them out of an expensive meal and cash gifts.

Another team targeted a recently deceased doctor who, they believed, had behaved improperly. They decided to doorstep several different members of his family and, in order to prevent them comparing notes, arranged for their home phones to be blocked so they couldn't call each other.

There was a gay man who was quoted in the paper supporting the outing of public figures who were secretive about their sexuality but then went on television to deny he supported the tactic: a reporter was sent to raid his dustbins to see if there was anything they could use to punish him for letting them down.

Barry Beardall was only one mechanism among many for trying to create stories that refused to happen on their own. While Beardall was trying to induce Frank Dobson's aides to engage in political corruption, one senior staffer remembers an experienced reporter coming to work for the paper and being baptised in fire when he was told to phone round all the candidates who were running to be Mayor of London to see whether they were taking money from dodgy foreigners. Talking to Glenda Jackson's office, the new reporter struck gold when he was told that only very recently a strange Russian had offered them a donation. As soon as he reported his success to the news desk, the executives started laughing, and he realised that the dodgy Russian was another *Sunday Times* reporter who had been tasked to set up the story for him to discover. According to this source, the new reporter complained bitterly, was hauled into an executive's office and warned that he was damaging his career. But he stood his ground and refused to write it.

With this same strategy of provoking stories instead of finding them, they attempted to take advantage of an interview that had been set up with the Tory minister Alan Clark. Instead of sending a reporter, the news desk inveigled a particularly pretty secretary into going to see him in the hope that the famously libidinous old rake might make a pass at her.

Reporters say it was common on a Friday night for the news desk to tell them that one of David Leppard's pieces needed a quote from an expert to fill a gap. They would be told to get on the phone and to keep phoning until they found somebody who would give them exactly the quote they wanted. 'It was like going into a restaurant and ordering this quote off the menu, and it had to be Exactly This. Eventually you would get somebody to say it – you might talk to them for forty-five minutes and use nine seconds of what they said, totally out of context, but as long as they said the words, technically it was OK to use it.'

In the midst of all this, the Insight team was toppling towards its demise. Although David Leppard seemed to be able to conjure funds out of the organisation, Insight had been suffering for years from the twin pressures of a mean budget and an endless demand for scoops. They had no more than £1,000 a week to spend, frequently trapping them in their role of Hindsight team.

In its last few years, the pressure on Insight produced a bizarre sequence of events which began just before the invasion of Iraq. An executive came up with the idea that, as soon as the fighting stopped, they should hire two former SAS men to smuggle two reporters into Iraq to find Saddam Hussein's weapons of mass destruction. That plan backfired badly when Saddam's foreign ministry somehow heard of the plan and threatened to kick out the *Sunday Times* reporter who was in Baghdad to cover the invasion. John Witherow cancelled the operation.

However, unbeknown to him, a few journalists, desperate to deliver big stories, decided to keep the plan alive, funding it partly with cash which they diverted from the news budget and partly with a considerable amount of money from one particularly eager young reporter's personal savings. This time, they succeeded in getting at least one of the ex-SAS men across the border into Iraq. He came back empty-handed but thought he might yet succeed. So they sent him in again, and again he came back empty-handed and roosted for a while in a City hotel at the journalists' expense. (A copy of his bill shows a deep attachment to the minibar.) Finally, tens of thousands of pounds later, they abandoned the operation.

This pressure reached a point where Insight's penultimate editor, Stephen Grey, was so busy churning out Hindsight pieces that he had to use his spare time to work privately on his best story – the allegation that the CIA were using Third World countries to torture suspected terrorists, an inquiry which eventually led Grey to write a book exposing the CIA's system of 'extraordinary rendition' flights.

Insight's final editor, Dean Nelson, as we have seen in Chapter 7, was reduced to hiring a reporter, David Connett, 'off the books' so that Connett could engage in 'dark arts' to procure stories and be deniable if he were caught. This was at the same time as David Leppard and another senior reporter, Rob Winnett, were renting an office in Clerkenwell to handle a trainee reporter, Claire Newell, who had signed up with a secretarial agency which supplied typists for government departments. From this vantage point, she was feeding back a succession of officially secret documents, any one of which could have landed her in jail if the government had chosen to prosecute Murdoch's paper.

In the summer of 2005, Murdoch's men finally and formally killed off the Insight team. All that remained of the unit which had exposed Kim Philby and thalidomide was the name, to be used as a logo on stories put together by newsroom reporters.

It should be said that, during the following year, the new arrangement scored one highly successful hit, when *Sunday Times* reporters uncovered the fact that the Labour Party had been raising funds through loans which, unlike donations, did not have to be declared; and that there was evidence that four men who had made loans totalling £5 million had been led to believe that they would be rewarded with peerages. This provoked a major police inquiry with the unprecedented result that the Prime Minister was twice questioned under caution, although no charges were brought.

It's extremely difficult to know precisely where to pin the blame for the long, slow demise of truth-telling at the *Sunday Times*. It's tempting to blame some of the reporters whose stories so frequently turned out to be false or distorted or unethical. But then again it's clear that they were working under unreasonable pressure and often found their work being rewritten. Some of that rewriting was legitimate, standard practice, designed simply to present the story in its sharpest possible form. Some of it clearly was not. And beyond that, in some circumstances, one would lay the blame at the editor's door, but it's clear that on the *Sunday Times* under John Witherow, the editor was not always aware of exactly what was going on.

Years ago, in an interview with an Australian journalist, Rupert Murdoch declared expansively: 'The buck stops with the owner, whether the presses break down, whether there are libels in the papers, or anything else.' Perhaps he is right.

Insight was killed in the end simply to save Murdoch's money. The managing editor, Richard Caseby, calculated he could save £300,000 by closing it down, including a saving of £130,000 in the first year.

The slow death of Insight was a saving for Murdoch's company. It was an incalculable loss for Fleet Street. As Harry Evans said when he looked back at the Philby story: 'If the press will not do this work, who else can?'

9. The Blinded *Observer*

A funny thing happened to the *Observer*'s US correspondent, Ed Vulliamy, in the autumn of 2002.

It started when he came up with a new contact – a former senior analyst in the Central Intelligence Agency named Mel Goodman. This was an interesting contact for two reasons. First, although Goodman had left the agency, he had kept his security clearance and had stayed in touch with his former colleagues and was able to get access to highly classified documents. Second, he had a big story: through these contacts, he knew that, contrary to everything that was being said by the American and British governments, the CIA were reporting that Saddam Hussein had no weapons of mass destruction.

Looking back at it now, that seems almost like a cliché, but in 2002 it was highly important. Only a handful of journalists had run stories to challenge the global Flat Earth reporting about Iraqi weapons; and those few dissenting stories were weakened by the fact that they were based on comments from unidentified officials. Goodman not only had the story direct from the CIA, he was willing to go on the record as a named source.

Vulliamy filed it all and waited for the impact which it was bound to have on the global debate about the impending war. The funny thing was that the *Observer* did not print it.

Over the following four months, as the cries for war became louder, Vulliamy filed it again. In total, he filed versions of Mel Goodman's revelations on seven different occasions. The *Observer*, however, did not print any of them.

A surviving copy of the seventh version, filed two weeks before the invasion in March 2003, reveals that it exposed much of what the world learned only slowly in the months and years that followed.

There was the intro clearly revealing 'assurances to the *Observer* by one veteran senior former CIA officer that Saddam Hussein possesses no weapons of mass destruction'.

There was the central charge of dishonesty: 'The official, talking to the *Observer* for some months now, accuses the Bush adminstration of "manipulating intelligence materials to make the case for war" – manipulation by the White House, Pentagon and other politically-appointed masters whom the officer accuses of deliberately "cranking up" and "making fabricated additions to" the work of CIA analysts over the threat posed by Saddam Hussein, his links to al-Qaeda and his alleged weapons of mass destruction.'

And there was Goodman, on the record: 'Speaking exclusively to the *Observer*, Melvyn Goodman was head of the CIA's Soviet desk during much of the cold war. In an interview four months ago, Goodman charged the Bush administration with "basing the case for war against Iraq on a shoot-the-messenger syndrome, ignoring the assessments by CIA analysts which do not support the case for war, and instead establishing intelligence cadres made up of political appointees who will tell the President what he wants to hear".'

This version of the story ran to more than 1,500 words and went into considerable detail. It summarised the conclusion of CIA analysts that there was no evidence of the claimed link between Saddam and al-Qaeda; relayed their scepticism about claims of Iraqi weapons; revealed that neither the CIA's 'front-row analysts' nor their colleagues in the State Department had any faith in the Iraqi National Congress, led by Ahmed Chalabi, whose information was still being taken seriously at this time; and named the political officials in the Pentagon and the State Department who were obstructing the flow of honest intelligence.

There were further powerful quotes from Goodman, the intelligence veteran: 'The entire enterprise is back to front from an intelligence point of view. President Bush will use whatever information suits him, and if he isn't getting it from the civil service, he arranges for people to give it to him. This leads to a cranking up of what the intelligence analysts actually find and to the politicisation of intelligence. It entails acute frustration among some of the best professional agents. You have to imagine what it is like for the analysts. You go to your political masters in the White House or Pentagon, and deliver what you know. They say: "We want this, not that. We want X, not Y. Go and get me Y."'

All of this flew in the face of the consensus account of Iraq's threat to the world and of its links with international terrorism. All of it subsequently proved to be true – when it was too late to influence the debate on the need for war.

Why did the *Observer* not print it?

Something important happened to the *Observer* in the build-up to the invasion of Iraq. The problem was not simply that they refused to print Mel Goodman's revelations. There were other stories of a similar kind which also struggled to make it into print. And the rejection of those stories occurred while the paper was engaged in publishing a sequence of high-profile, high-volume falsehoods about the alleged threat from Iraq, some of which went far beyond false claims that were made in other media. As the deadline for invasion drew nearer, the paper declared its support for war.

This was a newspaper which historically had positioned itself on the left of centre and had taken some pride in its willingness to swim against the mainstream, to confront the power elite if that was what its principles demanded. Most famously, the *Observer* had stood out against the British invasion of Suez in 1956, despite courting the scorn of the government and the loss of some of its more conservative readers and advertisers.

And yet this newspaper which had thrived on scepticism was seduced into accepting unproven and extravagant claims; this flagship of the left was towed along in the wake of a determinedly right-wing American government; on this crucial, long-running story, the essential role of journalism, to tell the truth, was compromised.

However shocking the *Observer*'s coverage may have been to some of its readers and some of its reporters, there is an important sense in which it was not an aberration. While the paper may well have lost touch with its roots, its performance was a classic example of some of the great underlying weaknesses in modern journalism.

★   ★   ★

Two months after Islamist terrorists used four planes full of civilians as flying bombs in New York City, Washington DC and Pennsylvania, the *Observer* announced that the men responsible for this massacre were linked to the Iraqi regime of Saddam Hussein. This was a big story, billed as 'A Focus Special', 2,500 words long, spread across two pages, with a thick black headline. And it was wrong.

It was wrong in its headline claim of an 'Iraqi connection' to the attacks of 11 September 2001. It was wrong in its central statement that the Iraqi regime had used its intelligence officers to liaise with the hijackers, wrong to imply that the regime had trained them. It was wrong in much of its detail.

The story was written by one of the *Observer*'s most experienced reporters, David Rose, a former crime reporter who had become a specialist in intelligence and terrorism. It was one of a sequence of high-profile and sometimes aggressive stories which he wrote in the nineteen months between those infamous attacks and the subsequent invasion of Iraq. Many of these stories were, at best, unproven; at worst, simply wrong. Like the 'Iraqi connection' story, they provided powerful ammunition for those who believed that force should be used against Iraq.

On 14 October, a month before his 'Iraqi connection' story, Rose had already used the front page of the *Observer* to name Iraq as the CIA's prime suspect for the five letters containing anthrax which had been sent to targets in the US. This is a contention for which no evidence has ever been produced. Even at the height of their attempts to prove a link between Saddam Hussein and international terrorism, the British and American authorities never produced any evidence or intelligence to link the Iraqi regime to the anthrax attacks.

In the months that followed his claims about the Iraqi connection, Rose produced a series of other stories containing claims which do not stand up to scrutiny. Some of them were presented in the context of lacerating attacks on those who opposed the American position.

In a comment piece in December 2001, arguing for the use of military force against Saddam Hussein, Rose defended the Iraqi National Congress, which was then the vehicle for American political ambitions in Iraq, complaining that 'foreign policy Arabists have briefed the media that the INC is a disorganised, divided rabble'. He then declared:

'In fact, it is supported by the overwhelming majority of Iraq's liberals and intellectuals, and has become by far the best source of information on what is actually happening there.' The INC's leader, Ahmed Chalabi, subsequently returned to Iraq where he failed conspicuously to attract support from a majority of liberals or intellectuals or anybody else; and his INC was exposed as the source of a steady flow of disinformation in the build-up to the war.

In January 2002, Rose complained about 'inaccuracies and glib assertions' in the media and went on to endorse the views of Laurie Mylroie, an American academic who was claiming that Iraq was responsible not only for the attacks of 11 September 2001, but also for the first bombing of the New York World Trade Center in 1993, the Oklahoma City bombing in 1995, the bombing of two US Embassies in East Africa in 1998 and even the crash of TWA flight 800 off the coast of Long Island in 1996. Mylroie's theories had been adopted and re-cycled by the neoconservatives in the Bush administration. An insight into her credibility is captured in *Against All Enemies*, the memoir of Richard Clarke, who advised four US presidents on counter-terrorism. Clarke describes a meeting in 2001 at which the then Deputy Secretary of Defense, Paul Wolfowitz, claimed that al-Qaeda must have had the support of a foreign government in its 1993 attack on the World Trade Center. He continues: 'I could hardly believe it, but Wolfowitz was spouting the Laurie Mylroie theory that Iraq was behind the 1993 truck bomb at the World Trade Center, a theory that had been investigated for years and found to be totally untrue.'

Later in 2002, Rose marked the anniversary of the 11 September attacks by assaulting the credibility of Scott Ritter, the former UN arms inspector who was warning that Saddam Hussein's regime possessed no weapons of mass destruction. As evidence against Ritter, Rose cited the testimony of an Iraqi defector named Adnan Saeed al-Haideri. The reality was that al-Haideri had failed a CIA lie detector test in December 2001, before his claims were fed to the world's media via the *New York Times*. After the war, when he was taken to Iraq by American intelligence, he was unable to find any of the weapons sites which he had claimed to know about. Scott Ritter's warnings turned out to be correct.

That same month, Rose reported as fact that Saddam Hussein had disposed of the husband of one of his mistresses by having the man thrown into prison and his assets seized. He also reported as fact that Saddam's son had raped this woman's fifteen-year-old daughter. He wrote: 'The *Observer* has seen evidence which corroborates her story, including copies of her passport and visa stamps, and photographs of one of her daughters with Saddam's son.' Clearly, this evidence did nothing to corroborate the key statements in the story. This woman, whose allegations were provided to the media by the Iraqi National Congress, subsequently claimed on US televison that she had personally seen Osama bin Laden visiting Saddam, and that Saddam liked to drink alcohol and smoke cigars while watching videos of his enemies being tortured. Rose now accepts that elements of her story appear to have been propaganda.

On 16 March 2003 – a week before the invasion – Rose reported that an alleged Spanish terrorist, Yusuf Galan, who had been accused of helping the 11 September conspirators, was said to have 'links with Iraqi officials', specifically that he had once been invited to a party by the Iraqi ambassador in Spain. Galan was eventually convicted and jailed for six years as a minor member of a terrorist organisation and not as a party to the 11 September conspiracy. Whatever was originally claimed by Spanish investigators, no evidence was ever produced to show that he had any connection of any kind with any Iraqi official, or that he had been invited to an Iraqi Embassy party, or that he had gone to the party (or that attending such a party would have been evidence of Iraqi involvement in his plans for terrorism).

Why? Why would such an able and experienced reporter produce so many stories which were not only factually wrong but which carried the flag for a policy which appeared to contradict so many of the principles which guided his newspaper?

A year after the war, in May 2004, Rose confessed in the *Evening Standard* that his enthusiasm for the invasion had been 'misplaced and naive'. 'I look back with shame and disbelief,' he said. Three weeks later, in the immediate aftermath of the *New York Times* publishing an account of its own failure to report the reality of the case for war against Iraq, Rose wrote a short and limited retraction of his work in the *Observer*, in which he acknowledged that he had become part of 'a calculated set-up, devised to foster the propaganda case for war'. But why? A glimpse of the answer was captured by Rose in his *Observer* retraction. He had, he said, been 'bamboozled'.

Reporters do not have to be dishonest to be wrong. They do not have to be the hirelings of governments or intelligence agencies to become the vehicles for their disinformation. They simply need to be vulnerable to manipulation.

In his sequence of stories, Rose relied on two different kinds of sources of information: defectors provided by the Iraqi National Congress; and officials of intelligence agencies, particularly the American CIA and the British MI6. Both led him astray.

After the war, it became notorious that the INC's collection of defectors had misled reporters, most notably some of those working for the *New York Times* and the *Washington Post*. Rose relied on the claims of five of these defectors. One, who spoke to him on condition of anonymity, told the truth, he believes. But this man did not contribute to any of his *Observer* stories. Two others – Mohammed Harith and Adnan Saeed al-Haideri, he now accepts, were liars – and had been recognised as liars by American intelligence before they were fed to the media by the INC. He now has doubts as to whether they were even genuine defectors.

The other two – Sabah Khodada and a man known as 'Abu Zeinab' – provided core information for Rose's 'Iraqi connection' story in November 2001, claiming that Saddam Hussein had been training Islamist terrorists at a camp called Salman Pak, and suggesting that the hijackers on 11 September had used techniques which were taught there. Rose still believes there is evidence that Saddam Hussein was training Islamic militants but acknowledges that there is no evidence that this was aimed at the West. The evidence of both men has been dismissed as unreliable by the CIA and by the US Defense Intelligence Agency and by subsequent official inquiries into the justification for the war. Rose now also recognises that, in spite of the US conducting the most far-reaching criminal investigation in the history of humankind, there is still no evidence to support the INC's claim that Saddam Hussein's regime were involved in the attacks of 11 September 2001.

For most of the rest of his false leads, Rose relied on intelligence sources. His story linking Iraq to the anthrax attacks was put up to him by James Woolsey, a former director of the CIA, who was one of the first hawks to argue publicly that the 11 Sepember attacks provided grounds to remove Saddam Hussein. In his 'Iraqi connection' story, Rose was steered by a senior official from the CIA who clearly did not agree with the analysts whose doubts were reflected by Mel Goodman. It was this official who persuaded Rose that there was 'significant Iraqi assistance and some involvement' in the 11 September attacks; and who provided Rose with two crucial contentions, both of which proved to be false.

First, this CIA source encouraged Rose to accept the claim, which had already been published elsewhere, that the supposed leader of the 11 September terrorists, Mohammed Atta, had flown to Prague in April 2001, five months before the attack, to meet an Iraqi intelligence officer, Colonel Mohammed al-Ani. Rose now accepts that this was wrong. There is fairly good evidence that Colonel al-Ani met an unknown young Arab man in Prague in April 2001; there is hard evidence that Mohammed Atta had visited Prague a year earlier, in June 2000; but there is no evidence that Mohammed Atta ever met Colonel al-Ani or any other Iraqi official in Prague or any other city.

The truth, as Rose subsequently came to accept, is that Czech intelligence officers had information that Colonel al-Ani had been seen meeting a young man of Arab appearance who was never identified. When Mohammed Atta's face was broadcast around the world after 11 September, one Czech source said that he thought Atta could have been this young Arab. This uncertain identification was passed up the tree in Prague and then disclosed to US intelligence who shared it with US politicians who rapidly stripped it of its uncertainty and leaked it to the media as a stick with which to beat Iraq.

The CIA source passed this stick to Rose. Rose trusted him. It is notable that he went further than other journalists who wrote about Atta's alleged link to Colonel al-Ani in Prague, claiming that Atta had made not one but two trips to meet the Iraqi intelligence colonel; and that he was not the only suspected al-Qaeda member who met al-Ani and other Iraqi agents in Prague. There is simply no evidence to justify any of this, and we now know that two months before the invasion of Iraq internal CIA reports said analysts were 'increasingly sceptical' about the alleged meetings – scepticism which was not passed on to David Rose by his senior CIA source.

Second, this same CIA official fed Rose the line that two other, unnamed 11 September terrorists also had meetings with Iraqi intelligence officers in the spring of 2001, in the United Arab Emirates. Rose checked the story with the INC, who confirmed it and identified the two hijackers as Marwan al-Shehri and Ziad Jarrah. The CIA official then confirmed the names. Rose now accepts that this too was wrong. Both the CIA and the INC were recycling the same uncorroborated information from the same poisoned source. Months later, when Rose complained to him, the senior CIA official backtracked fast and said this had been merely 'a preliminary conclusion'.

The contribution of British intelligence to the 'Iraqi connection' story was more confused. Two different MI6 officers gave Rose entirely contradictory accounts of what was happening. Rose had dealt with MI6 before. Years earlier, in 1992 when the existence of the agency had been finally officially acknowledged by the British government, its then chief, Sir Colin McColl, had lunch with the then editor of the *Observer*, Donald Trelford. McColl suggested that, in its new slightly public form, MI6 was willing to open up a formal channel to talk to the press and he asked if the *Observer* might like to appoint a reporter to liaise with the agency. Trelford suggested David Rose, who was then the paper's home affairs correspondent. That afternoon, Rose received a phone call inviting him to tea at the Ritz Hotel, where he met MI6's first 'director of public affairs'.

Rose had stayed in touch with MI6, enjoying an access which was denied to reporters who had not been nominated as official liaison points. By the time he came to write his Iraqi connection story, he had dealt with at least three directors of public affairs and had come to know several senior officers.

It was one of these operational officers who told him that 'there was a view in MI6' that Iraq was behind the 11 September attacks. However, when Rose went to the director of public affairs, he was told that that was not correct. Rose then went back to the operational officer who said that the official line was disinformation, designed to distance MI6 from a US policy with which they did not agree. Rose's subsequent line in his story that 'Whitehall sources made clear that parts of British intelligence had reached the same conclusion' was designed to reflect this division, although it failed to capture MI6's outright denial.

Looking back on all this in his short retraction in the *Observer*, Rose wrote: 'To any journalist being offered apparently sensational disclosures, especially from an anonymous intelligence source, I offer two words of advice: *caveat emptor.*'

This does not quite deal with the issue. The idea that anonymous intelligence sources were unaccountable and prone to manipulate reporters was hardly news to Rose. Any experienced reporter knows that. (As we have seen, in Chapter 6, intelligence agencies have a history of involvement in feeding propaganda to the mass media.) Rose himself had heard an MI6 officer speaking quite openly about 'using the press'; and, several years earlier, one of the MI6 directors of public affairs had tried to feed him a story about the former Nigerian dictator, Sani Abaja, investing money in Cambridge University – a story which Rose checked and found to be entirely fictitious. And yet, in the build-up to war, he recycled key claims which they made to him and which he could not check.

Rose now feels particularly bitter towards the senior CIA official who misled him, a man to whom he was introduced by a former CIA agent who recommended him as a reliable informant. Rose told me: 'I have never come across a source who I assumed instinctively was the gold standard, because of his position, who I've felt so badly let down by. I thought this was an impeccable source, so I was predisposed to believe him. If it hadn't been for him, I would never have been so inclined to believe the INC.'

The truth that scarcely dares to raise its head here is that most reporters routinely accept unchecked statements from official sources. This is the easiest method for PR and propaganda to enter the news. Some reporters sometimes, if they have the time, will try to check. In the early days of the campaign for war, the *Observer's* foreign affairs specialist, Peter Beaumont, ran a long analysis of the intelligence on Iraqi weapons, which was a model of sceptical reporting, laying out the claims and exposing their weaknesses as well as their strengths. But most reporters most of the time will reproduce what they are told by official sources, because they are 'predisposed to believe' them. Usually, this turns out to be a safe bet: even if the official story is wrong, it will look right because everybody else is running it; and usually it won't be proved wrong, because those who attack it will lack the instant credibility of the official sources who are backing it.

Rose's position with his pre-war stories, however, was particularly weak. Although he was following the consensus line on the threat from Saddam Hussein, he was more or less out on his own with much of the detail of what he was writing. His official sources were divided among themselves, and when he needed their support, they ran for cover. But most of all, he was wrong.

In part, perhaps, this goes back to the nature of the man, that he has all the self-confidence of great reporters but less of the judgement. His stories did not simply explore the evidence of Saddam Hussein's guilt. They persistently overstated the case and then hunted down and battered some of those who opposed it. In retrospect, Rose admits that he signed up to a cause in which he believed and became too 'gung-ho'.

But the core point here is that ultimately the only secure defence for a reporter is to be right and provably so. If the reporter is obstructed – by personal weakness or by the nature of the organisation for which he works – he may suffer. Being duped is a professional hazard but the cruel reality, as John Pilger put it in an interview about the reporting of the build-up to the Iraqi war, is that: 'Our job is not to be duped.'

Rose misled his readers. He also misled his editor. However, in this saga of manipulation, Rose was not the only target, nor the only victim.

Roger Alton has never claimed to be a political animal. His style is too intense, bordering on manic, at best full of charm, at worst eye-wateringly clumsy. His passions are far from government, much closer to sport and women, both of which he pursues with obsessive energy. In newspaper terms, he is a desk man, a brilliant subeditor who can project stories on a page, a good commissioner of interesting tales. But not political.

This was reflected in a story that went round the *Observer* newsroom after he was appointed editor in July 1998 and found himself being invited to go round to Downing Street for a quiet chat with the Prime Minister. 'Fuck,' said Alton, who swears when he breathes. 'I can't meet the Prime Minister. I'm just a fucking sub.'

In his anxiety, so the story goes, he turned to the *Observer*'s then political editor, Patrick Wintour, and persuaded him to come with him to help him handle the conversation. So it was that a few days later, Alton turned up in Downing Street with Wintour by his side, and waited nervously outside the Prime Minister's study. David Miliband, then running the Prime Minister's policy unit, walked by and said hello to Wintour, who introduced him to his new editor.

'So, what sort of changes do you plan to make to the paper?' asked Miliband, who was evidently looking for some kind of political insight.

Totally bereft of an answer, Alton reverted to type, stammering: 'Bit more sex on the front page. More sport. That kind of thing.'

Alton's relative innocence in politics might not have become so important if Patrick Wintour had stayed at the *Observer* and continued to offer guidance. As it was, some eighteen months later, Wintour left to become political editor at the *Guardian*. Even then, things might have run smoothly if, as everybody expected, the job had passed to Wintour's deputy, Andy McSmith, an able and experienced political correspondent.

McSmith, however, was shocked a few weeks later to be phoned at home by Alton who told him that the job had gone to a journalist with no significant track record in political reporting, Kamal Ahmed, the *Guardian*'s media editor. McSmith was so furious that he could barely speak and slammed the phone down on Alton. The next day he went to see him – insulted at losing the job; baffled that it had gone to a man who had no real experience at all of Westminster; aghast at the idea that he would have to take orders from somebody whom he was simultaneously teaching. He asked his editor why he should accept this. 'Well, you'll be a better human being,' replied Alton in what may have been intended as a joke. McSmith resigned.

Now, the editor who lacked political experience had lost both his political editor and his political correspondent. And the new man, Kamal Ahmed, had even less experience of government than he did.

Alton was not worried: it would be a good thing, he argued, to open up the claustrophobic Westminster village by putting in a political editor who was not trapped in a web of loyalties. Ahmed was not worried: he had been a journalist for nine years and he was sure he could cope. But the difficulties were soon clear.

As soon as he started the new job, in April 2000, Ahmed struggled. He had no network of backbench contacts. He did not even know the basic routine in the House of Commons. One backbench Labour MP who had previously been a Cabinet minister was surprised to find that Ahmed was trying to set up a meeting for Wednesday at noon without realising that this clashed with Prime Minister's Questions, the most important slot in the weekly parliamentary diary. Some of the other political correspondents, possibly out of solidarity with the jilted Andy McSmith, made little effort to help him – even when they heard that Whitehall PR specialists were privately competing with each other to see who could slip Ahmed the biggest fib.

During Ahmed's first month in the Westminster snakepit, the *Observer* ran a sequence of stories which turned out to be misleading as various political back-stabbers passed the new political editor material without too much scruple about whether it was true or false.

Sources in Ireland told him that the Northern Ireland Secretary, Peter Mandelson, was being brought back to London during the coming summer. That ended up on the front page with a feature inside. It never happened: Mandelson stayed in Belfast until the following January when scandal forced him to resign.

A senior source in the Labour Party told him that Ken Livingstone, who was then running to become Mayor of London against the official Labour candidate, faced a special investigation for breaking spending rules in his campaign. That ended up on an inside news page. It never happened: the Labour Party produced no evidence of Livingstone breaking the rules, and there never was an investigation.

A source close to Gordon Brown told him there was to be 'a multi-billion-pound package of measures to tackle Britain's crippling transport crisis'. Some of this did happen. There really were two new tram schemes and some extra cash for the west coast mainline rail route. But the rest – all the other tram schemes, the double-decker trains, the superinterchanges where motorway traffic would switch to public transport, the motorway lanes reserved for buses – none of that happened at all. To add a little personal insult to editorial injury, according to a veteran political correspondent, Brown dispatched a civil servant to warn a senior journalist at the *Observer* that he was less than impressed by the new man's grasp of politics.

Soon, Ahmed was so depressed that he went to the executive editor, Andy Malone, and told him he wanted to resign. Malone persuaded him to stick with it a little longer. Ahmed did, and, since he is hardworking and ambitious, he came up with a solution to his problems. He made friends with Downing Street and, in particular, with the Prime Minister's press secretary, Alastair Campbell.

This relationship was to become the source of great controversy. Some other political correspondents and some of Ahmed's colleagues at the *Observer* became alarmed that he was being used as a conduit for government announcements. 'He was just like Alastair's jug,' according to a ministerial adviser who deals with the press. 'Alastair poured stuff into him, and he poured it out into the *Observer*.' Ahmed, however, did not see it that way at all. He believed that it was part of his job to 'reflect government thinking' and that by getting close to Downing Street, he was picking up good stories for the paper.

Looking back at Kamal's coverage, you can see that certainly there were a lot of stories which simply announced government plans. Downing Street was under pressure over Europe, and it was Ahmed who announced the new European enforcer with 'sweeping powers' to control European policy across all departments. The government was in trouble over rising figures for violent crime, and it was Ahmed who announced 'sweeping new powers' for police to close down bad pubs. So, too, when the government was in trouble because GM seeds from Canada had contaminated crops in Britain; or when the government was in trouble because Oxford University had rejected a state school student even though she had six A levels: Ahmed was there to pass on the Downing Street line.

Ahmed's copy began to betray a striking enthusiasm for Tony Blair. When Campbell told him that the Prime Minister might take part in televised debates with other party leaders during the next election,

Ahmed opened his story with the words: 'He is the telegenic Prime Minister, the man who can be trusted to say the right thing in front of the cameras. Now it looks as though he could put his talents to good use.' When Campbell gave him advance notice of a controversial speech about the National Health Service, Ahmed said nothing about the intense opposition to government plans, only that 'Blair will spearhead a campaign to modernise the National Health Service. He believes the traditional establishment running it needs shaking up.'

In the *Observer* office Ahmed was soon a much more confident figure, brandishing his link to Alastair Campbell, perhaps merely as a joke, perhaps as a badge of power. Colleagues recall him blandly declaring at news conferences that he couldn't tell them what he would be writing for that week's paper until he had spoken to Alastair. 'In this job, you really only need one contact,' was a regular quip, they say. One journalist reported finding him lurking behind his shoulder as he was writing a story and Ahmed explaining, 'Alastair likes to know what we're all doing.' Ahmed insists he never said any of these things, although he does remember commenting on anti-government stories at conference, saying, 'Better get clearance for that.'

It is not that Ahmed was a government patsy. He did run some stories which embarrassed the government. But by choosing to see it as his job to 'reflect government thinking' inevitably he opened the door to a government which was highly adept at manipulating reporters and particularly keen to insert its message into the columns of the *Observer*, a paper which is read widely by Labour Party members and backbench MPs. Beyond that: on key issues, Ahmed personally and loudly supported the government; he was clearly excited by his contact with the Prime Minister, inclined to let slip that the PM had shared a beer with him or asked his opinion on something; and with Downing Street's help, he had survived his uncomfortable arrival in Westminster. The result was that some of Ahmed's colleagues warned the *Observer* news desk that the political editor seemed to be in danger of crossing the line from independent reporter to Downing Street's ally. One senior executive recalls the news desk rejecting some of his stories as 'government puffs' and urging him to include more material to challenge what he was being told by his official sources.

It is clear he was not always checking the truth of what he was being given. In July 2000, he used the front page of the *Observer* to report that the government was about to give schools in England and Wales 'their biggest cash injection ever' – an extra £5.5 billion over three years. A simple check would have told him that that could not be true, since £5.5 billion was substantially less than the extra £9.7 billion which had been given to education for the previous three years. Early in the following year, he ran a front-page story about a speech which the Prime Minister was due to give to a party conference in Glasgow, predicting seven different points which he would make. If he had asked for an advance text of the speech, he would have discovered that six of these points were wrong. Alastair Campbell's deputy, Lance Price, later confessed that he had had only the vaguest idea what points the Prime Minister planned to make in his speech, so 'I'd made some up'.

But Ahmed stuck to his work, convinced that he was right to stay close to the heart of government, reassured that he was landing good stories for the paper, and strongly defended by his editor, Roger Alton, who soon adopted Ahmed as a friend and as a political guide, to whom he turned for guidance and support.

And then the campaign for war began.

It was fascinating, but not surprising, when many months after the invasion, a leaked memo disclosed the thinking inside Downing Street. The memo was written to the Prime Minister by his foreign policy adviser, Sir David Manning, on 14 March 2002, summarising a conversation with the then US national security adviser, Condoleezza Rice: 'I said that you would not budge in your support for regime change, but you had to manage a press, a Parliament and a public opinion that was very different than anything in the States.'

As a single, particularly clear example of what this meant, we now know that, on the day after that memo was written, the Joint Intelligence Committee circulated a secret summary of its best information on Saddam Hussein's weaponry. This summary warned repeatedly that intelligence on this subject was 'poor','very little' and 'sporadic and patchy'. It went on to pitch the estimated threat at a conspicuously low level, reporting its judgement that Iraq had retained some biological agents, that 'it may retain some stocks of chemical agents' although the sources for this view were said by defence intelligence to be 'dubious', and that Iraq's earlier attempts to procure nuclear weapons had been frozen by sanctions. A parallel advice to ministers concluded that 'Saddam has not succeeded in seriously threatening his neighbours'.

However, in the following two or three weeks, the need to 'manage public opinion' saw the Prime Minister give an interview to Australian television in which he delivered an unqualified warning, shorn of his intelligence agencies' doubts, that 'we know that he [Saddam] has stockpiles of major amounts of chemical and biological weapons'. He also told the House of Commons without equivocation that Saddam was 'developing weapons of mass destruction . . . He is a threat to his own people and to the region.' And, on a visit to the United States, he boldly declared to reporters: 'We know he has been developing these weapons. We know that those weapons constitute a threat.' That last story ran on the front page of the *Observer*, under Kamal Ahmed's byline.

This was a dangerous time for the paper. It was one thing for the government to 'manage' right-wing newspapers, but the respected left-wing *Observer* – the newspaper that was read by the very Labour Party members and backbench MPs who were most likely to give the government a headache over the war – that really would be a prize. Senior journalists at the *Observer* say Alastair Campbell was dogged in his efforts to turn the paper around. Ahmed was a prime target. So, too, was his editor.

Campbell stayed in regular contact with Roger Alton. There were times when Alton submitted copy to be included in leader comments which, other journalists believed, had come straight from Alastair Campbell's email messages. The press secretary also arranged further informal chats for Alton with the Prime Minister himself, including an intimate lunch in the early autumn of 2000 from which, according to colleagues, Alton returned full of determined support for the campaign against Saddam. The previously nervous editor became so relaxed about his contact with the Prime Minister that he took to imitating Tony Blair at news conferences. When the Iraqi threat was discussed, he liked to put on his Tony voice and describe how he had seen things that made the hair stand up on the back of his neck. He also became more open about his own right-wing gut instincts, knocking back ideas which struck him as left-wing with a dig at one of north London's most notoriously sandal-wearing neighbourhoods: 'It's a bit Crouch End, isn't it?'

A more experienced or more cynical political editor might have steered Alton away from the government's line. As it was, Kamal Ahmed also became an open advocate in the office of the government's argument on Iraq. Both men accepted as true statements from Downing Street which were clearly calculated to mislead. Over the following months, as the momentum towards war gathered weight, the *Observer* provided its readers with a steady dribble of falsehood and distortion, leaked into its columns from Downing Street.

At the next US summit, in September, the *Observer* reported a series of extravagant claims from the 'resolute' Prime Minister that Saddam had 'stocks of biological and chemical weapons that had not been accounted for'; that his weapons of mass destruction would be targeted at British interests; and that 'on the nuclear sites, there has been a lot of activity going on'. All this ran into the paper without qualification or criticism.

Blair was allowed to corroborate his claims by declaring: 'We only need to look at the report from the International Atomic Energy Agency this morning showing what has been going on at the former nuclear weapons site to realise that.' If the *Observer* had checked to make sure that the Prime Minister was telling the truth about this IAEA report, they would have found out that there was no such report. There was not even a report that the Prime Minister had misconstrued. There just was no IAEA report at all. There was a story in the *New York Times*, published the day before the Prime Minister made these remarks, and it did claim that 'a United Nations official said today that international weapons inspectors had identified several nuclear-related sites in Iraq where new construction or other unexplained changes had occurred since their last visit nearly four years ago'. In the classic churnalist pattern, that story had been picked up by Reuters and spread around the world. However, even as that was happening, the IAEA was denying it. From their headquarters in Vienna, they issued a statement which could not have been clearer: 'With reference to an article published today in the *New York Times*, the International Atomic Energy Agency would like to state that it has no new information on Iraq's nuclear programme since December 1998 when its inspectors left Iraq.' And yet, twenty-four hours later, in spite of that clear denial, the Prime Minister, with assistance from the front page of the *Observer*, was adding falsehood to falsehood.

In that same story, the paper recycled its briefing from Downing Street, that 'the Prime Minister believes public opinion over Iraq will harden with the publication tomorrow of a report by the International Institute for Strategic Studies in London'. Citing 'officials at Number 10', it faithfully reported that the ISS report would 'concentrate on whether Iraq is supporting terrorist organisations around the world with weapons or finance'. If the *Observer* had checked to make sure that Downing Street was telling the truth about this report, they would have found out that, in fact, the ISS report had nothing at all to say on that subject of Iraq's supposed support for terrorist organisations. The *Observer* also claimed that the report would 'give details of Saddam's attempt to rebuild his nuclear capabilities since the ending of UN weapons inspections in 1998'. It didn't do that either. The ISS report did say that Saddam had had the opportunity to rebuild his nuclear capability and took it for granted that he would want to, but it offered no information at all on any attempts which he might have made to do so.

The same day saw the paper carry an admiring account of the Blair–Bush relationship which was 'so crucial to peace', confiding that, according to 'one No 10 official', even on his holiday the previous month, 'Tony read new evidence about Iraq pretty much every day'. Later that month, the *Observer* was one of a handful of papers who were given a Downing Street briefing which hyped the contents of a dossier on Iraqi weapons due to be published that week which, in turn, hyped the contents of intelligence reports which, in turn, were entirely wrong on crucial points. This ran on the front page, without qualification or criticism.

The paper went on to run an attack on the leading parliamentary opponent of the war, Robin Cook; a long interview with the Prime Minister, allowing him to switch the focus to domestic issues before his party conference; a declaration that 'post-Saddam Iraq' had been 'mapped out by the allies'; an announcement that the Prime Minister was sending

Lord Guthrie to Turkey as 'a safe pair of hands' to ensure their support; and an attack on the views of the then Foreign Secretary, Jack Straw, who had fallen out of step with Downing Street; as well as regular repeats of the government's certainty that 'we know he has WMD'.

All of these stories were substantially the work of the government, engineering coverage to 'manage public opinion'. All of them carried Kamal Ahmed's byline. Some of them contained significant falsehood or distortion.

However, it needs to be said that this is not just about Ahmed. Other *Observer* reporters contributed to these stories. *Observer* executives, particularly the editor, chose to publish them. Beyond that, although Ahmed may have developed a special enthusiasm for Downing Street, media outlets all over the world were also running false and distorted stories.

It is squarely within the conventions of modern journalism to report the speeches and comments of political leaders and to reproduce material selected and provided by their PR staff. It is clear that if journalism is required to focus its attention on the behaviour of the state, then that makes sense. But if journalism is also required to tell the truth, it makes no sense at all to carry this material without qualification or criticism or attempt to check its truth. But that is what happens.

Taken together with David Rose's flawed reporting, Downing Street's work with Kamal Ahmed and Roger Alton meant that *Observer* readers were slowly soaked in disinformation. But, just as important, the newspaper's own internal thinking was stained too. Senior journalists at the paper say there was a perception that some reporters were 'on message' while others were not. 'A barrier prevented some stories getting prominence,' according to one. 'There was definitely a circle of resistance that I felt was wrong.'

It was against this background that the paper repeatedly rejected Ed Vulliamy's stories about Mel Goodman and his discovery of the truth about what CIA analysts were saying about the supposed threat from Saddam Hussein. Looking back now, it is clear that there was a horrible continuum here: the process of distortion which Mel Goodman was trying to expose was precisely the same process which had infiltrated the *Observer*'s reporting and thinking and which led to Goodman's own exposé being rejected. And, as we will see, there were further, equally worrying incidents in the weeks immediately before the invasion.

It should be said that this was not some kind of Stalinist censorship. The *Observer* did run anti-war columns on its comment pages. Some anti-war stories did make it onto the news pages; some of them were important. But the reality is that, as a result of sustained and often subtle manipulation, the paper was being steered in a direction which it would not otherwise have taken. This finally became unavoidably clear on Sunday morning, 19 January 2003, when the *Observer* formally came out in favour of war.

A long leader, which considered the arguments on both sides, concluded: 'We find ourselves supporting the current commitment to a possible use of force.' Notably, this leader accepted the American contention that Saddam possessed weaponry which posed a threat to the wider world; and furthermore it supported the Americans in their willingness to use force even if they lacked the backing of the UN Security Council.

Readers reacted with a torrent of letters. Some supported the leader, but many were angry, a mood captured by one who wrote: 'I couldn't believe my eyes when I read your weaselly, disgraceful, morally and intellectually dishonest editorial, in which you support Blair's Iraq policy.' Some in the newsroom felt equally strongly. They acknowledged that there was a reasonable and honourable argument for removing the Iraqi dictator to end his repressive rule, but they worried that this particular leader comment was taking a line which betrayed the newspaper's historic principles, as though somebody had crept in and stolen their moral anchor. Journalists on the *Observer*'s daily sister paper, the *Guardian*, were angry, and some of them raised it at a subsequent staff meeting with Liz Forgan, the chair of the Scott Trust which owns the *Guardian* and the *Observer*.

There are some at the *Observer* who believe that this leader was the product of some subtle manoeuvring in the office. During the week before it appeared, at the regular Wednesday conference, Roger Alton had made his own pro-war view clear. A day later, he had taken aside a senior journalist who would be involved in deciding the final leader line and asked him: 'Would it be controversial if we took this line?'

The journalist wasn't sure what he meant. 'You mean an anti-war line?'

'No, no,' said Alton. 'We've got to stand shoulder to shoulder with the Americans.'

Having thus advertised his own position, Alton then took the unusual step of failing to turn up to the main leader conference on Friday, at which the paper's final line would be decided. He said it was just bad luck; he had something else he had to do. There are some who believe he was being much cleverer than that – that he had made it clear what he wanted and that, by staying away from his own leader conference, he made it impossible for opponents to challenge him. And they noted that the first draft of the leader was written not by one of the regular leader writers, but by David Rose, who worked directly for Alton, not for the news desk.

Six senior *Observer* journalists gathered that Friday to make the decision. Only one of them – the political columnist Andrew Rawnsley – spoke in favour of the American plan, and, since Rawnsley habitually saved his best shots for his own column, his impact was limited. One other, Ben Summerskill, remained neutral, because it was his job to write the leader that emerged. The other four – the former editor and economics columnist Will Hutton, the acting comment editor Barbara Gunnell, the regular columnist Mary Riddell and the deputy editor Paul Webster – were all more or less opposed. And yet they sanctioned the leader along the lines which the absent editor wanted.

It may be that this was a victory for subtle manoeuvring. But the real difficulty for the six journalists at that meeting was that, with the best will in the world, like so many other journalists, they didn't really know what they were talking about. How could they? The *Observer* had not only failed to discover the truth for itself about the Iraqi threat but, working on a particularly difficult and well-obscured subject, it had been manipulated into believing significant falsehoods. The reality is that, like so many journalists, they did not know what was true; they merely thought they did.

Another funny thing happened a few weeks after that leader was written, although the chain of events had begun unnoticed several months earlier, in November 2002, at an anti-war meeting in Bristol.

One of the speakers at that meeting was Yvonne Ridley, a former *Sunday Express* journalist who had become the subject of a world news story in September 2001, when she was reported to have been taken hostage by the Taliban as US forces prepared to invade Afghanistan. Subsequently, she had converted to Islam and become an outspoken peace campaigner and political activist.

As the meeting in Bristol ended, Ridley was approached by a woman who claimed to be working at the Government Communications Headquarters in Cheltenham. Since GCHQ is a highly secret spying organisation, which specialises in intercepting all forms of communication, Ridley was suspicious, fearing this might be some kind of trap. She told the woman she would leave her business card for her on a shelf in the room and, if ever she wanted to talk, she could phone and introduce herself as 'Isabelle'.

Three months later, in early February 2003, Isabelle called. Ridley arranged to meet her, in Patisserie Valerie in Soho. They made small talk for a while, and then Isabelle handed over a piece of paper. Ridley read it. 'Bloody hell,' she said.

The document was an email which appeared to have come from the National Security Agency, the US equivalent of GCHQ, an organisation so secret that it has been nicknamed the No Such Agency. It suggested that, a few days earlier, the NSA had started spying on six key members of the Security Council of the United Nations. These were the six countries whose support the United States needed if it was to pass its famous 'second resolution' endorsing military action against Iraq. The document recorded an NSA instruction that, in breach of international law and in spite of all diplomatic protocol, the six delegations were to have all phone calls from their homes and offices recorded and their email traffic intercepted and copied.

Realising that police would try to trace the source of the document, Isabelle had cut off the header at the top of the email, but she allowed Yvonne Ridley to scribble out some details from the header on to the back of the piece of paper.

Ridley saw that this was an enormously important story. Conceivably, it could even change the outcome of the UN Security Council's vote on the second resolution. Her first move was to take it to Chris

Hughes, a senior journalist at the *Daily Mirror*. Hughes, however, was unable to confirm that the document was genuine and so, three days later, he couriered it back to her, and she took it to Martin Bright, the home affairs editor at the *Observer*, with whom she had dealt in the past. This caused several problems.

The first problem with the story was simply to confirm that it was true. Bright worked with the foreign affairs specialist, Peter Beaumont, and the US correspondent, Ed Vulliamy, trying to find intelligence sources who would confirm that this spying operation was taking place or, failing that, at least to find confirmation that the man who was said to have sent the email from the NSA, Frank Koza, did indeed exist and was indeed in a position to be organising such an operation.

The second problem was the 'circle of resistance' to anti-war stories. As soon as the three reporters started work on the NSA document, some senior executives started airing their doubts about it. They said Yvonne Ridley was an unreliable source. They drew attention to the fact that the header had been cut off. Kamal Ahmed was particularly sceptical. According to one source: 'He was running around the office going, "Hitler diaries, Hitler diaries,"' reviving the memory of the humiliation of the *Sunday Times* in 1983 when they published a forgery claiming to be the diary of Adolf Hitler. He may or may not have been joking.

By now, there was some ill feeling in the office between Ahmed and reporters who opposed the war. A few weeks earlier, at the end of January, there had been a controversial incident on the Prime Minister's plane as he flew to Washington DC. A group of political reporters were flying with him at the back of the plane, and several noticed that Alastair Campbell emerged from the front section, where he was sitting with the Prime Minister, and called Ahmed forward to join them. Nobody would have known what passed between them if Ahmed had not returned to the office in London in the following week, claiming that Campbell had shown him a new summary of alleged intelligence on Iraqi weaponry and consulted him on how best to use it as a media story. This summary was what came to be known as the 'dodgy dossier'.

The dossier in itself was immediately a source of trouble for Ahmed. He, along with other political reporters in the Prime Minister's party, found it slipped under their hotel doors in Washington in time for them to file stories for their papers on Sunday 2 February. In his story that day, Ahmed described it as 'new intelligence documents released by Downing Street' and went on to say that it was 'based on information from MI5, MI6 and the Security Services'. In fact, it was nothing of the kind. It was a collection of a few scraps of raw intelligence with a hearty mix of publicly available material which had been downloaded from the Internet and hyped by Downing Street press officers. We now know that intelligence agencies complained bitterly that their names were being used to give credibility to assessments which they had never seen. The foreign secretary, Jack Straw, was particularly alarmed that he knew nothing of the dossier until he read about it in the papers.

In filing a false story, Ahmed was in the same trouble as other reporters that weekend who once again had been misled by Downing Street. However, in allowing himself to be consulted about the dossier by the Prime Minister's press secretary, Ahmed was on his own. As word of Ahmed's involvement spread through the *Observer* office, some of his colleagues started asking hostile questions. Was it right for an independent reporter to get into that kind of relationship with the government? And if the Prime Minister's press secretary had to have some feedback from a reporter, why did he choose Kamal Ahmed? When the sheer dodginess of the dossier eventually became clear, the news desk asked Ahmed to write a story about it, focusing, among other things, on the fact that he had been asked his opinion about it while not even the intelligence agencies who were supposed to have written it or the Foreign Secretary himself had been consulted. Ahmed then denied emphatically that he had given Campbell any advice on the dossier and refused to write about it.

This incident encouraged the perception that Ahmed had crossed the line from independent reporter to Downing Street aide. This was reinforced when word spread through the office that, as the paper was being prepared on Saturdays, Ahmed was regularly phoning Alastair Campbell to read out extracts from the news list with the result that the government would be aware of any controversial stories which the paper was planning to run the next day. This was in no way normal behaviour for a journalist. Ahmed insists that this never happened. But I have spoken to one of his colleagues who has no doubt at all that he personally and repeatedly witnessed Ahmed doing precisely this.

It was against this background that Martin Bright, Peter Beaumont and Ed Vulliamy were trying to confirm that the NSA had been intercepting phone calls from the six key members of the Security Council. *Observer* staff say they have a clear memory of Kamal Ahmed making it very clear that he thought that the story should not appear, 'dropping poisonous stink bombs' as one journalist put it. This was clearly spooking Roger Alton, who was worried about the story, not so much because it was anti-war in its implications but because he felt it was unsafe: this was not an anodyne story from an official source but an explosive allegation which might blow up in his face.

Beyond that, several senior sources felt that the paper's strong line in favour of the war was now infecting editorial judgements. At the sixth attempt, on the same day that Ahmed ran his misleading story about the dodgy dossier, Ed Vulliamy had finally managed to slip a small fraction of his story from the CIA veteran Mel Goodman into the paper – as the final two paragraphs of a 1,200-word story on page 16. And these senior figures noted that while pro-war stories had been allowed to float into the paper without being properly checked, the NSA story was being subjected to an intense grilling.

Two weeks passed. The three reporters on the NSA story had reached the point where, after speaking to intelligence experts, they believed the document was genuine, but still they could not get their story into the paper. Then Vulliamy talked his way through the NSA switchboard and, to his delight, found himself speaking to the office of Frank Koza. He managed to confirm that Koza was the NSA's Defense Chief of Staff, responsible for regional targets, and was indeed in a position to write an instruction like this.

Even now, the story was stalled. Late on Saturday afternoon, 1 March, Roger Alton was still fretting about whether or not to run it, until Peter Beaumont took him out into the stairwell of the office and made it very clear that the story was checked and solid and had to run. Alton agreed.

The story finally appeared the following day, 2 March. The front-page headline declared: 'SECRET DOCUMENT DETAILS AMERICAN PLAN TO BUG PHONES AND EMAILS OF KEY SECURITY COUNCIL MEMBERS'. It named Angola, Cameroon, Chile, Mexico, Guinea and Pakistan as targets of the spying.

Some who were involved felt frustrated by the delay in finally getting the story into print: 'If we had gone with it two or three weeks earlier, it might have made a difference. There was an ideological resistance to it. It could have stopped the war. And that's why the document was leaked to us.' (That week, police arrested Katherine Gunn, a twenty-eight-year-old worker at GCHQ, who had provided the document which 'Isabelle' took to Yvonne Ridley.)

But the problems in the *Observer* office were not yet over.

In New York, Vulliamy started talking to senior delegates from some of the six nations who were being spied on. He turned the conversation round to their plans for voting on the second resolution. This was a supremely important vote. Without it, the United States and its allies would lack the legal and political cover which they had sought for their invasion. Just as important in the British context, without that resolution, the Prime Minister risked losing his own vote which was due in the House of Commons. His support within the Labour Party was crumbling. Four Cabinet ministers and six parliamentary aides were on the point of resigning their posts. Backbench MPs were in rebellious mood. Downing Street needed that resolution. Or, at the very least, they needed the party to continue believing that the resolution would be passed.

Five of the fifteen nations on the Security Council had already declared they would vote against the resolution. If three others joined them, the US and UK could not get the majority they needed. Talking to the delegates of the six key nations, Vulliamy discovered that Chile, Mexico and one other who spoke on condition of anonymity had already decided to vote against. The resolution would fail. He filed his story from New York, for the paper of Sunday 9 March.

In the London office, however, Ahmed spoke to Alastair Campbell in Downing Street. Ahmed had already written a story several weeks earlier helpfully reporting about the resolution that 'Britain is certain it will be passed, not unanimously, but probably 13–2, with Syria and

Germany against'. This was part of a concerted media campaign on both sides of the Atlantic to pretend that all was well at the UN. Now Campbell told Ahmed that, contrary to what Vulliamy was filing, they still expected the UN resolution to go through and they were still working on the six key nations. Then Tony Blair phoned Roger Alton.

Ahmed and the deputy editor, Paul Webster, were called into Alton's office to join the conversation on the speakerphone. Blair reassured them that there was no problem with the second resolution. It was a 'keep your peckers up conversation', according to one source. The three executives emerged from Alton's office, laughing that Blair had said 'Hey, guys' so many times that it might have been Rory Bremner on the other end of the line, impersonating the Prime Minister.

The next day, 9 March, the *Observer* carried a front-page story about the progress of the UN resolution, written by Kamal Ahmed. It made absolutely no reference at all to Vulliamy's first-hand findings from the key nations. Instead, it told *Observer* readers: 'Downing Street was bullish last night about the chances of getting the required nine votes to pass the resolution. Sources close to Blair said that all the diplomatic effort would be aimed at persuading the key "middle six" countries – Pakistan, Angola, Cameroon, Guinea, Mexico and Chile – to support the resolution.'

A longer story by Ahmed inside the paper also was written as though all six of the key nations remained undecided. 'The British Government is confident it can persuade enough [to come] on board,' it said, before adding one single line which reflected what Vulliamy had filed. 'Noises from the UN are less certain,' it said.

Events proved that Vulliamy's unpublished story was right. The Prime Minister and his press secretary were wrong (and, courtesy of intercepting phone calls at the UN, had every reason to know they were wrong). And the *Observer*'s story was also wrong.

On that same weekend, Vulliamy filed for the seventh and final time his story about Mel Goodman and the CIA, quoted at the beginning of this chapter. That, too, failed to make it into the paper.

Eleven days later, in the early hours of Thursday 20 March, London time, the first air-raid siren wailed over Baghdad.

10. *Mail* Aggression

On a bright sunny day in July 1992, two young women from south London walked out of the Royal Courts of Justice into a crowd of reporters and photographers. Michelle and Lisa Taylor had just spent the best part of a year in prison, starting to serve a life sentence for murdering a friend called Alison Shaughnessy. Now, the highest criminal court in the land had quashed their conviction and released them to return to their lives.

Years passed. Both of the sisters got married and started families and sank back into a welcome obscurity. Then suddenly, on 24 June 2000, the *Daily Mail* returned to the story with a three-page spread, written by Jo Ann Goodwin, with a large headline: 'WHY I BELIEVE THEY ARE MURDERERS'. Next to a picture of Michelle and Lisa Taylor, a second headline added: 'WHEN THESE SISTERS WERE CLEARED OF A BRUTAL KILLING, THEY POSED AS VICTIMS. NOW A DAMNING *MAIL* DOSSIER CASTS NEW DOUBT ON THEIR INNOCENCE.'

This story is worth examining, because it is a model of a certain kind of reporting. And, as we will see, it is a model which is particularly associated with the *Daily Mail*. This involves something rather like the work of a gardener, who digs out and throws away weeds and stones and anything else which he does not want and then plants whatever he fancies. The story, in other words, is a model of the subtle art of distortion. Aggressive distortion.

One considerable group of facts which stood in the way of Jo Ann Goodwin's story was clustered around that hearing in the Court of Appeal at the Royal Courts of Justice. I was there on the day that the Taylor sisters were released, because I had written about their case. The three judges did not simply give in to some clever nit-picking by the defence: they hurled that case out of court to the sound of a humble apology from the prosecution and with a ringing rebuke for two groups of people whom they blamed for a serious miscarriage of justice – the police and also the press, specifically including the *Daily Mail*. The lead judge, Lord Justice McCowan, spoke at length about three serious flaws in the original trial of the sisters.

First, he pointed to the evidence of the only witness who could place the Taylor sisters at the scene of the crime. This was Dr Michael Unsworth-White, a neighbour of the murdered woman, who told the original trial that he had seen two girls who were somewhat like the sisters running from the victim's house at about the time of the killing. However, on the eve of the appeal, defence lawyers searching through boxes of unused evidence had come across a record of Dr Unsworth-White's first account to police of what he had seen, in which he had said that these girls had been walking, not running – and that one of them had been black. The Taylor sisters are white. This was, said Lord Justice McCowan, 'a very remarkable change of story' and, furthermore, one that had been concealed by police at the sisters' trial.

Second, Lord Justice McCowan dealt with an incident during the trial when the defence had hinted at the possibility that Dr Unsworth-White was interested in claiming a reward for his information. There had been protests from the prosecution that this was quite baseless, and the defence were forced to apologise in front of the jury, a move which clearly was likely to have damaged their credibility while bolstering the credibility of Dr Unsworth-White. Now, it had become clear that, in truth, the doctor had indeed applied for the reward and furthermore that the police had always known this. This withholding of evidence, Lord Justice McCowan said, was 'of course, completely wrong'.

Third, he turned to the press and castigated the 'unremitting, sensational, inaccurate and misleading' reports which had been published during the trial, with the clear risk that any juror who read them would be turned against the Taylors. 'What in fact they did was not reporting at all. It was comment, and comment which assumed guilt on the part of the girls in the dock.' He announced that he was formally referring five daily newspapers, including the *Daily Mail*, to the Attorney General, with a view to their being prosecuted for contempt of court: 'The press is no more entitled to assume guilt in what it writes than a police officer is entitled to convince himself that a defendant is guilty and to suppress evidence, the emergence of which he fears might lead to a defendant's acquittal.'

Faced with all this, the Crown had thrown in the towel, not merely declaring that they would drop their opposition to the sisters' being freed but, in a highly unusual step, publicly and formally apologising to the Court of Appeal for the way that the case had been conducted.

The findings of the Court of Appeal were clearly important. They were also highly obstructive to a story which wanted to claim that the sisters were guilty. Jo Ann Goodwin had the answer. She simply chucked almost all of it out. Right at the end of her three-page story, she referred to Dr Unsworth-White's racial confusion about what he had seen, adding none of Lord Justice McCowan's comments, and informed her readers that it was 'unbelievable' that the court had been influenced by this. No mention of the judge's comments on the seriousness of this concealment of evidence. No mention of the concealment of the truth about that witness's interest in the reward. No mention at all of five newspapers, including her own, being blamed for reporting which was so bad that they had been formally referred for prosecution. With almost all of the troublesome facts about the appeal thrown on to the compost heap, Goodwin then planted at the top of her story one bright, shining falsehood. 'Michelle and Lisa Taylor were freed on a legal technicality,' she told her readers.

This easy omission of uncomfortable facts ran through the story. Goodwin reran the prosecution case, describing it as 'hard to refute', and simply ignored almost all of the defence case. The police claimed that Michelle Taylor had killed Alison Shaughnessy out of jealousy, because she had married Michelle's former boyfriend. Goodwin reported this as though it were a fact: 'She was obsessed by him and terrified of losing him.' She did not report the defence reply that Michelle had lost interest in John Shaughnessy many months before the killing and had a new boyfriend. Goodwin reported that Michelle's diary 'provided ample evidence of her hostile feelings towards Alison'. She did not report the defence reply that in the whole diary, there was only one sentence expressing hostility to Alison Shaughnessy and that this had been written many months before the murder. She reported that Lisa Taylor's fingerprints had been found in Alison Shaughnessy's flat, but did not report the defence reply that this was simply because Lisa had been there weeks earlier, helping her father who is a cleaner.

In one particularly striking passage, Goodwin dealt with the witness who most powerfully established the innocence of the two sisters – their friend, Jeanette Tapp. Goodwin, however, introduced Jeanette as the source of 'the most damaging evidence' against the sisters and told her readers simply that Jeanette had originally told police that she had been with both sisters at the time of the murder but had then withdrawn her story. This was, Goodwin concluded, an attempt by the sisters 'to manufacture a false alibi'. Goodwin, however, did not tell her readers that Jeanette Tapp had told her story to the police not once but three times and in increasing detail, right down to the brand of cigarettes she had been smoking with the sisters and the subjects of the conversation they had been having; and that she had finally changed her story only after four detectives raided her room at 5.40 one morning, arrested her on a charge of conspiracy to murder, spent two hours and fifty-five minutes with her before sitting her down in front of a tape recorder, at which point she declared that all her previous statements had been false – and the police dropped the charge of conspiracy to murder against her. Goodwin dealt with all this by simply chucking it out of her story and telling her readers, in relation to Jeanette's new story: 'It is hard to see why she should lie.'

But it was Bernard O'Mahoney who, according to Goodwin, was the 'key to the case'. He was introduced to her readers honestly enough as 'a 40-year-old ex-gangster' with convictions for violence. Goodwin explained that Mr O'Mahoney had happened to wander into the Taylor sisters' original trial, had thought that they 'radiated innocence' and so had decided to befriend them. After their conviction, she said, he had worked on their appeal and then, when they were released, he had started writing a book about the case with Michelle. He had fallen in love with her and left his wife. But one day, looking through some legal documents, he had found a letter from the sisters' lawyers, written before their original trial, which said that Michelle Taylor had made 'certain admissions' with the result that Lisa Taylor was being advised to become a prosecution witness against her. O'Mahoney had then confronted Michelle with this clear evidence of her guilt, and Michelle had made a tearful confession. Goodwin continued: 'All his efforts to free the Taylor sisters had been built on a lie. The woman with whom he had fallen in love had ruthlessly used and deceived him. Furious at the betrayal, he left Michelle and returned to his family – his book about the Taylors abandoned, his loyalty to their cause destroyed.'

This would indeed have been 'the key to the case' if it had been the truth. What Goodwin knew but did not tell her readers was that O'Mahoney was a con man, specialising in befriending high-profile prisoners and selling titbits to the press. For example, at the same time as he was writing letters to Michelle Taylor in prison, he was also writing to the Yorkshire Ripper, Peter Sutcliffe, posing as 'Belinda Cannon', sending him 'big, juicy hugs'. O'Mahoney passed Sutcliffe's replies to a woman friend, who then put on a wig and attempted to sell them to the *Sunday People* for £4,000. Goodwin also knew but did not tell her readers that throughout the time that he was befriending the Taylor sisters, Mr O'Mahoney was secretly selling stories about them to Gary Jones, who was first at the *Daily Mirror* and then at the *News of the World*.

And Goodwin knew but did not say that, by the time O'Mahoney spoke to her for her current story in the *Mail*, he had become involved in a bitter feud with the Taylors. The Taylors said this was because Michelle had found out that he was cheating on her, had thrown him out and fallen into a long wrangle about who owned the book which they had been writing. O'Mahoney had made threatening phone calls and delivered sneering notes to the sisters, while Lisa Taylor's husband had made threatening calls in reply; someone had slashed the tyres on the Taylors' cars; and both sides had complained to the police.

The 'key to the case', in other words, was a man with a track record of deceit; who specialised in lying for the sake of newspaper stories; and who had a clear personal motive to damage the Taylor sisters. His claims were so contentious that no newspaper could rely on them without strong corroboration. The difficulty for Jo Ann Goodwin was that there was no corroboration at all. Instead, there was powerful secondary evidence to confirm that his story about the damning legal letter and Michelle's tearful confession was false.

He claimed the letter was from the Taylors' solicitor, but the solicitor, Michael Holmes, furiously denied this as 'spiteful, damaging and untrue'. And, indeed, it was hard to explain why any solicitor would jeopardise his career by putting forward a false defence for clients whom he knew to be guilty, especially after confirming their guilt in writing. When he was confronted with this denial long before Jo Ann Goodwin's story, O'Mahoney had shifted his ground and said the letter was from a legal clerk, a claim which foundered on the same obstacles.

It was even harder for O'Mahoney to explain why he had never told the police about Michelle's supposed confession. On his own account, during his feud with the Taylors, he had gone to see the police and made a statement which was calculated to cause them damage, claiming that he had fabricated evidence to help them. And yet he had never hinted at this dynamite revelation, that one of the sisters had now admitted the murder. To any reporter who was interested in checking the story, this was very hard to explain. Indeed, it raised the clear possibility that Mr O'Mahoney had not mentioned it to the police in that interview, because he had not yet dreamed it up. But Jo Ann Goodwin had no room for any of this in her story and simply reproduced Mr O'Mahoney's highly contentious claims in detail as though they were statements of fact.

There was more of this kind of distortion, much more, in Goodwin's long story. The *Daily Mail*, however, went ahead and published, with devastating results for the Taylor sisters, who, eight years after their release, now found themselves being pointed at in the street and treated with suspicion at their children's schools. They tried to fight back. They went to lawyers to sue for libel. The lawyers explained that there was no legal aid for libel, but they would consider running the case at their own expense, claiming a fee only if they won. At the same time, the sisters turned for recompense to the Press Complaints Commission, the industry body appointed to enforce good practice in British newspapers. The PCC, however, told the Taylors that they could not complain if they were also suing. So the family divided their action: the sisters worked with the lawyers to see if they could sue on a no-win, no-fee basis, while their parents pursued a complaint through the PCC.

Faced with a formal complaint, it was open to the *Daily Mail* to review its story, to recognise that it was deeply distorted and inaccurate and to publish the truth. The paper, however, chose to back Jo Ann Goodwin. In correspondence with the PCC, the paper's executive managing editor, Robin Esser, dismissed Mr and Mrs Taylor's complaint. 'I do not imagine the PCC wants to get into an extended debate if we can avoid it. What must be clear is that this was a carefully researched article, with many supporting documents, and that the writer took huge care to be accurate . . . The essential point is that I can see no breach of the code in what we have published.'

The Taylors fought on. The libel lawyers, having examined the paperwork, finally told the sisters that the case was going to be so complex and so expensive that they could not risk pursuing it without any fee. Unable to use the courts, the Taylor sisters were then told they could not go through the PCC either, because more than a month had passed since the *Mail* story. And so they relied on the complaint from their parents, which was being processed by the PCC.

It was a big case. Several thousand people every year complain to the PCC, but very few complain about anything as serious as an accusation of murder. The PCC's slogan is that its service is 'fast, free and fair'. Months passed; the *Mail* stood its ground; the Taylors kept fighting with help from the libel lawyers, Bindman & Partners, who supported them without being paid; I supplied a witness statement. Finally, on 26 September 2001, the PCC's full commission met to deliver its ruling, and its ruling was . . . that it would make no ruling.

In a lengthy statement, headed without apparent irony with the word 'Decision', the PCC simply refused to make any judgement at all about whether the *Mail's* story had been accurate. It did so, first, on the grounds that its rules do not require it to consider complaints from third parties, even though they had allowed the complaint to run for fifteen months before enforcing this rule against the Taylor sisters' parents. Second, they argued that Mr and Mrs Taylor had 'made no specific complaint under the PCC code against the article taken as a whole', even though Mr and Mrs Taylor had complained in writing in several letters of 'numerous inaccuracies' and 'many inaccuracies and distortions' in the *Mail* story. Third, they declared that it was not for them to consider the case when the Taylors 'had the option of taking proceedings for defamation', even though the legal costs had already blocked this route.

It is an extraordinary feature of the Press Complaints Commission that, unlike other watchdog bodies who rule on complaints from the public about professional groups such as lawyers and doctors, the PCC rules on almost no complaints at all. We looked back through ten years of PCC records and found that they had received a total of 28,227 complaints from members of the public. These covered not only inaccuracy but also invasion of privacy, harassment, the unethical treatment of children and other alleged breaches of the PCC's code of conduct. And yet the records show that the PCC refused to consider ruling on 25,457 of them: just over 90% of those complaints were rejected on technical grounds without the PCC even investigating their content.

The obstacles that were placed in the way of the Taylors' complaint turn out to be common. Over the ten years, nearly 1,000 others were rejected because they were not made quickly enough. Nearly 2,000 others were rejected because they were made by third parties. The idea that the Mr and Mrs Taylor did not make a complaint about 'the article as a whole' reflects the experience of nearly 7,000 others who were told that in some way their complaint did not fit within the PCC's code. The suggestion that the Taylors should take their complaint elsewhere was one of more than 6,000 where complainants were told they were outside the PCC's remit. Many thousands of others (the statistics aren't clear) were rejected because they were not 'formalised' by the complainant.

Only 2,770 complaints were 'accepted for investigation' – just 9.8% of the total number of complaints made. Most of those, 2,322, were then 'resolved' when the newspaper reacted to the PCC's acceptance of the complaint by agreeing to apologise or to publish a clarification. Only 448 complaints – 1.6% of the total – succeeded in persuading the PCC to make a formal adjudication. And the PCC then rejected more than half of them (251). Out of 28,227 complaints that were sent to the PCC over the ten-year period, just 197 were upheld by an adjudication. That is 0.69%. The PCC was set up by the news-papers who are the subject of these complaints.

Since most complainants – like the Taylor sisters – find that the courts are closed to them by the sheer expense of suing, this leaves newspapers in a position of some considerable security. The *Daily Mail* has a special place here.

The first thing to recognise about the *Daily Mail* is that it is the most successful and powerful newspaper in Britain.

While others spent years watching crowds of their readers walk away, the *Mail* carried on pulling them in, utterly defeating its old rival, the *Daily Express*; swallowing another rival, the *News Chronicle*, as well as its own sister paper, the *Daily Sketch*; easily resisting the brief threat from a new challenger, *Today*; overhauling even the red-top *Daily Mirror*. Along the way, it has spawned a Sunday sister paper and started producing special editions in the Irish Republic. Every year for the past fifteen years, it has turned in a substantial profit – no other mid-market or quality newspaper in Britain has anything like that track record. This financial strength has allowed it to protect its jour-nalists from the kind of cuts which have done such damage elsewhere, leaving the *Mail* as arguably the most potent news-gathering machine in Britain.

That commercial success is linked to its outstanding political influ-ence. It is because it has these resources that the *Mail*, more than any other paper, is in a position to release reporters from churnalism and break big stories which will be picked up and run by the rest of Fleet Street, often recycling the *Mail*'s angle as well as its choice of subject. Government pays attention to the *Mail*.

I've had the chastening experience of publishing long stories on public policy, only to be told by senior civil servants: 'Very interesting, but it won't make the slightest difference. Now, if you were on the *Mail* . . .' The Prime Minister, Tony Blair, was exposed to some jeering in July 2000, by the leaking of an internal memo in which he had listed 'touchstone issues' on which he felt an urgent need to connect with the 'gut British instinct' of voters. The volume of the jeering rose sharply when it became clear that his perception of British instincts was an uncanny echo of a leader column which had been published by the *Daily Mail* shortly before he wrote his memo. Politicians work hard socially as well as politically to make the *Mail* their friend. Gordon Brown caught the tone in a videoed message for Paul Dacre's tenth anniversary as editor: 'Paul Dacre has devised and delivered one of the great newspaper success stories. He also shows great personal warmth and kindness as well as great journalistic skill.'

The second thing to recognise about the *Mail* is that, more than any other newspaper in Britain, it deals in falsehood and distortion. There is a glimpse of this in our review of the records of the Press Complaints Commission. In among the thousands of cases which had fallen by the way, we drew up a league table of complaints which had succeeded, either because the PCC had eventually adjudicated against a newspaper, or because the paper had agreed some kind of resolution to satisfy the complainant. This showed that, over that time, only four papers had suffered more than fifty successful complaints – *The Times*, the *Mirror*, the *Sun* and, comfortably ahead, with 153 successful complaints about its reporting, the *Daily Mail*. The average number of successful complaints for the rest of Fleet Street was forty-three for each paper. On that basis, over that ten-year period, the *Daily Mail* has been provoking justifiable complaint about unethical behaviour at just over three times the rate of the other national titles.

Not all of these successful complaints against the *Mail* involved false-hood and distortion. There is a recurrent theme of invading privacy – of Tony Blair's schoolboy son; of a ten-year-old girl whose father was targeted by the *Mail* for his affairs with teenagers; of the Aga Khan and his wife, who were photographed on the deck of their yacht (the *Mail* said that if they wanted their privacy, they should stay below deck). In one case, they published a photograph which allowed the victim of a sexual assault to be identified.

But inaccuracy was the most common theme, in cases such as those of Mark Fenwick, whose photo was used to illustrate an article on the National Front (he had nothing to do with the National Front);

Mr and Mrs Riley, whose son's death was linked by the *Mail* to alcohol abuse (he had no alcohol at all in his blood); Mr Sorrell, whose daughter was said to be a topless dancer (she wasn't); Princess Michael of Kent, who was accused of spending £30,000 on a fur coat (she hadn't); Sarah Scott, who was said to have admitted having an affair with the Deputy Prime Minister, John Prescott (she hadn't admitted it and she hadn't had the affair).

Sometimes, this is a matter of the *Mail* taking the truth and distorting it – attacking the BBC by misquoting an internal memo; criticising a High Court judge by misquoting from a speech he had made. In others, the problem is pure falsehood – the prisoner who was falsely said to have been given legal aid to sue because he had missed his breakfast; the man who was falsely accused of running a feud with his neighbours; the married couple who were falsely described as treating their twelve-year-old daughter so badly that she had run off with a US marine.

With most of these successful complaints, the *Mail* resolved the problem by publishing a 'clarification', usually with far less prominence than the original story. In April 2006, for example, the paper ran a story almost as big as their coverage of the Taylor sisters which attacked Robin Spark, son of the novelist Muriel Spark, claiming that he had 'bled' his mother of the money for which she had worked. Robin Spark complained that this was not true and after seven months of pushing through the PCC, the *Mail* eventually conceded that its claim had been entirely false. The original story was 2,092 words long; the clarification was just eighty-one words.

In the same way, we looked into the small number of cases where a complainant has the financial backing to pursue a libel action against a newspaper. This provided a similar glimpse of the *Mail*'s attachment to inaccuracy. In February 2001, the paper paid £100,000 in damages to Sir Alan Sugar after running a story which accused him of being 'miserly' during his period as chairman of Tottenham Hotspur football club. Oddly, they had had to pay damages to a previous chairman, Irving Scholar, after running a story accusing him of hypocrisy. Sir Alan emerged from the High Court and declared: 'Newspapers destroy people's lives. They take the mickey out of people just to increase their circulation. My victory today, I hope, will help to stop that.' It didn't stop the *Mail*.

They went on to accuse the American film producer, Steve Bing, of hiring private investigators to destroy the reputation of his former lover, Liz Hurley (the *Mail* admitted the story was untrue and paid damages); the actress Nicole Kidman of having an affair with her co-star, Jude Law, during the filming of *Cold Mountain* (the *Mail* admitted the story was untrue and paid damages); the actress Diana Rigg of hating men and giving up her career (after she complained, the *Mail* ran a second article along similar lines before admitting the story was untrue and paying damages); the actor Rowan Atkinson of needing five weeks' treatment in a clinic for depression (the *Mail* admitted the story was untrue and paid damages); the actor Sir Michael Caine of having a facelift (the *Mail* admitted the story was untrue and paid money to a charity of Sir Michael's choice); the actress Sharon Stone of leaving her four-year-old son alone in her car while she dined out in a restaurant (the *Mail* admitted the story was untrue and paid damages); the singer Sir Elton John of banning guests at a charity function from talking to him (the *Mail* admitted the story was untrue and paid damages); the TV presenter Noel Edmonds of behaving unprofessionally and unreasonably over the course of his career (the *Mail* admitted the story was untrue, paid damages and agreed to serialise Edmonds' new book); one of their own journalists, Glenys Roberts, of conducting a vendetta against a restaurant near her home (the *Mail* admitted the story was untrue and paid damages); the actor Hugh Grant of destroying his relationship with Jemima Khan by flirting with other women (the *Mail* admitted the story was untrue and paid damages to Marie Curie Cancer Care); the BBC *Newsnight* producer Thea Rogers of stalking a colleague (the *Mail* admitted the story was untrue and paid 'substantial damages').

Some of these stories by the *Daily Mail* are not just false, they plunge a dagger into the reputation of their subject. After the death of the celebrated barrister George Carman, in January 2001, the paper ran a vicious attack on his companion, Karen Phillips, in which they claimed that she had manipulated Carman into altering his will in her favour, as he lay dying. 'The mistress of manipulation,' they called her, adding that she had not been concerned for Carman's health at all, only in gaining financially. She complained and received a letter containing still more attacks on her character. But she fought on and, eventually, the *Mail* admitted the story was untrue and paid damages. Sally Becker had a similar experience. She had become so famous for her work in Bosnia, rescuing sick children from the war, that she was known as 'the Angel of Mostar' – until the *Mail* got hold of her and told its readers: 'She was no angel.' The paper claimed that she was being sued by volunteers who worked for her, because she had defied the advice of local police and taken them on a route which had risked their lives. She complained and found herself the target of yet more stories in the paper attacking her character. But she fought on and eventually, after more than three years of argument, the *Mail* admitted the story was untrue and paid damages.

Looking back at these cases – at the PCC and in the courts – a pattern begins to emerge: facts are swept aside or distorted; the story is published; the subject of the story then complains and is confronted by the wealth and cleverness of the *Mail* which will fight them right up to the point of final defeat, when, if need be, it will surrender and offer some kind of deal. And then the pattern repeats. It repeats because the penalty is no match for the rewards of the behaviour which is being penalised.

The *Mail* is deriving at least some of its commercial and political success precisely from the fact that it can play fast and loose with the facts and frequently have no fear of the consequences: the PCC bails them out; the victim can't afford to sue; or, if the victim does sue, the paper can live with the cost. It's like watching a footballer who, finding himself the last man between his opponent and his gaping goal, will deliberately foul the opponent in order to protect that goal, calcu- lating that it is worth it even if he is punished by the referee. Brilliant and corrupt, the *Daily Mail* is the professional foul of contemporary Fleet Street.

A lot of people misunderstand the *Mail*. They see it as a right-wing rag driven by an addiction to the Conservative Party and to the defence of the rich and powerful. That is not where the drive comes from at all.

When he was interviewed about his job by the House of Commons' Public Administration Committee in March 2004, Paul Dacre said: 'My job is to edit my newspaper, to have a relationship with my readers, to reflect my readers' views and to defend their interest.' This is a particular view of an editor's role, not necessarily the one which would be identified by all other editors, but it perfectly describes the moral engine which drives the *Daily Mail*.

More than any other paper, the *Mail* identifies with the world of its readers; more than any other, it embodies the five rules for increasing revenue, described in Chapter 4. With story after story, they tell it to sell it. I have never met a *Mail* journalist who did not marvel at Paul Dacre's ability to know instinctively, immediately and entirely clearly what his readers want to be told about the world – the facts, the values, the moral panics.

The striking thought in Piers Morgan's comment to his chief executive, that 'the readers are never wrong – repulsive, maybe, but never wrong' is echoed less crudely in a memo from Paul Dacre to his proprietor in October 1997. In the memo, which was subsequently leaked to *Private Eye*, Dacre was defending one of his then columnists, Andrew Alexander, against Lord Rothermere's complaint that he was a political dinosaur. Dacre told him: 'I suspect that Andrew Alexander *is* a dinosaur but then I am pretty sure that a great number of our readers are too.' So, Alexander stayed in place.

The *Mail* is a perfect commodity, designed to be sold to a particular market, of lower-middle-class men and women. Its addiction is to them; and if, in order to speak for their interests, the *Mail* must attack, it will. Black people, poor people, liberals and all kinds of lefties, scroungers, druggies, homosexuals: they will all be attacked. And if it is necessary to attack, too, the rich and the powerful and any political party, including the Conservatives, then so be it. It sells its readers what they want to see in the world. That behaviour might make it unpopular with a mass of people who do not happen to share those values, but it would not in itself be a cause for complaint about its journalism. Newspapers are allowed to make judgements about what is important.

The difficulty for the *Mail* is that in its relentless pursuit of that commercial agenda, it has developed a striking willingness to cut the corners of journalistic integrity, to inject the facts with the falsehood and distortion which will please its readers. And if that involves publishing a few clarifications or even paying occasional damages, so be it. Look, for example, at their coverage of race and immigration.

I spoke to a man who had worked for the *Daily Mail* for some years as a senior news reporter. He said:'They phoned me early one morning and told me to drive about three hundred miles to cover a murder. It was a woman and her two children who'd been killed. I got an hour and a half into the journey, and the news desk called me on my mobile and said,"Come back." I said,"Why's that?"They said,"They're black."'

I talked to another journalist who has spent many years working for the *Mail*. She said: 'I did a thing about an American couple who were living as crofters in Scotland – Sutherland, I think. They were white, but the woman had got children from a former marriage, and they were mixed race, so that story was dropped by the features editor. It happens once or twice – you write a story and it doesn't go in because the people are black, then you realise. There was another time I had to do a story about a vet in east London who was looking after homeless people's animals. I spent two days looking for her, because she travelled around. I finally found her, she came out holding this Old English sheepdog, it would have been great, but she was black. I said, "Sorry – no story."'

This was a consistent theme. Perhaps I have been unlucky, but I have never come across a reporter from the *Daily Mail* who did not have some similar story, of black people being excluded from the paper because of their colour. A district reporter told me he would call up from Manchester to tell the news desk a story, 'and they would always ask:"Are they our kind of people?" i.e. "Are they white, middle class?" Or more often it would be: "Are they of the dusky hue?" And if they were of the dusky hue, then they didn't want the story.'

I mentioned this to another reporter, who has spent several decades on the *Mail*, and he immediately named the senior news executive who was most keen on the 'dusky hue' euphemism. And this is not a thing of the past. While I was writing this book, I spoke to a local news agency who had just had the *Daily Mail* news desk on the phone, checking out a murder on their patch and asking if the victim was white or black so that they could decide whether they wanted the story.

The reasons for this are slightly subtle. There is an element of pure naked racism. The feature writer who had had the problem with the homeless persons' vet told me she had heard a very senior, rather famous *Mail* journalist on the phone to the West Indies. (I won't name him, because he is dead.) She said he was having trouble booking a hotel room and resorted to addressing the receptionist as a slave, shouting down the phone: 'Who's your owner?' Yet another *Mail* reporter, a young man who worked there for a year, told me he had been amazed at the openness of the racism in the office: 'You'd often hear people using the word "nigger" or "nig-nog" – really shocking. It's the senior people who do it, not Dacre, but some of the other older ones: "Oh, it's the nig-nogs again." There is definitely a racist environment.'

But there is something else more important at work here – the *Mail's* urgent desire to feed its readers with the world they want to believe in. As one very experienced *Mail* journalist put it: 'They don't want a multicultural society, they want to go back to the 1950s.' Paul Dacre reflected this when he was questioned by the Public Administration Committee. He told them that his paper had a lot of readers from ethnic minorities: 'They are our kinds of people, the aspirational members of their community, and we have a very good relationship with them. I would say the *Mail* is always highlighting their successes.'

This means that black people can, in fact, make it into the paper, providing they fit into a *Mail*-friendly stereotype. A reporter who worked there for years and who has Jamaican relatives told me: 'Certainly, it is just a routine thing to keep out stories where the principals turn out to be black, but the *Mail* can embrace people from ethnic minorities providing they are respectable, short-back-and-sides people, who are trying to be British in a traditional way.' She cited the case of the black soldier, Johnson Beharry, who had been awarded the Victoria Cross in March 2005, whom the *Mail* were happy to treat as a hero.

A more famous case is that of Stephen Lawrence, the black schoolboy whose murder in August 1993 remains unpunished after bungling by London police. The *Daily Mail* famously – and courageously – named his five alleged killers on its front page in February 1997. One of those directly involved says that the *Mail's* approach to the story began by being hostile. They sent their only black news reporter, Hal Austin, to interview the dead boy's father, Neville Lawrence, with instructions to run a story attacking the groups who were campaigning for a new inquiry into the murder. 'We don't want rent-a-mob left-wingers – that was the line.' During that interview, Neville Lawrence realised that Austin's editor was the Mr Dacre for whom he had done some plastering in Islington some years earlier. By the time Austin sat down to write his story, the highly respectable Neville Lawrence had contacted Dacre, and the news desk told him to change the line: 'Do something sympathetic.'

The other black stereotype which makes it into the *Mail* is the criminal. As a crude check on this, we analysed the pictures which appeared on the paper's news and feature pages over a nine-month period and logged the race of their subjects. We found two things. First, they were overwhelmingly of white people – a daily average of thirty photographs of white faces to only one of black (i.e. Afro-Caribbean). This is roughly in line with the population as a whole. But then we analysed the nature of the black people who were being shown in the photographs. And what was striking was that while some showed sportsmen, entertainers, asylum seekers and figures in crowds, far more than anything else the *Mail's* photographs of black people showed the faces of criminals. Lots and lots of black criminals: 64% of the pictures of black people in our sample of the *Mail* were of muggers and murderers and rapists, which is hugely out of line with the population as a whole – but absolutely on target for the world view of *Mail* readers.

Just as Stephen Lawrence became an acceptable example of a young black man, so Winston Silcott became an icon for a bad black. This started when he was wrongly accused of being involved in the murder of PC Keith Blakelock during the Tottenham riots in October 1985 and then picked up new energy when he was released from that sentence by the Court of Appeal in November 1991. One *Mail* journalist who was directly involved told me: 'Winston Silcott – we were trying to stitch him up with a photo of him with evil eye. The whole thing was to make Silcott out to become a demon. That became a *Mail* campaign to blame Silcott for the death of Keith Blakelock. Even with the new forensic evidence which confirms his innocence, they won't let go. Winston Silcott remains a demon.'

This clearly matters immediately because it is recycling and re-inforcing a falsehood, that black people are bad. And since it is matched by the pattern of exclusion of black people from stories of ordinary life, the effect is all the stronger. It matters, too, because it has a direct feed into political issues around race, and since the *Mail* enjoys a peculiarly powerful political impact, this ends up feeding into government policy. This is particularly clear in the paper's treatment of immigration.

I used a media database to pull up a small, random sample of stories from the *Daily Mail* which mentioned the word 'asylum seeker' or 'migrant'; and, where they were based on accessible source material, I went back to that material and checked their accuracy. I found that – as with the Taylor sisters – the paper was falling back on falsehood and distortion to project its line.

For example, in July 2003, the *Mail* ran a story which informed its readers: 'Asylum seekers infected with the Aids virus are putting public health at risk, MPs will warn today. A growing number of asylum seekers and migrants to the UK are infected with Aids or the HIV virus, says a parliamentary report.' I went back to the parliamentary report on which this story was based, to check what it said.

The report, by the all-party parliamentary group on Aids, turned out to be a detailed argument which precisely contradicted the *Mail* line. The MPs noted that, among the heterosexual population, 90% of new cases of Aids had been contracted in sub-Saharan Africa. But it went out of its way to explain that this was not a problem caused by asylum seekers. Those who were infected came from countries which tended not to produce asylum applications (South Africa, Uganda, Zambia); those who had applied for asylum tended to come from countries with very low HIV rates (Iraq, Afghanistan). Zimbabwe was the one exception, with high asylum and high HIV. Africans in the UK with Aids were just as likely to be students, tourists and workers on work permits, the MPs said.

The report did highlight a threat to public health – but not from asylum seekers, as the *Mail* claimed. The threat, according to the MPs, came from the policies which had been introduced by the government to placate right-wing newspapers. The system for dispersing asylum seekers meant that if any of them were suffering from Aids, they were likely to be sent to places with inadequate health care; and the cuts in their benefits and access to the NHS were likely to make their health even worse. They identified the source of the problem as media reports which created 'a self-perpetuating cycle whereby, as the public's perception of the extent of the problem increases, so policymakers respond with increasingly punitive policies'. Which did not stop the *Mail* from using the MPs' report to perpetuate the cycle still further.

A month later, the *Mail* was behaving in a similar way with a story about a report from *The Economist* on the impact on London of an influx of foreign workers. The *Economist* report was almost entirely good news: the influx had given London the highest growth rate in the country; 67% of these foreign workers were from high-income countries; many of them were better educated than most Londoners; they were particularly diligent workers; and, by pushing up the price of houses, they had allowed a mass of Londoners to fufil their dream of selling up and moving to the countryside which, in turn, had boosted the economy of rural towns. But in the hands of the *Mail*, this became bad news about the usual enemy.

The *Mail* opened its story with two sentences which were 100% fiction: 'London has become the immigration capital of the world, according to a report. More foreigners are now settling in London than even New York or Los Angeles.' Nothing like that appeared in the *Economist* report. The story went on to insert a killer paragraph, which was also pure *Daily Mail*, based on nothing at all from *The Economist*: 'Hundreds of thousands of illegal migrants, as well as failed asylum seekers, have set up home in the capital in the past ten years.' The *Mail* then cemented the distortion by including the *Economist's* reference to small 'villages' of Poles, Algerians, Moroccans, Kosovans and Albanians – but chucking out the *Economist*'s specific reference to the real origin of many of these workers, that 'the Europeans and Americans are all over central London'.

Having changed the subject of the story, the *Mail* then changed the angle, omitting almost all of the good news which ran through the *Economist* report and selecting those few sentences which recorded the disadvantages of this influx: the pressure on public services, and the problems of first-time buyers who were being priced out of the housing market. The good news in *The Economist* that Londoners could now afford to move out and live the rural dream was stood on its head by the Mail claiming that these foreigners were 'forcing many Londoners to flee the capital as property prices soar'. The *Economist* report ended on an upbeat note: 'The government understands how migration has driven London's economy, and London has driven Britain's.' The *Mail* story ended by quoting the head of Migrationwatch UK, Sir Andrew Green, that these were very serious developments: 'We are aggravating congestion and weakening the cohesion of our society.'

Nothing excuses this kind of journalism. And, in the absence of effective regulation from the Press Complaints Commission, nothing stops the *Mail* from indulging in it.

There was a court hearing which caught the *Mail*'s eye. It could have been reported like this: 'A High Court judge yesterday moved to protect children who have fled from rape, murder and massacre in war zones. In a ruling which was welcomed by refugee groups and specialist lawyers, Mr Justice Burnton attacked local authorities who have denied housing to refugee children simply because they could not prove they were under 18.' The *Mail* reported it like this: 'The beleaguered immigration system was dealt another blow yesterday when a High Court judge made it harder for officials to catch fraudulent young asylum seekers.'

The *Mail* ran an investigation into the easy availability of false identity papers. They could have linked this to all kinds of people who might want to cheat the system – professional fraudsters, benefit fiddlers, escaped prisoners, wanted criminals, runaway fathers, runaway sex offenders, undischarged bankrupts, defrocked priests, disqualified drivers and discredited journalists – but they focused the entire front-page story and inside spread on 'bogus asylum seekers and fanatics'.

The paper wrote about old people's homes which were closing to become hostels for asylum seekers. The reality was that the law required a higher standard of housing for old people, and the local councils were refusing to fund refurbishment; asylum seekers, however, could legally still be housed in substandard accommodation. In the hands of the *Mail*, this became two stories, headlined: 'WHAT KIND OF COUNTRY DO WE LIVE IN WHEN FRAIL OLD LADIES ARE TURNED OUT OF THEIR HOME TO MAKE WAY FOR FIT YOUNG ASYLUM SEEKERS?' and 'WIDOWS ORDERED OUT, THEN ASYLUM SEEKERS MOVE IN'.

The distortion runs into the leader columns. One, in November 1998, headed 'Wolves posing as sacrifical lambs', combined a startling absence of evidence with language which bordered on incitement to hatred. And this commentary was based on almost no facts at all. To highlight this volatile combination, I've put brackets around the claims of fact on which the *Mail* was relying:

> Scores of those who come to these islands claiming sanctuary commit the most heinous of crimes, even as they plead to stay. (Just how many it is impossible to say. For no official records are kept.) But a *Mail* investigation has thrown up (more than 40 cases of asylum seekers in the last year alone who were found guilty in the Crown Courts of London) of every serious form of depravity in the book from rape to heroin dealing.
>
> (Doubtless, they represent no more than a small and vicious minority) of the tens of thousands of bogus claimants still worming their way into Britain. But no breed of migratory villain is more vile than the wolf who masquerades as a sacrificial lamb. They pose as victims while violating those who take them in. They pollute good race relations and poison the cause of genuine refugees from overseas terror.
>
> It is monstrous that they should ever have been given house room within our shores in the first place. It is a scandal that no preliminary checks were required to be made as to whether they had criminal records in their countries of origin before they were let

loose here. We have more than enough home-grown crime of our own without meekly opening our door to any and every foreign predator who pretends to be a fugitive from persecution. For how much longer must Britain's immigration authorities be typecast as the Suckers of the Western World?

At one point, the Association of Chief Police Officers became so concerned about this kind of journalism that they published a report, warning that 'ill-informed adverse media coverage' was heightening tensions and increasing resentment of asylum seekers. They warned: 'Racist expressions towards asylum seekers appear to have become common currency and "acceptable" in a way which would never be tolerated towards any other minority group.' Ultimately, this was producing the risk of 'significant public disorder', the chief police officers warned. The *Mail* ran a story about this, which picked up on the risk of 'significant public disorder' but simply chucked out any mention of the media role in provoking it. Instead, they highlighted a minor theme in the report about conflict within refugee communities; cited a case in Kent where two Kosovars had been accused of murdering 'a man thought to be an asylum-seeker'; and inserted the idea that a curfew could be imposed on asylum seekers to stop them provoking local disorder.

This pattern of distortion also includes rejecting stories which do not fit the template. In September 2006, an Angolan refugee, Manuel Bravo, was denied asylum even though his parents had been killed and his sisters raped and murdered. He and his thirteen-year-old son, Antonio, were taken to Yarl's Wood detention centre to await deportation. There, while his son slept in the same cell, Manuel Bravo hanged himself. He knew that if his son was an orphan, he would be saved from being sent back to violence in Angola. He left a note: 'Antonio. I am really sorry. I don't [want] you [to] come to Angola to suffer.' That came down the supply line from the coroner's court to the news factory. Some other papers ran it. Not the *Daily Mail*.

It was the same when the Governor of the Bank of England suggested that East European migrants were helping to keep down inflation; when an inquest heard how Elmas Ozmico, aged forty, had died in detention after pleading with immigration officers for nineteen hours for medical help; when the Institute for Public Policy Research reported that migrants were paying more tax and costing less in public spending than their British-born equivalents; when the UN High Commissioner for Refugees complained that asylum seekers 'have been turned into faceless bogeymen by an unscrupulous popular press'; when the Refugee Council reported that destitute asylum seekers were being refused NHS treatment even when they were suffering from cancer or on the verge of giving birth; when Ernst & Young reported that migration was having a positive impact on the UK economy; when Amnesty International and Refugee Action reported that asylum seekers had been made so destitute by government policy that some were sleeping in phone kiosks and public toilets. Other papers ran these stories. Not the *Daily Mail*. The readers wouldn't like it.

There is something else which *Mail* journalists all talk about, which is Paul Dacre's aggression.

A woman who edited a section of the paper told me: 'They call him the Vagina Monologue because he calls so many people a cunt. He would stalk through the newsroom – it's ten to eight in the evening, the paper is ready to go, and he's shouting "What the fuck is this, you cunt, there's not a fucking brain in this office" – tearing up pages. Everybody shrinks to the size of a dwarf when he does that, trying to get out of the way. I used to take the page in to him at the end of the day, which was terrifying – it's the biggest office in the universe, you sink into the shagpile carpet, he's got a desk like Napoleon's, all the sofas are low down, all designed to impress. He used to just rip the page up. He would put the knife into a story – "This is shit!"'

Another woman, who edited a different section, said: 'He could turn on the charm with women. I went for my interview with him, and the champagne came out and he was gently flirtatious. He is also an extraordinary bully. It is terrifying if you go in to see him with your page. He keeps you waiting and then goes, "Rubbish, rubbish." It's like going to see the headmaster.'

Dacre's aggression is the fuel in the *Daily Mail*'s engine. One of its effects is simply that *Mail* journalists are in no doubt that they are expected to beat the opposition. As a former news reporter put it: 'The *Mail* man is always supposed to be the first on the doorstep, and the last to leave. You talk to everybody, you write everything down, you file everything back to the office. You just keep filing.' Dacre works long hours, so everybody else works long hours. He works Christmas Day, so they do too. (There was a famous row one Christmas when Dacre swore furiously at a journalist who had dared to go out for lunch.)

A senior reporter who worked for Dacre for many years told me: 'The *Mail* is meticulous, it never stops. By nine in the morning, the news desk have read every word of every paper and cut out every line which might need following. The penalties for failing are condign. When you are sent on a story, you have to perform every single time.'

It is under this kind of pressure that *Mail* reporters have turned to the Dark Arts (Chapter 7) and other desperate measures. One former staffer told me of an incident when a frantic show-business writer was so frightened of missing a story that she smashed the window of a celebrity's car to get the information she needed. I've come across several cases where a *Mail* reporter has managed to beat the opposition on a story with a crucial quote which shows every sign of having been fabricated. The paper's former New York correspondent, Daniel Jeffreys, eventually lost his job after filing eyewitness accounts of several events he had not seen.

This drive to beat the opposition is backed with the paper's huge resources. When there is a big story running, the *Mail* will throw money at it and will often beat the competition to the new angle.

There was a striking example of this in November 1995 when Princess Diana gave her famous interview to the BBC's *Panorama* programme and admitted that she had had an affair with James Hewitt. Reporters descended on Hewitt's home in Devon. The *Mail* sent a team of three in a chauffered car. One of them succeeded in evading the rest of the pack to find a side door, through which he slipped an envelope offering Hewitt a guaranteed payment of £250,000 with a possible £1million, depending on what he had to say. With the chance of success in front of them, the *Mail* team checked into a local hotel so that Hewitt could meet them there and, fearful that the opposition might see him and steal him, they simply booked every single room in the place, to keep it empty. (Nevertheless, Hewitt failed to take the bait.)

But this aggression also creates a kind of moral cowardice in the office as a whole. The bullying cascades down through the levels. *Mail* staff agree that Dacre reserves the worst of his outbursts for his executives. One recalled: 'An editor, a middle-ranking guy, came up to him with a project and, in front of the whole newsroom, Dacre started railing at him. At one point he said, "You're just a bag of piss."' Another described a young man who was given a senior job on the features desk: 'He couldn't do it. Everything went awry. Dacre got hold of him, called him a cunt in front of other men. He used to do it at conference and every night when they were putting the paper to bed. This guy just cracked. He would be in tears. There was a Christmas party where his wife was saying that Dacre had given him a nervous breakdown. In the end, they just kicked him upstairs.' Another journalist recalled a different features executive who was treated with similar verbal violence. 'He was very victimised. He had no courage. He used to say to me in the evening: "Well, that's another day we won't have to live again."'

While some executives crumple, others take the bullying and pass it on down the line. An experienced reporter recalled an incident involving a senior executive who routinely found himself on the receiving end of a vagina monologue from Dacre. This executive was dealing with a legal complaint and told a young woman reporter that he needed some paperwork from her, but she was sent out on a story before she had a chance to get it to him. 'When she finally got back, the executive started shouting and swearing at her, in front of the whole newsroom – "you fucking cunt". It was like he was Dacre's ventriloquist dummy.'

Resistance is not welcome. A journalist who had done well at the *Mail* told me that he got fed up and handed in his resignation and was then summoned in to Dacre's office: 'This was only the second time I'd really had a conversation with him. It was uncomfortable. He took his shoes off and laid out on the sofa in his office and was very paternal – "You've been under a lot of pressure, take some time off, think about it and you'll change your mind, talk to your family." He said I could be the next Geoffrey Levy, which was a horrifying prospect. The next day, I rang the news desk and said: "I am going to leave." They went and told Dacre and came back to me and said: "Paul says you're a complete cunt." Then I had a friend who got a job at the *Mail* and my name came up, and she was told I had left because I had had a nervous breakdown! A little bit later, I wrote a story in another paper, which referred to something I'd done at the *Mail*. That day, I got a call from the news desk, telling me in no uncertain terms that I was to keep my mouth shut. It was really quite threatening.'

A young graduate who wanted to be a reporter had an even brusquer introduction to *Mail* discipline. Adam Macqueen signed on with an employment agency and was sent to work in the paper's promotions department. He was quite pleased, thinking he might learn something about reporting. However, the agency sent in a summary of his previous work experience, which revealed that he had put in some time at *Private Eye*. That day, he was told to go and not to return and further- more that he would never be employed again by any of the *Mail* titles.

The reporters and subeditors who are on the bottom layer of this cascade of bullying end up succumbing to a kind of moral cowardice, shrinking from punishment and making the most of the available rewards. Over and over again, *Mail* reporters shrugged and tried to explain: 'You just have to put up with it and take the money and be miserable. The *Mail* pays well, you get a car and health cover and a pension – it's like an institution. People sell their soul.' And another: 'I'm a willing soldier. I don't have the luxury of judging the paper's ideas. I'm well paid, I get to write big stories. I don't admire the racism. My only recourse if I don't like it, is to leave.' And another: 'It's constant fear versus good money.'

The reporters who stay rapidly learn how to survive and prosper: they anticipate the required distortion. One who spent years at the *Mail* said: 'You knew instinctively what was required. There was no one that took you into a room and said, "Right, you have to stick it to this sort of person but not that sort of person." If you got it wrong, you wouldn't get into the paper or they would rewrite your copy, so you did learn that way.'

A specialist writer with many years at the paper told me: 'You become so inculcated with all of the doctrine that you know instantly what you are supposed to write. You forget the extent to which you are blinkered. It is hard to put your finger on it. You probably do get chemically changed by the experience.' One of their former news reporters said: 'On 60/70% of stories, you are not aware of it; but, on touchstone issues, you knew that the headline had been written before the story came in and your job was to make the facts fit.'

And if, by chance, reporters come up with the wrong angle, it is reversed before it gets into print, either because the copy itself is rewritten or because the headline changes the angle. 'Dacre kills with headlines,' as one long-term *Mail* reporter put it. Sometimes, this happens for purely commercial reasons, simply to turn a small story into a big one. An anodyne feature about the biography of Otto Frank, father of Anne Frank, who died in a Nazi concentration camp, was transformed by a headline which asked 'DID ANNE FRANK'S FATHER BETRAY HER?' The story produced not one single word of evidence to suggest that Otto Frank had betrayed any of his family in any way; indeed, it reported that they were betrayed by an anti-Semitic petty criminal. The *Mail* dealt with the problem a week later by publishing a short letter of complaint from the Anne Frank Trust, on page 68.

At other times, the killer headline changes the angle to enforce the *Mail*'s political line. There was a huge row in the office in July 2003, when Dacre decided to attack political correspondents from other newspapers for failing to ask tough questions of Tony Blair at one of his monthly press conferences. According to somebody who was close to the *Mail* news desk at the time, an instruction was passed to the paper's own political correspondent, Paul Eastham, to write a story describing the other political writers as 'toadies'. Eastham refused.

The news desk then obtained a transcript of the press conference, which is published by Downing Street, and gave it to a junior reporter with an instruction to list ten political specialists who were at the conference and to give them a 'toady rating' according to their alleged tendency to ask the Prime Minister soft questions. This was written and sent to Eastham, who sent it back with a single line typed across the top: 'This should not be published.'

The news desk then called Eastham and instructed him to write an introduction to this 'toady list' and, faced with his continuing protests, promised Eastham that, if he did so, they would make it clear that he was not the author of the list. Eastham filed an introduction. Dacre then ran it under the following headline:'Evasion and the toadies of medialand: Ruthlessly stage-managed, yesterday's presidential press conference was fixed to avoid honest answers (and yes, you guessed it, the Mailman was sidelined). By Paul Eastham.' Eastham's prominent byline was followed by the introduction which he had finally written – and also by the toady list which it now appeared that he had also written.

When the *Mail* was published the next day, the political correspondents who had been named as toadies complained bitterly, and Eastham resigned in writing. Dacre panicked and sent his chauffeur with a personal letter to Eastham, begging him to stay and promising never to do such a thing again. Eastham agreed to withdraw his resignation but subsquently found himself sidelined and then passed over for a promotion. He eventually left the paper.

The practical effect of all this is that these reporters become open conduits through which the *Mail* pours down its aggression on its chosen targets. Its quest to reflect the moral and political values of its lower-middle-class readers frequently goes beyond mere reporting, taking on the shape of a punitive campaign against anybody who says or does anything which challenges those values.

Lady Brittan, wife of the former Conservative Home Secretary, Leon Brittan, found herself a target when, in August 2002, as chair of the National Lottery's Community Fund, she approved a grant for the National Coalition of Anti-Deportation Campaigns. The *Mail*, high on its anti-immigration horse, denounced her as 'queen of the loony lotto grants' and 'a quango queen'; her husband as a 'fat cat'; her colleagues on the lottery board as 'sanctimonious politically-correct twits', 'unelected quangocrats' and 'politically correct do-gooders'; their decision as 'offensive beyond belief', 'a disgrace', 'bizarre', 'outrageous' and 'scandalous'. Four times in ten days, they encouraged their readers to 'vent their justified anger' by writing to Lady Brittan; and each time, they published her address at the Community Fund's office. She then received a torrent of what she described as 'hate mail', some of it threatening.

The idea of a stable family is somewhere close to the heart of *Mail* values. This means, for example, that women who choose work rather than child-rearing can become targets for Paul Dacre's aggression, although there is a delightful story about Dacre coming unstuck on this. In a *Sunday Telegraph* feature about the former *Mail* editor, David English, Vicki Woods recalled a morning conference at the *Mail* when she was editor of the Femail pages and Dacre was still the news editor: 'One morning, Paul Dacre bossily said that the news-desk had got a fabulous story that should be handled by the Femail editor. I bridled on cue. "Apparently," said Paul, "the country is losing billions of pounds every year because women are turning up an hour or two late for work. There's a very serious survey been done, and I think there's a serious point to make." Oh, yeah? Why are they late to work? "Well, apparently they're staying late in bed because (cough) they're having sex in the mornings." It was a gift. I said: "So who are they having sex with? Each other?" And David shouted, "Bang to rights, Mr Dacre!"'

But now he is editor, Dacre gets his way, and *Mail* aggression rains down on anybody who fails to conform to his idea of family life. This often makes targets of social workers, who incur twice the aggression because they not only interfere with family life but represent the 'nanny state'. In the autumn of 2005, the paper ran a long campaign against Essex County Council social workers whom they accused of ordering the adoption of two young children simply because their parents were 'too slow'.

In truth, of course, the case was much more complicated than that. An appeal against the council's decision went to the High Court, where Mrs Justice Pauffley explained at length that there were 'manifold difficulties' in the family: the oldest child had already suffered 'significant emotional harm'; both were at risk of further emotional and physical harm; the risk was so great that, even with extensive support, 'the parents were found to be unable to protect the children from significant harm or meet their welfare needs'; visits by the parents to the children in care had had to be stopped after the mother attacked one of the social workers and the father threatened other social workers with a car bomb and a hired assassin; the council had made prolonged attempts to enable the children to stay with their parents but these had left the children exposed to potential harm; and the oldest child had made clear progress in all areas of development since she had been taken into care. In the hands of the *Mail*, all this was reduced to the simple and scandalous proposition that, as its first headline put it, 'YOU'RE NOT CLEVER ENOUGH TO HAVE CHILDREN, SO WE'RE TAKING THEM AWAY'. The children had been 'stolen by the state'; the social workers were 'child snatchers' and 'child stealers'.

The High Court took the unusual step of publishing Mrs Justice Pauffley's judgement in an attempt to stop media distortion of the case, but aggression continued to pour through the *Mail*'s coverage – 'rampant destruction of family life by the state', 'cruelty beyond forgiveness', 'an experiment in social engineering', 'betrayal of the stolen children'. In Essex, the head of the social services department started receiving messages from *Mail* readers: 'Adolf Hitler would be proud of you – I bet you leave the real abusers alone – too much like hard work . . . Shame on you – you are a disgrace to a disgraceful profession.' One of the social workers was accosted in the street.

In the familiar pattern, the council tried to sue for libel and discovered that, as a council, it had no legal right to do so. It turned to the Press Complaints Commission with a five-page letter, listing inaccuracies and omissions. The PCC rejected the complaint, arguing that, although the *Mail* had ignored many of the facts in the High Court judgement, this was acceptable, because the paper was simply giving its view of the facts – an argument which, on the face of it, would allow any newspaper to ignore any facts which obstructed any story. The council appealed and continued to complain. In a final letter to them, the PCC director, Tim Toulmin, captured the nature of the PCC's remit: 'I realise that the council feels that the newspapers have reported this case unfairly, but it is not for the PCC to make judgements about fairness.'

The *Mail*'s aggression on the subject of the traditional family also makes a target of gay men and women. The paper was apparently happy to support the Conservative MP Michael Portillo in his attempt to become leader of his party in 2001 – until he admitted he had had gay relationships in the past and told a meeting of Tory MPs that he would consider changing Section 28, the controversial law which then restricted free discussion of gay relationships in schools. The *Mail* drenched him with hostility.

As commander of police in Brixton, south London, Brian Paddick found two bullseyes on his forehead: he is gay and he took a liberal line on the policing of cannabis. In March 2002, the *Mail on Sunday* paid £100,000 to his former lover for a story which claimed that Paddick had allowed him to smoke cannabis in their flat and that Paddick had smoked joints with him more than a hundred times. The *Daily Mail* picked this up and used it as a stick to beat Paddick, calling him 'the camp commander', 'commander crackpot' and 'an icon for our moral decadence', running a series of stories which attacked his policy on drugs, repeatedly referring to his homosexuality and suggesting this would allow him to escape unpunished. 'I suppose we must be thankful he's not a black homosexual, in which case he'd have been metaphorically bullet-proof,' one *Mail* columnist wrote.

Although his former lover had undoubtedly smoked cannabis in their flat, Paddick vehemently denied allowing him to do so or doing so himself. Following an independent police inquiry, the Crown Prosecution Service decided not to prosecute, and the Metropolitan Police neither censured nor reprimanded him. A legal action for breach of confidence ended in December 2003 with the *Mail on Sunday* confessing that the allegation that Commander Paddick had smoked cannabis was simply false; the paper paid more than £350,000 in costs and damages. Despite its numerous references to this allegation, the *Daily Mail* never told its readers that it had turned out to be incorrect.

It was the *Mail*'s campaign against cannabis which saw them, in February 2002, report the death of James Hynard with the headline: 'CANNABIS HORROR – TEENAGER MADE TO FEEL INVINCIBLE BY DRUG STABS HIMSELF TO DEATH IN FRONT OF HIS FATHER'. Two further *Mail* stories in the following seven days referred back to this case. It took three months of complaint from the Hynard family, during which they supplied the *Mail* with the coroner's report, before, on 2 May, the paper published a short clarification on page 31 in which they admitted that James Hynard had not been high on cannabis when he died and that in fact he had been suffering from the sudden onset of a psychotic illness. The coroner had specifically explained at the inquest, which the *Mail* claimed to be reporting, that drugs had not been a factor in the teenager's death.

In similar vein, the paper's campaign against 'binge drinking' in 2002 saw them fabricating a helpful story. A young woman, who worked for a PR company and who came to be known as Miss A, was approached by the *Daily Mail* to help with a story on the balance between work and leisure. Miss A and two friends agreed to meet a *Mail* reporter in a bar in central London for an interview and photographs. The subsequent story presented the women as part of 'the epidemic of young women binge drinking'. 'Are you a functional alcoholic?' asked the headline. 'Are you on the slippery slope?' echoed the picture caption. As a result of this coverage, Miss A lost her job with the PR company but managed to find solicitors who agreed to sue the Mail on a no-win, no-fee basis. Eventually, they admitted the story was false and paid damages.

All kinds of left-wingers have found themselves on the receiving end of aggressive *Mail* stories which turn out to be Flat Earth news. During the Thatcher years, the *Mail* joined other right-wing newspapers in exposing the 'political correctness' of 'loony left councils' – Hackney, which said the word 'manholes' was sexist and renamed them 'access chambers'; Camden, which said the word 'sunshine' as a form of address was racist; Haringey, which said the old nursery rhyme 'Baa Baa Black Sheep' was racist and banned it. All these stories were fiction. Which did not stop the *Mail* running the Baa Baa Black Sheep story again in March 2006, when a nursery class in Oxfordshire was said to have banned it as racist. That was fiction too. (They had simply been using the rhyme to teach the children colours – 'Baa Baa Yellow sheep, have you seen the sun?' and so on.)

The *Mail* accused Fiona Millar, partner of Tony Blair's former press secretary, Alastair Campbell, of handing out gold watches to staff at their children's primary school. That was fiction. When the former miners' leader Arthur Scargill agreed to give an interview to the paper in February 2001, a reasonably straightforward feature was given a killer headline: 'ROAR OF THE DINOSAUR: ARTHUR SCARGILL, THE MAN WHO DESTROYED TRADE UNIONISM IN BRITAIN, IS MAKING A COMEBACK

AT 63. DEFIANT AS EVER, HERE HE REVEALS WHY HIS WIFE LEFT HIM AFTER 37 YEARS OF MARRIAGE.' That not only turned the story against Scargill, it also tricked *Mail* readers: the story, in truth, contained no kind of explanation at all from Scargill about his marital problems.

When anti-capitalist demonstrators fought with police at the G8 Summit in Genoa in July 2001, the *Mail* moved in, looking for the leftist ringleaders. They chose a freelance journalist, Mark Covell, who had been so badly beaten by police that he was hospitalised with broken ribs and a punctured lung. A *Mail* reporter cheated her way into his hospital room; other *Mail* reporters doorstepped his mother in England to collect negative quotes; and the paper then produced a front-page story which falsely accused him of having organised the riot. In truth, he had had nothing to do with it.

Covell could not afford to sue for libel but found a lawyer who agreed to sue the *Mail* for breach of privacy, for which he could get legal aid. The paper resisted, denied all wrongdoing and even claimed that they had trespassed in his hospital room in order to draw attention to his maltreatment by the Italian police. Finally, with Covell clearly willing to take them to court, the *Mail* sent him a formal letter of apology and paid his legal costs and damages.

In the course of serving its readers, the *Daily Mail* has had a significant impact on almost every political issue of the day – Europe, crime and policing, the NHS, binge drinking, the MMR vaccine, GM foods, asylum and immigration, drugs, fuel tax, homosexuality, trade unionism, human rights. In so far as it is simply making moral judgements about what is important, its work is entirely legitimate. In so far as it allows its special relationship with inaccuracy to distort those issues, it clearly is not. In that case, the effect of the *Mail*'s professional foul is not merely to mislead its readers about the state of the world but to distort the whole political process.

It is here – with the political impact of media – that Flat Earth news is at its most frightening. The *Mail*'s peculiar aggression means that it is unusual in the news factory: it is more likely than any other title to pick on a story and push it so hard that churnalists on other titles pick it up and run it too; and its tendency to pursue a single issue with relentless anger, regardless of inaccuracy, makes it more likely than any other outlet to frighten government into changing their policy, whether for better or worse.

People sometimes say that government listens to the *Daily Mail* because it is 'the voice of Middle England', but that's just another easy cliché. It's the aggression that makes the *Mail* powerful. I know of nothing anywhere in the rest of the world's media which matches the unmitigated spite of an attack from the *Daily Mail*. And since it is part of an industry in Britain whose sole attempt at regulation is an organisation which rejects more than 90% of complaints without even considering their content, that aggression is free to cripple reputations, free to kill ideas, regardless of justice, regardless of truth.

At the end of his book, *What the Media are Doing to Our Politics*, John Lloyd quotes an unnamed senior Labour politician (whose way of speaking is strikingly reminiscent of Tony Blair's) who told him: 'The *Daily Mail* is an extraordinary product. It springs from the head of Paul Dacre who has the kind of prejudices and beliefs no one knows about. I won't go into them. But he is accountable to no one. He has absolute and unaccountable power.'

But the *Mail* is simply achieving from inside the news factory what other powerful voices are achieving with such ease from outside. Across the developed world, newspapers and broadcasters have succumbed to the logic of commercialism. As a result they are more likely to generate falsehood and distortion themselves, more likely to recycle falsehood and distortion which has been generated by manipulative outsiders, less likely to tell the truth.

As Paul Dacre himself put it, when he gave evidence to the Public Administration Committee in the House of Commons about the role of journalists: 'Our job, and I do not want to be pompous, is to be guardians of the truth.'

And – if you check – you'll find that the truth is that the Earth is not flat.

Epilogue

'Journalists used to question the reasons for war and expose abuse of power. Now, like toothless babies, they suckle on the sugary teat of misinformation and poop it into the diaper we call the six o'clock news.'

Kent Brockman, TV newsreader, The Simpsons

So, what is to be done?

In an imaginary world, we might demand that media products should be treated like food products which are required to carry a clear label to inform consumers of their contents. To translate this idea across to the media industry, we would need somebody to stump up a lot of cash to run a parallel news organisation, which would sample the output of each newspaper and broadcaster, check it for accuracy, and then produce a rolling average for, say, the preceding six months, so that each media outlet could be required to display prominently the percentage of its stories which had turned out to be false or distorted.

We could reinforce the impact by running annual Flat Earth News awards for 'Falsehood of the Year' (to be known as the Millennium Bug Award); 'Grocer of the Year' for the media corporation which had forced most stories out of its overworked reporters; 'The Most Gullible Use of Propaganda'; 'The Most Illegal Use of Private Investigators'; and a Paul Hucker Award for the most widely repeated PR nonsense.

In that imaginary world, we would force media owners to provide decent levels of staffing; resurrect the network of front-line reporters which once covered the country and indeed the globe; rewrite the conventions of reporting to give truth primacy over the news factory's pragmatic rules of production; retrieve the news agenda from PR and propaganda; bury the Press Complaints Commission and give media victims a genuine right to the truth; reform our media laws and give all honest reporters a genuine public-interest defence.

If all that were to happen, we might have a chance of realising the vision described by Ignacio Ramonet, editor-in-chief of *Le Monde Diplomatique*, in January 2005, when he tried to explain his hopes for his own publication: 'We intend to stay faithful to the fundamental principles of our way of making news. That means slowing down the acceleration of media; opting for journalism that can illuminate the darker areas of present reality; interesting ourselves in situations that are not in the media's spotlight, but that can help us to a better understanding of the international context; offering even more complete, deep-ranging and better-documented supplements on major contemporary issues; going to the heart of those issues with rigour and seriousness; presenting news and information not often published and, indeed, often concealed; and daring to go against the tide of the dominant media.'

In the real world, however, it is highly unlikely that we will find any way of bringing the media back on track. It would be a little easier if the essential problem were simply that proprietors were imposing their editorial line on their journalists. If that were the case, we might focus all our effort on tackling the overbearing political power of the media proprietors – an extremely tough fight but possibly a fight that could be won. As it is, we are dealing with a system that is running out of control, with the logic of commerce randomly overwhelming the requirements of reporting. A conspiracy can be broken; chaos is harder to control.

That is not to say that the real world is entirely without hope. The former CBS TV journalist Charles Lewis conjured up a small miracle in the United States in 1989 by creating the Center for Public Integrity. He completely bypassed all the traps of commercialism by raising money from foundations and individuals, and setting up the centre as a non-profit organisation. It now has forty journalists and 240 part-time researchers who tackle tough, time-consuming, expensive investigations – and then give the results away to the mass media and to anybody else who is interested. To date, they've produced more than three hundred investigative reports and fourteen books and collected a wallful of awards. Charles Lewis believes there is a model here which can be used in other countries.

There are still some safe havens which we might be able to protect. Some of them are inside the BBC whose public funding gives it some slight protection against commercialisation. And certainly there is a battle worth fighting to defend the BBC against the relentless pressure from Rupert Murdoch to privatise it and reduce it to the ghetto status of public broadcasting in the United States.

And, of course, there is the Internet. Bloggers and citizen journalists do uncover untold stories. There was a very telling incident in the winter of 2005 when, a full year after General Metz's men stormed into Fallujah, it was revealed that his troops had been firing white phosphorus shells not as a source of light but, in breach of the international convention on chemical weapons, as a means of burning insurgents alive. That story emerged, despite official denials from the US State Department, because bloggers found and circulated evidence from an article in a US Army magazine called *Field Artillery*, which had been published in March 2005. As the story finally made it into the mass media, the director of Global News at the BBC, Richard Sambrook, was asked by *Press Gazette* why it had been left to bloggers to dig out the truth, and he replied that 'deadlines and resources dictated that it would always be the case that individuals could find information or have information that the main news organisations would not get'. What an admission! Huge organisations whose sole purpose in life is to gather news are too busy with their churnalism to find out what is happening.

But, against that, the Internet is also functioning as a kind of information madhouse, frantically repeating whatever fragments of 'news' happen to make it into the blogosphere, much of it nonsense which echoes that damning line from H. L. Mencken, that 'the central belief of every moron is that he is the victim of a mysterious conspiracy against his common rights and true deserts . . . [He] ascribes all his failures to get on in the world, all of his congenital incapacity and damfoolishness, to the machinations of werewolves assembled in Wall Street or some other such den of infamy.' Much of it is peddled by global news websites with all of the inherent weaknesses which we have seen. And more and more websites and chat rooms are being penetrated by PR activity. (PR Newswire, for example, sells its clients a service called Search Engine Visibility to help them hike the prominence of their stories.)

The real promise of the Internet, however, is not that it is a means of allowing individuals to beat the mass media but that it could liberate the mass media from churnalism. By delivering news electronically, the Internet has the potential to slash the costs of production, reducing or completely removing the heavy costs of printing and distributing conventional newspapers. If those savings were recycled back into the newsrooms, to employ more journalists, we could start to reverse the process which has made the media so vulnerable to Flat Earth news. But that sounds suspiciously like the imaginary world again. So far, media owners have shown every sign of grasping electronic delivery as yet another chance to cut costs and increase revenue without putting anything back into journalism.

All this matters deeply to our world and the way that we run it. There is a great passage in a book by John Nichols and Robert McChesney, called *It's the Media Stupid*, in which they consider the impact of the commercialised media on the culture of their societies:

> This is a generation that is under pressure from the media it consumes to be brazenly materialistic, selfish, depoliticized and non–socially minded. To the extent one finds these values problematic for a democracy, we all should be concerned. The commercial media system is the ideological linchpin of the globalizing market economy.
>
> Consider the case of the Czech Republic. Only a decade ago the young generation led the 'Velvet Revolution' against the communist regime under the slogan 'Truth and love must prevail over lies and hatred.' Ten years later, even the *Wall Street Journal* acknowledged that the Czech Republic had turned into a demoralized morass, where 'an unnerving dash to the free market' had created a society awash with greed, selfishness, corruption, and scams.

They add:

> The type of political culture that accompanies the rise of the corporate media system worldwide looks to be increasingly like that found in the United States: in the place of informed debate or political parties organizing along the full spectrum of opinion, there will be vacuous journalism and elections dominated by public relations, big money, moronic political advertising and limited debate on tangible issues. It is a world where the market and commercial values

overwhelm notions of democracy and civic culture, a world where depoliticization runs rampant, and a world where the wealthy few face fewer and fewer threats of political challenge.

I'm afraid that I think the truth is that, in trying to expose the weakness of the media, I am taking a snapshot of a cancer. Maybe it helps a little to be able to see the illness. At least that way we know in theory what the cure might be. But I fear the illness is terminal.

Fifty years ago, in *The Hidden Persuaders*, the excellent Vance Packard, himself a journalist, recognised the threat while it was still gathering force, and he emerged with a cry of optimism. 'We can choose not to be persuaded,' he urged. Fifty years on, I'm not so sure.

At the Columbia School of Journalism in New York, they display the words of the former newspaper proprietor and editor, Joseph Pulitzer: 'A cynical, mercenary, demagogic, corrupt press will produce in time a people as base as itself.' He was probably right.

Index

Index

Index

243, 252, 254; roadmap 247; UK intelligence and 244–5

Information Research Department: disinformation/propaganda spread by 231–2, 234–5; MI6 and 234

Ingram, Martin 278

Insight team, history of 275–6, 287–328

International Herald Tribune 164, 205n, 210, 216

Internet 32, 38, 40, 42, 49, 50; anti-abortionist websites and 109; blogging on 223, 395; news coverage on 49, 50, 63, 69–73, 223, 395; news media revenue through 63; newspaper price wars and 62; news plagiarism through 106–7, 395; PA repackages news for 83; Press Association and 74–84; pseudo-websites on, listed, 222–4, 240, 252

invasion of privacy 279–86

Iran: Afghan terrorist links to, claimed, 207, 217; misinformation about 224; MI6 and 233–4; nuclear weapons programme of 224

Iraqi National Congress (INC), disinformation from, 238, 332–5, 337–8

Iraq War 20, 35, 119, 132, 135, 139–41, 148, 176, 329, 330; al-Zarqawi and 205, 207, 212; Centcom and 246; Combined Press Information Centre (Baghdad) 255; Downing Street dossier and 199–201, 352–4; Gilligan report on 121, 199–201, 277; Hutton and 121, 173; Iraqi insurgency and 213–15; MI6 'intelligence' and 232–3; neocons need for 212; Operation Mass Appeal and 231–2; political/military PR and 89, 167, 244; 'pro-democracy' media of 238; 'Remember Freedom' TV campaign and 179; story fatigue of 120; US case for 208–13, 218–19, 333; VX nerve agent and 233; *see also* Gulf War; WMD

Islam 100, 128, 136, 205, 206–18

Israel: Gaza Strip and 167–8; intelligence from 232, 297, 299; lobbying from 123–5, 140; nuclear weapons illegally developed by 296–301; Psychological Warfare Unit set up by 231; Shin Bet and 297; Vanunu and 296–301, 311

issue management 185–6

I-teams 117

ITN 82

ITV 50, 66–7, 70, 134–5

Izvestiya 231

Jackson, Bennett 127

Jackson, Glenda 325

Jackson, Paul 135

Japan Times 226

Jarvis, Sian 201

Jay, Peter 138

Jebb, Susan 170

Jeffreys, Daniel 380

John Paul II, Pope 143–4; assassination attempt on 229

Johnston Press 65

Jones, Alan 91

Jones, Alan Gwynne *see* Chalfont, Lord

Jones, Gary 361

Jordan, al-Zarqawi claims made by 206–8, 211, 212, 216

journalism: accuracy of 32, 70–3, 102–3; churnalism and 59, 69–70; commercial interests and 52, 61; computer-program-generated 107; critical v. compliance 108; 'electric fence' deterrence to 122–5; excellence in 108; higher education and 56; objectivity of 109–14; primary purpose of 51; purpose of 113; sleuthing and 83; speed of 69–73; terminology used in 53; tradition of 133; truth-telling 62, 206, 311, 328

journalists: actors posing as 176; becoming VJs 67; CIA and 227–8; code of conduct of 282; collusion with politicians 19, 44; Columbia School of Journalism and 397; communist spies and 44; contacts used by 55–6, 84; courage displayed by 205, 205n; decline of 97–8; diaries of 56–60; downgrading of 65–9;

'electric fence' deterrence to 122–5; false expectations of 55–6; freelance 65–6, 88; ignorance displayed by 350; MI6 and 231, 233–4; non-existent German spies and 44; objectivity of 109–14; police corruption and 266–79; PR companies and 87; privacy, and double standards of 265–6; Response Source used by 197; shorthand skills of 72; stories attributed to 52, 53; terminology used by 53; *The Simpsons* and 391; working conditions of 54–60, 65–9, 81–2, 95, 115, 147, 203

Jowell, Tessa 174

July 2005 attacks 35

Karmy-Jones, Riel 262

Kay, Richard 271

Kaznacheyev, Aleksandr 226

Kean, William 115

Kelling, George 39

Kelly, David 199, 276–7

Kelly, J. Michael 221

Kempster, Doug 270

Kenny, Mike 172

Kerry, John 175

KGB: Agent Boot story and 323–4; CIA and 226, 293; FBI and 293; MI6 and 293

Khodada, Sabah 335

Khomeini, Ayatollah 29

Khrushchev, Nikita 226

Kimmitt, Mark 213, 214, 216

King, Alan 262

King, George 310

King, Martin 269

Kingston, Tom 269

Kinnock, Neil 198

Klein, Calvin 167

Knight Ridder 101, 119–20

Knightley, Phillip 100, 289, 292–3

Kolbe, Maximilian 183

Korean War 114–16, 120

Koskinen, John 11

Kovach, Bill 45, 117

Koza, Frank 352, 354

Kurds, al-Zarqawi claims made by, 207, 209, 212, 216

Kuwait, Gulf War and, 221

Kyoto Protocol 171, 187, 188, 190

La Republica 231

Larry King Live 218

LA Times 10, 97, 119, 120, 142, 208

Lashmar, Paul 235

LATIN (news agency) 226

Lawrence, Neville 373

Lawrence, Stephen 373

Lawson, Nigel 66

le Carré, John 235

Le Monde Diplomatique 108, 393

Leahy, Terry 131

Leeds Evening Post 81

Leigh, David 280–1

Leitch, David 288–90, 294

Lenin, Vladimir 44

Lennox, Jenny 82

Leppard, David 316–27

Lesbian Avengers 312–16

Leslie, John 83

Lester, Julius 128

Levene, Ray 271

Levy, Geoffrey 126, 382

Levy, Michael (Lord) 277–8

Lewinsky, Monica 175, 184

Lewis, Charles 394

Lewis, Dan 171

Lewis, Justin 4, 35

libel law 121, 122

Index

racism and 20; Rupert Bear and 22; Star TV and 19, 21; UK newspapers acquired by 18, 20, 110, 296, 302; Vietnam War and 20; Wapping and 61, 301
Murray, Charles 39
Murray, Craig 217
Murray, Jim 134
Murrell, Hilda 125–6
Myers, Richard 219, 242, 252
Mylroie, Laurie 333

Napoleoni, Loretta 205n, 210
Nation 166
National Star 164
National Union of Journalists (NUJ) 81–2, 284
National Velvet 30
NATO 25; dispute within 242; PR and 242; strategic communications and 237, 241
Nature 195
NatWest 158, 161, 163
Nazif, Ahmed 249
NBC: CIA and 228, 229; Fallujah reports by 251
Near and Far East News Agency, MI6 and 234
Neil, Andrew 21–2, 298–303, 311, 313–15, 321; Aids reporting and 312; Gibraltar 'car bomb' reports and 306; memoir of 305
Nelson, Dean 275–6, 327
neocons 33, 36, 171, 212
neutrality 112–13, 131–2
New Yorker 141, 232
New York Herald Tribune, CIA and 228
New York Newsday 99
New York Times 346–7; al-Zarqawi stories by 207, 212–14, 216; Abu Sifa story by 120; Afghan War reports by 148; bin Laden and 34; CIA and 227–9, 333; Cold War reports by 225; David Rose and 334; destruction of America and 128; fictitious news in 13, 224; HonestReporting campaign against 124; INC misled 335; Jayson Blair and 13; job losses at 96; Judith Miller and 121; misinformation about USSR spread by 44; news recycling by 107; Nicaragua Contra reporting by 130; Shia 'death squad' story by 119; Vietnam War coverage by 129; Washington Post swaps notes with 147; Y2K reports by 10
New York Tribune 166
New Zealand Listener 106
Newcastle Evening Chronicle 50
Newell, Claire 327
Newkirk, Ingrid 167
News Chronicle 54, 60–1, 68, 365
News Corporation 96
news factories 32, 59, 64, 69–3, 84, 90, 102–3, 113, 139, 150–2, 171; al-Zarqawi story and 205–17
News International, police corruption and 271
News of the World 18, 197, 274, 278, 312, 361; police corruption and 269–71, 274, 278; Prince William's voicemail messages and 285–6; Whittamore and 262
Newsnight 121, 129, 145, 172, 368
newspaper proprietors 15–23, 55, 62–4, 98; cost-cutting era of 142
news portals 107
news sound bites 141, 177
news stories/sources: accuracy of 32, 70–3, 102–3, 142–3; artificially created 173; balance in 131–3; Benji the Binman 279–82, 324; celebrities targets for 133, 261, 263, 265, 270–2, 279, 284; Christian belief reported as fact 143–4; concerning black people 127–8; 'Crocodile Dundee effect' on 106; distortion of 94, 106, 153; fictitious nature of 96, 176; 'food labelling' for 393; foreign, lack of, 99, 117; 'just add water' nature of 117; neutrality in 112; non-reporting of 78–9, 94, 106, 115, 129; objectivity in 109–14; politicians targets for

279–82, 316–26; Press Association and 74–84; recycling of 71, 103, 107; repackaging of 81, 83, 117; scrutiny of 147; skewing of coverage of 117–18
Newsweek 10, 100; CIA and 228, 229
Newton, Max 17–18
Nichols, John 396
Nicholson, Leslie 292–3
'Ninja Turtle' syndrome 145–7, 148, 161
Nixon, Richard 2, 178
Nobel Prize 131
non-stories: animal rights 79; First World War 44; gay foster parents 78; local government 79; New Zealand 105–6; non-reporting 36–7; pension funds 79; pseudo-evidence and 173; Queen Mother's death 143; reporting 33–4, 168; Scotland Yard 78; UN list 36
Noriega, Manuel 238
North, Gary 26
Northcliffe, Lord 15
Noye, Kenneth 270
NSA 351–2, 354
nuclear testing 129

objectivity 109–14
Observer 3, 4, 14, 19, 147, 337, 352–5; al-Zarqawi stories by 205n, 210; Cambridge spy ring and 294; CIA contacts with 329–31; David Rose and 334–5, 338, 348; government line reflected by 343–50; *Independent on Sunday* swaps notes with 147; Iraq War reporting by 209, 329–39, 344–50; MI6 and 235; misleading stories in 341; Queen Mother's death and 142–3; Suez crisis and 331; Whittamore and 260
Official Secrets Act 122, 293
Ogilvy & Mather 176
Okinawa Morning Star 226
Oliver, James 235
O'Mahoney, Bernard 360–2
Orwell, George 112
Outfoxed 21
'oven-ready' news 81
Overselling Climate Change 192, 194
Oxford Research Group 43
Oxford Times 195
Ozmico, Elmas 378

Pace, Peter 218
Packaging Politics 86, 89
Packard, Vance 155, 177–9, 256, 397
Paddick, Brian 387
Page, Bruce 17, 140, 288, 290, 292–4, 301
Palestine 123–5, 140, 168
Palestine Media Watch 123
Panorama 144, 380
Paris Match 227
Paterson, Chris 106–8, 135–6
Patten, Chris 19, 199
Pauffley, Mrs Justice 385–6
Pecke, Samuel 55
Pell, Benjamin *see* Benji the Binman
Penkovsky, Oleg 226
Penrose, Barrie 268, 309, 314
perception management 241
PETA, fabrication of news by, 167
Philadelphia Inquirer 99
Philby, Eleanor 294
Philby, John 294
Philby, Kim 235, 287–96, 300, 320, 324, 327
Phillips, Karen 368
Phillips, Melanie 193
Pianko, Adam 165
Pike, Otis 225, 227